Images of
Mathematics
Viewed Through
Number, Algebra,
and Geometry

5/7/15

To Jim
with my highest regards
Bob

Images of
Mathematics
Viewed Through
Number, Algebra, and Geometry

Robert G. Bill

Library of Congress Control Number:		2014907846
ISBN:	Hardcover	978-1-4931-9831-3
	Softcover	978-1-4931-9832-0
	eBook	978-1-4931-9830-6

This book was printed in the United States of America.

Rev. date: 12/11/2014

To order additional copies of this book, contact:
Xlibris
1-888-795-4274
www.Xlibris.com
Orders@Xlibris.com
618082

TABLE OF CONTENTS

To my wife Susan,
and my three sons Sam, George, and Tim

FOREWORD

Does the world need another book introducing the non-specialist to the world of mathematics beyond that found in typical high school presentations? There are indeed myriads of books: some have a recreational approach; some are specialty books with a particular focus (books on π, e, 0, etc.); and some books are without (or almost without) any mathematical formulas, meant to give a flavor of the allure and scope of mathematics. Alternatively, there are books of an encyclopedic nature, or books focusing on details of specific episodes and techniques in the development of mathematics which may leave the reader amongst a beautifully luxuriant thicket, but without giving a sense of the broader directions of mathematics. In this book, using secondary school math skills as a base, I wish to add to the literature which focuses on some of the broader themes of mathematics. I hope to engage those of you who are just learning high school mathematics or those who have completed it, moved on, and still wonder what mathematics is all about. In both cases, I believe that by taking advantage of the math training that you have already acquired, broad mathematical themes can be explored and experienced, creating a greater appreciation of one of humanity's greatest creations.

Basics of number systems, algebra, and geometry are being put or have been put into your tool kit in high school with much of the motivation for these subjects supplied through problem solving. Moreover, it is explained that the development of mathematical fluency is an absolute requirement for those seeking careers in science, engineering, or other quantitative disciplines. And so it is. But mathematics is also, in its own right, one of the great creative and intellectual achievements of humanity. I believe that the typical introductory math training provides the skills necessary to allow the fundamental sources and directions of mathematics to be developed and illustrated in a systematic way. Furthermore, I believe this can be accomplished by focusing primarily on illustrations of concepts rather than on the many detailed calculation methods required for problem solving.

Unlike many other books for the non-specialist of mathematics, I have included in my presentation lots of equations, proofs, and abstract concepts. I have selected this approach because mathematics at its core is abstract with symbolic representation as its language. Developing a comfort with such an approach is essential to enjoying and understanding the meaning of mathematics. My hope is that this book will provide an opening to the world of mathematics beyond just a qualitative sense of wonder and to inspire and enable you to continue on to the wider, more advanced literature of mathematics such as exemplified by the referenced works or available through a search of subjects on the internet. I firmly believe that mathematics is not just for the practitioners, just as the arts are not for the artist alone. Independent of its extraordinary usefulness, mathematics can provide unique pleasures and insights for the mind.

For those of a more practical nature, a better acquaintance with some of the great themes of mathematics will provide motivation beyond that typically encountered in school. Also, a broader view along with the skills acquired will facilitate an understanding of mathematical details that are otherwise often only understood as sets of rules.

The subject matter presented here is at an introductory level in keeping with the mathematics of an inquisitive student in high school. At this level, the subjects presented, although selected to illustrate major themes in mathematics, are necessarily very preliminary and incomplete in nature in that entire books have been written covering just individual sections. You should view this book as a friend telling you about things to look out for on your upcoming trip. Thus, this book is not meant to replace more specialized works, but to give you an entrée to those works which are typically aimed at those who have already begun to specialize in mathematics.

Topics explored here include: the relationship of the real numbers to the integers and rational numbers, the uncountability of the irrational numbers, complex numbers, logic and proofs in math, the world of non-Euclidean geometries, vectors, tensors, matrices, and paths from sets of the real numbers to the exotic world of topology. These topics would lead in the twentieth century to controversies over the meaning of mathematics, the subject of my final chapter. I emphasize that these topics are developed starting with only introductory math as a basis without assuming prior knowledge of advanced mathematics techniques. New techniques and concepts are developed, building from chapter to chapter.

In addition, to the subjects mentioned above, I have included an introduction to the calculus. This is a subject which typically is only taught to those considered gifted in mathematics. I do not see why all students should not be familiar with the basic concepts (again, in contrast to the complex manipulations) as the calculus can be motivated with geometric approaches and is the gateway to much of science. I have not included the subjects of probability, statistics, and discrete mathematics which have added their own important themes to mathematics, but do not fit as smoothly into unity of the other topics as presented here.

This book is meant to be read with care, but mostly with the pleasure that comes with understanding and new insights. A careful reading is meant to provide all the necessary details to follow the conceptual developments. By working through all of the arguments, my hope is to give you not only the feel of the extraordinary scope of mathematics, but to actually experience it. In writing this book, I have frequently made use of phrases such as, "we will now see" or "we can determine . . . ." By "we", I mean that you are following along with me in my line of reasoning. In cracking the hard nut of an argument, I hope you, like Archimedes, will experience your own eureka moments. If you are moved in this way and this book makes it possible to continue your journey in mathematics as one of life's pleasures, then my efforts will have served their purpose.

R. G. B.
March, 2014

Chapter 1

IN THE BEGINNING

"Mathematics may be defined as the subject in which we never know what we are talking about nor whether what we are saying is true." —*Bertrand Russell* [i]

"Mathematics as an expression of the human mind reflects the active will, the contemplative reason, and the desire for aesthetic perfection. Its basic elements are logic and intuition, analysis and construction, generality and individuality." —*Richard Courant* [ii]

1.1   Hidden in plain sight

Mathematics has been part of the human drama from the beginning of civilization. Mathematics and its companion, science are often contrasted with the arts. The former subjects being seen as objective, concrete, logical, and sources of universal knowledge while the arts are viewed quite differently as subjective, intuitive, and capable of creating and communicating personal knowledge. However, mathematics and science in common with the arts can be seen as developing from the tension between the explorations of the external world and those of the inner world of imagination and consciousness. The history of mathematics is full of triumphs of the imagination, sometimes motivated by the need to solve a practical problem or a desire to improve our description of the universe, but also by the urge

---

i Bertrand Russell (1872-1970)—British philosopher, mathematician, social activist; famous for attempting a comprehensive analysis of the foundations of mathematics (*Principia Mathematica* [Math References 36] with Alfred North Whitehead, first published in 1910); known publicly for his activism including support of pacifism in World War I, the anti-Vietnam War movement, and nuclear disarmament (quote cited in Kline, *Mathematics, The Loss of Certainty*, p.251 (for full citation details see Math References 18).
ii From the preface of Courant, Robbins, and Stewart, *What is Mathematics*, [Math References 8]. Richard Courant (1888-1972)—German born applied mathematician and founder of a renowned mathematics institute at New York University later named the Courant Institute of Mathematical Sciences.

to create a new abstract world with beauty and structure satisfying to the discoverer. These new imaginative worlds of mathematics have been found to be the very language needed to describe the physics of the one real world that we live in. That the physical universe is rational and can be understood and described in the language of mathematics is to my mind, a deep mystery and marks humanity's imagination as a central element of the universe.

All of this is to suggest that humanity's epiphanies of imagination are the common source of art, mathematics and science. I believe we often fail to see this because it seems necessary for every generation to retrace the paths to the truths of the arts, with individuals rediscovering, modifying, and defining their own version of that truth. In contrast, math and science are knowledge bases that continually build upon the discoveries of the past. We take them for granted since before even becoming adults, we learn mathematical and scientific truths that took thousands of years for humanity to finally grasp. As we go forward in the pages that follow, I ask you to remember that like all works of art, the search for structure and relationship in mathematical form has been part of humanity's great imaginative journey.

My aim here is to describe some of the broad themes of mathematics as illustrated and implied by the details of introductory mathematics skills, that is, those tools which you with your teachers' guidance worked hard to acquire starting with your very first acquaintance with numbers. These tools include: a familiarity with the number system (integers, fractions, real numbers, the decimal system), the operations of arithmetic (addition, subtraction, multiplication, and division), elementary algebra with rules for solving simple equations in one or two variables, graphing straight lines in a coordinate system and representing them as equations, and an introduction to elements of plane geometry (points, lines, and figures such as triangles and circles) along with the ability to make simple arguments about the relationships of geometric figures.

Our introductory math skills are embedded within a much broader theoretical framework which is typically hidden by a focus on details rather than conceptual foundations. We will start with numbers, the foundation of mathematics you are probably most familiar with, building number systems using the methods of proof (the axiomatic method) that you were introduced to in that other early foundation of mathematics, Euclidean geometry, Then, looking more closely at geometry, we will explore the broader view of geometry that was inherent in the axiomatic method, yet lay dormant for over two thousand years. We will see that embedded within the axiomatic method were the seeds that would grow into new geometries, algebras, and entirely new mathematics as represented by the calculus, set theory, and topology. That these foundations and their generalization have led to the creation of entirely new ways for formulating mathematical ideas is the major theme presented here.

This book is not a history of mathematics. However, the unfolding of the story of how our understanding of mathematics developed over the ages helps to clarify the important themes of mathematics and gives context to our journey. Moreover, the manner in which math is introduced in schools in many ways retraces these historical developments. For these reason, I will give in this first chapter a brief discussion of selected historical developments that shed light on the concepts presented in this book. Details of the subjects mentioned in this historical context will then be explored in the following chapters. (In the endnotes, as indicated by Arabic numeral superscripts, citations are given for supporting references where more details may be found. Often, details are also available with a different perspective among the other references that I cite. Where I have added parenthetical comments as footnotes, I have indicated these by Roman numeral superscripts.)

1.2   The story so far; an outline of the history of mathematics[iii]

1.2.1   Ancient origins of counting, geometry, and algebra

The first encounter with mathematics by our ancient ancestors was undoubtedly with counting. Wolf bones from 30,000 years ago,

---

iii The literature of the history of mathematics is vast. I have focused particularly on four references where more details can be found as indicated in the endnotes and footnotes. Each reference has its particular viewpoint and area of coverage. Much of the discussion here on ancient mathematics is summarized from the highly readable coverage of ancient numeration, calculation, and geometry by Bunt, Jones, and Bedient. *The Historical Roots of Elementary Mathematics* (for full citation details, see Math References 6). In this work clear examples of number systems and calculation methods are provided. Ball, *A Short Account of the History of Mathematics* [Math Reference 3] a classic first published in 1908, provides an encyclopedic description of

discovered in 1937 in excavations, showed markings with notches, not surprisingly, in groupings of five.[1] Suffice it to say that these artifacts suggest the idea of counting and the use of five as a precursor for the concept of a number base. Thus, it is fitting that we will start our journey with numbers in Chapter 2.

With the advent of the historic period, written notation for numbers occurred as documented through the discovery of ancient Egyptian papyri and clay tablets from the civilizations of Mesopotamia. For example, about 4,000 years ago in Egypt, symbols were introduced for the powers of 10 up to 1,000,000.[2] In the Egyptian number system, the position of the symbols would not be critical, and no symbol for zero existed or was necessary. If the symbols for 1, 10, and 100 were, respectively,[iv] |, ∩, and ℰ, then 321 would be expressed as ℰ ℰ ℰ ∩∩ |. The system was a decimal system in the sense that when the number of a symbol type increased to ten, it was replaced by the next symbols, for example ten |'s became ∩.

The Egyptians developed techniques using their symbols for addition, subtraction, multiplication, use of fractions in which the numerator was unity (except for the the fraction 2/3), and division. However, the methodologies for employing these arithmetic operations were supplied through specific examples of practical calculations without the development of a more general approach. Other types of example problems demonstrated approaches for determining unknowns in simple algebraic problems.[3]

The Babylonian number system from about the same period was a sexagesimal (base 60) positional system, conceptually similar to our decimal system (base 10) with the first fifty nine numbers using a symbolic system like that of the Egyptians. Like our decimal system the number of units of a given power of 60 depended on the placement of the symbols. However, in the earliest forms of their number system, it did not have a place holder like our zero, and ambiguities could occur. The precise quantity needed to be implied by the context in which the number was employed. A method of

---

the contributions of virtually all significant mathematicians up to the mid nineteenth century. A more up-to-date and narrative history, paralleling that of Ball, is given by Merzbach and Boyer, *A History of Mathematics*, [Math References 24]. Kline, *Mathematics, the Loss of Certainty* [Math References 18] provides a philosophical view of the developments, controversies, and critiques of mathematics into the twentieth century.

iv The form of the hieroglyphic symbols is from Bunt, Jones, and Bedient, p. 6.

separating the numbers associated with the various powers of sixty was eventually developed about 300 BC; however, it was not conceived of as a number like our zero.[4]

Mathematical techniques were developed by the Babylonians with some steps towards greater generalization than provided by Egyptian approaches. These techniques included: the arithmetic operations, approximations of square roots (even for some cases that we know of as irrational numbers—numbers that cannot be expressed as the ratio of two integers), and solutions to simple algebraic problems, including the forms of the quadratic equation with positive solutions, and cubic equations of the form $ax^3 + bx^2 = c$, with a, b, and c being specific positive numbers.[5] Solutions of cubic equations were unknown to the Egyptians. However, as in the case of Egyptian mathematics, the emphasis was on practical rules to solve specific problem types. A good illustration of this approach and its drawbacks is an example given below of the Babylonian solution to a problem equivalent to solving the quadratic equation, $11x^2 + 7x = 6\ 1/4$. The Babylonians expressed problems geometrically, so this problem might have been expressed as find the side of a square for which eleven times its area plus seven times its side equals 6 1/4. I think by trying to follow the ancient instructions that you will clearly see the difficulties posed to advancing mathematics and problem solving by the use of specific verbal instructions compared to the modern general symbolic approach. (Note that the Babylonians would have expressed numbers with decimal fractions such as 6.25 as 6 15 in their sexagesimal system since $15/60 = 0.25$.)

> *"You take 7 and 11. You multiply 11 by 6 15 and it is 1 8 45 [1 · 60 + 8 + 45/60]. You halve 7 and obtain 3 30. You multiply 3 30 and 3 30. You add the result, 12 15 to 1 8 45 and the result 1 21 [81] has 9 as its square root. You subtract 3 30, which you multiplied by itself, from 9 and you have 5 30. The reciprocal of 11 does not divide. What shall I multiply by 11 so that 5 30 results? 0 30 is its factor. 0 30 is the side of the square [x = 30/60]."*[v]

---

v Cited (p. 195) in Kriwaczek, Paul, *Babylon, Mesopotamia and the Birth of Civilization*,[Other Citation Sources 12], a fascinating general account of the ancient civilizations and cultures of Mesopotamia from Sumer to the fall of Babylonia. In the above problem, if you associate the specific quadratic equation with $ax^2 + b\ x = c$, then you will see the Babylonian solution

In geometry, the Egyptians were concerned with areas and volumes of geometric figures and as with arithmetic methods, provided examples, in some cases incorrect. Their method for determining the area of a circle implies a reasonable approximation for π (256/81 or 3.16 . . .). They were aware of the right triangle, and of specific lengths of sides which produced them, for example: 3, 4, 5.[6] Similar, comments could be used to summarize the achievements of the Babylonians in geometry.[7] Thus at this point in history, the ideas of numeration, the operations of arithmetic, simple solutions of algebraic type problems (however, without a symbolic approach), and some elements of geometry, including quantification of area and volume had appeared.[vi] A notable aspect of this knowledge is its practical character emphasizing the transmission of knowledge through specific examples. For the development of general approaches with results based upon proofs, progress would await new and revolutionary insights introduced by the Greeks.

1.2.2   Classical Greece and the science of deduction

A new approach to mathematics began with Thales of Miletus (640-550 BC). Thales changed the focus of mathematics from methods of determining specific mathematical results to generalized geometrical statements.[8] For example, he stated that the angles at the base of an isosceles triangle are equal. Although some of the statements were considered to be proven, the general approach of deducing theorems from accepted statements was only achieved through the studies of Pythagoras (569-500 BC)[9], his school, and its followers. The discoveries of followers of the Pythagorean School would be further developed and systematized a number of times but most famously by Euclid (330-275 BC) in his classic *Elements*.[10] Euclid

---

technique as implementing one solution of the quadratic formula with a = 11, b = 7, and c = 6 15 (6.25):

$$x = (-b/2 + \sqrt{\left(\frac{b}{2}\right)^2 + ac}\,)/a.$$

In the last step, one gets x=5 30/11, so the Babylonian asks *"What shall I multiply by 11 so that 5 30 results?"* Many other examples of the Babylonian approach to solving quadratic equations are given in Bunt, Jones, and Bedient, pp. 51-58.

vi Similar developments in mathematics also occurred in the ancient communities in China and India; see Merzbach and Boyer, pp. 175-189; see also pp. 3-5 for brief discussion of the Mayan number system.

followed a deductive or axiomatic approach to mathematical truth developed over many years and clarified by among others, Aristotle (384-322 BC).[11] In this approach statements called propositions or theorems could only be proved from previously proven statements which ultimately must be traced back to what might be thought of as self-evident truths, called axioms or postulates (for example all right angles are equal to one another) and common notions (common notions having a broader scope than the geometric postulates, for example, if equals be added to equals the wholes are equal). In addition, definitions were also necessary to complete the system. The first two definitions in *Elements* are: a point is that which has no parts, and a line is a length without breadth. Such was the acceptance of this approach that for over 2,000 years Euclid's geometry was considered to be the only valid representation of physical space. However, numerous mathematicians during this time period sought to show that Euclid's fifth postulate (called the Parallel Postulate),[vii] being much less intuitively obvious than the other postulates, was unnecessary; that is, it could be proved from the other postulates. As a result of these efforts, in the nineteenth century it would finally be understood that such a proof is impossible and that the self-evident truths were merely postulates which could be replaced by other consistent postulates giving rise to non-Euclidean geometries.[12] Thus Euclid's geometry was not only a pillar of mathematics, introducing the axiomatic method, but would ironically through its diminished status become a gateway to a world of new mathematics. We will look closely at the axiomatic approach and non-Euclidian geometries in Chapter 4.

Although Euclid's *Elements* are primarily associated with geometry, the common notions can also be seen as the glimmerings of a future axiomatic approach for the algebra of numbers. The Pythagoreans and their followers had early on become so enamored with the relationships of the natural numbers (positive integers) that they would seek to understand the underlying principles of the

---

[vii] "That, if a straight line falling on two straight lines makes the interior angles on the same side less than two right angles, the two straight lines, if produced indefinitely, meet on that side on which are the angles less than two right angles," Heath, *Euclid, The thirteen Books of the Elements*, Vol. 1 (Books I and II), p. 155, {Math References 15]. This as discussed in Chapter 4 is equivalent to the more commonly known postulate, *Through a given point P not on a line l there is one and only one line in the plane of P and l which does not meet l (see Section 1.2.5.2 and 4.3.4).*

universe in terms of them.[13] This viewpoint would survive well into the Renaissance, constraining investigators such as the astronomer Johann Kepler (1571-1630)[14] in his views of acceptable descriptions of the universe. Only the undeniable nature of the planetary observations would finally cause him to abandon his theories based on natural numbers.[viii] Of more permanent value to mathematics was the exploration by the Greeks of mathematical properties of the natural numbers, for example, as described in *Elements*: the discovery of prime numbers (numbers only divisible by themselves and one), the Euclidean Algorithm for determining the greatest common divisor, the Fundamental Theorem of Arithmetic (which proved that natural numbers consisted of a unique product of prime numbers), the infinite number of primes, and thus, more generally the beginnings of the discipline of number theory. These results would be significant as a starting place for the properties of the rational numbers (numbers expressed as the ratio of two integers (Chapter 2).

The interpretation of algebraic relations of numbers was characteristically given a geometric interpretation by the Greeks of the classic period; for example, the product of two integers, $n \cdot m$, could be viewed geometrically as the area of a rectangle with sides n and m. However, within this interpretation were the seeds to destroy the Pythagoreans view of the primacy of the natural numbers in the universe. As early as the time of Pythagoras, it may have been known that the length of the diagonal of a square with sides of unity could not be represented as a ratio of natural numbers; that is $\sqrt{2}$ is an irrational number.[15] Such a discovery created a crisis for Greek philosophy. For this reason geometrical representations of numbers and of their algebraic relations were favored rather than the explicit acknowledgement of numerical approximations of the irrational numbers, such as employed by the Babylonians. We retain some of this reaction in our expressions: x-square and x-cube for respectively, x^2 and x^3. Probably for these reasons, the development of Greek algebra was hindered. Exceptions to this general tendency could be found at the Schools of Alexandria in Egypt from about 300 BC to 600.

---

viii Kepler discovered his three laws governing planetary motions of the solar system from the precise observations of Tycho Brahe. Kepler's first law states that planets move in elliptical orbits. This was contrary to his notion that the motions would be described in terms of the five regular polyhedra. Kepler's laws would be crucial in the development by Isaac Newton of the Universal Law of Gravitation; see Kline, pp. 36-40.

Particularly noteworthy for this discussion is Diophantus (ca. 350) who developed a primitive symbolic approach to algebra in which words used to specify quantities and operations were abbreviated.[16] With this technique, he provided a general solution for some quadratic equations, solutions for one form of cubic equation, and algebraic solutions to a variety of word problems. When the roots were irrational or negative, the solutions were rejected; thus, expressing a concern with the reality of these numbers which would continue well into the eighteenth century.[17] Also noteworthy were his methods for determining solutions with rational numbers for equations of two or three variables (indeterminate equations) including solutions for some forms of simultaneous equations. Others of this period would also continue the development of algebra using the practical approach begun by the Egyptians and Babylonians. However, little interest was taken in its logical foundations in sharp contrast to deductive geometry. No proofs were given for the solution techniques. The development of an axiomatic approach to numbers and their properties would not begin until the nineteenth century.

1.2.3   Harbingers of modern mathematics; innovations in number and algebra

With the end of the Western Roman Empire in the fifth century and the relative stagnation of mathematics in the continuing Byzantine Empire (Eastern Roman Empire), innovation in mathematics would move eastward to the communities of the Indian sub-continent and those of the Islamic civilization developed after the seventh century. In India, about the sixth century, a positional decimal system, reducing the required symbols for numbers, was introduced. The addition of zero, perhaps about 200 years later, completed the Indian decimal system. Techniques, analogous to current practice, were developed for the arithmetic operations. In addition to the positive integers and fractions, Indian mathematics used irrational numbers and incorporated negative numbers, along with associated rules for their use. As in the past, however, the rules were developed pragmatically and with analogies to the operations of the natural numbers. Other contributions were the development of trigonometric functions along algebraic lines rather than the geometrical interpretations such as those of Ptolemy of Alexandria.[ix] Also, initial steps were taken towards symbolic algebra similar to Diophantus.[18]

The spread of the Islamic communities in the seventh and eighth century brought them into contact with the mathematics of the Hindus. By the end of the eighth century, they were familiar with the Hindu numerical notation, arithmetic, and algebra.[x] Among the greatest of the contributors to Islamic mathematics was Muhammad ibn Musa al-Khwarizmi (ca. 780-ca. 850). His name, al-Khwarizmi, would come down to us in English as algorithm, evolving in its meaning from referring to the decimal system as explained in his works to more general procedures for calculations. The origin of the word algebra comes from the title of his work, *Hisob al-jabr wa'l muqabalah* which refers to the rules for manipulating equations (translated as restoration and reduction as in transposition of terms in an equation to form a solution). The work includes: rules for solution of quadratic equations with positive solutions, geometric interpretations of the algebraic rules, products of $(x \pm a)$ $(x \pm b)$ (modern notation), expressions involving squares, or square roots and, despite rejecting negative solutions to equations, rules for signed numbers: for example, $(-a) \cdot (-a) = a^2$.[19] Another significant step was the use of decimal representations for fractions by Jamshid al-Kashi (ca. 1380-1429). Surprisingly, decimal fraction had not been used in the Hindu number system.[xi] Although symbolic algebra was not used in this work, it was the initial source for the introduction of the decimal system and algebra into Europe. Other Islamic mathematicians through the fifteenth century would continue to contribute following the pragmatic path of algebra, however without introducing other major innovations.

Europeans first became aware in the twelfth century of the mathematics of the Islamic communities through the Moorish schools of Granada, Cordova, and Seville.[20] For the next 300 years, the primary mathematical activity was absorption and spread of the knowledge

---

ix Ptolemy (ca. 90-168) is famous for his astronomical treatise, the *Almagest*, in which he describes the motion of the sun and planets about the earth using epicycles; Ball, p.96-99.

x Details on Islamic mathematics from the seventh to twelfth century are summarized from Merzbach and Boyer, pp.203-222.

xi Merzbach and Boyer, p. 192. Decimal fractions had been employed in China possibly as early as 1400 BC Ibid. p. 180. However, their late introduction by al-Kashi is a reminder of the frequent isolation of developments in mathematics.

of the Greek, Hindu, and Islamic world. By the middle of fifteenth century, this was accomplished throughout much of central and western Europe through books prepared by European scholars from Greek and Islamic sources.

From the mid fifteenth to the mid seventeenth century, advancements were made by European scholars along the previously established directions of algebra. For example Nicholas Tartaglia (1500-1557) solved cubic equations of the form: $x^3 + qx = r$ (modern notation).[21] He also provided a technique for determining the coefficients of the expansion of $(1 + x)^n$ from the coefficients of: $(1 + x)^{n-1}$. Girolamo Cardan (1501-1576), who had without permission published Tartaglia's solution for cubic equations as his own, published solutions for additional forms of cubic equations.[22] He discussed the nature of the solutions, including negative and what became known as complex numbers (solutions involving terms with square roots of negative numbers) along with the usual discussion of positive solutions. He noted that the complex numbers would appear in pairs although he described them as "ingenious though useless".[23]

Throughout this period, the development of algebra continued with the same pragmatic approach lacking theoretical foundations that had characterized its development since the time of the Egyptians and Babylonians. The contrast with the deductive structure of geometry must have been apparent. Most likely, the lack of an effective algebraic notation, along with the clarity that it would bring, was in part to blame. Over time innovations in symbolic representations were added. The contributions of François Viète (1540-1603) were notable in this regard as particularly adding symbolic structure and the use of symbols for unknowns and for generalized known quantities that would lead to modern algebra notation.[24] Fitfully over time, such innovations as symbols for the arithmetic operations, equality, powers of variables, and abbreviations of trigonometric functions would be created such that by the middle of the seventeenth century the structure of algebraic notation would be recognizable in its intent, if not completed, to modern eyes.[25]

Arguably the most significant innovation of the first half of the seventeenth century was the creation of a bridge between geometry and algebra through the development of analytic geometry. As is often the case, major new insights may be independently discovered. However, priority appears to be given to René Descartes (1596-1650) as attested to, at least in terms of common attribution, through the naming of coordinates referred to perpendicular axes as Cartesian. Descartes recognized the possibility of describing geometric curves in the plane through equations of these coordinates and thus, geometric properties would be embedded in algebraic descriptions.[26] In forming a relationship between the points of the Cartesian plane and numerical coordinates, Descartes assumed, certainly without appreciation for his farsighted assumption, that there was a one-to-one correspondence between points of a line and real numbers. Of course, he could not know this as he had no formal understanding of either negative or irrational numbers.[27]

Prior to Descartes, Pierre de Fermat (1601-1665) had similar insights which were closer in application to modern analytic geometry; however, his results were not published in his lifetime.[28] Both men investigated geometric properties such as the tangent (slope of a curve at one point) and its normal (perpendiculars to the tangent lines) to curves. The reduction of geometry to algebraic functions would ultimately lead to common foundations in numbers for geometry and algebra (Chapters 5).

1.2.4   On the shoulders of giants; calculus and the beginnings of mathematical analysis[xii]

New mathematical techniques continued to be developed throughout the first half of the seventeenth century. For example, Fermat and Isaac Newton's mentor Isaac Barrow (1630-1677) developed techniques using infinitesimals[xiii] for determining tangents to curves.[29] Similarly, methods involving essentially the summation of infinitesimals in the determination of the area under curves were developed by Bonaventura Cavalieri (1598-1647) and Fermat, following in the footsteps of Archimedes (287 BC-212 B.C).[30] These undoubtedly contributed to the discovery of the calculus which will be discussed below. However, the greatest impetus to the development of the new mathematics was the inspiration that came from the desire to explain the fundamental workings of the universe. The mathematical and scientific discoveries of Isaac Newton (1642-1727)[31] and Gottfried Leibniz (1646-1716)[32] in the second half of the seventeenth

---

xii In a letter Newton wrote, "If I have seen farther than Descartes, it is because I have stood on the shoulders of giants," Merzbach and Boyer, p. 358.
xiii Infinitesimals along with their use were poorly defined and in the absence of rigorous methods for their use were employed informally as quantities smaller than any specified quantity.

century would lead to a spectacular expansion of mathematical and scientific knowledge that would be central to the development of physics until the beginning of the twentieth century and remain vital to engineering to the present.

Newton was a beneficiary of a scientific revolution that had been initiated by three developments: the theory of Nicolaus Copernicus (1473-1543) which shifted the sun to the center of the solar system; the three laws of Kepler describing the planetary motions; and the astronomical observations with a telescope by Galileo Galilei (1564-1642).[33] Galileo's observations supported Copernicus' system through the example of a mini-solar system in the moons revolving about Jupiter, and the observation of phases of Venus, similar to those of the moon, which supported the description of Venus revolving around the sun as an inner planet.[xiv]

Newton would explain the planetary motions, the orbit of the moon, as well as motion of falling objects and projectiles at the earth's surface through his three laws of motion and his universal law of gravitation. To do this he would develop, as part of what would become known as the calculus, an analytical method to determine the changes in motion under the force of his universal gravity.[34] In addition to Galileo's astronomical contributions to the ongoing revolution in science, Galileo also had developed the relationships with time of the velocity and distance of a uniformly accelerated object (such as under the force of gravity near the earth's surface) and verified the relationships experimentally through observations of the time of descent of bodies sliding down inclined planes.[35] Newton's mathematical approach calculated the velocity as what he termed the fluxion (time rate of change) of distance, which he termed a fluent (flowing quantity).[36] This was calculated, in essence, through the device of determining the average velocity over decreasingly small time increments or infinitesimals, which unfortunately were not precisely defined by either Newton or Leibniz[37]. Alternatively, the problem could be described geometrically as one of determining the tangent at given times of the curves of distance versus time. Similarly, acceleration could be calculated as the fluxion of velocity (in this case the fluent). Independently, Leibniz would develop the same technique

---

xiv Drake, Stillman, *Discoveries and Opinions of Galileo*, translated by Stillman Drake, [Other Citation Sources 4]; a translation by Drake of Galileo's letters describing his observations of Jupiter and Venus, among others, see pp. 51-58, pp. 93-94.

using different notation and terminology which would through its greater ease of manipulation become that of modern usage in the calculus. In Leibniz's terminology, the velocity and acceleration are, respectively, the derivative of distance and velocity. Acceleration is therefore a second derivative of distance.

Newton's second law of motion, as expressed in one form, says that the net force in a given direction on an object is equal to the product of the mass of the object and its acceleration in that direction. As acceleration is the derivative of velocity, the determination of velocity from a known force such as gravity involves finding the function whose derivative is the acceleration (generated by the known force). The genius of Newton and Leibniz was to show that the determination of the velocity was directly related to the determination of the area under the curve of acceleration versus time. (Recall that the insight that the area under a curve could be obtained as the infinite sum of infinitesimal areas was anticipated by Cavalieri and Fermat.). In Leibniz's terminology, the velocity was the integral of the acceleration. Surprisingly therefore, the problems of determining tangents (derivatives) and areas under curves (integrals) were, inverse processes. This is described by the Fundamental Theorem of Calculus and will be discussed in Chapter 8.

The calculus techniques of Newton and Leibniz along with Newton's Laws of Motion and Universal Law of Gravitation would be extended and exploited to successfully describe an unprecedented number of physical phenomena. Of particular importance was the extension of the calculus to describe problems with variations in three dimensions and time. These formulations are known as partial differential equations. Just to mention a few examples, Jean Le-Rond D'Alembert (1717-1783)[38] developed the wave equation, explaining the phenomena of traveling waves; Leonhard Euler (1707-1783)[39] established the equations of hydrodynamics which bear his name, Joseph Louis Lagrange (1736-1813)[40] initiated a generalization of Newton's equations of motion, central to theoretical physics, in terms of generalized coordinates and generalized kinetic and potential energies, and Pierre Laplace (1749-1827)[41] developed his equation for gravitational potential energy which bears his name. A form of this equation has application to among others: solid and fluid mechanics, heat conduction, mass diffusion, and electricity and magnetism. Insight into the extension of calculus to such three dimensional problems is given in Chapter 8.

The advances in physics generated by the approach of calculus were also accompanied by numerous significant advances in mathematics. Newton had developed the binomial theorem (without proof) which allowed functions of the form, $(1 + x)^{m/n}$, where m and n are integers, to be expressed as an infinite series. [42] An example of an infinite series is given below:

$$(1-x)^{-1} = 1/(1 - x) = 1 + x + x^2 + x^3 + x^4 + \ldots \qquad (1.1)$$

Such forms were often easier to manipulate term by term with the calculus than the original function; however, as with the calculus and algebra in general, no logical foundations had been established. Despite the lack of a fundamental understanding of infinite series, mathematicians pragmatically, moved forward treating the infinite series in a manner similar to ones with a finite number of terms. Sometimes this would work—other times, not. For example, for x=1/2, the infinite series noted above equals 2 just as the function $1/(1 - x)$ does; while for $x > 1$, the series diverges (does not equal any finite number), although $1/(1 - x)$ is a normal function. Newton developed infinite series for the trigonometric functions of sine and cosine (Section 4.3.4), Euler[43] for the irrational numbers of π and e.[xv] Using the infinite series representations, Euler could easily show the important relationship:

$$e^{i\theta} = \cos(\theta) + i\sin(\theta) = a + bi, \qquad (2.1)$$

with $i = \sqrt{-1}$ (Euler, late in his life, introduced this notation) and the variable θ in radians (recall. the arc length of a semi-circle of radius r is π r; i.e., π radians corresponds to a circular sector of 180°). Note that the result of 2.1 is what is known as a complex number with a real part, a = cos (θ), and an imaginary part, b =sin (θ). The Euler relation will be discussed in Sections 6.4 and 8.2.2 after the introduction of complex numbers in Chapter 3.

---

xv The irrational number e (2.71828 . . .), as designated by Euler, was shown by him to be the limit as n becomes indefinitely large (n→∞) of $(1+\frac{1}{n})^n$. It is the base for natural logarithms (ln) in the same way 10 is the base for common logarithms (log). (For example, ln e² =2 and log 10² = log 100 =2). The expression for e was first encountered by Jacques Bernoulli in the problem of continuously compounded interest; Merzbach and Boyer, pp., 286-289, 393, and 408-410. Limits will be discussed in Chapters 5 and 6.

The area of mathematics dealing with the processes involving infinity, infinite series, infinitesimals, and the concepts of integration and the derivative came to be known as analysis. In the absence of rigorous foundations for analysis, enormous progress was still made using pragmatic approaches in solving physical problems and exploring the theoretical implications of the new techniques. However, critics questioned the validity of the calculations. An example of the criticism of the new techniques can be illustrated with the derivative. If the derivative of the distance versus time curve was conceived of as being obtained from the distanced moved in an infinitesimal time, the resulting derivative could reasonably be interpreted as 0/0. Bishop George Berkeley attacked Newton's analysis, writing that Newton's fluxions (or derivatives in Leibniz's terminology) . . . *"are neither finite quantities, nor quantities infinitely small, not yet nothing. May we not call them the ghosts of departed quantities?"*[44]

A significant portion of the nineteenth century efforts in mathematics would be devoted to developing a rigorous foundation for the calculus. Before this could be completed, however, the foundations of the real numbers, including the irrational numbers such as $\sqrt{2}$, would also have to be built. These ideas would shift the focus to increasingly abstract concepts, in contrast to the scientifically or practically based sources of inspiration for algebra and the calculus. The real numbers will be developed in Chapters 3 and 6 prior to the discussion of the calculus in Chapter 8.

1.2.5   Castles in the air; the age of foundation building and abstraction[xvi]

1.2.5.1 *The real number system*

With advances in calculus techniques at the very core of scientific progress in such areas of physics as mechanics, electricity, magnetism, and heat transfer, clearly there was a need to put the methods based on the infinitesimals that Newton had described as *"evanescent divisible quantities"*[45] on a more formal and logical foundation. Numerous mathematicians made attempts; however, the greatest progress in developing these foundations was due to Augustin

---

xvi "If you have built castles in the air, your work need not be lost; that is where they should be. Now put the foundations under them." From: Thoreau, Henry David, *Walden or Life in the Woods*, p. 209.[Other Citation Sources 16].

Louis Cauchy (1789-1857).[46] Cauchy replaced the concept of the infinitesimals with a formal definition of limit. He applied this concept to the continuity of a function (as implied by relationships such as distance versus time), the derivative, and the integral as an infinite summation process, as well as to infinite series. Cauchy described the limit process by noting that:

> *"When the successive values attributed to a variable approach indefinitely a fixed value so as to end by differing from it by as little as one wishes, this last is called the limit of all others.*[47]

The mathematical formulation of this concept and its application are discussed in Chapters 5 and 6.

Cauchy's concept of limit would eventually lead through the work of others to a full understanding of the real numbers. Going back to antiquity, no formal foundation had been established for numbers and operations that applied to numbers. The lack of clear meaning of the real numbers which included the irrational numbers was vital not only to the calculus to which they applied, but also to the foundations of mathematics. In their attempts to formulate rigorous foundations for the calculus, mathematicians searched for functions that would test their new theoretical bases for the calculus. For example Karl Weierstrass (1815-1897), who made Cauchy's concept of limit mathematically precise, formed a function that is continuous everywhere and nowhere differentiable (that is, there are no tangents to the curve).[48] Georg Bernhard Riemann (1826-1866) investigated functions with discontinuities with a view to determining conditions in which integrals could be obtained. Among the functions he investigated is one which is discontinuous at infinitely many points in an interval yet its integral exists. His efforts would result in the formulation of integration now known as the Riemann integral. Perhaps the most pathological function was that imagined by Peter Dirichlet (1805-1859).[49] The Dirichlet function $f(x) = \begin{cases} b, & \text{for x irrational} \\ a, & \text{for x rational} \end{cases}$ is nowhere continuous or differentiable, but with a full understanding of the real numbers and an appreciation of their meaning for integration, the function would ultimately be integrated through the more comprehensive technique of Lebesgue integration (Henri Lebesgue, 1875 1941).[50] (Note that for continuous functions, all of the integration techniques from Newton on would give the same area under the curve as expected.)

The key to the development of a foundation for the real numbers was the understanding of the differences between the rational numbers and the irrational numbers which together form the real numbers. Both the rational numbers and real numbers are characterized as what is known as an ordered field, and therefore follow the same algebraic rules with regard to the common arithmetic operations and ordering given by relations such as a is less than b (a < b). Moreover, for both rational and real numbers, there are infinitely many numbers between any two selected numbers. The differences between the rational and real numbers were first made clear by Richard Dedekind (1831-1916).[51]

Dedekind noted that the rational and irrational numbers could be distinguished through the concept of a cut separating the set of rational numbers into two sets of numbers. The sets are defined by the condition that all the rational numbers are contained within one or the other set with each set containing at least one number, and that all of the numbers of one set, call it A, are less than those of the second set, B. Only one real number can be defined by this cut in the sets of numbers. If the cut is such that set A has the largest number (or B has the smallest), then the cut defines a rational number. If A has no largest rational number and B no smallest number, then the cut defines an irrational number. As a classic example, if the set A consists of the rational numbers r with r^2 less than or equal to 2, then there is no largest rational number within A (no matter how close r^2 is to 2, a larger rational number can be selected.), and no smallest in B.

The Dedekind cuts defining the rational and irrational numbers can be visualized geometrically as the continuous number line. With that picture, one is reminded that the irrational number $\sqrt{2}$ may be represented geometrically as the line segment which is the diagonal of a square whose sides are unity. The Dedekind cuts and the real numbers are discussed in detail in Chapter 3.

The definitions of Dedekind for rational and irrational numbers are equivalent to alternative postulates of the sets of real numbers. One such postulate is the Least Upper Bound Property which states that: If a nonempty set of elements of the real numbers has an upper bound, then it has a least upper bound.[52] For example, if we take the set of rational numbers whose square is less than 2, we will see in Chapter 2 that there is no least upper bound. The Least Upper Bound Property, crucial to the difference between the rational and real numbers and to what is known as the completeness of the real numbers, will be explored in Chapter 2, 3, and 6 and in the context of set theory in Chapter 9.

Georg Cantor (1845-1918)[53] would continue the evaluation of numbers in sets. Indeed the concept of sets of numbers would become central to the foundations of mathematics. Particularly controversial were his investigations of infinite sets. His method of analysis would make it clear that infinite sets such as the even numbers, integers, and rational numbers could be considered as being of the same order of infinity; i.e., each could be put into a one-to-one correspondence with the natural numbers. For this reason such sets are known as countably infinite or denumerable. In contrast, the real numbers were shown to be uncountably infinite, leading to the implication that there are "more" irrational numbers than rational numbers. Such consideration would lead Cantor to transfinite numbers which characterize the nature of infinite sets even beyond the infinity of the real numbers.[54] These ideas will be explored in Chapters 3 and 9.

1.2.5.2 Euclid's fifth postulate and the birth of new geometries

During the same period when Cauchy was developing more rigorous foundations for the calculus, the two thousand year old search for improvements in Euclid's geometry would end with a dramatic undercutting of geometry's claim as the premier example of rigor in mathematics and only true representative of physical space. As previously mentioned, since the time of Euclid, mathematicians had sought to show that Euclid's fifth postulate[xvii] could be proved from the other postulates and was thus unnecessary. Euclid, perhaps concerned about the nature of his fifth postulate, did not employ it in proofs until his twenty ninth propositions.[55] However, over the centuries, mathematicians would find that their "proofs" of the fifth postulate were just restatements of Euclid's fifth postulate in other forms. For example, most students today know the fifth postulate in the form as stated by John Playfair (1748-1819):

> "Through a given point P not on a line l there is one and only
> one line in the plane of P and l which does not meet l."[56]

The use of the fifth postulate, known as the Parallel Postulate, is necessary to prove Euclid's thirty second proposition[57] that the sum of

---

xvii See footnote vii (Section 1.2.2)

the angles of a triangle is 180° and the famous Pythagorean Theorem[58] (Euclid's forty seventh proposition) which states that in a right triangle the square of the hypotenuse equals the sum of the squares of the adjacent sides).

Two mathematicians who accepted that Euclid's Parallel Postulate is independent of the other postulates were Nikolai Lobachevsky (1793-1856) and John Bolyai (1802-1860).[59] Each, independently, replaced Euclid's Parallel Postulate with the postulate which in its essentials said that for a given point P not on a line l, there is **more than one line** in the plane of P and l which does not meet l. They then explored the consequences of this new postulate leading to a new geometry sometimes known as hyperbolic geometry. Of particular note are the consequences that the sum of the angles of a triangle is less than 180°, similar triangles (triangles with the same angles) are congruent, and that not surprisingly, relationships analogous to those of trigonometry and the Pythagorean Theorem differ from their Euclidean counterparts. However, all of the propositions of Euclid which do not use his Parallel Postulate are true in this new geometry.

Riemann in 1854 delivered a lecture at the University of Göttingen broadening the traditional view of geometry through a generalization of the concept of a mathematical space.[60] Consistent with the far broader consequences of Riemann's insight is that if Euclid's Parallel Postulate is replaced with the postulate that no lines are parallel, a different geometry results in which the sum of the angles of a triangle is greater than 180° and that this sum approaches 180° as the area of the triangle approaches zero. One interpretation of the new geometry termed elliptic is that it is consistent with the geometry of the surface of a sphere. The new geometries eventually made it clear that the postulates of Euclid are not self-evident truths, but hypotheses which if followed logically lead to the geometric system of Euclid. Different hypotheses would lead to different geometries. However, this axiomatic approach did not apply simply to geometry. It might also be employed to provide the foundations for all mathematics. This was the dream going into the twentieth century. In the final chapter, the limitations of the axiomatic method discovered in the twentieth century will be discussed The axiomatic approach inherent in the formation of the different geometries will be discussed in Chapter 4, along with examples from non-Euclidean geometry.,

With the introduction of these new geometries, it was natural to ask about their relationship to physical space. Carl Friedrich Gauss (1777-1855)[61] had anticipated in letters to colleagues the existence of non-Euclidean geometries and attempted to evaluate the sum of angles of triangles formed by three mountain peaks. However, he was not successful at reaching a conclusion due to experimental errors. Gauss never published his views on non-Euclidean geometry, perhaps due to the controversy that would attend such publication when it was generally thought that Euclidean geometry was the only possible geometry.[62] However, Gauss did introduce new concepts in geometry that were important for the future developments. Gauss initiated concepts leading to differential geometry which evaluated the local properties of curved surfaces. He developed a mathematical formulation for the local curvature and its relationship to the parameters determining the surface.

Gauss's concept of local curvature would be extended by Riemann when he generalized the concept of non-Euclidean geometries through a locally varying measure of distance on a surface, closely related to curvature.[63] The mathematical entity known as a tensor, which may be thought of as a generalization of a vector (an entity such as velocity with magnitude and direction indicated in three dimensional spaces by three components) would be central to differential geometry and form the mathematical apparatus for Einstein's Theory of General Relativity. Chapter 7 will introduce the concepts of vectors and tensors.

1.2.5.3 New algebras—new approaches

Algebra, since the earliest time, lacked solid foundations, progressing pragmatically as new problems came to the fore. To meet the needs of newly developed physical theories such as those of fluid and solid mechanics, new mathematical entities and techniques for applying them to problems, had to be established. One example of a physical concept requiring new mathematics is that of stress in fluids or solids. The concept of stress requires more components than a vector such as velocity because stress must indicate not only the direction in which the internal force per unit area is applied to a solid or fluid, but also the direction (orientation) of the surface to which the stress is applied. While velocity requires three components, one for each direction of space, stress is described by nine components in what could described as an array called a tensor.

William Hamilton (1805-1865) and Hermann Grassmann (1809-1877) developed different approaches to these formulations; however a common characteristic of the new algebras which they created were arrays for which products did not commute (ab ≠ ba).[64]

Exploring more generally the algebra of multi-component arrays called matrices (Chapter 7), Arthur Cayley (1821-1895) observed the same lack of the commutative property.[65] Mathematicians were surprised as they had assumed that the commutative property, with its connections to numbers and arithmetic, would be present. With the creation of new algebras which were useful in physical problems, systems of algebra like the new geometries could be seen as sets of propositions that followed from their postulates. The usefulness of the resulting system, therefore, would depend upon experience of its use with the intended application.[xviii]

The logical structures supporting algebra had been investigated long before the concerns brought about by matrices. Evariste Galois (1812-1832) defined the properties of an algebraic structure termed a group as part of his work on the solvability of polynomials. Unfortunately, his work was virtually unknown as it was not published until sixteen years after his tragic death in a duel.[66] An example of a group is the integers under the operation of addition. The postulates that define integers as a group under addition are: 1) the addition of any two integers is an integer (closed under addition), 2) the grouping of numbers in a sequence of addition is not important (associative property: $(a + b) + c = a + (b + c)$, 3) the addition of zero to any integer leaves that integer unchanged (existence of an identity element, in this case 0), and 4) existence of an inverse number such that for all integers, an integer and its inverse add to the identity element, $(a + (-a) = 0)$.[67] These properties define many diverse sets and their operations and are the basis for determining propositions that hold for all groups. Integers have the additional commutative property, $a + b = b + a$, so it is a commutative or Abelian group.

Dedekind continued Galois' development of an abstract axiomatic basis for algebra. Dedekind introduced the algebraic structure known as a field composed of a system with two binary operations forming two groups in which the operations are distributive (for example, $a(b + c) = ab + ac$).[68] Both the rational and real numbers have the properties of a field, the difference being the addition of the Least Upper Bound Property for real numbers, as mentioned previously.[69]

---

xviii Commenting that the usefulness of an algebraic system needs to be tested by experience, Henri Lebesgue pointed out that determining whether one plus one equals two may depend on the context. For if one puts a lion and a rabbit in a cage, one will not find two animals in the cage later (Kline, p. 92).

The new understanding of analysis, geometry, and algebra made it seem to many mathematicians toward the end of the nineteenth century that an axiomatic approach could be used to form a solid foundation for all of mathematics. With a bridge established between geometry and algebra through analytic geometry, establishing the foundations of analysis and algebra from numbers would provide in principle such a foundation. Weierstrass called this program the arithimetization of analysis. One aspect of this program was the building up of the real numbers from the natural numbers. In some sense, this was a return to the Pythagoreans' dream of the primacy of number in the universe. A significant start in this program was the statement of the fundamental postulates by Giuseppe Peano (1858-1932) forming the axiomatic basis of the natural numbers and the properties of their binary operations.[70] On this foundation, the integers could then be constructed with the addition of zero and the negative integers, followed by the rational numbers as ratios of integers, and the real numbers, with the irrational numbers defined by the Dedekind cuts. As Caspar Wessel (1745-1818) and later Gauss, and Robert Argand (1768-1822) recognized, complex numbers could be represented as Cartesian coordinates of real numbers in a plane with the ordinate being imaginary.[71] Thus, the complex numbers could also be built from the foundation of the natural numbers. (Chapter 3)

The apparent successes of the axiomatic approach seemed by the end of the nineteenth century to be leading to an age when mathematics could be said to rest on absolute foundations of truth. As part of this program of perfecting mathematics, David Hilbert (1862-1943) revised Euclid's plane geometry, clarifying assumptions, correcting logical errors, and removing meaningless definitions. Hilbert's axiomatic geometry was initiated with undefined terms (point, line, plane, on, between, and congruent) with definitions for segment, intersection, triangle (and related definitions such as sides, vertices, etc.) and fourteen postulates which relate the undefined terms.[72] Hilbert's geometry, starting with undefined terms, is, therefore, abstract and does not require the identification of its conclusions with the usual intuitive model of geometry. Hilbert in discussing the need to approach geometry abstractly stated that *"One must at all times be able to replace 'points, lines, planes' by 'tables, chairs, beer mugs.'"*[73] This is to say that other interpretations for point, line, and plane that fit the definitions and postulates would be acceptable models and alternative applications.[xix]

---

xix This is the sense of Bertrand Russell's comment cited in footnote i.

1.2.6 The ongoing story of mathematics: limitations and rich possibilities

Just as Hilbert had strengthened geometry through the axiomatic method, he recognized that there were issues with the axiomatic method itself which needed to be strengthened. Perhaps the most pressing question was whether contradictory conclusions might be obtained by using different combinations of the postulates from within a system. Hilbert referred to a system in which contradictions could not occur as consistent.

Of comparable importance was the question of whether every statement within a mathematical system could be shown to be true or false. Hilbert called an axiomatic system complete if there are no undecidable statements. Hilbert believed that consistency and completeness could be shown, but this and other philosophic questions discussed below would lead to struggles in the first half of the twentieth century bringing into question Hilbert's view of the perfectibility of mathematics.[74]

A major step in the arithimetization of mathematics was taken with Peano's axiomatic approach to the natural numbers which could be used as a foundation for the real and complex numbers. However, others searched for even more fundamental foundations. Alfred North Whitehead (1861-1947) and Bertrand Russell (1872-1970) sought to base all of mathematics on principles of logic (logistic approach). They initiated their system with axioms of logic from which all else would be derived.[75] An introduction to logic is given in Chapter 4. The logistic approach would be quite controversial. Since the time of Aristotle, rules of logic had been assumed in deriving postulates; however for many, mathematics, because of its extraordinary success at describing the physical world, seemed to require external input from experiences beyond simply pure logic.

Another approach followed from Dedekind's and Cantor's descriptions of the real numbers in terms of sets. Ernst Zermelo (1871-1953) and Abraham Fraenkel (1891-1965) established axioms for set theory which could be used as a foundation for mathematics and competed with the logistic approach.[76] In both the logistic and set-theoretic approach, critics considered there to be serious defects. Both approaches made use of infinite sets which were not accepted as proper by many leading mathematicians. Also the use of existence proofs which did not provide a method for constructing the mathematical entity in question was also not acceptable to all.

In both cases, it was argued that mathematical entities that were outside human experience and intuition were not proper foundations for mathematics. Yet other problems were raised by paradoxes of logic. Russell provided one example of a paradox using sets with the property of containing themselves along with the other member sets. The paradox was illustrated by Russell in the form of the question, if a barber shaves only those who do not shave themselves, does he shave himself?[77] Reflecting on this statement, it is clear that the answer cannot be said to be true or false. Such paradoxes struck at the heart of logic as a foundation of mathematics. Thus what Hilbert might have imagined at the beginning of the twentieth century as a golden age of mathematics was instead one of controversies and lively debate.

As serious as the issues discussed above were, they were overshadowed by an even more alarming discovery concerning the foundations of mathematics. Recall that Hilbert believed that an axiomatic system could be shown to be consistent and complete. However, in 1931, Kurt Gödel (1906-1978) published a paper proving that the consistency of a mathematical system such as that of Whitehead and Russell could not be established and that there are statements which are not decidable in a consistent mathematical system.[78] Thus in a single paper, Gödel had put an end to Hilbert's dream:

> *". . . to eliminate once and for all the questions regarding the foundation of mathematics in the form in which they are now posed, by turning every mathematical proposition into a formula that can be concretely exhibited and strictly derived, thus recasting mathematical derivations and inferences in such a way that they are unshakable and yet provide an adequate picture of the whole science."*[79]

The implications of the debate on the foundations of mathematics and the limitations discovered by Gödel are discussed in the context of the meaning and direction of mathematics in the final chapter.

Was this the end of progress in mathematics?—Hardly. Despite the impossibility of fulfilling Hilbert's dream, mathematics continued to expand its theoretical scope while continuing to play its crucial historic role of providing the language needed for theoretical physics, engineering, and other quantitative disciplines such as economics. An arbitrary list that one might obtain through a casual internet search of twentieth century mathematicians might reveal the following great contributors to mathematics and just a few of examples of their contributions to applied problems: Andrei Kolmogorov (turbulent fluid mechanics), John von Neumann (computer architecture, game theory), Roger Penrose (general relativity, black holes), René Thom (catastrophe theory), Stanislaw Ulam (Monte Carlo methods of computation), and Norbert Wiener (cybernetics—feedback in control systems). Even this small list gives a sense of the unique expressive capability of mathematics.

New areas of mathematics would appear in the twentieth century at an unprecedented pace. As an example of one of the most important of these new areas, topology is introduced briefly in Chapter 9. Topology can be considered to be a generalization of geometry and space with origins in the set theories of Cantor and the related set concepts applied to the real numbers. As early as the first half of the nineteenth century, geometry had been investigated by A. F. Mobius (1790-1860) in terms of the abstract effects of various types of transformations.[80] Mobius classified transformations depending on the geometric characteristics which remained the same (congruence, similarity, preservation of parallel lines, etc.). This approach would be extended by Felix Klein (1849-1925)[81] in a more general way by evaluating geometries using group theory to characterize transformations in terms of the properties of figures that would remain invariant. However, in topology, space as defined by Maurice Fréchet (1878-1973)[82] became even more general, consisting of abstract sets of points and their relationships. Concepts of neighborhoods, open and close intervals, and their connectedness, which find their place in sets of the real numbers and in the concept of limit, would have a more general meaning in these abstract spaces (Chapter 9). The further generalization of geometry was revolutionary. A current search of the internet would generate a considerable list of conferences and papers with abstract studies in topology along with applications for topology.

The struggle in mathematics over its foundations in the twentieth century raises the question of why mathematics has continued to be successful. The simplest answer is that its abstract methods are grounded rigorously in logic and experience. When approached with imagination and intuition, but with an understanding of the foundations and their limitations, mathematics has proved to have an extraordinary capability to describe, comprehend, and project the relationships and interactions of systems whether of the real world or the imagination.

This brief outline of the history of mathematics started with concerns with counting and problems of geometry. The history of mathematics is in part the history of how these ideas were extended, developed to solve new problems, and generalized to produce abstract systems with sometimes unforeseeable future applications. Although mathematics has become more abstract, the inspiration of individual imagination and experience has remained vital. I believe that even this short history has shown that mathematics has been one of the great intellectual achievements of humanity. Let us now take a closer look.

Chapter 2

A UNIVERSE OF NUMBERS

"All is number."—motto of the Pythagorean school[xx]

"God made the integers; all the rest is the work of man."—Leopold Kronecker[xxi]

2.1   Counting one at a time; the natural numbers

2.1.1   Introduction

Our first encounter with mathematics is with the natural numbers and counting. We probably remember as a small child seeing picture books which introduced us to the alphabet followed by pictures introducing us to numbers. We saw perhaps the picture of a single sea lion with the number 1, a pair of dogs with the number 2, a trio of tigers with the number 3 . . . all the way up to perhaps a dozen ducks with the number 12. We would certainly not appreciate that we had just been introduced to some of the most fundamental ideas of mathematics. In identifying "twoness" with the image of a pair of dogs, we encounter the abstraction that a collection or set of two dogs has the number two in common with any other set for which a one-to-one matching can be made with each dog and members of the other set. The set consisting of your two hands (to pet each dog, of course) is such a set. The number two is identified with all such sets which form what is called an equivalence class. "Two" is just the name of the equivalence class. As we shall see in Chapter 3, this is essentially Cantor's approach for cardinal numbers and assessing the size of infinite sets. Also, as we view the pictures, we are introduced to the

---

xx We know little of the life of Pythagoras, but the devotion of his followers to numbers as the essence of the universe is unquestioned; Merzbach and Boyer, pp. 44-45.

xxi Leopold Kronecker (1823-1891) Professor of University of Berlin with contributions in number theory, arithmetization of algebra, and analysis. He rejected mathematics that involved non-finite processes, for example, the transfinite numbers of Cantor; quote cited in Merzbach and Boyer, p.542-543.

ordering principle; the tigers come after the dogs which come after the sea lion. We recognize the order of the numbers as the abstract act of counting: 1, 2, 3 . . . In recognizing order, we encounter Cantor's idea of the ordinal number, the first number, second number, etc. We also encounter the traditional relationship of greater than: there are more tigers than dogs and more dogs than sea lions. Reaching ten trucks, say, we may have also noticed that there are now two numbers that make up ten, thus we are introduced to decimal representation and the number zero which is a place holder for the one's unit and indicates that there are no "ones". In this way we are introduced to natural numbers, eventually learning about their rules of arithmetic resulting from the operations of addition and multiplication.

Our first goal in Chapter 2 will be to present a set of postulates (also known as axioms) that can generate the natural numbers that are consistent with our intuition and experience with counting. These are the postulates of Giuseppe Peano. From the postulates, the rules of arithmetic will be derived. The concept of a postulate goes back to the classical Greeks and their geometry. As noted in the history outline, the postulates were thought to be self-evident truths which we now consider to be postulates on which we build a logical system of mathematics. From this starting point, the relationship of Peano's Postulates to those algebraic rules for addition and multiplication that you learned in school will be demonstrated. Ultimately, the postulates for the natural numbers will be expanded upon to build the integers, the rational numbers, real numbers, and finally the complex numbers.

First, however, I will present examples of some of the familiar algebraic rules of natural numbers in the guise of a very simple model. The model is not meant to prove any of the rules of the natural numbers, but just to remind you visually of their meaning and to give a sense of their reasonableness in preparation for the proofs that follow.[xxii].

We might identify our usual symbols for natural numbers by the following sets of dots:

$$\{\bullet\} = 1, \{\bullet\bullet\} = 2, \{\bullet\bullet\bullet\} = 3, \{\bullet\bullet\bullet\bullet\} = 4, \{\bullet\bullet\bullet\bullet\bullet\} = 5, \{\bullet\bullet\bullet\bullet\bullet\bullet\} = 6 \ldots \quad (2.1)$$

Then, we can define addition, +, through the following:

$$\{\bullet\} + \{\bullet\} = \{\bullet\bullet\}, \{\bullet\bullet\} + \{\bullet\} = \{\bullet\} + \{\bullet\} + \{\bullet\} = \{\bullet\bullet\bullet\}, \ldots \quad (2.2)$$

---

xxii A model could be based rigorously on the fundamentals of set theory which is discussed in chapter 9. However, this is not our purpose here.

Here the equality signs indicates the ability to match each specific symbol, •, on the left hand side of the equality sign with a specific one on the right. We could define addition of any two numbers through successive use of the above definition.

Now, from an example using our model, we can illustrate the associative property of addition. This property along with the commutative property tells us that the addition of numbers does not depend on the order of addition. For example, we know that 3 + 4 + 5 = 4 + 5 + 3.

Addition is a binary operation, we can add as many numbers as we want, but we add two numbers at a time. We will use the convention that addition within parentheses is performed first. The associative property is illustrated by the following example: (2 + 3) + 1 = 2 + (3 +1). Using variables k, m, and n which can take on the value of any natural number, we have the general property that, (k + m) + n = k + (m + n). Now let us use our simple model to see that this is reasonable by comparing (2 + 3) + 1 with 2 + (3 +1).

In our model:

$$(\{\bullet\bullet\} + \{\bullet\bullet\bullet\}) + \{\bullet\} = \{\bullet\bullet\bullet\bullet\bullet\} + \{\bullet\} = \{\bullet\bullet\bullet\bullet\bullet\bullet\}$$

and

$$\{\bullet\bullet\} + (\{\bullet\bullet\bullet\} + \{\bullet\}) = \{\bullet\bullet\} + \{\bullet\bullet\bullet\bullet\} = \{\bullet\bullet\bullet\bullet\bullet\bullet\} \tag{2.3}$$

Using one of Euclid's common notions from *Elements*, that things equal to the same thing are equal to each other, (known as the transitive property), it is clear that:

(2 + 3) + 1 = 2 + (3 + 1) since both are equivalent to {••••••}.

Similarly we can see in our model an example of the commutative property, m + n = n + m. Let us compare:

2 + 3 with 3 + 2

$$\{\bullet\bullet\} + \{\bullet\bullet\bullet\} = \{\bullet\bullet\bullet\bullet\bullet\} = \{\bullet\bullet\bullet\} + \{\bullet\bullet\} \text{ or} \tag{2.4}$$

3 + 2 = 2 + 3

Multiplication[xxiii] can be modeled through repetitive addition. Below this is illustrated along with the commutative property for multiplication (n x m = m x n):

$2 \times 3 = 6$ $\{\bullet\bullet\bullet\} + \{\bullet\bullet\bullet\} = \{\bullet\bullet\bullet\bullet\bullet\bullet\} = \{\bullet\bullet\} + \{\bullet\bullet\} + \{\bullet\bullet\} = 3 \times 2$ (2.5)

or geometrically like the Greeks with rectangles with sides that that are 2 by 3 or 3 by 2:

$2 \times 3 = 6$ and $3 \times 2 = 6$ (2.6)

The associative property for multiplication, $(k \cdot m)\, n = k(m \cdot n)$ could be illustrated by extending the arrays, such as those above, into three dimensions. For example (4x3) x2 could be viewed as a cuboid 4 rows high by 3 columns wide and 2 rows deep. Rotating the cube allows us to look at it as 4x(3x2) and of course the number of cells is the same.

The operation of multiplication over a sum of two numbers can be defined through the distributive property, $k\,(l + m) = k \cdot l + k \cdot m$. An example of the distributive property is shown below along with the model:

$2\,(3 + 1) = 2\,(4) = 8$ and $2(3 + 1) = 2 \times 3 + 2 \times 1 = 6 + 2 = 8$

$(\{\bullet\bullet\bullet\} + \{\bullet\}) + (\{\bullet\bullet\bullet\} + \{\bullet\}) = (\{\bullet\bullet\bullet\bullet\}) + (\{\bullet\bullet\bullet\bullet\}) = \{\bullet\bullet\bullet\bullet\bullet\bullet\bullet\bullet\}$
$(\{\bullet\bullet\bullet\} + \{\bullet\bullet\bullet\}) + (\{\bullet\} + \{\bullet\}) = \{\bullet\bullet\bullet\bullet\bullet\bullet\} + \{\bullet\bullet\}   = \{\bullet\bullet\bullet\bullet\bullet\bullet\bullet\bullet\}$

(2.9)

Geometrically, this could be shown as:

+   =   = $\bullet\bullet\bullet\bullet\bullet\bullet\bullet\bullet$ (2.10)

---

xxiii Note, multiplication between two numbers, n and m, is indicated, variously, as n x m, nm, $n \cdot m$, or n (m). When the operation of addition and multiplication occur in the same expression, such as mn + jk, this will be taken to mean (mn) + (jk).

The distributive property, among many other things, also allows us to simplify mental multiplication. For example, $5(2,034) = 5(2,000) + 5(34) = 10,000 + 170 = 10,170$.

One other property that we will encounter is the closure property. This simply means that the addition or multiplication of any two numbers is also a number. This should seem obvious in our simple model.

With these reminders of the closure, associative, commutative, and distributive laws, let us take a look at the road ahead.

2.1.2   The roadmap from the natural to the real and complex numbers

Our immediate goal will be to prove the closure, associative, commutative, distributive, and order properties as direct consequences of Peano's Postulates for the natural numbers. Peano wanted to provide a foundation for the real number system on the natural numbers. As we shall see, in addition to the natural numbers, the real numbers include: integers formed by adding zero and negative numbers to the natural numbers; ratios of integers called rational numbers; and irrational numbers such as the square root of 2, which cannot be formed as a rational number.

You know already that the natural numbers are not sufficient for the many types of problems that mathematics is called upon to solve. If we designate the variable, x, as an unknown quantity (a tradition started by Descartes)[83], then there are no natural numbers that satisfy the following equations:

$$x + 5 = 5 \tag{2.11}$$

$$x + 5 = 3 \tag{2.12}$$

$$5x + 3 = 5 \tag{2.13}$$

$$x \cdot x = 2 \tag{2.14}$$

$$x \cdot x = -2 \tag{2.15}$$

In order to solve these types of equations, we will need to expand our numbers beyond the natural numbers. In this process we will first create the integers which will allow us to solve equations 2.11 and 2.12; followed by the rational numbers to solve equation 2.13; the real numbers to solve equation 2.14; and finally, the complex numbers to solve 2.15. At each step, we will define the new numbers in terms of the old. The integers will be defined in terms of the natural numbers, the rational numbers in terms of the integers, and so forth. At each step we will have to add a new property, but we will do it in such a way so that we do not lose the previous number systems and their properties.

When we wish to expand from the rational numbers to the real numbers; however, we will encounter a fundamental difference between them that relates to their nature as collections which have an infinite number of members. We will therefore delay the definition of the real (and complex numbers which are based on the real numbers) to Chapter 3 where we discuss the properties of infinite collections. But to get started, we will build our foundations in the natural numbers by proving their properties from Peano's Postulates. The proofs of the major properties are noted as theorems (another common name is proposition); while less significant proofs needed in the proof of a theorem are traditionally known as lemmas.

A key part of all of the theorems is the notion of equality.[xxiv] In every case the form of one algebraic structure is proved to be equivalent to another structure, for example the associative property of addition, $(a + b) + c = a + (b + c)$. Therefore, before we prove these theorems, I would like to discuss the mathematical meaning of equality. In Section 2.1.1, we identified equality through a matching principle as in $\{\bullet\bullet\} + \{\bullet\bullet\bullet\} = \{\bullet\bullet\bullet\bullet\bullet\}$. However, it may be more broadly defined as an example of an equivalence relation. Relations between two objects x and y may be symbolically represented as xRy. For example, if x and y represent people, and the relationship R stands for "is the full sibling of" then if x is the sibling of y, then y is the sibling of x. Thus, whenever xRy is true, we have yRx. In this case, the relation has the property of symmetry. If y is also the sibling of z, then x is the sibling of z. This is an example in which the relation is transitive. Symbolically, if xRy and yRz, then xRz. In order to be an equivalence relation, in addition to symmetry, and transitivity, the relation must also be reflexive, that is, xRx must be true. In our example, x cannot be the sibling of himself or herself, therefore the relationship, "is the full sibling of" is not an equivalence relation.

The definition of equality based on forming a one-to-one correspondence between members of sets can be used as an equivalence relation with variables such as x, y, and z representing classes of sets

---

xxiv If you think the meaning of equality is obvious, ask someone what is the meaning of the phrase, ". . . all men are created equal . . . ."

since: x = x; also, if x = y, then y = x; and if x = y, y = z, then x = z. Other examples of equivalence relations are similarity of triangles (triangles with equal angles) and congruence of triangles (triangles which may be made to coincide through translation and rotation).

An important property of equivalence relations is that it apportions the sets on which the relation acts into unique equivalence classes, therefore equality between representations of the equivalence classes signifies that we can substitute one side of the equality by the other. With this further understanding of "=," let us now look at the natural numbers through postulates which bring to mind our intuitive ideas of numbers and counting.

2.1.3   Peano's Postulates for the natural numbers[xxv]

From only five postulates and four definitions, all of the theorems of arithmetic for natural numbers can be derived. Peano's axiomatic system begins with undefined terms as did Hilbert's axiomatic system for geometry. These are: natural number, successor, and the symbol 1. He then states the five postulates, the unproven statements that define relationships between the undefined terms.

The five postulates (ℕ1-ℕ 5) for the natural numbers are:

ℕ1 1 is a natural number.

ℕ2 Each natural number n has exactly one successor denoted by n^+.

ℕ3 1 is not a successor to any natural number.

ℕ4 If $n^+ = m^+$, then n = m; for a given number, it is the successor of a unique number.

ℕ5 If S is a set of natural numbers that contains 1, and if whenever n is member of S then n^+ is a member of S, then S contains all the natural numbers.

---

xxv Eves, *Foundations and Fundamental Concepts of Mathematics*, p.191 [Math References 11]; see also, Meserve, Bruce E., *Fundamentals Concepts of Algebra*, pp. 8-13 [Math References 25]. I have followed Eves approach to Peano in starting with 1 as the first natural number. Other authors start with 0 which provides a more concise development of number systems (see fn. xxviii in Section 2.2.1) although as discussed in the history outline, 0 is a much later concept than the counting numbers.

In order to apply these postulates to the normal rules of arithmetic for natural numbers, we need to define operations of addition and multiplication. Starting with addition indicated by the traditional symbol "+," it is reasonable to identify the successor to a number, n^+ with the operation of adding one; that is,

Definition ℕ1: $n + 1 = n^+$

Furthermore, we define the operation of adding two natural numbers as:

Definition ℕ2: $m + n^+ = (m + n)^+$

Similarly, we define the operation of multiplication through two definitions:

Definition ℕ3: $n \cdot 1 = n$

Definition ℕ4: $n \cdot m^+ = n \cdot m + n$

That the postulates and definitions embody our intuitive ideas of the natural numbers, counting and arithmetic seems plausible from the examples below:

$1^+ = 1 + 1 = 2, 2^+ = 2 + 1 = 3, 3^+ = 3 + 1 = 4 \ldots$

$2 + 2 = 2 + 1^+ = (2 + 1)^+ = 3^+ = 4 \ldots$

$1 \cdot 1^+ = 1 \cdot 1 + 1 = 2, 2 \cdot 2 = 2 \cdot 1^+ = 2 \cdot 1 + 2 = 4 \ldots$

More significantly, from these four definitions and the five postulates, we can prove for the natural numbers that the operations of addition and multiplication always produce unique natural numbers (the closure property) and follow the associative, commutative, and distributive properties. Furthermore, we will prove that the natural numbers are ordered; that is for any two natural numbers n and m one and only one of the following conditions must be true: n is equal to m, n is less than m, or n is greater than m ($n = m$, or $n < m$, or $n > m$).

The main approach to proving these results is through postulate ℕ5 which is called the postulate of mathematical induction.

Specifically postulate ℕ5 describes conditions for which a set can be shown to include all of the natural numbers. From this postulate, it follows that if a statement can be shown to be true for the natural number, n = 1, and true for n + 1 if it is assumed to be true for n, then it must be true for all the natural numbers.

One way of envisioning postulate ℕ5 is to think of it in terms of a long line of dominoes each one balanced upright on its end and lined up close to the next. We could associate each domino with a natural number, n. Suppose now that we can show that no matter which domino, n, is knocked over that it will cause the next in line, n^+, to fall. If we then knock over domino 1, we can be certain that all the dominoes in the line will fall over; that is the dominoes (if we have an unlimited supply) can represent the natural numbers.

The following example will illustrate proof by induction. Suppose we wish to prove that the sum of the first n natural numbers, S_n, starting with 1, is equal to n (n +1)/2; that is,

$$S_n = 1 + 2 + 3 + 4 + \ldots + n = n\,(n+1)/2$$

First let us look at the simple case of n=1. The sum $S_1 = 1$.

$n(n + 1)/2 = 1(1 + 1)/2 = 1$, so our formula checks for n=1.

Now our hypothesis is that the sum up to n, S_n, is equal to n(n + 1)/2. We must show using this hypothesis that the sum up to n^+, S_{n^+} is equal to $n^+(n^+ +1)/2$. Using Definition 1 and the assumption for S_n,

$$S_{n^+} = S_{n+1} = S_n + n+1 \;=\; n\,(n+1)/2 + n + 1$$
$$= (n^2 + n + 2n +2)/2$$
$$= (n^2 + 3n + 2)/2$$
$$= (n + 1)\,(n + 2)/2$$
$$= n^+\,(n^+ +1)/2$$

Thus, $S_n = n(n+1)/2$ is true for all n since it is true for n = 1 and true for n^+ if it is true for n.

In developing proofs, in addition to the postulate of induction, other types of logical argument will also be used. In Chapter 4, we will go into more details about logical arguments with the discussion of the axiomatic method in geometry; however, I will briefly review here some of the details of logical argument that you probably have encountered in geometric proofs. One of the most common logical types of argument in science or mathematics is one described by Aristotle, known as a syllogism. A syllogism logically connects the truth of a series of statements called implications. In your geometry classes, you would typically start a proof with a statement that is a given condition of the theorem to be proved. This would be followed by theorems or postulates that are linked to the given condition and lead to other theorems, and so forth until the proof was complete. In the following example, I will denote such statements symbolically as p, q, and r. A simple syllogism would be: if p implies q and q implies r, then p implies r.[84] Such a chain of statements can be extended to any number.

Related to statements such as the implication p implies q are situations in which q implies p, also. In this situation, p is true only if q is true and vice versa. Other verbal phrases to indicate this relationship are: p is a necessary and sufficient condition for q, and p is true if and only if q is true. To prove that a statement p is a necessary and sufficient for the statement q, you must prove p implies q and q implies p. Further to this discussion, I remind you that if the statement p implies q is true, the converse statement, q implies p, is not necessarily true: If the postman is on my porch, then my dog barks loudly, is, unfortunately, true; however, if my dog barks loudly, then the conclusion that the postman is on my porch is not necessarily true.

Another argument form that will be employed is known by the names: indirect proof, proof by contradiction, and reductio ad absurdum (Latin for reduction to absurdity). In this argument form, in order to prove a statement, it is assumed that the statement is false. If following this assumption, a contradiction occurs, then the statement is true.[85]

Perhaps the most straightforward of the methods of proof is proof by cases. In that method one simply looks at all the possible situations that can arise and show that the desired conclusion occurs in each. The use of such a method, of course, requires the ability to identify all possible cases.

As a concluding point to this brief review of methods of proof, I note that by tradition from the times when Latin was the universal academic language of the West, the end of proofs were traditionally marked Q.E.D., for "quod erat demonstratum" for "what was required to prove". Of course, the original statement was in Greek (ὅπερ ἔδει δεῖξαι).[86] I will keep this convention to make it clear that the proof is indeed finished (should you be uncertain about that) and to remind us that we owe this form of knowledge to the ancient Greeks via Rome.

2.1.4   Consequences of Peano's postulates

The major theorems (closure, associative, commutative, and distributive) that follow from Peano's five postulates will now be proved.[xxvi] Because these are the foundations for all the other number systems, I shall develop them in some detail. As we go forward to other number systems, we will need to add additional postulates to those of Peano, but the consistency of these expanded sets of postulates with the major theorems developed here will always be traceable back to the natural numbers. For this reason, I trust you will be patient in following the proofs so that you trust in the results and see the connection with the previous intuitive description of these theorems.

Except where noted, all proofs about the natural numbers are by mathematical induction. In these proofs, first the theorem is shown to be true for n=1. Then we make the hypothesis that the theorem is true for the natural number n. Using this hypothesis we must then show that the theorem is true for n's successor n^+. If we can do that then, the proof is complete.

Theorem ℕ1 (Closure Property for Addition): If m and n are natural numbers, there is a natural number, k, such that $m + n. = k$

For n = 1: $m + 1 = m^+$ (Every number has a   Definition ℕ1
                                        successor)

$\Rightarrow$ true for n = 1.

Hypothesis for n: $m + n = k$.

Must show: $m + n^+ = k^+$

$\qquad\qquad m + n^+ = (m + n)^+$ Definition ℕ2

$\qquad\qquad\qquad = k^+$ By hypothesis

True for n= 1 and for n^+ if true for n $\Rightarrow$ Theorem ℕ1 is true for all n. Q.E.D.

---

xxvi Starting with Peano's Postulates, Landau [Math References 20] develops comprehensively the properties of the natural numbers, integers, rational numbers, real numbers, and complex numbers. The abbreviated approach given here is similar to that of Landau; however, unlike the presentation here, Landau does not introduce the negative numbers until he has completed the development of the positive integers and rational numbers.

Theorem ℕ2 (Closure Property for Multiplication): If m and n are natural numbers, there is a natural number, k, such that m · n. = k

<u>For n = 1</u>: m · 1 = m	Definition ℕ3
⇒ true for n = 1.	
<u>Hypothesis for n</u>: m · n = k.	
<u>Must show</u>: m · n⁺ = natural number	
$\quad\quad\quad$ m · n⁺ = m · n + m	Definition ℕ4
$\quad\quad\quad\quad\quad$ = k + m	By hypothesis
For every natural number, m and	
k, k + m is a natural number	Thm. ℕ2: Closure for Addition

True for n= 1, and for n⁺ if true for n ⇒ Theorem ℕ2 is true for all n. Q.E.D

Theorem ℕ3 (Associative Property of Addition): (k + m) +n = k + (m +n)

<u>For n= 1</u>: (k + m) +1 = (k + m)⁺	Definition ℕ1
$\quad\quad\quad\quad\quad$ = k + m⁺	Definition ℕ2
$\quad\quad\quad\quad\quad$ = k + (m +1)	Definition ℕ1
$\quad\quad\quad\quad\quad$ ⇒ true for n = 1	
<u>Hypothesis for n</u>: (k + m) +n = k + (m +n)	
<u>Must show</u>: (k + m) + n⁺ = k + (m + n⁺)	
$\quad\quad\quad$ (k + m) + n⁺ = (k + m) + n +1	Definition ℕ1
$\quad\quad\quad\quad\quad$ = k + (m + n) +1	By hypothesis
$\quad\quad\quad\quad\quad$ = k + (m +n) ⁺	Definition ℕ1
$\quad\quad\quad\quad\quad$ = k + (m + n⁺)	Definition ℕ2

True for n= 1 and for n⁺ if true for n ⇒ Theorem ℕ3 is true for all n. Q.E.D.

The following lemma is proved as an aid in proving the Commutative Property of Addition.

Lemma ℕ1: 1 + n = n +1

<u>For n = 1</u>: 1 + 1 = 1 + 1 ⇒ true for n=1	
<u>Hypothesis for n</u>: 1 + n= n +1	
<u>Must show</u>: 1 + n⁺ = n⁺ + 1	
$\quad\quad\quad$ 1 + n⁺ = (1 + n)⁺	Definition ℕ2
$\quad\quad\quad\quad\quad$ = (n + 1)⁺	By hypothesis
$\quad\quad\quad\quad\quad$ = (n⁺)⁺	Definition ℕ1
$\quad\quad\quad\quad\quad$ = n⁺ +1	Definition ℕ1

True for n= 1 and for n⁺ if true for n ⇒ Lemma ℕ1 is true for all n. Q.E.D.

Theorem №4 (Commutative Property of Addition): $m + n = n + m$

<u>For $n = 1$:</u> $m + 1 = 1 + m$ Lemma №1
$\Rightarrow$ true for n=1
<u>Hypothesis for n:</u> $m + n = n + m$
<u>Must show:</u> $m + n^+ = n^+ + m$

$$\begin{aligned}
m + n^+ &= m + (n + 1) & &\text{Definition №1}\\
&= (m + n) + 1 & &\text{Thm. №3: Associative}\\
&= (n + m) + 1 & &\text{By hypothesis}\\
&= n + (m + 1) & &\text{Thm. №3: Associative}\\
&= n + (1 + m) & &\text{Lemma №1}\\
&= (n + 1) + m & &\text{Thm. №3: Associative}\\
&= n^+ + m & &\text{Definition №1}
\end{aligned}$$

True for $n = 1$ and for n^+ if true for $n \Rightarrow$ Theorem №1 is true for all n. Q.E.D.

The following two lemmas are proved as aid in proving the Commutative Property of Multiplication.

Lemma №2: $m^+ \cdot n = m \cdot n + n$ (compare with Definition №4.)

<u>For $n = 1$:</u> $m^+ \cdot 1 = m^+$ Definition №3
$\qquad\qquad\quad = m + 1$ Definition №1
$\qquad\qquad\quad = m \cdot 1 + 1$ Definition №3
$\Rightarrow$ true for $n = 1$.
<u>Hypothesis for n:</u> $m^+ \cdot n = m \cdot n + n$
<u>Must Show:</u> $m^+ \cdot n^+ = m \cdot n^+ + n^+$

$$\begin{aligned}
m^+ \cdot n^+ &= m^+ \cdot n + m^+ & &\text{Definition №4}\\
&= m \cdot n + n + (m + 1) & &\text{By hypothesis;}\\
& & &\text{Definition №1}\\
&= m \cdot n + (n + m) + 1 & &\text{Thm. №3: Associative}\\
&= m \cdot n + (m + n) + 1 & &\text{Thm. №4: Commutative}\\
&= (m \cdot n + m) + (n + 1) & &\text{Thm. №3: Associative}\\
&= m \cdot n^+ + n^+ & &\text{Definitions №1, №4}
\end{aligned}$$

True for $n = 1$ and for n^+ if true for $n \Rightarrow$ Lemma №2 is true for all n. Q.E.D.

Lemma №3: $1 \cdot n = n \cdot 1$

<u>For $n = 1$:</u> $1 \cdot 1 = 1 \cdot 1 \Rightarrow$ true for $n = 1$
<u>Hypothesis for n:</u> $1 \cdot n = n \cdot 1$
<u>Must show:</u> $1 \cdot n^+ = n^+ \cdot 1$

$$1 \cdot n^+ = 1 \cdot n + 1 \qquad \text{Definition N4}$$
$$= n \cdot 1 + 1 \qquad \text{By hypothesis}$$
$$= n + 1 \qquad \text{Definition N3}$$
$$= n^+ \qquad \text{Definition N1}$$
$$= n^+ \cdot 1 \qquad \text{Definition N3}$$

True for n= 1 and for n^+ if true for n $\Rightarrow$ Lemma N3 is true for all n. Q.E.D.

Theorem N5 (Commutative Property of Multiplication): $n \cdot m = m \cdot n$

For n = 1: $m \cdot 1 = 1 \cdot m$ Lemma N3
$\Rightarrow$ true for n=1
Hypothesis for n: $n \cdot m = m \cdot n$
Must Show: $n^+ \cdot m = m \cdot n^+$

$$n^+ \cdot m = m \cdot n + m \qquad \text{Lemma N2}$$
$$= m \cdot n^+ \qquad \text{Definition N4}$$

True for n= 1 and for n^+ if true for n $\Rightarrow$ Theorem N5 is true for all n. Q.E.D.

Theorem N6 (Distributive Property): $k\,(m + n) = k \cdot m + k \cdot n$

For n = 1: $k\,(m + 1) = k \cdot m^+ = k \cdot m + k = k \cdot m + k \cdot 1$

Definitions N1, N4, N3

$\Rightarrow$ true for n=1
Hypothesis for n: $k\,(m + n) = k \cdot m + k \cdot n$
Must Show: $k\,(m + n^+) = k \cdot m + k \cdot n^+$

$$k\,(m + n^+) = k\,(m + n)^+ \qquad \text{Definition N2}$$
$$= k\,(m + n) + k \qquad \text{Definition N4}$$
$$= (k \cdot m + k \cdot n) + k \qquad \text{By hypothesis}$$
$$= k \cdot m + (k \cdot n + k) \qquad \text{Thm. N3: Associative}$$
$$= k \cdot m + k \cdot n^+ \qquad \text{Definition N4}$$

True for n= 1, and for n^+ if true for n $\Rightarrow$ Theorem N6 is true for all n. Q.E.D.

The distributive property, proved in Theorem N6, is sometimes referred to as the left distributive property as the multiplier is to the left of the quantity in parentheses. The right distributive (Theorem N6a—see below) may be proved in a similar manner.

Theorem N6a (Distributive Property - right): $(m + n)k = m \cdot k + n \cdot k$

Robert G. Bill

Theorem ℕ7 (Associative Property of Multiplication):
$(k \cdot m) n = k (m \cdot n)$

<u>For n= 1</u>: $(k \cdot m) \cdot 1 = k \cdot m = k (m \cdot 1)$ Definition ℕ3
$\Rightarrow$ true for n=1
<u>Hypothesis for n:</u> $(k \cdot m) n = k (m \cdot n)$
<u>Must show:</u> $(k \cdot m) n^+ = k (m \cdot n^+)$

$$(k \cdot m)n^+ = (k \cdot m)n + (k \cdot m) \qquad \text{Definition ℕ4}$$
$$= k (m \cdot n) + (k \cdot m) \qquad \text{By hypothesis}$$
$$= k (m \cdot n + m) \qquad \text{Thm. ℕ6: Distributive}$$
$$= k (m \cdot n^+) \qquad \text{Definition ℕ4}$$

True for n= 1 and for n^+ if true for n $\Rightarrow$ Theorem ℕ7 is true for all n. Q.E.D.

We have proved some of the most significant of the consequences of Peano's Postulate which form the basic rules of algebra while illustrating the power of the postulate of induction to obtain these results. We now need to establish the order properties which are fundamental to our intuitive understanding of numbers and counting. The order properties (of which Part I is frequently referred to as the Trichotomy Law) consists of three related parts. We shall prove Part I, the other two follow easily using the definitions of greater than (>) and less than (<) given below.

Definition ℕ5: If $m = n + k$, then m is said to be greater than n or $m > n$.

Definition ℕ6: If $n = m + j$, then m is said to be less than n or $m < n$.

Similar definitions of inequality will be used later on for integers, rational numbers, and real numbers. The theorem establishing properties can be proved with the help of the following lemma (see Appendix A for proof of the lemma along with proofs for other supporting lemmas):

Lemma ℕ4(2): $m \neq m + n$

Theorem ℕ8 (Order Property): For natural numbers m and n,

I.   Only one of the following three cases is true: 1) $n = m$, 2) $n = m + k$ ($n > m$), or 3) $m = n + j$ ($m > n$)
II.   If $k < m$ and $m < n$, then $k < n$.
III. If $m < n$, then $m + k < n + k$

We first prove for Part I, that only one of the three cases is possible.

<u>Indirect proof by cases</u>

<u>Hypothesis</u>: case 1, 2, and 3 are all true.

> If case 1) is true; then,
> for case 2) $n = m = m + k$ which cannot be true;   Lemma $\mathbb{N}4(2)$
>
> for case 3) $m = n = n + j$ which cannot be true   Lemma $\mathbb{N}4(2)$

Therefore a contradiction occurs and, all three cases cannot be true at the same time. If case 1) is true, then case 2) and case 3) are false.

<u>Hypothesis</u>: case 2) and case 3) are both true, then:
$$n = m + k = n + j + k \text{ which is false.}   \text{Lemma } \mathbb{N}4(2)$$

Therefore a contradiction occurs and, either only case 2) is true or only case 3) is true. We have shown that only one of the cases is possible for a given m and n.

Now we must show that given any natural number m that any n satisfies one of the three cases of Theorem $\mathbb{N}8$.

<u>Proof by Induction:</u>

<u>For $n = 1$:</u>

case 1): if $m = 1$, then case 1) is true	Equivalence Relation
case 2): $1 = m + k$, cannot be true	Postulate $\mathbb{N}3$
case 3): $m = 1 + j = j^+$	Thm. $\mathbb{N}5$: Commutative, Definition $\mathbb{N}1$

Therefore, case 3) is true if m is the successor of some number j which is true for any m. (other than $m = 1$, covered in case 1).
$$\Rightarrow n = 1 \text{ satisfies case 1 or case 3 for any m}$$

<u>Hypothesis</u>: For a given m, n satisfies one of the three cases
<u>Must show:</u> n^+ satisfies one of the three cases:

case 1: if $n = m$, $n^+ = m^+ = m+1$	Postulate $\mathbb{N}4$, Definition $\mathbb{N}1$
	Satisfies case 2 with $n^+ > m$

case 2: if $n = m + k$ $(n > m)$, then $n^+ = (m + k)^+ = m + (k + 1)$.

Postulate $\mathbb{N}4$, Definition $\mathbb{N}1$
Satisfies case 2 with $n^+ > m$

case 3: if $m = n + j$ $(m > n)$,

     let: $j = p + 1$ Thm. $\mathbb{N}1$: Closure

     $m = n + p + 1 = n^+ + p$ Thm. $\mathbb{N}5$: Commutative, Definition $\mathbb{N}1$

For $j \neq 1$, satisfies case 3 with $m > n^+$; for $j = 1$, $m = n^+$.

$\Rightarrow$ true for $n = 1$ and for n^+ if true for $n \Rightarrow$ Theorem $\mathbb{N}8$ is true for all n.

Q.E.D.

We have now completed proofs of theorems based upon Peano's Postulates which demonstrate the connection between algebraic rules and the natural numbers we first learned for counting. These theorems that you probably are more familiar with as rules of algebra, I will designate as the Canonical Postulates for Natural Numbers because they could equally serve as a definition of the natural numbers. Peano's Postulates can be shown to be implied by the Canonical Postulates and the associated definitions of addition and multiplication.[87] Going forward, knowing that the Canonical Postulates are a consequence of Peano's Postulates, we will use these postulates as a base to expand upon in building the integers, rational numbers and the real numbers.

2.1.5 Canonical Postulates for the Natural Numbers:[88]

$\mathbb{N}_c 1$ **(Closure Postulate for Addition):** If m and n are natural numbers, there is a natural number, k, such that $m + n. = k$

$\mathbb{N}_c 2$ **(Closure Postulate for Multiplication):** If m and n are natural numbers, there is a natural number, k, such that $m \cdot n. = k$

$\mathbb{N}_c 3$ **(Associative Postulate of Addition):** $(k + m) + n = k + (m + n)$

$\mathbb{N}_c 4$ **(Associative Postulate of Multiplication):** $(k \cdot m) \cdot n = k \cdot (m \cdot n)$

$\mathbb{N}_c 5$ **(Commutative Postulate of Addition):** $m + n = n + m$

$\mathbb{N}_c 6$ **(Commutative Postulate of Multiplication):** $m \cdot n = n \cdot m$

$\mathbb{N}_c$ **7 (Distributive Postulate):** $k\,(m+n) = k \cdot m + k \cdot n$

$\mathbb{N}_c$ **8 (Identity Element for Multiplication):** There exists a natural number, 1, with $n \cdot 1 = n$.

$\mathbb{N}_c$ **9 (Induction Postulate)** S is a set of natural numbers that contains 1, and if whenever n is member of S then $n + 1$ is a member of S, then S contains all the natural numbers.

$\mathbb{N}_c$ **10 (Order Postulate):** For natural numbers j, k, m and n,

I. Only one of the following three cases is true: 1) $n = m$, 2) $n = m + k$, or 3) $m = n + j$,
    $(n = m, m < n, \text{ or } m > n)$.
II. If $k < m$ and $m < n$, then $k < n$.
III. If $m < n$, then $m + k < n + k$.

Given that all of the above canonical postulates have been proved from those of Peano, you might now ask if they are all needed to define the natural numbers. The answer is that some of the postulates are unnecessary. To define the natural numbers, we do not need the commutative postulates, $\mathbb{N}_c$ 5 and $\mathbb{N}_c$ 6, the associative postulate for multiplication, $\mathbb{N}_c$ 4, and Parts II and III of the order postulate $\mathbb{N}_c$ 10. These can be derived from the other postulates. I include them because they are frequently included as part of the algebraic structure known as a field which is the structure of both the rational and real numbers.

One other reason for including unnecessary postulates such as the commutative property is that it allows one to more quickly become familiar with useful algebraic manipulations rather than to depend on more basic properties. Two common examples of theorems that are often included as postulates are the cancellation theorems for addition and multiplication that allow simple equations to be solved. We will prove the cancellation theorem for addition with a proof by contradiction using the canonical postulate of order. The cancellation theorem for multiplication (see Theorem $\mathbb{N}$10 below) may be proved in a similar manner.

Theorem $\mathbb{N}$9 (Cancellation Property for Addition):
If $n + k = n + m$, then, $k = m$

<u>Indirect proof by cases using the Order Postulate $\mathbb{N}_c$ 10:</u>

<u>Hypothesis</u>: If n+ k = n + m, then
Either case 1) k = m, case 2) k = m + j, or case 3) m = k + p is true
$$\text{Order Postulate } \mathbb{N}_c 10$$

Suppose case 2) is true: k = m + j, then

$$\begin{aligned}
n + k &= n + (m + j) & &\text{Equivalence Relation}\\
&= (n + m) + j & &\text{Associative Postulate } \mathbb{N}_c\, 3\\
&= (n + k) + j & &\text{By hypothesis}
\end{aligned}$$

Contradiction by Lemma $\mathbb{N}4(2)$, $\Rightarrow$ k $\neq$ m + j

Suppose case 3) is true: m = k + p, then

$$\begin{aligned}
n + m &= n + (k + p) & &\text{Equivalence Relation}\\
&= (n + k) + p & &\text{Associative Postulate } \mathbb{N}_c\, 3\\
&= (n + m) + p & &\text{By hypothesis}
\end{aligned}$$

Contradiction by Lemma $\mathbb{N}4(2) \Rightarrow$ m$\neq$ k + p,
Therefore k = m. $\text{Order Postulate } \mathbb{N}_c 10$

$$\text{Q.E.D.}$$

Theorem $\mathbb{N}10$ (Cancellation Property of Multiplication):
If $n \cdot k = n \cdot m$, then, k = m

The cancellation theorems for addition and multiplication allow us to immediately solve the following types of simple equations:

$$3 + x = 5 = 3 + 2 \Rightarrow x = 2$$

and

$$6 \cdot x = 12 = 6 \cdot 2 \Rightarrow x = 2$$

Before leaving the natural numbers, the important rules for exponentiation with natural numbers need to be defined.

2.1.6   Exponentials in the natural numbers

Definition $\mathbb{N}7$: $n^1 = n$ and $n^{k+1} = n^k \cdot n$

Examples: $2^2 = 2 \cdot 2 = 4, 2^3 = 2^2 \cdot 2 = 2 \cdot 2 \cdot 2 = 8$

$$n^4 = n^3 \cdot n = n \cdot n \cdot n \cdot n$$

Using the postulate of induction the following theorems of exponentiation can also be easily proved.

Theorem ℕ11: $(nm)^k = n^k \cdot m^k$

Example: $(2 \cdot 3)^2 = 2^2 \cdot 3^2 = 36$

Theorem ℕ12: $n^k \cdot n^j = n^{k+j}$

Example: $3^2 \cdot 3^1 = 3^3 = 27$

Theorem ℕ13: $(n^j)^k = n^{j \cdot k}$

Example: $(2^5)^2 = 2^{10} = 1024$

So to recap, what have we accomplished? Starting with Peano's Postulates which mirror our intuitive ideas of counting, we have established the defining algebraic postulates of natural numbers. From these the familiar algebraic rules of the cancellation properties of addition and multiplication follow. Despite the impressive array of postulates, we still cannot solve, among many others, the simple equation: $5 + x = 3$. For this we will need to extend our numbers to the integers.

2.2   Going negative; building the integers

As noted in the previous section, despite our accomplishments, we have no solution to problems within the natural numbers such as $5 + n = 3$ or for that matter, $5 + n = 5$. In fact, we could prove using Peano's Postulates that there is no natural number that we could substitute for n that would make these statements true. Undoubtedly you know that what we need to solve the equations mentioned above are the negative numbers and zero. The addition of these to the natural numbers forms the integers.

Another way of looking at this problem is in terms of the properties that form what is known as a group. Recall from our history outline that in order to meet the requirements for a group with respect to the operation of addition (Section 1.2.5.3) that it must have an identity element e such that $n + e = n$ and inverse numbers n^- such that $n + n^- = e$. Thus the natural numbers do not form a group. In our example above, if we had an additive inverse for 5, call it 5^-, we could show for our problem $5 + x = 3$ that $x = 3 + 5^-$, but simply introduc such numbers doesn't tell us how they relate to the natural numbers or the algebraic rules for their use. Our goal is to define the additive inverses (which will become the negative numbers) and the identity element for addition (zero) in terms of the natural numbers and their operations of addition and multiplication. The resulting integers will also have the closure, commutative, associative, and distributive properties. These new numbers called the integers $\mathbb{I}$ will include the natural numbers $\mathbb{N}$.

2.2.1   Adding the identity element and inverse numbers

We have shown with the natural numbers that whenever $m > n$, we can solve a problem such as $n + x = m$. Indeed this is the definition of what we mean by greater than and allows us to express this result verbally as m is greater than n by x. Now we know that there are many different pairs of natural numbers n and m for which m is greater than n by the same number, for example, $5 + 2 = 7$, $30 + 2 = 32 \ldots$ This suggests another way to define numbers as a pair of natural numbers. For natural numbers m, n with $m > n$, if $n + x = m$, then we will make the hypothesis that we can associate the natural number x with the pair [m, n]. The idea of expressing numbers in terms of the natural numbers m and n is that we want to expand the properties of the new numbers using the proven properties of the natural numbers. As you probably noticed, for the symbol [m, n], I could have used the traditional symbol for the operation of subtraction, "−," but at this time the operation of subtraction is not defined. The comma is simply a separator. and [m, n] simply designates a number for which $m > n$.

Now we might ask, if we have two of these new numbers, [m, n] and [k, l] how do we know if they are equal. Looking at our specific examples above, $5 + 2 = 7$ and $30 + 2 = 32$, you may notice that $7 + 30 = 5 + 32$. This suggests the following rule for natural numbers k, l, m, and n with $m > n$ and $k > l$:

[m, n] = [k, l] if and only if $m + l = k + n$.

far all that we have done is create a new way to express natural s because we have restricted our new numbers [m, n] to the n. We now remove this restriction, allowing $m \leqq n$, and see numbers have the properties of an identity element and verse while maintaining the algebraic properties of the s. We also need to define the operations of addition and multiplication which must be shown to be consistent with those operations in the natural numbers.

Definition I1: The integers, $\mathbb{I}$ are defined as the ordered pairs of the natural numbers, [m, n].

Definition I2: Two integers, [m, n] and [k, l] are equal if and only if m + l = n + k.

Definition I3: The operation of addition between pairs of integers is defined by: [m, n] + [k, l] = [m + k, n + l].

Definition I4: The operation of multiplication between pairs of integers is defined by: $[m, n] \cdot [k, l] = [m \cdot k + n \cdot l, m \cdot l + n \cdot k]$.

If the new numbers are to be useful, then the following three theorems must follow from Definitions I1 to II4 and the properties of the natural numbers:[xxvii]

Theorem I1 (Equivalence Relation): The equality of the integers is an equivalence relation.

Theorem I2: (Closure, Associative, and Commutative Properties of Addition): The integers are closed under addition which is commutative, and associative.

Theorem I3 (Closure, Associative, Commutative, and Distributive Properties of Multiplication): The integers are also closed under multiplication which is commutative, associative, and distributive over addition

I will not give a complete proof of these theorems, but I will illustrate how they are easily proved using the definitions and properties of

---

xxvii In addition to the three theorems, the definition of the integer operations must also be shown to be what is known as being well-defined, that is the operations of addition and multiplication must give unique results when one member of an equivalence class is substituted for another. In the case of addition, this means if [a, b] = [a', b'] and [c, d] = [c', d'] then [a, b] + [c, d] = [a', b'] + [c', d'] and for multiplication, [a, b] · [c, d] = [a', b'] · [c', d']. This is shown by Eves, p. 191. Operations for rational, real, and complex numbers discussed later are similarly well defined.

the natural numbers $\mathbb{N}$. Starting with Theorem $\mathbb{I}1$, the symmetric property of the equivalence relation is proved below. With proof that the definition of equality for the integers is an equivalence relation, the infinite number of integers formed by ordered pairs of natural numbers such as [m, n] = [4, 2] = [102,100] = . . . are an equivalence class which as we will see is equivalent for this case to the natural number 2.

Theorem $\mathbb{I}1$(Symmetry): If the integer [m, n] = [k, l] then [k, l] = [m, n]

[m, n] = [k, l]	By hypothesis
m + l = n + k	Definition $\mathbb{I}2$
n + k = m + l	Equivalence Relation in $\mathbb{N}$
k + n = l + m	Commutative Postulate $\mathbb{N}_c$ 5
[k, l] = [m, n]	Definition $\mathbb{I}2$

Q.E.D.

The method of proof for Theorem $\mathbb{I}2$ is illustrated below for the commutative property of addition.

Theorem $\mathbb{I}2$ - Commutative Property of Addition: [k, l] + [m, n] = [m, n] + [k, l]

[k, l] + [m, n] = [k + m, l + n]	Definition $\mathbb{I}3$
= [m + k, n + l]	Commutative Postulate $\mathbb{N}_c$ 5
= [m, n] + [k, l]	Definition $\mathbb{I}3$

Q.E.D.

Theorem $\mathbb{I}3$ for the operation of multiplication is again a direct result of the closure, associative and commutative properties of the natural numbers. The method of proof is illustrated below for the commutative property of multiplication. The proof of the distributive property is given in Appendix B.

Theorem $\mathbb{I}3$ - Commutative Property of Multiplication:
[˙ [m, n] = [m, n] · [k, l]

l = [k · m + l · n, l · m + k · n]	Definition $\mathbb{I}4$
= [m · k + n · l, m · l + n · k]	Commutative Postulate $\mathbb{N}_c$ 6
[m, n] · [k, l]	Definition $\mathbb{I}4$

Q.E.D.

These illustrative proofs should make you comfortable with the idea that the new numbers will maintain the properties of the natural numbers. We will now go forward with our goal of finding the forms for an identity element for addition and additive inverses. As a first step, I remind you that the form of the new numbers is not unique by noting that for example the natural number 2 corresponds to [5, 3} = [32, 30]. This is generalized in the following theorem.

Theorem I4: For any integer, [m, n] = [m+ k, n +k]

m + n = n +m	Commutative Property N_c 5
(m + n) +k = (n + m) +k	Cancellation Property of Addition Theorem N9
m + (n + k) = n + (m + k)	Associative Postulate N_c 3
[m, n] = [m + k, n + k]	Definition I2

Q.E.D.

With this observation, we wish to see if our new numbers have the flexibility to include an identity element for addition and an additive inverse. Let us first look for the identity element for addition. Theorem I4 above suggests that we associate the identity element with [k, k] since [m+ k, n +k] = [m, n] + [k, k].

Theorem I5 (Additive Identity Element, Zero): For any integer, [m, n], the integer [k, k] = [k + j, k+ j] is an additive identity element such that [m, n] + [k, k] = [m, n]. The integer [k, k] is called zero.

[m, n] + [k, k] = [m + k, n + k]	Definition I3
= [m, n]	Theorem I4

Q.E.D.

The following property of zero also follows from the natural numbers.

Theorem I6: [k, k] · [m, n] = [k, k].

[k, k] · [m, n] = [k · m + k · n, k · m + k · n]	Definition I4

and

[k · m + k · n, k · m + k · n] = [k, k] since k · m + k · n + k = k · m + k · n + k	Definition I2

Q.E.D.

Our next step is to identify the additive inverses for every integer, [m, n]; that is, we would like to find the integer [i, j] such that [m, n] + [i, j] = [k, k]. Using the definition of addition we desire that the following be true:

[m, n] + [i, j] = [m + i, n + j] = [k, k]

For this to be true, we must have by Definition I2 of equality:

m + i + k = n + j + k.

By the cancellation theorem for natural numbers, Theorem N9:

m + i = n + j or by the commutative property of the natural numbers

i + m = j + n.

Finally, Definition I2 requires that:

[i, j] = [n, m].

Thus the additive inverse of [m, n] is [n, m].

Formally we have the following theorem and proof establishing additive inverses for all integers. Notice that all we have essentially done in the proof below is to reverse the process by which we discovered the additive inverse. This is typical of the way proofs are discovered in contrast to clairvoyantly going from the hypothesis to the conclusion.

Theorem I7 (Additive Inverse): For any integer, [m, n] there exists an additive inverse, [n, m] such that [m, n] + [n, m] = [k, k].

[m, n] + [n, m] = [m +n, n +m]	Definition I2
= [m + n, m +n]	Commutative Postulate N_c5
Let m + n = k, then [m, n] + [n, m] = [k, k]	Closure Postulate N_c1

Q.E.D

Now that we have established the algebraic properties of the integers along with the existence of an identity element for addition and an additive inverse, we want to show that the natural numbers are embedded within the integers. After a bit of reflection it should be clear that we can match the natural number, m, with the integer [m + k, k]. This may be illustrated by comparing the operations of addition and multiplication for natural numbers with their integer representations. For the natural numbers, let m + n = p. The corresponding expression for integers is:

[m + k, k] + [n + k, k] = [m + n + k + k, k + k]	Definition I3
= [m + n + k, k] + [k, k]	Definition I3

$$= [m + n + k, k] \qquad \text{Theorem II5}$$
$$= [p + k, k] \qquad \text{By hypothesis}$$

Similarly, letting $m \cdot n = r$:

$[m + k, k] \cdot [n + k, k] = [m \cdot n + q, q],$
with $q = mk + nk + k^2 + k^2$, \qquad Definition II4
$$= [r + q, q]$$

In regard to the operation of multiplication within the integers, it is also easily proved that the identity element for multiplication is $[1 + k, k]$ by showing that the product of an integer $[m, n]$ with the identity element of multiplication is $[m, n]$. However, there is no multiplicative inverse for $[m, n]$ such that $[m, n] \cdot [i, j] = [1 + k, k]$ except for $[m, n] = [1 + k, k]$.

We have identified a correspondence between the natural numbers and the integers as, $n \leftrightarrow [n + k, k]$ which we shall now designate as the integer N. We shall designate the integer $[k, k]$ as 0 which can be considered to be part of an expanded set of the natural numbers, called the whole numbers. The integer 1 is the successor to 0.[xxviii] With the introduction of 0, $[n + m, m] = [n, 0] = N$.

The additive inverses introduce new numbers, called the negative numbers. We shall designate the additive inverse of $N = [n, 0]$ as $-N = [0, n]$, hence:

$$N + (-N) = 0$$

We define the operation of subtraction as addition of an additive inverse:

$$N + (-N) = N - N = 0.$$

---

xxviii The number one can easily be shown to be the successor of zero: $0^+ = 0 + 1 = [k, k] + [1 + m, m] = [1 + m + k, m + k] = 1$. Rather than starting the natural numbers with 1 as the only number which does not have a successor, one could begin the development of numbers with the whole numbers, which include the natural numbers and 0. The postulates of the whole numbers would then include: $n + 0 = 0 + n = n$. The postulate of induction would use 0 instead of 1 as a base. An approach for the development of numbers starting with the whole numbers is given by Thurston, H. A., *The Number System* [Math References 34] and Hamilton, A. G., *Numbers, sets, and axioms*, pp. 1-50, [Math References 13].

In general,

$$N + (-M) = N - M = [n, 0] + [0, m] = [n, m]$$

The last statement shows that the comma separator in [n, m] may be replaced with the symbol of subtraction, that is, [n − m] and is consistent with its use for the operation of subtraction. The correspondence of the natural numbers within the integers and the existence of the negative numbers are summarized in the following two theorems:

Theorem 18: The integers [n + m − m] = [n − 0] = N, form the positive integers and correspond to the natural number n. The identity element of addition, [k − k] = 0. The natural numbers along with their properties are contained within the integers. (The natural numbers are said to be isomorphic with the positive integers.)

Theorem 19: Each positive integer [n + m − m] = [n − 0] = N has an additive inverse, [m − n +m]= [0 − n] which is designated as −N with N + (−N) = 0.

The integers [m, n + m] = [m − (n + m)] = − N form the negative numbers.

The order of the inverse numbers can be established; we have:

−1 + 1 = [0 − 1] + [1 − 0] = [1 − 1] = 0, therefore. 0 is the successor of −1 and −1 < 0.

Similarly, −2 + 1 = [0 − 2] + [1 − 0] = [0 −1] = −1 therefore, −1 is the successor of −2 and −2 < −1.

Thus the natural numbers within the integers form an infinite increasing sequence from zero with their inverses forming and infinite decreasing sequence:

. . . −3, −2, −1, 0, 1, 2, 3 . . .

At this stage, it is appropriate to mention the relation of the integers to the number line. The number line, which is a geometric concept, recalls the Greek view of numbers as units of length, at least the positive numbers. We can associate an arbitrary length to represent the interval from 0 to 1. Moving to the right of 1, one unit length, we encounter 1's successor 2, and so forth. The negative numbers can then be conceived as moving to the left starting from 0 as the predecessor to -1. Despite this simple model of the negative numbers, well into the nineteenth century the legitimacy and meaning of negative numbers would be questioned by mathematicians[89] with full understanding not coming until the real numbers consisting of the rational and irrational numbers were rigorously defined. The development ahead of the rational numbers (Section 2.4) and real numbers (Section 3.2) will provide the numbers to fill in the gaps of the number line between the integers.

Taking into account the new properties of integers consistent with the Postulates for the natural numbers, $\mathbb{N}$, we may now list below the twelve canonical postulates for the integers.

2.2.2   Canonical Postulates for Integers

$\mathbb{I}_c 1$ **(Closure Postulate for Addition):** If M and N are integers, there is an integer, K, such that $M + N = K$.

$\mathbb{I}_c 2$ **(Closure Postulate for Multiplication):** If M and N are integers, there is an integer, K, such that $M \cdot N = K$.

$\mathbb{I}_c 3$ **(Associative Postulate of Addition):** $(K + M) + N = K + (M + N)$.

$\mathbb{I}_c 4$ **(Associative Postulate of Multiplication):** $(K \cdot M) \cdot N = K \cdot (M \cdot N)$.

$\mathbb{I}_c 5$ **(Commutative Postulate of Addition):** $M + N = N + M$.

$\mathbb{I}_c 6$ **(Commutative Postulate of Multiplication):** $M \cdot N = N \cdot M$

$\mathbb{I}_c 7$ **(Distributive Postulate):** $K (M + N) = K \cdot M + K \cdot N$

$\mathbb{I}_c 8$ **(Identity Element for Multiplication):** There exists an integer 1 with $N \cdot 1 = N$.

$\mathbb{I}_c 9$ **(Identity Element for Addition):** There exists an integer 0 with $N + 0 = N$.

$\mathbb{I}_c 10$ **(Additive Inverse):** For any integer N, there exists an additive inverse $-N$ such that $N + (-N) = N - N = 0$.

$\mathbb{I}_c$**11 (Order Postulate):** For integers M, N, and J > 0, K >, 0:

    I.   Only one of the following is true: M = N, N = M + K, or M = N + J, (M = N, M < N, M > N).

    II.   If K < M and M < N, then K < N.

    III.   If M < N, then M + K < N+ K

    IV.   If M > 0 and N > 0, then M · N > 0

$\mathbb{I}_c$**12 (The Integers as an Extension of the Natural Numbers):** The natural numbers are isomorphic with the positive integers (N > 0).

Postulates $\mathbb{I}_c$1 through $\mathbb{I}_c$ 8 correspond to Postulates $\mathbb{N}_c$1 through $\mathbb{N}_c$8 for the natural numbers. They are only modified by indicating that they now apply to integers. The new integer properties are given in Postulates $\mathbb{I}_c$9 and $\mathbb{I}_c$ 10 expressing the existence of an additive identity element and the existence of additive inverses. The Order Postulate $\mathbb{I}_c$11 has been modified from $\mathbb{N}_c$10 by the addition of Part IV to account for the introduction of zero and negative numbers. The Induction Postulate, $\mathbb{N}_c$9 is replaced by Postulate $\mathbb{I}_c$12 noting that the positive integers and their properties are isomorphic with the natural numbers.

2.2.3   Working with the integers

From the above postulates we can prove the cancellation theorems of addition and multiplication.

Theorem $\mathbb{I}$10 (Cancellation Property for Addition): If N+ K = M + K, then N = M

With the postulate for an additive inverse within $\mathbb{I}$, this is trivial in that adding (−K) to both sides of the equation immediately yields N = M. The cancellation property for multiplication is proved using the Order Postulate ($\mathbb{I}_c$11) in Appendix C.

Theorem $\mathbb{I}$11 (Cancellation Property for Multiplication)
If K · M = K · N, then N = M

The introduction of the negative numbers, complicates the relations of inequality (Order Postulate IV). The following theorems and corollaries should clarify the impact of negative numbers on order in operations involving multiplication.

Theorem $\amalg$12: For integers M, N, if M > N, then, −M < −N.

M > N   By Hypothesis
M = N + P (with P >0)   Order Postulate $\amalg_c$11
M + (−M) + (−N) = N + P + (−M) + (−N)

                                                  Cancellation Theorem $\amalg$10
−N = −M+ P   Associative Postulate $\amalg_c$3, Commutative Postulate $\amalg_c$5,
                                                       Additive Inverse $\amalg_c$10
−N > −M   Order Postulate $\amalg_c$11

                                  Q.E.D

For example: 5 > 2 and −2 > −5; 5> −2 and 2 > −5.

The corollary below is a consequence of simply letting N = 0 in Theorem $\amalg$12. (A corollary is a theorem that follows immediately from another theorem.)

Corollary $\amalg$1: For integers M > 0, −M < 0.

More generally, multiplying an inequality by a negative number changes the sense of the inequality.

Theorem $\amalg$13: For integers M, N, and K > 0, if M > N, then −K · M < −K · N.

M > N, K > 0   By hypothesis
−K < 0   Corollary $\amalg$1
M = N + P (with P > 0)   Order Postulate $\amalg_c$11
K · M = K · N + K · P   Distributive Postulate $\amalg_c$7

K · M + (−K ·M) + (−K · N) = K · N + P + (−K ·M) + (−K · N)
                                          Cancellation Property: Theorem $\amalg$10

−K · N = (−K · M) + K · P   Additive Inverse $\amalg_c$10[xxix],
                                                    Postulates $\amalg_c$3 and $\amalg_c$5
K · P > 0   Order Postulate $\amalg_c$11
−K · M < −K · N   Order Postulate $\amalg_c$11

                                  Q.E.D.

---

xxix Theorem $\amalg$14, given below, shows that the additive inverse of K · N, which is −(K · N) = K · (−N). Theorem $\amalg$15 which can be similarly proved, states that −(K · N) = −K · N.

With the above theorems and corollaries, the following postulate, which can be proved to be equivalent to the Order Postulate I_c11, should appear plausible. There are analogous order postulates for rational and real numbers.[90]

I_c**11a (Alternate Order Postulate):** There is a collection I_p of the integers I, not containing 0, such that if $M \neq 0$, then only one of the following is true: M is a member of I_p or—M is a member of I_p. If M and N are members of I_p then M + N and M · N are members of I_p. The collection I_p is known as the positive integers. The remaining non-zero rational numbers make up the negative numbers.

An alternative definition for the relationship of inequality which is equivalent to that of I_c11 is given below:

Definition $I5$: If M and N are members of I_p and M+ $(-N) > 0$, then M > N.

From the canonical postulates we may easily establish the elementary rules of algebra for the negative (signed) integers.

Theorem $I14$: $-(M \cdot N) = M \cdot (-N)$

$M(N + (-N)) = M \cdot 0 = 0$	Additive Inverse I_c10, Theorem $I6$
Also, $\quad M(N + (-N)) = M \cdot N + M \cdot (-N)$	Distributive Property I_c7
Therefore, $\quad M \cdot N + M \cdot (-N) = 0$	Equivalence Relation
$M \cdot N + (-(M \cdot N)) = 0$	Additive Inverse I_c10
$-(M \cdot N) = M \cdot (-N)$	Cancellation Property: Theorem $I10$

Q.E.D.

Similarly, starting with $(M + (-M))N = 0$ and the right distributive property,we can establish the following associated theorem:

Theorem $I15$: $-(M \cdot N) = (-M) \cdot N$.

Let us now determine the rule for the product of two negative numbers.

Theorem $I16$: $(-M) \cdot (-N) = M \cdot N$

$(-M)(N + (-N)) = (-M) \cdot 0 = 0$	Additive Inverse I_c10, Thm. $I6$
$(-M)(N + (-N)) = (-M \cdot N) + (-M) \cdot (-N))$	Distributive Postulate I_c7
$-(M \cdot N) + (-M) \cdot (-N) = 0$	Equivalence Relation: Theorem $I14$
$-(M \cdot N) + M \cdot N = 0$	Additive Inverse I_c10
$(-M) \cdot (-N) = M \cdot N$	Cancellation Property: Theorem $I10$

Q.E.D.

You will recognize these results in the elementary rules of algebra that the product of a negative number and a positive number is negative (for example, $-4 \cdot 3 = -12$) and the product of a negative number and a negative number is positive, for example:

$(-4) \cdot (-3) = 12$. We also note that $-1 \cdot N = -N$ and $-1 \cdot (-N) = N$.

We can now solve problems of the type that began our search for negative numbers:

$5 + X = 3$

Adding the inverse of 5 to each side of the equation, we have:

$(-5) + 5 + X = (-5) + 3$

$((-5) + 5) + X = -1(2 + 3) + 3$

$0 + X = -2 + (-3 + 3)$

$X = -2.$

We also can now solve problems such as:

$2X + 7 = 19$

$2X + 7 + (-7) = 19 + (-7)$

$2X = 12 + (7 + (-7))$

$2X = 2 \cdot 6$

$X = 6$

However, what about: 2X + 7 =18 which can be simplified as above to 2X =11. Here the cancellation theorem for integers cannot help us as 11 does not have 2 as a factor. The determination of those cases in which the cancellation theorem can be applied will lead us in the next section to understand the factors called prime numbers.

2.3   Prime time

As a start, let us look more closely into problems in which the cancellation theorem for multiplication can be applied such as $2X = -6$. Within the integers, we may rewrite the number -6 as a product of factors: $2X = 2 \cdot (-3)$ and then use the cancellation theorem to give the answer $X = -3$. In order to know when the cancellation theorem for multiplication can be used with the integers, we need a method to determine such factors for any integer. For this purpose we will need to revisit the natural numbers.

2.3.1   Prime numbers and the sieve of Eratosthenes

As noted in Chapter 1, the school of Pythagoreans took a great interest in the properties of the natural numbers. Euclid incorporated their results and additional discoveries in his *Elements* in which he stated definitions for even, odd, prime, and composite numbers, among others.[91] Characteristically for the Greeks, prime and composite numbers were defined in geometrical terms; however, in modern terms, a prime number is one whose only factor is one and itself, a composite number being the product of prime numbers. These numbers are the foundation for the discipline of number theory.

A method for determining the prime numbers up to any given number was given by Eratosthenes of the Alexandrian School (275-194 BC).[92] The method, known as the Sieve of Eratosthenes, can be imagined by noting that if you multiply by 2 the sequence of positive integers starting at 1, the resulting sequence 2, 4, 6, 8, 10 . . . clearly consists of composite numbers with a factor of 2. Moving on to 3, the products formed with the sequence of natural numbers are: 6, 9, 12, 15. These numbers are also clearly composites. The next number that has not been identified as a composite is 5 with the sequence of products: 5, 10, 15, 20 . . . . Visually, we can imagine this process by striking every other number starting with 2 in a list of numbers of interest, every third number after 3, and every fifth number after 5, continuing until all necessary numbers have been evaluated. The result is shown below with all of the numbers up to 50 so struck shown in bold and underlined.

1, 2, 3, **4**, 5, **6**, 7, **8**, **9**, **10**, 11, **12**, 13, **14**, **15**, **16**, 17, **18**, **19**, **20**, **21**, **22**, 23, **24**, **25**, **26**, **27**, **28**, 29, **30**, 31, **32**, **33**, **34**, **35**, **36**, 37, **38**, **39**, **40**, 41, **42**, 43, **44**, **45**, **46**, 47, **48**, **49**, **50**

Thus, the prime numbers are those that are left which up to 50 are: 2, 3, 5, 7, 11, 13, 17, 23, 29, 31, 37, 41, 43, and 47.

You may have noticed in going through this process that only prime numbers up to 7 needed to be evaluated. In general to evaluate the prime numbers up to N, one only needs to evaluate prime numbers up to the largest positive integer, $M \leqq \sqrt{N}$ (or $M^2 \leqq N$).[xxx] This follows from the statement that every composite number N has a prime number less than or equal to $\sqrt{N}$. We can prove this in an indirect proof by assuming that all the prime factors of N are greater than $\sqrt{N}$. For example, if N is a composite number, then under our assumption, it must be equal to some product, PK with P, a prime number, and K numbers greater than $\sqrt{N}$. For this to be true with M defined as noted above, $M + 1 \leqq P$, and $M + 1 \leqq K$, that is, $(M + 1)^2 \leqq PK = N$. This contradicts the assumption that M is the largest integer for which $M^2 < N$. Thus, a useful property of number theory (NT) is that we need only evaluate prime numbers up to $\sqrt{N}$.

Theorem NT1: If a positive integer, N, is composite, it has a positive prime factors P such that $P^2 \leqq N$.

2.3.2   An infinite number of primes

From Definition ℕ2 of Peano, we know that every positive integer has a successor and therefore the number of integers is unlimited or infinite. This raises the question of whether there are an infinite number of prime numbers. Euclid in *Elements* proved that there are an infinite number of prime numbers essentially as follows.[93]

---

xxx We will denote positive square roots of a number N, as $\sqrt{N}$. Further discussion of exponents is found in Sections 2.4.6 and 3.4. Here we only need know that $\sqrt{N^2} = N$, for example, $\sqrt{49} = \sqrt{7^2} = 7$.

Let us assume that there are N prime numbers, the largest prime number being P_N. We can form the positive integer K as the product of the N prime numbers, that is:

$$K = P_1 \cdot P_2 \cdot P_2 \cdot P_2 \cdot P_2 \ldots P_{N-1} \cdot P_N.$$

Now K has its successor, K +1 which will not have any of the prime numbers as a factor. and therefore must be prime. This contradicts our assumption; hence:

Theorem NT2: There is no largest prime number.

2.3.3 The Fundamental Theorem of Arithmetic

We are seeking to determine the factors of composite numbers, as an aid to using the cancellation theorem for multiplication. Euclid in *Elements* after showing that every integer must be a prime or composite[94] showed that this factorization is unique.[95]

Suppose the composite integer K may be factored in two ways with N factors of prime numbers P_i (I = 1 to N)and M factors of prime numbers P'_j (j = 1 to M).

$$K = P_1 \cdot P_2 \cdot P_3 \cdot P_4 \cdot P_5 \ldots P_{N-1} \cdot P_N. = P'_1 \cdot P'_2 \cdot P'_3 \cdot P'_4 \cdot P'_5 \ldots P'_{M-1} \cdot P'_M$$

P_1 must be a factor of K, hence a factor of the product of the P's. Since both sets of factors are prime numbers, P_1 must equal one of the P's; thus they can be cancelled. This can be continued until there are no factors left or the remaining factors must equal one. Hence the factorizations are the same (except for order).

Theorem NT3 (Fundamental Theorem of Arithmetic): Every positive integer can be uniquely factored into a product of prime numbers.

2.3.4 The division algorithm

The final property of the positive integers that we will explore is known as the division algorithm, which anticipates our development of the rational numbers. The algorithm is implicit in the Axiom of Eudoxus (died ca. 355 BC) which states that given two unequal natural numbers, m and n, with m > n, n can be repeatedly subtracted from m until there is a remainder k less than n.[96] This is equivalent to the following theorem:

Theorem NT4 (Division Algorithm): Given two positive integers, M and N with M > N, there exists positive integers, K and L with L < N such that M = K · N + L.

2.3.5   The Euclidean Algorithm

A useful tool for determining the greatest common factor between two positive integers is the Euclidean Algorithm which makes repeated use of the division algorithm. A useful way to visualize the algorithm is to take the approach of the classical Greeks and interpret the division geometrically. Suppose we wish to determine the greatest common factor between two numbers, say, 420 and 1176. We can think of these numbers as being represented by a rectangle with sides 420 and 1176 in length as shown in the accompanying figur.

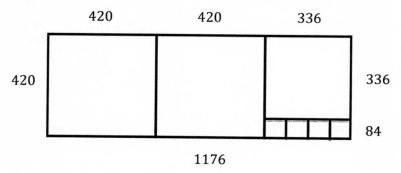

The rectangle's length is first divided into as many squares with sides 420 units long as possible—in the diagram we can see two. The remainder of the length of the rectangle is 336 units, forming a a smaller rectangle of dimensions 336 by 420. Only one square 336 by 336 can be placed in this space leaving a rectangle of dimensions 84 by 336 units. This can be divided exactly into four squares 84 units on a side.

It is clear that 84 is an exact divisor of 420 and 1176, since the row of squares 84 by 84 is and exact divisor of 336 and when the row of these squares is added to the 336 by 336 square, it fills out a rectangle 420 by 336.

This geometric process can be expressed algebraically for this specific case, providing another way to see that 84 is a common factor.

$$1176 = 2 \cdot 420 + 336 \tag{2.12}$$

$$420 = 1 \cdot 336 + 84 \tag{2.13}$$

$$336 = 4 \cdot 84 + 0 \tag{2.14}$$

Through substitution of 2.13 into 2.12 followed by 2.14, we have:

$$1176 = 2 \cdot (1 \cdot 336 + 84) + 336 = 3 \cdot 336 + 2 \cdot 84 = 3(4 \cdot 84) + 2 \cdot 84 = 14 \cdot 84.$$

Now suppose there is a common divisor of 1176 and 420 greater than 84, say x. If x is a common divisor of 1176 and 420, then it must divide $(1176 - 2 \cdot 420) = 336$. Therefore, x is also a common divisor of 336. Similarly, x must then be a common divisor of $(420 - 1 \cdot 336) = 84$. Since x is assumed to be greater than 84, we reach a contradiction as x cannot be a divisor of 84. Thus, the greatest factor that can divide the rectangle of dimensions 420 by 1176 is 84. A similar approach can be used to show that the Euclidean Algorithm provides the greatest common divisor of any two natural numbers. Euclid proved this result in Propositions 1 and 2 of Book VII of his *Elements*.[97] Of course the Euclidean Algorithm must agree with the result that we would obtain by determining 1176 and 420 as products of their prime numbers.

$$1176 = 2^3 \cdot 3 \cdot 7^2 \qquad 420 = 2^2 \cdot 3 \cdot 5 \cdot 7$$

Comparing the products of the prime numbers that form the composite numbers 1176 and 420, we see that they have in common the product: $2^2 \cdot 3 \cdot 7 = 84$ in agreement with the result of the Euclidean Algorithm.

Suppose we wish to find the greatest common factor between 1176 and $420 + 1 = 421$. We follow the same algorithm:

$$1176 = 2 \cdot 421 + 334$$

$$421 = 1 \cdot 334 + 87$$

$$334 = 3 \cdot 87 + 73$$

$$87 = 1 \cdot 73 + 14$$

$$73 = 5 \cdot 14 + 3$$

$$14 = 4 \cdot 3 + 2$$

$$3 = 1 \cdot 2 + 1$$

$$2 = 2 \cdot 1 + 0$$

Thus the greatest common factor is 1. That is to say 1176 and 421 have no factors other than 1 in common. A key insight into the algorithm is that the remainder at each step must decrease as the divisors decrease in size, eventually reaching zero. In the example above, the sequence of remainders is: 334, 87, 73, 14, 3, 2, 1, 0 each being less than its associated divisor: 421, 334, 87, 73, 14, 3, 2, 1.

An interesting consequence of the Euclidean algorithm is that if k is the greatest common factor between two natural numbers m and n, then there exists integers A and B so that: $k = A \cdot m + B \cdot n$. This type of problem is known as a Diophantine problem (after Diophantus). Such problems arise naturally in cases where only integer solutions make sense. A detailed discussion of the Euclidean Algorithm and Diophantine problems is given by Meserve[xxxi] as part of an introduction to number theory. Other introductory subjects within number theory include formulas and distributions for prime numbers, modular arithmetic[xxxii], and many other relationships between integers. A classic problem of number theory for centuries was Fermat's Last Theorem. Fermat stated without proof that no natural numbers can be found for x, y, and z such that: $x^n + y^n = z^n$, if $n > 2$. Finally in 1995, the proof was provided in two papers by Andrew Wiles solving one of mathematics most famous problems.[98] (In contrast, for $n = 2$, Euclid had shown that there were an infinite number of solutions.)[99] Another famous example of a problem of number theory is that known as the Goldbach Conjecture. In a letter to

---

xxxi Meserve, pp. 58-97.

xxxii Modular arithmetic deals with systems in which a number m is said to be congruent with a number j modulo n if $m = k \cdot n + j$, where j, k, m, n are integers. The most common example of such a congruence are the hours as indicated on a clock which are modulo 12, (the hour after noon is 1); Ibid., pp. 83-84.

Euler, Christian Goldbach stated that every even integer greater than 2 is the sum of two prime numbers.[100] The validity of the conjecture remains unknown.

Our introduction to some elements of number theory has been brief. However, having met our goal of understanding the factorization of the integers, we can determine those cases in which the cancellation theorem for multiplication can be used to solve problems such as M · X = N. We now return to the problem of solving equations such as 2X = 11 in which there are no solutions within the integer numbers.

2.4   Divide and conquer; the rational numbers

We recognize that in order to solve problems such as $2 \cdot x = 11$, our number system must once again expand taking us beyond the integers. We know that there is no integer that can solve this equation since $2 \cdot 5 = 10 < 11$ and $2 \cdot 5^+ = 2 \cdot 6 = 12 > 11$. We need a number between 5 and its successor, 6.

2.4.1   Using the group concept to add a multiplicative inverse

We solved problems such as $3 = 5 + x$, by introducing additive inverses. If we could create multiplicative inverses, then we could solve equations such as $2 \cdot x = 11$. Denoting the multiplicative inverse of 2 as 2^*, we would have $2^* \cdot 2 = 1$. Therefore,

$$2^* \cdot 2 \cdot x = x = 2^* \cdot 11.$$

We will expand the integers to the rational numbers, $\mathbb{R}$, so that each integer, N within $\mathbb{R}$. except 0 will have an inverse N^* with $N^* \cdot N = 1$. Now, if you look closely at the canonical postulates for the integers (Section 2.2.2), you will see that the integers form what is termed a group with regard to the operation of addition (Section 1.2.5.3). Specifically, the canonical postulates associated with addition, $\mathbb{I}_c1$(closure), $\mathbb{I}_c3$ (associative property), $\mathbb{I}_c5$, (commutative property), $\mathbb{I}_c9$ (identity element), and $\mathbb{I}_c10$ (additive inverse) form an additive commutative group. However, the integers do not form a group with regard to the operation of multiplication, since there is no multiplicative inverse. The multiplicative inverse is exactly the property that we wish to add. Since the group concept is entirely general, we can structure new numbers with the operation of multiplication using the additive group structure as a template. The new numbers, which we will call rational numbers, will be formed from the integers in a manner similar to the way in which we formed the integers from the natural numbers.

Let us replace in our definitions of integers, the operational symbol for addition, +, with that for multiplication, ·, the identity element for addition, 0 with that for multiplication, 1, and the natural numbers with the integers. The integers were formed from the ordered pair of natural numbers, [m − n]. The rational numbers will be developed using the ordered pairs of Integers, [M / N] where the "/" is initially simply a separator between the integers and is not yet symbolic of a binary operation.

The approach outlined above, suggests the definitions of the rational numbers shown in the next table in the right hand column. The corresponding forms for the integers forming the basis of the rational numbers are shown in the left hand column. Notice that the integers are embedded within the rational numbers just as the natural numbers are embedded within the integers. (For the Additive Group, 0 is considered to be a member of the extended natural numbers.)

Additive Group	Multiplicative Group
$[i - j] = [m - n]$ if $i + n = j + n \rightarrow$	$[I / J] = [M / N]$ if $I \cdot N = J \cdot N$
$[i - j] + [m - n] = [i + m - j + n] \rightarrow$	$[I / J] \cdot [M / N] = [I \cdot M / J \cdot N]$
$n \leftrightarrow [n + k - k] = [n - 0] \rightarrow$	$N \leftrightarrow [N \cdot K / K] = [N / 1]$
$0 \leftrightarrow [k - k] = [0 - 0] \rightarrow$	$1 \leftrightarrow [K / K] = [1 / 1]$
$-N = [k - n + k] = [0 - n] \rightarrow$	$N^* = [K / N \cdot K] = [1 / N]$

With these considerations, the rational numbers, $\mathbb{R}$, will now be formally developed starting with definitions.

Definition $\mathbb{R}$1: rational numbers $\mathbb{R}$ are defined as the ordered pairs of the integers [M / N] with $N \neq 0$.

Definition $\mathbb{R}$2: Two rational numbers, [M/ N] and [K/ L] are equal if and only if $M \cdot L = N \cdot K$.

Definition $\mathbb{R}$3: The operation of multiplication between pairs of rational numbers is defined by: $[M / N] \cdot [K / L] = [M \cdot K / N \cdot L]$.

Definition $\mathbb{R}4$: The operation of addition between pairs of rational numbers is defined by: $[M / N] + [K / L] = [(M \cdot L + K \cdot N) / N \cdot L]$.

The form for the definition of the operation of addition will be clarified after we introduce an identity element for multiplication. The definition of addition for the rational numbers will be shown to be consistent with the properties of the integers. We now develop the properties of the rational numbers following the same approach as we used for the integers.

2.4.2   Algebraic properties of the rational numbers

Theorem $\mathbb{R}1$ (Equivalence Relation): Equality within the rational numbers is an equivalence relation.

Theorem $\mathbb{R}1$ follows directly from the properties of the integers. As an example, the symmetric relation is proved below. Note that only definitions and the properties of the integers are used in the proof:

Theorem $\mathbb{R}1$(Symmetry): If the rational number $[M/N] = [K/ L]$ then $[K/ L] = [M/ N]$

$[M/ N] = [K/ L]$	By hypothesis
$M \cdot L = N \cdot K$	Definition $\mathbb{R}2$
$N \cdot K = M \cdot L$	Equivalence Relation for $\mathbb{I}$
$K \cdot N = L \cdot M$	Commutative Postulate $\mathbb{I}_c 6$
$[K / L] = [M / N]$	Definition $\mathbb{R}2$

Q.E.D.

It can easily be shown that the new rational numbers have closure, commutative and associative properties under the operation of multiplication and addition since the integers have these properties.

Theorem $\mathbb{R}2$ (Commutative Group under Multiplication): The rational numbers are closed under the operation of multiplication, which is commutative and associative; there exists an identity element for multiplication; and every rational number, except the identity element for addition, has a multiplicative inverse.

I will illustrate how these group properties follow from the definitions of the rational numbers and postulates of the integers with proofs for the commutative property, the existence of an identity element and a multiplicative inverse.

Theorem $\mathbb{R}2$ (Commutative Property for Multiplication): For [M / N] and [K/ L] in $\mathbb{R}$, [M / N] · [K / L] = [K / L] · {M / N]

[M / N] · [K/ L] = [M · K / N · L]	Definition $\mathbb{R}3$
= [K · M/ L ·N]	Commutative Postulate $\mathbb{I}_c$ 6
= [K/ L] · [M/ N]	Definition $\mathbb{R}3$

Q.E.D.

We want to confirm the definition of the identity element for multiplication.

Theorem $\mathbb{R}2$ (Identity Element for Multiplication): There exists an identity element in $\mathbb{R}$ for multiplication [M / M}, such that [K/ L] · [M/ M] = [K / L].

[K/ L] · [M/ M] = [K · M/ L· M]	Definition $\mathbb{R}3$
= [K/ L] since K · M · L = L · M · K	
	Definition $\mathbb{R}2$, Postulates $\mathbb{I}_c$ 4, $\mathbb{I}_c$ 6

Q.E.D.

With the identity element for multiplication now defined, we can confirm the existence of a multiplicative inverse.

Theorem $\mathbb{R}2$ (Inverse for Multiplication): For rational numbers [M/ N] with M, N $\neq$ 0, there exists a multiplicative inverse [N/ M], such that [M/ N] · [N/ M/] = [M/ M].

[M/ N] · [N/ M] = [M · N/ N · M]	Definition $\mathbb{R}3$
= [M/ M] since M · N · M = M · N · M	Definition $\mathbb{R}2$

Q.E.D.

Note that the cancellation property for multiplication follows as a direct consequence of the existence of multiplicative inverse.

Theorem $\mathbb{R}3$ (Cancellation Property for Multiplication): If [M/ N] · [I/ J] = [K/ L] · [I/ J] then [M/ N] = [K/ L]

This follows immediately from:

$[M/N] \cdot [I/J] \cdot [J/I] = [K/L] \cdot [I/J] \cdot [J/I]$;

hence,

$[M/N] = [K/L]$.

Q.E.D.

Now we want to see that the rational numbers also form a group under the operation of addition.

Theorem $\mathbb{R}4$ (Commutative Group under Addition): The rational numbers are closed under the operation of addition, which is commutative and associative; there exists an identity element; and every rational number has an additive inverse.

As in the case of the operation of multiplication, I will illustrate how these group properties follow from the definitions of the rational numbers and postulates of the integers with proofs for the commutative property, the existence of an identity element and an additive inverse.

Theorem $\mathbb{R}4$ (Commutative Property for Addition): For $[M/N]$ and $[K/L]$, $[M/N] + [K/L] = [K/L] + [M/N]$.

$$
\begin{aligned}
[M/N] + [K/L] \quad &= [(M \cdot L + K \cdot N)/N \cdot L] && \text{Definition } \mathbb{R}4 \\
&= [K \cdot N + M \cdot L / L \cdot N] && \text{Postulates } \mathbb{I}_c 5, \mathbb{I}_c 6 \\
&= [K/L] + [M/N] && \text{Definition } \mathbb{R}4
\end{aligned}
$$
$$\text{Q.E.D.}$$

Theorem $\mathbb{R}4$ (Identity Element for Addition): There exists an identity element for addition, $[0/N]$, with $N \neq 0$, such that $[K/L] + [0/N] = [K \cdot N + 0 \cdot L / L \cdot N] = [K \cdot N / L \cdot N] = [K/L]$.

This, as shown above, follows immediately from the definition of the addition of rational numbers and the properties of 0 in $\mathbb{I}$. We can now show that there is an additive inverse for the rational numbers.

Theorem ℝ4 (Inverse for Addition): For every rational number, [M/ N], there exists an additive inverse, [−M/N], such that [M/ N] + [−M/ N] = [0/ N].

$$
\begin{aligned}
[\text{M}/\text{ N}] + [-\text{M}/\text{ N}] \quad &= [\text{M} \cdot \text{N} + (-\text{M} \cdot \text{N})/ \text{N} \cdot \text{N}] &&\text{Definition } \mathbb{R}4 \\
&= [\text{N } (\text{M} - \text{M})/ \text{N} \cdot \text{N}] &&\text{Postulate } \text{I}_c\, 7 \\
&= [0 / \text{N} \cdot \text{N}] &&\text{Postulate } \text{I}_c\, 10, \text{Thm. I}6 \\
&= [0 / \text{N}] &&\text{Definition } \mathbb{R}2 \\
&\qquad\qquad \text{Q.E.D.}
\end{aligned}
$$

The one remaining canonical algebraic property that exists for the natural and the integers is the distributive property. The distributive property relates the operation of multiplication over addition. Recall that the distributive property was a key part of the theorems used to determine the sign of products of the integers, for example, $(-\text{M}) \cdot (-\text{N}) = \text{M} \cdot \text{N}$ In order to help us with the proof of the distributive property for the rational numbers, we will first prove another property of addition:

Lemma ℝ1: For [I / J] and [K / J] in ℝ, [I / J] + [K / J] = [I + K / J].

$$
\begin{aligned}
[\text{I} / \text{J}] + [\text{K} / \text{J}] &= [\text{I} \cdot \text{J} + \text{K} \cdot \text{J} / \text{J} \cdot \text{J}] &&\text{Definition } \mathbb{R}4 \\
&= [\text{J } (\text{I} + \text{K}) / \text{J} \cdot \text{J}] &&\text{Postulates } \text{I}_c 6, \text{I}_c\, 7 \\
&= [\text{J}/ \text{J}] \cdot [\text{I} + \text{K}/ \text{J}] &&\text{Definition } \mathbb{R}3 \\
&= [\text{I} + \text{K}/ \text{J}] &&\text{Theorem } \mathbb{R}2 \\
&\qquad\qquad \text{Q.E.D.}
\end{aligned}
$$

Note that in the above proof, if I + K = J, then [I / J] + [K / J] = [J / J] which is consistent with the idea of [I / J] as a fraction. This is a result of the definition of addition. Further insight into the relation between [I / J] and fractions is given by the development of the expression for [M / N] + [K / L] using Lemma ℝ1:

$$
\begin{aligned}
[\text{M}/\text{N}] + [\text{K}/\text{L}] &= [\text{L} / \text{L}] \cdot [\text{M} / \text{N}] + [\text{N} / \text{N}] \cdot [\text{K} / \text{L}] &&\text{Theorem } \mathbb{R}2 \\
&= [\text{L} \cdot \text{M} / \text{L} \cdot \text{N}] + [\text{N} \cdot \text{K} / \text{N} \cdot \text{L}] &&\text{Definition } \mathbb{R}3 \\
&= [\text{M} \cdot \text{L} / \text{N} \cdot \text{L}] + [\text{K} \cdot \text{N} / \text{N} \cdot \text{L}] &&\text{Commutative Property } \text{I}_c 6 \\
&= [\text{M} \cdot \text{L} + \text{K} \cdot \text{N}/ \text{N} \cdot \text{L}] &&\text{Lemma } \mathbb{R}1
\end{aligned}
$$

Thus, our definition of addition is consistent with the definitions of multiplication and the identity element through Lemma ℝ1. The definition may also be viewed as illustrating the addition of fractions using a common denominator (in our proof, $N \cdot L$). As a specific example, we have:

$$[3/5] + [1/2] = [3 \cdot 2 + 5 \cdot 1 / 5 \cdot 2] = [11 / 10]$$

Here, we can see the familiar rule for adding fractions.

We now show that the definition of addition is consistent with the distributive property:

Theorem ℝ5 (Distributive Property): For rational numbers $[I/J]$, $[K/L]$, and $[M/N]$, $[I/J] \cdot ([K/L] + [M/N]) = [I/J] \cdot [K/L] + [I/J] \cdot (M/N)$

$[I / J] \cdot ([K / L] + [M / N])$

$\quad = [I / J] \cdot ([K \cdot N + M \cdot L / L \cdot N])$ Definition ℝ4

$\quad = [I \cdot (K \cdot N + M \cdot L) / J \cdot (N \cdot L)]$ Definition ℝ3

$\quad = [I \cdot (K \cdot N) + I \cdot (M \cdot L) / J \cdot (N \cdot L)$ Postulate $\mathbb{I}_c 7$

$\quad = [I \cdot (K \cdot N) / J \cdot (N \cdot L)] + [I \cdot (M \cdot L) / J \cdot (N \cdot L]$ Lemma ℝ1,

$\quad = [N / N] \cdot [(I \cdot K) / (J \cdot L)] + [L / L] \cdot [(I \cdot M) / (J \cdot N]$ Def. ℝ3, Post.$\mathbb{I}_c 4$, $\mathbb{I}_c 6$

$\quad = [I / J] \cdot [K / L] + [I / J] \cdot [M / N]$ Thm ℝ2, Definition ℝ3

$\quad\quad\quad\quad\quad\quad$ Q.E.D.

2.4.3   Order and the rational numbers

With the addition of the multiplicative inverse to the properties that were satisfied for the integers, the rational numbers form the mathematical structure that is known as a field. The integers, not having this property are known as a ring (two groups without an inverse for one of its two operations). The remaining property that needs to be investigated is the order property. This property which is also satisfied by the rational numbers establishes the rational numbers as an ordered field.

As shown below, the order property is stated exactly the same as that for the integers, replacing references to the integers with rational numbers.

Theorem ℝ6 (Order Property): For rational numbers $[K/L]$, $[M/N]$, and $[P/Q]$:

I.   Only one of the following is true: $\{M / N\} = [K / L]$, $[M / N] > [K/L]$) or $[K / L] > [M / N]$.

II.   If $[K / L] < [M / N]$ and $[M / N] < [P / Q]$, then $[K / L] < [P / Q]$.

III.   If $[M / N] < [P / Q]$, then $[M / N] + [K / L] < [P / Q] + [K / L]$
IV.   If $[M / N] > 0$ and $[K / L] > 0$, then $[M / N] \cdot [K / L] > 0$

Just as in the case of the integers, operations of multiplication for inequalities of rational numbers require some care with the negative numbers. In the simple case in which the rational numbers are all formed from positive integers, K, L, M, N, P, then it is clear using the definition of inequality of the integers and our understanding of rational numbers as fractions that if:

$K \cdot L > M \cdot N$
$[K / N] > [M / L]$

However, if, for example, $N < 0$, then similar to Theorem I13, the definition of inequality leads to a reversal with $[K / N] < M / L]$.

For example, $2 \cdot 3 > 4 \cdot (-5)$ and therefore $[3/4] > [-5/2]$, but $[2/-5] = [-2/5] < [4/3]$.

Depending on the sign of K, L, M, and N, the relation of $[K / N]$ to $\{M / L\}$ can be determined by recalling that as with the integers the inequality is reversed when multiplying by a negative number. As a result, the general relation for K, L, M, and N can be summarized as: $[K / N] > [M / L]$ if $K \cdot L^2 \cdot N > M \cdot N^2 \cdot L$.[101]

2.4.4   Rational numbers and the integers

We now identify the integers within the rational numbers. For every integer N, we have:

Theorem $\mathbb{R}$7: The rational numbers $[N \cdot M/ M] = [N/ 1]$, correspond to the integers N which are embedded within the rational numbers along with their properties.

Examples: $N + M \leftrightarrow [N/1] + [M/1] = [N \cdot 1 + M/ 1 \cdot 1] = [N + M / 1]$

$N + (-M) = N - M \leftrightarrow \{N/ 1\} + [-M/ 1] = [N \cdot 1 + (-M) \cdot 1 / 1 \cdot 1] = [N - M / 1]$

$N \cdot M \leftrightarrow [N/1] \cdot [M/ 1] = [N \cdot M/ 1 \cdot 1] = [N \cdot M/ 1]$

We will simplify the notation, dropping the brackets for the rational numbers and designate the general rational number, [M/N] as a variable such as $X = m/m$ with integers within the rational numbers indicated by using the lower case variables. As X is a rational number, ultimately expressible as the ratio of two integers, such expressions as X / Y is a legitimate expression with Y also being a rational number. For example:

If $X = k / j$ and $Y = m / m$, then

$1 = Y \cdot (1 / Y) = (m / m) \cdot (1 / Y)$ and $(1 / Y) = m / m$.

$X / Y = (k / j) / (m / m) = (X / 1) \cdot (1 / Y) = (k / j) \cdot (m / m) = (k \cdot m) / (j \cdot m)$.

The identity elements for addition and multiplication are 0 and 1, respectively. The rational number m/m is restricted to $m \neq 0$. This restriction is required because for all $m \neq 0$,

if $m = 0$ and $m/m = X$, then

$m = m \cdot X = 0$,

which contradicts $m \neq 0$.

The form $0/0$ is not allowed since if:

$0/0 = X$

$0 = 0 \cdot X$ which is true for any X.

The form $0/0$ is therefore indeterminate.

We have established the properties of the rational numbers through Definitions $\mathbb{R}1$ to $\mathbb{R}4$ and Theorems $\mathbb{R}1$ to $\mathbb{R}6$ which use only the properties previously established for the integers. We can now define the rational numbers through a set of postulates incorporating these definitions and results.

2.4.5   Canonical Postulates for the Rational Numbers

$\mathbb{R}_c$ 1. (Commutative Property for Addition): For X and Y rational numbers, $X + Y = Y + X$.

$\mathbb{R}_c$ 2. (Commutative Property for Multiplication): For $\mathbb{X}$ and $\mathbb{Y}$ rational numbers, $\mathbb{X} \cdot \mathbb{Y} = \mathbb{Y} \cdot \mathbb{X}$.

$\mathbb{R}_c$3. (Associative Property for Addition): For $\mathbb{X}$, $\mathbb{Y}$, and Z rational numbers, $(\mathbb{X} + \mathbb{Y}) + Z = \mathbb{X} + (\mathbb{Y} + Z)$

$\mathbb{R}_c$4. (Associative Property for Multiplication): For $\mathbb{X}$, $\mathbb{Y}$ and Z rational numbers, $(\mathbb{X} \cdot \mathbb{Y}) \cdot Z = \mathbb{X} \cdot (\mathbb{Y} \cdot Z)$

$\mathbb{R}_c$ 5. (Identity Element for Addition): There exists an identity element for addition, $\mathbb{0}$ such that $\mathbb{X} + \mathbb{0} = \mathbb{X}$.

$\mathbb{R}_c$6. (Identity Element for Multiplication): There exists an identity element for multiplication, $\mathbb{1}$, such that $\mathbb{X} \cdot \mathbb{1} = \mathbb{X}$.

$\mathbb{R}_c$7. (Inverse for Addition): For every rational number, $\mathbb{X}$, there exists an additive inverse, $-\mathbb{X}$ such that $\mathbb{X} + (-\mathbb{X}) = \mathbb{X} - \mathbb{X} = 0$.

$\mathbb{R}_c$8. (Inverse for Multiplication): For every rational number $\mathbb{X} \neq \mathbb{0}$, there exists a multiplicative inverse, $\mathbb{1} / \mathbb{X}$, such that $\mathbb{X} \cdot (\mathbb{1} / \mathbb{X}) = \mathbb{1}$.

$\mathbb{R}_c$9. (Distributive Property): For $\mathbb{X}$, $\mathbb{Y}$ and Z rational numbers, $\mathbb{X}(\mathbb{Y} + Z) = \mathbb{X} \cdot \mathbb{Y} + \mathbb{X} \cdot Z$

$\mathbb{R}_c$10. (Order Property): For rational numbers $\mathbb{X}$, $\mathbb{Y}$ and Z,

I.   Only one of the following is true: $\mathbb{X} = \mathbb{Y}$, $\mathbb{X} < \mathbb{Y}$, $\mathbb{Y} > \mathbb{X}$.
II.   If $\mathbb{X} < \mathbb{Y}$ and $\mathbb{Y} < Z$, then $\mathbb{X} < Z$.
III.   If $\mathbb{X} < \mathbb{Y}$, then $\mathbb{X} + Z < \mathbb{Y} + Z$
IV.   If $\mathbb{X} > 0$ and $\mathbb{Y} > 0$, then $\mathbb{X} \cdot \mathbb{Y} > 0$.

As with the natural numbers and integers, there is more than one way to express the postulates. The ordering property can also be expressed as the following statement[xxxiii]:

$\mathbb{R}_c$ 10a. (Alternate Order Property): There is a collection $\mathbb{R}_p$ of the rational numbers, $\mathbb{R}$, not containing $\mathbb{0}$, such that if $\mathbb{X} \neq \mathbb{0}$, then only one of the following is true: $\mathbb{X}$ is a member of $\mathbb{R}_p$ or $-\mathbb{X}$ is a member of $\mathbb{R}_p$.

---

xxxiii Eves, p. 180, see also Thurston, p. 27. The postulate given in $\mathbb{R}_c$10 is discussed as part of the definition of a field in Labarre, A. E., Jr., *Intermediate Mathematical Analysis* [Math References 19].

If $\mathbb{X}$ and $\mathbb{Y}$ are members of $\mathbb{R}_p$, then $\mathbb{X} + \mathbb{Y}$ and $\mathbb{X} \cdot \mathbb{Y}$ are members of $\mathbb{R}_p$. The collection $\mathbb{R}_p$ is known as the positive rational numbers. The remaining non-zero rational numbers make up the negative numbers.

An alternative and equivalent definition for the relationship of inequality follows:

Definition $\mathbb{R}5$: If $\mathbb{X}$ and $\mathbb{Y}$ are members of $\mathbb{R}_p$, and $\mathbb{X} + (-\mathbb{Y}) > \mathbb{0}$, then $\mathbb{X} > \mathbb{Y}$.

As in the case of $\mathbb{I}_c 11a$, I shall not prove the equivalence of the $\mathbb{R}_c 10$ and its alternate $\mathbb{R}_c 10a$; however, the existence of additive inverse assures that for every $\mathbb{X}$, there is a $-\mathbb{X}$ and if $\mathbb{X} > 0$, then $(-\mathbb{X}) < 0$. Postulates $\mathbb{R}_c 1$ to $\mathbb{R}_c 9$ define the rational numbers as the algebraic structure called a field. The addition of Postulate $\mathbb{R}_c 10$ means that the rational numbers are an ordered field.

2.4.6   Rational exponents

As with the natural numbers, we would like rules for exponentiation for the rational numbers. Recall the following definitions and theorems for exponents that are natural numbers (Section 2.1.6):

Definition $\mathbb{N}7$: $n^1 = n$ and $n^{k+1} = n^k \cdot n$

Theorem $\mathbb{N}11$: $(nm)^k = n^k \cdot m^k$

Theorem $\mathbb{N}12$: $n^k \cdot n^j = n^{k+j}$

Theorem $\mathbb{N}13$: $(n^j)^k = n^{j \cdot k}$

Just as in our development of the rational numbers, we want to keep our definition for exponents with rational numbers consistent with the rules for the natural numbers. Theorem $\mathbb{N}12$ requires exponents to be additive for the natural numbers. We extend this to the rational number with the following definition:

Definition $\mathbb{R}6$: $\mathbb{X}^m \cdot \mathbb{X}^n = \mathbb{X}^{m+n}$

Noting that, $\mathbb{X}/\mathbb{X} = \mathbb{1}$, we make the following definition for the multiplicative inverse of $\mathbb{X}$:

Definition $\mathbb{R}7$: $(1/\mathbb{X})^m = \mathbb{X}^{-m}$

Thus,

$\mathbb{X}/\mathbb{X} = \mathbb{1} = \mathbb{X}^1 \cdot \mathbb{X}^{-1} = \mathbb{X}^{1-1}$, and

$\mathbb{X}^m / \mathbb{X}^m = = \mathbb{X}^m \cdot \mathbb{X}^{-m} = \mathbb{X}^{m-m} = \mathbb{X}^0$ which leads to:

Definition $\mathbb{R}8$: $\mathbb{X}^0 = \mathbb{1}$.

Note that $\mathbb{0}^0$ is not defined as $(\mathbb{0}/\mathbb{0})$ is indeterminate.

We note that the negative numbers were previously introduced in the integers, but we did not extend the exponents to the negative integers at that time. Given that $1/X$ is not defined within the integers; negative exponents also could not be defined.

We would like the above definitions of exponents to be applicable to rational numbers such as, $\mathbb{p}/\mathbb{q}$; however the meaning of $\mathbb{X}^{p/q}$ is not clear. To interpret the meaning of this number let us appeal to Theorem N13: $(n^j)^k = n^{j \cdot k}$. We provisionally extend this to rational exponents through the following conjecture:

$(\mathbb{X}^p)^{1/q} = \mathbb{X}^{p/q}$.

If we take $\mathbb{X} = \mathbb{2}$, with $\mathbb{p} = \mathbb{q} = \mathbb{2}$, then we have: $(\mathbb{2}^2)^{1/2} = \mathbb{2}^{2/2} = \mathbb{2}^1 = \mathbb{2}$. You are probably familiar with this as 2 being the positive square root of 4 or $2 = \sqrt{4}$. Similarly, $\mathbb{8}^{1/3} = \sqrt[3]{2^3} = \mathbb{2}$ that is 2 is the cube root of 8. However, in general we do not know how to interpret numbers such as $\mathbb{2}^{p/q}$. Our example suggest that if $x^2 = \mathbb{2}$, then $x = \mathbb{2}^{1/2}$. In Section 2.6, we will find out that there is no rational number, $\mathbb{m}/\mathbb{m}$ that fits this description. Thus until we extend our numbers to the real numbers, our exponents are limited to the integers.

We have determined the structural basis for the rational numbers going back to the natural numbers. Extending the natural numbers to the integers and then to the rational number has allowed us to solve any problem that can be put into the form: $\mathbb{a}x + \mathbb{b} = \mathbb{0}$. This is known as a linear problem. Using the additive and multiplicative inverses, we now know that the postulates for the rational numbers allow for the solution $x = -\mathbb{b}/\mathbb{a}$.

We have focused on the basis for the rules that govern our number systems. In the next section, we will look into how numbers can be represented by the decimal notation to take practical advantage of our understanding of the number system. In addition to the practical significance of the decimal systems, the efficient representation of numbers by decimals will also help us to understand the extension of the rational numbers to the real numbers.

2. 5   Ten is enough; decimal representation

Our decimal number system and the associated rules of arithmetic are learned after much hard work in school. Afterwards, we take it entirely for granted, using it without much thought as to its meaning. But as I discussed in Chapter 1, the decimal number system was arrived at only after thousands of years with inputs across continents and civilizations. Just to give a sense of the advancement in calculation brought about by the decimal system try the simple problem of adding say 86 and 63 with Roman numerals. You will recall from school that 80 is represented as C (100) less XX (20), that is XXC; 6 as V (5) plus I (1) or VI, so 86 is XXCVI. The number 63 is 60 as L (50) plus X(10) and three 1's, hence 63 is LXIII. The problem therefore might look something like this:

$$
\begin{array}{r}
\text{XXCVI} \\
\underline{\text{LXIII}} \\
\text{CXLIX}
\end{array}
$$

Try the addition yourself. I believe that you could imagine rules for addition with Roman numerals, but it is clearly less systematic than addition in the decimal system. Multiplication would be a horror. It is therefore not surprising that Roman numerals were used primarily to record results with the arithmetic operations performed mechanically with an abacus.[102]

Roman numerals were a major step backwards from the positional sexagesimal (60 based) system of the Babylonians. The Babylonians understood that by using a sexagesimal system they only needed symbols for 1 to 59 with greater numbers being built from the powers of 60 as for example 86 (decimal) $= 1 \cdot (60)^1 + 26 \cdot (60)^0 = 1\ 26$ and $63 = 1 \cdot (60)^1 + 3 \cdot (60)^0 = 1\ 3$. And so returning to our addition problem: $86 + 63$ (decimal) $= 1\ 26 + 1\ 3 = 2\ 29 = 2 \cdot (60)^1 + 29 = 149$ (decimal). The Babylonian system required the ability to add or multiply any two numbers up to 59 and they had clay tablets (early math aids) to help with this.[103] I believe most of us would prefer remembering our multiplication and addition tables only up to 9. Also, as previously noted in Chapter 1, for apparently hundreds of years, the Babylonians did not have the number zero to indicate the absence of a power of 60, so that $3610 = 1 \cdot (60)^2 + 10$ could look like 1 10 which could easily be misinterpreted. Finally, like our decimal system the Babylonians also could indicate fractions in terms of portions of their base 60. So for example our 1.5 would be $1\ 30 = 1\ 30 \cdot 60^{-1}$. With this background, let us look more explicitly into the decimal number system, looking first into the representation of the integers and then the representation of rational numbers.

2.5.1   Integers in different bases.

Any positive integer M may be represented in terms of a positional base system such as the decimal or sexagesimal system. In base b, M may be expressed as:

$$M = a_n \cdot b^n + a_{n-1} \cdot b^{n-1} + \ldots + a_1 \cdot b^1 + a_0 \cdot b^0.$$

The division algorithm is used to determine a_0, that part of M which is not a multiple of b; a_1, that part of M which is not a multiple of b^2 and so forth. I will illustrate this by expressing the decimal number $2{,}365 = 2 \cdot 10^3 + 3 \cdot 10^2 + 6 \cdot 10^1 + 5 \cdot 10^0$ in base 8 (octal system). To determine the octal equivalent, we begin by dividing 2,365 by 8 to obtain that part of our number which is not a multiple of a power of 8:

$$2365 = 295 \cdot 8 + 5$$

Now we divide 295 by 8 to determine that part which is not a multiple of 8^2,

$$295 = 36 \cdot 8 + 7.$$

Continuing, we divide 36 by 8,

$$36 = 4 \cdot 8 + 4,$$

and

$$4 = 0 \cdot 8 + 4.$$

Hence $2,365 = 4 \cdot 8^3 + 4 \cdot 8^2 + 7 \cdot 8^1 + 5 \cdot 8^0 = 4 \cdot 512 + 4 \cdot 64 + 7 \cdot 8 + 5$
$= 4475$(octal).

This can also be seen by direct substitution from above:

$295 = 36 \cdot 8 + 7 = (4 \cdot 8 + 4) \cdot 8 + 7$

$2,365 = 295 \cdot 8 + 5 = ((4 \cdot 8 + 4) \cdot 8 + 7) \cdot 8 + 5 = (4 \cdot 8 \cdot 8 \cdot 8) + (4 \cdot 8 \cdot 8) + (7 \cdot 8) + 5$.

As another example, I will determine the binary (base 2) equivalent of 100(decimal). In the binary system, the only numbers are 0 and 1.

$100 = 2 \cdot 50 + 0$

$50 = 2 \cdot 25 + 0$

$25 = 2 \cdot 12 + 1$

$12 = 2 \cdot 6 + 0$

$6 = 2 \cdot 3 + 0$

$3 = 2 \cdot 1 + 1$

$1 = 2 \cdot 0 + 1$

Therefore, 100(decimal) = 1100100(binary)

$$= 1 \cdot 2^6 + 1 \cdot 2^5 + 0 \cdot 2^4 + 0 \cdot 2^3 + 1 \cdot 2^2 + 0 \cdot 2^1 + 0 \cdot 2^0$$

$$= 64 + 32 + 0 + 0 + 4 + 0 + 0 = 100\text{(decimal)}$$

The decimal system is the key to easily learned methods for the arithmetic operations. However, it is so engrained in our minds from training that we perform these arithmetic operations without even being aware of the commutative, associative, and distributive properties upon which the calculation depends. Let's look at a simple multiplication:

$$
\begin{array}{r}
45 \\
\times\ 7 \\
\hline
315
\end{array}
$$

If you think carefully about the process by which you perform this simple calculation, I believe you will see that it includes roughly the following steps which you perform rapidly, barely noticing them as you briefly store interim results in your memory like the 3 that you carry to the 10's place from the multiplication of 7 x 5:

$$7(5 + 4 \cdot 10) = 7 \cdot 5 + 7 \cdot 40$$
$$= (5 + 3 \cdot 10 + 7 \cdot 4 \cdot 10)$$
$$= (5 + 3 \cdot 10 + 28 \cdot 10)$$
$$= (5 + 31 \cdot 10)$$
$$= (5 + 1 \cdot 10 + 3 \cdot 10 \cdot 10)$$
$$= 315$$

Thus in this simple example, we can see the role of the positional decimal system and the role of the commutative, associative, and distributive propertie to provide effective means of multiplication. Similar examples could be presented for the other arithmetic operations. Let us now look at the role of the decimal system in representing fractional numbers.

2.5.2   Rational numbers in the decimal system

Now that we have looked at representing numbers greater than one in the base 10 system, it is easy to extend it to fractional parts of numbers less than 1. We simply take advantage of the negative exponents that are available as part of the rational numbers. We write then for $0 < p/q < 1$:

$$p/q = a_{-1}/10 + a_{-2}/100 + a_{-3}/1000 + \ldots$$

$$= a_{-1} \cdot 10^{-1} + a_{-2} \cdot 10^{-2} + a_{-3} \cdot 10^{-3} + \ldots$$

or in decimal notation,

$$p/q = 0.a_{-1} a_{-2} a_{-3} \ldots$$

From our experience with long division, we are familiar with two types of results: one in which the result can be expressed with a finite number of numerals, and one where the process of long division is unending with a repeating set of numerals. Examples of both types are shown next:

```
   0.750              0.666...           0.2727...
4)3.000            3)2.000            11)3.000
   28                 18                   22
   20                 20                   80
   20                 18                   77
   00                 20...                30
                                           22
                                           80
                                           77
                                           30...
```

These results raise the following questions: when can a rational number be expressed as a decimal with a finite number of numerals (as in the example, 3/4 = 0.750), what is the relationship between rational numbers and decimal numbers with an unending, repeating sequence of numerals, and can all rational numbers be expressed as decimal numbers?

The first question is easily disposed of by noting that if a rational number, p/q, is represented by a decimal with n decimal places then it can be written as a fraction with a denominator of 10^n. In our example above, 3/4 = 0.75 = 75/100. More generally, considering the ratio of p and q with all common factors cancelled, then all of the factors of q must be in the factors making up $10^n = 5^n \cdot 2^n$ for some n. For example:

$$3/250 = 3/(5^3 \cdot 2) = (2^2/2^2) \cdot 3/(5^3 \cdot 2) = 12/(5^3 \cdot 2^3) = 12/1000 = 0.012$$

Whereas $3/255 = 3/(5 \cdot 51) = 0.01176470588235294117647058882$ 35294 . . . , as 51 is not a factor of 10^n. However, note that the digits 1176470588235294 form a repeating sequence of numerals.

In regard to decimal numbers with patterns of repeating numbers, let us look at the example of 3/11 = 0.27272727 . . .

The nature of the decimal representation may be clearer by rewriting it in the form below:

$$S = 3/11 = 0.27(1 + 10^{-2} + 10^{-4} + 10^{-6} + \ldots$$

The infinite sum in the parentheses is known as a geometric series in which each successive term is multiplied by 10^{-2}. If we look at just the first n terms in the finite sum, S_n, then:

$$S_n = 0.27((10^{-2})^0 + (10^{-2})^1 + (10^{-2})^2 + (10^{-2})^3 + \ldots + (10^{-2})^{n-1}),$$

Now since this is a finite sum, we can use our usual operations for rational numbers:

$$10^{-2} \cdot S_n = 0.27(10^{-2} + 10^{-4} + 10^{-6} + 10^{-8} + \ldots + 10^{-2n}), \quad \text{therefore,}$$

$$S_n - (10^{-2} \cdot S_n) = S_n(1 - 10^{-2}) = 0.27(1 - 10^{-2n}) \quad \text{or}$$

$$S_n = 0.27(1 - 10^{-2n})/(1 - 10^{-2}) = \frac{0.27}{0.99}(1 - 10^{-2n})$$

If we take more and more terms in the sums S_n, that is for greater and greater n, then 10^{-2n}, gets smaller. In fact for any small positive number that we think of, we can always find an n that makes 10^{-2n} even smaller. As we will discuss in Chapter 6, we can say that the limit of 10^{-2n} as n increases beyond any given number is 0 or symbolically, $\lim_{n \to \infty} 10^{-2n} = 0$. Taking this into account, we have.

$$S = \lim_{n \to \infty} S_n = 0.27/0.99 = 3/11$$

We have shown that our non-terminating, repeating decimal is consistent with a rational number in the limit. Using the same approach as above, we can derive a general expression for the geometric series with $-1 < x < 1$, and any constant c:

$$S = c + cx + c\,x^2 + c\,x^3 + c\,x^4 + \ldots$$

$$S = c\,(1 + x + x^2 + x^3 + x^4 + \ldots$$

$$S_n = c\,(1 + x + x^2 + x^3 + \ldots + x^{n-1})$$

$$x \cdot S_n = c(x + x^2 + x^3 + x^4 + \ldots + x^n)$$

$$S_n - (x \cdot S_n) = S_n(1 - x) = c\,(1 - x^n)$$

$$S_n = c\,(1 - x^n)/(1 - x),$$

Because for $-1 < x < 1$, $\lim_{n \to \infty} x^n = 0$.

$$S = \lim_{n \to \infty} S_n = c/1 - x$$

Now that we have shown how to deal with an infinite repeating decimal properly, let us take a simple visual and intuitive approach, closely related to our formal approach, for another infinite repeating decimal.

$S = 0.2510101010\ldots$

$10{,}000S = 2510.10101\ldots$

$100 \cdot S = 25.101010\ldots$

$10{,}000 \cdot S - 100 \cdot S = 2485$

$9{,}900 \cdot S = 2{,}485$

$S = 2{,}485/9{,}900 = 497/1980$ which is a rational number.

Our final question from the beginning of this section is whether all rational numbers can be represented by decimal numbers. In answering this question, we shall again use the algorithm for long division. Let us first go back to the simple example of 3/11. When we do long division our first step for a number less than 1 is to determine the number of tenths, followed by hundredths, thousandths . . .

```
      0.2727...
  11)3.000
     22
     80
     77
      30
      22
       80
       77
       30...
```

The tenths are found explicitly as below by finding how many times 11 goes into 30 or $(10 \cdot 3)$. The division algorithm shows that there are 2 tenths with a remainder of 8:

$10 \cdot 3 = 2 \cdot 11 + 8.$

We now find how many hundredths there are in the remainder;

$10 \cdot 8 = 7 \cdot 11 + 3$, so there are 7 hundredths. Continuing we have,

$10 \cdot 3 = 2 \cdot 11 + 8$, and there are 2 thousandths,

$10 \cdot 8 = 7 \cdot 11 + 3$, and 7 ten thousandths, and so forth.

Hence, $3/11 = 0.2727\ldots$

In general for, $\qquad 0 < p/q < 1$:

$10 \cdot p = a_{-1} \cdot q + r_1$, with $0 \leq r_1 < q$

$10 \cdot r_1 = a_{-2} \cdot q + r_2$, with $0 \leq r_2 < q$

$10 \cdot r_2 = a_{-3} \cdot q + r_3$, with $0 \leq r_3 < q$, continuing as necessary.

Solving for the remainders, r_n and substituting, we would find that:

$p/q = a_{-1} \cdot 10^{-1} + a_{-2} \cdot 10^{-2} + a_{-3} \cdot 10^{-3} + \ldots + a_{-n} \cdot 10^{-n} + \ldots$ Since the remainders, r_n at each step are less than q, there are only q possibilities for the remainders. Eventually one of the remainders must be repeated and then the sequence repeats from that point on as in our example of $3/11$.

We may regard all rational numbers as non-terminating decimal sequences of repeating numerals, if we regard rational numbers such as $1/4$ as equal to $0.25000\ldots$ or $0.24999\ldots$. As the sequence of 9's in the latter form continues without end, it is as close to 0.25 as we wish. In Chapter 6, we will discuss more formally how this infinite sequence can be considered equal to 0.25 as a limit.

We have now shown that all rational numbers may be represented by our decimal system (the non-positive numbers are simply the negative of their positive counterpart). However, as discussed in the previous section, there are numbers such as $2^{1/2}$ which cannot be represented as rational numbers and their decimal representation does not result in a repeating sequence. This is the subject of our next section.

2. 6 The crisis of missing numbers

The problems of numbers that could not be represented as the ratio of two natural numbers, arose as we have mentioned in the history outline from considering the length of the hypotenuse of a right triangle. Consider first a right triangle with sides of length 3 and 4. (See the next figure.)

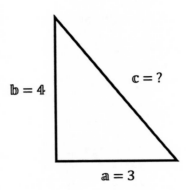

From the Pythagorean Theorem which we will prove in Chapter 4:

$$c^2 = a^2 + b^2$$

Or here, $$= 3^2 + 4^2$$

$$= 25$$

$$c \cdot c = 5 \cdot 5$$

Hence, $$c = 5$$

Notice that $c = -5$ is also a solution since $(-5) \cdot (-5) = 25$, but it does not make sense in the context of a solution which is the length of the hypotenuse of triangle.

We could also try out our guess for rational exponents here:

$$c^2 = 25$$

$$(c^2)^{1/2} = (5^2)^{1/2}$$

and $$c = 5.$$

Everything seems to be fine since 25 is the square of 5; however, except in similar obvious cases, the question arises as to whether for all rational numbers c, $c^{1/2}$ can be represented as a rational number. (Here I remind you again that the traditional symbol for the positive square root of a number, say in this case $25^{1/2}$ is $\sqrt{25} = 5$.)

The Pythagoreans famously encountered this problem in the right triangle with sides equal to 1. In this case, $c^2 = 2$. With our new tool for representing numbers, decimals, let us see what happens when we try and represent c as a decimal number.

To do this let us set up a table where we approximate c by finding a sequence of numbers, starting first with the greatest integer such that $c_0^2 < 2$. We hope to increase accuracy by continuing the approximation by increasing the number of decimal places in steps, for example c_1 is the largest approximation with one decimal place.[xxxiv] We can bracket the accuracy of c, by at the same time finding the smallest numbers, d_m having the same number of decimal places as c_n with $d_m^2 > 2$. Perhaps a pattern of repetition will occur as with the rational numbers.

m	c_m	$c_m^2 < 2$	d_m	$d_m^2 > 2$
0	1	1	2	4
1	1.4	1.96	1.5	2.25
2	1.41	1.9881	1.42	2.0164
3	1.414	1.999396	1.415	2.00225
4	1.4142	1.99996164	1.4143	2.00024449

Very quickly, our approximation procedure becomes quite accurate. Two important features of the table that will become important when we define irrational numbers are that each of the approximations is a rational number and that the c_m's form a sequence of numbers increasing in magnitude although still in each case with $c_m^2 < 2$. We might hope that if we continue the process that we will find a rational number whose square is exactly two. Unfortunately, you could work at this forever and never find that number. We know this because the Pythagoreans proved that such a number does not exist as a rational number. The proof by contradiction cited by Aristotle is surprisingly simple.[xxxv]

---

xxxiv Simon Stevin (1548-1620), who spread the use of decimal fractions, anticipated our understanding of irrational numbers by approximating them with increasing accuracy using rational numbers; Kline, 114; Merzbach and Boyer, pp. 282-285.

xxxv The proof of the irrationality of $\sqrt{2}$ has been cited in the past as Proposition 117 of Book X in Euclid's Elements (see Ball, p. 60); however, it

Let us assume that $2^{1/2}$ is rational. Then $2^{1/2}$ must be equal to the ratio of two natural numbers with $p/q = 2^{1/2}$. We can assume that p and q have no factors in common since if they did the common factors would cancel.

If $p/q = 2^{1/2}$, then

$$(p/q)^2 = (2^{1/2})^2$$

$$p^2/q^2 = 2$$

$p^2 = 2 \cdot q^2$, therefore, p^2 being a multiple of 2, it must be an even number.

If p^2 is an even number, then p must also be an even number.

Let $p = 2 \cdot m$, for some natural number, m within $\mathbb{R}$, then

$$p^2 = (2 \cdot m)^2 = 2 \cdot q^2$$

$$4 \cdot m^2 = 2 \cdot q^2$$

or

$q^2 = 2 \cdot m^2$ which means as in the case of p that q is an even number.

This contradicts the assumption that p and q have no factors in common; hence, $2^{1/2}$ cannot be equal to the ratio of two natural numbers, that is, $2^{1/2}$ cannot be a rational number. Numbers that cannot be represented as the ratio of two integers are called irrational numbers.

Similar arguments for the square root of any prime number can be developed by again assuming that the square root of the prime number is a rational number. In these cases a contradiction will result due to the unique prime factorization of composites. Since there are an infinite number of primes, there must be an infinite number of irrational numbers. That is a lot of "missing" numbers.

Irrational numbers such as $\sqrt{2}$ are part of a class of numbers called algebraic numbers since they are solutions to algebraic equations such as $x^2 = 2$. However, there are other irrational

---

is now thought to be a later addition although undoubtedly discovered much earlier by the Pythagoreans, Heath, Vol. 3, Book X, p. 2, [Math References 17].

numbers which do not arise in this way. Perhaps, the most famous of these numbers is designated as the Greek letter π. This irrational number which equals the ratio of the circumference of a circle to its diameter is one of the irrational numbers which does not occur as the solution to an algebraic equation. Such irrational numbers are known as transcendental numbers. What is most remarkable is that that once we define what "more" means, we will find that there are more irrational numbers than rational numbers and of the irrational numbers more transcendental numbers than algebraic irrational numbers. Thus, if with think of the line as representing the rational numbers, there are more holes in the line than numbers. (Surprisingly, as we shall see, there are as many rational numbers as algebraic irrational numbers.)

We will find in the next chapter that just as the integers and natural numbers are embedded within the rational numbers, the real numbers will be defined to contain all of our previously encountered numbers and include the irrational numbers. Therefore, the complete sets of numbers that make up the natural numbers, integers, rational numbers, and irrational number all contain an infinite number of members. Before we can define the real numbers, we will have to understand how to compare the "infinities" represented by the various classes of numbers. The difference between the rational numbers and the real numbers will allow us to identify any position on the real number line with a number. It will have no holes such as $2^{1/2}$. That every point on a line can be associated with a real number should not be too surprising when we consider that the Pythagoreans hypotenuse with length of $2^{1/2}$ is a real side of a real triangle. What we will need to do is to define the property that will allow the real numbers to represent that line in contrast to the rational numbers.

Chapter 3

COUNTING TO INFINITY

". . . all numbers are infinitely many; all their roots infinitely many; all squares infinitely many; that the multitude of squares is not less than that of all numbers, nor is the latter greater than the former. And in final conclusion, the attributes of equal, greater, and less have no place in the infinite, but only in bounded quantities."—Galileo Galilei[xxxvi]

"I see it, but I don't believe it."—Georg Cantor[xxxvii]

3.1. Comparing infinities

We proved in the previous chapter that no rational number could satisfy the equation, $x^2 = 2$. However, we found that we could get very close to the desired result through a sequence of approximations of rational numbers that got ever closer to the desired solution with each new approximation greater than the previous one. As we shall see, an unlimited number of approximations whose square is less than two could be calculated, each having the same characteristic of getting closer than the previous approximation.

This suggests that if we can imagine an infinite number of such approximations that we could indeed define a number that meets our requirements. In order to follow such an approach, we must have some understanding of what we mean by infinity.

We have already encountered infinity in our various collections of numbers, or to use the terminology of mathematics, sets of numbers. Starting with the natural numbers, we know that no matter how great the number that we choose, say n, there is always a number that is

---

xxxvi Galileo showed an early appreciation for the difficulties inherent in the concept of infinity in his *Two New Sciences*, but could not resolve the apparent paradoxes of there being as many squares as natural numbers. [Other Citation Sources 9], p.41.

xxxvii Cantor wrote this in a letter to Richard Dedekind describing his work on infinite sets in which he mentioned his astonishingly non-intuitive discovery of a one-to one correspondence between the points of a line and the points of a plane; cited in Kline, p. 201.

greater. The most obvious of these numbers is the successor to n required under Peano's Postulates which we designated as n^+. Since the natural numbers are embedded within the integers, and the integers within the rational numbers, each of these is also an infinite set.

While reflecting on these infinite sets, it is natural to ask if there are fewer even or odd numbers than the entire set of natural numbers. Or since every natural number has an additive inverse within the integers forming the negative numbers, do the integers form a larger set than the natural numbers? Or again, how does the set of all rational numbers compare with either the natural numbers or the integers?

Cantor approached this problem by applying the principle that two sets are the same size, termed equivalent, if a one-to-one correspondence can be established between the members of the two collections. A one-to-one correspondence for two sets of objects $\mathcal{A}$ and $\mathcal{B}$ is established if each object in $\mathcal{A}$ is paired with a single object in $\mathcal{B}$ and conversely.[104] Cantor identified the size of the set of objects with what he termed its cardinal number. For finite collections, these are our familiar numbers. The cardinal number for your eyes is two. Cantor's genius was to extend this concept to infinite sets. In doing so, he extended the idea of infinity from merely a potential that was never attained as widely accepted since the time of Aristotle[105] to the concept of a set which contains the entire infinite collection of numbers. As revealed in the quote of Poincaré at the beginning of Chapter 9, this was unquestionably controversial. However, with time it has become one of key approaches to mathematical analysis. We will now take a first look at the implications of Cantor's concept of infinite sets. We will return to this in Chapter 9 when a fuller description of sets has been given.

With a little imagination, the natural numbers $\mathbb{N}$ can be easily matched up with the positive even integers $\mathbb{E}$, positive odd integers $\mathbb{O}$, the negative numbers $\mathbb{N}_-$, and integers, $\mathbb{I}$, as shown below:

$\mathbb{N}$	1	2	3	4	5	....
$\mathbb{E}$	2	4	6	8	10	....
$\mathbb{O}$	1	3	5	7	9	....
$\mathbb{N}_-$	−1	−2	−3	−4	−5	....
$\mathbb{I}$	0	1	−1	2	−2	....

A more explicit method of showing the one-to-one correspondence is by defining a relationship between the sets. We can do this through an expression in which substitution of the natural numbers, n = 1, 2, 3, . . . , will generate the other sets of numbers. Such an expression is known as a function. The following functions will generate the desired sets:

For n = 1, 2, 3, 4, . . .

$\mathbb{E}(n) = 2 \cdot n$

$\mathbb{O}(n) = 2 \cdot n - 1$

$\mathbb{N}_-(n) = -n$

$$\mathbb{I}(n) = \begin{cases} n/2 \text{ for } n = 2, 4, 6 \ldots \\ (1-n)/2 \text{ for } n = 1, 3, 5 \ldots \end{cases}$$

We can see by either approach that there is the "same" number of natural numbers as even numbers, odd numbers, or integers or more briefly, the sets are termed equivalent. A defining characteristic of infinite sets is that it is possible to select only portions (subsets) of the set to form a new set which is still infinite—our even and odd sets as subsets of the natural numbers are examples. When an infinite set such as those above can be put into a one-to-one correspondence with the natural numbers, it is said to be countably infinite or denumerable. A set that is finite or countably infinite is sometimes termed countable.

Since the integers are embedded within the rational numbers, it is natural to compare the rational numbers with the integers and natural numbers. One major difference is that the rational numbers have a property known as denseness. A set of numbers is characterized as dense if between any two numbers there is another number in the set. In the case of the natural numbers and integers, no such number exists between numbers such as 5 and 6. Another way of saying this is that unlike the natural numbers or integers, any particular rational number does not have a specific successor. An obvious example illustrating denseness for rational numbers, say x and y, is the number $(x + y)/2$. We could continue and find a number between x and $(x + y)/2$ and so forth. Thus, there is an infinite number of rational numbers between any two rational numbers.[xxxviii]

---

xxxviii The property of denseness is an extension within the rational numbers of what is known as the Archimedean Property for the natural numbers: if $m < n$, there is a natural number k such that $k \cdot m > n$. This is intuitively evident from the unbounded nature of the natural numbers. Within the rational numbers this may be interpreted by noting that for any rational

The property of denseness that characterizes the rational numbers would seem to imply that there are more rational numbers than the natural numbers. To test this thought, however, we need to have a way to tabulate the set of rational numbers similar to the tables above for the natural numbers and integers. Then we can see if it is possible to have a one-to-one correspondence with the natural numbers. Recall that we generated the rational numbers from pairs of integers, [M/N]. This suggests that a systematic scheme to list all possible pairs of integers would do the job. Such a scheme was developed by Cantor to meet this need for the positive rational numbers.

The scheme in the next figure goes through all the combinations of pairs of positive integers; hence all positive rational numbers are represented. A systematic way to match the natural numbers with the rational numbers is indicated by the directed lines.

$$\rightarrow$$

$$
\begin{array}{lllll}
1/1 & 2/1 & 3/1 & 4/1 & 5/1 \ldots \\
1/2 & 2/2 & 3/2 & 4/2 & 5/2 \ldots \\
1/3 & 2/3 & 3/3 & 4/3 & 5/3 \ldots \\
1/4 & 2/4 & 3/4 & 4/4 & 5/4 \ldots \\
1/5 & 2/5 & 3/5 & 4/5 & 5/5 \ldots \\
\end{array}
$$

Counting the rational numbers in the order indicated and leaving out repeated numbers establishes the one-to-one correspondence of natural numbers with the positive rational number as shown in the table below:

$\mathbb{N}$	1	2	3	4	5	6	7	8	...
$\mathbb{R}_p$	1/1	1/2	2/1	3/1	1/3	1/4	2/3	3/2	...

number $\varepsilon < 1$, there is a number m such that $m \cdot \varepsilon > 1$ or $1/m < \varepsilon$. When we define what we mean by the limit process in Chapter 5, we will see that this means that $1/m$ approaches 0 for increasing m. Thus, there is no smallest rational number greater than 0, an example of the denseness property.

The same kind of pairing could also be generated between the natural numbers and just the negative integers. To provide a pairing of the natural numbers and all of the positive and negative rational numbers, each pairing of a positive rational number can be followed by a pairing with its additive inverse. The only missing rational number then is zero. If we think of the natural numbers as being the room numbers of a hotel with a countably infinite number of rooms then in this hotel (known as the Hilbert Hotel for David Hilbert's use of this imagery[xxxix]— see also Section 3.5), we can always make room for another guest such as Mr. Zero by asking each guest to move up one room, as there are plenty of rooms. Thus, the rational numbers can be put into a one-to-one correspondence with the natural numbers as in the table below:

$\mathbb{N}$	1	2	3	4	5	6	7	8	9	10	11	12
$\mathbb{R}$	0/1	1/1	−1/1	1/2	−1/2	2/1	−2/1	3/1	−3/1	1/3	−1/3	...

Thus, Cantor proved that like the integers, the rational numbers are countably infinite.

The discovery that the natural numbers, integers, and rational numbers form infinite sets of the same size is surprising, but does not seem to have gotten us closer to defining a new property that would allow us to include $\sqrt{2}$ into an extended number system. One clue is the difference between the decimal representation of rational numbers and our attempts at a decimal representation of $\sqrt{2}$. In the case of the rational numbers, the representation required an infinite sequence of digits, but we showed that after an initial sequence, the digits would always form a repeating pattern. Given that we proved that $\sqrt{2}$ is not a rational number, it is clear that if it can be represented as a decimal, it must also require an infinite sequence (otherwise, it would be a rational number) and the sequence cannot form a repetitive pattern. With these two observations, and the experimental observation that our approximations with rational numbers get closer and closer to satisfying $x^2 = 2$, we shall identify in the next section, a single property that will allow us to fill in all the holes in the number

---

xxxix David Hilbert's imagery of the hotel with a countably infinite number of rooms is described in the physicist George Gamow's book on modern science, *One, Two, Three, Infinity*, pp. 17-18, [Math Reference 9]; see also Amir D. Aczel's history of infinity, *The Mystery of Aleph*, pp. 55-56, [Math References 1].

line while keeping all the useful properties we developed for the rational numbers.

3.2   Filling in the missing numbers; the field of the real

Our goal of building number systems and their algebraic rules began on the firm foundation of the natural numbers and counting. We have gone far, but we are stuck at the same impasse as the Pythagoreans. We, like they, want to know, how can the length of the hypotenuse of a right triangle with unit sides be represented with numbers and what rules apply to such numbers.

It is useful to go back to geometry and its picture of the right triangle that started the crisis with the Pythagoreans. In the next figure, I have shown a right triangle with unit sides placed on the familiar x-y coordinate system. The horizontal leg of the triangle on the x-axis is of unit length and therefore has coordinates (1, 0). The vertical length is also unit length; hence the upper vertex of the triangle has coordinates (1, 1). If we drew a circle using a compass with its center at the origin of the coordinate system (the left vertex of the triangle) and radius equal to the hypotenuse of the right triangle, the circle would intersect the x-axis at a point whose distance from the origin according to Pythagoras' Theorem was the length of the hypotenuse, $2^{1/2}$. However, as we have seen, $2^{1/2}$ is not a rational number. This point does not appear to be special and certainly deserves its own number.

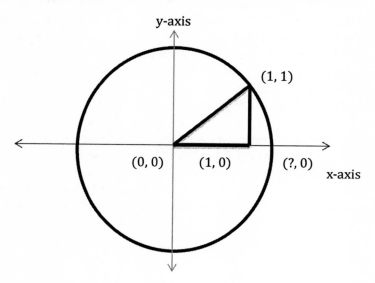

If we think about our drawing carefully, we realize it is an approximation to an ideal geometric description. Any drawing will require lines of some thickness. With a straightedge, compass, and pencil (the classical instruments of the Greeks included a stylus to mark some kind of tablet, but feel free to use paper and pencil in your thoughts), our precision is limited by the thickness of the pencil point. We can imagine that as the point becomes finer and finer, the length of the triangle sides and the hypotenuse becomes more precise, similar to our improved approximations to $\sqrt{2}$ in the table of Section 2.6. Ultimately it would seem, the ideal result would only occur with a pencil point of zero thickness. This reminds us of Euclid's definition of a point as that which has no parts. Another way of thinking about $\sqrt{2}$ in connection to the drawing above is that as we move in the positive direction from the origin (0, 0) on the x-axis passing by all the points that are positive integers and rational numbers, we will pass ever closer to $\sqrt{2}$ eventually passing on and beyond it. We wish to associate every point of the x-axis with a number. Defining the meaning of irrational numbers such as the $\sqrt{2}$ to fill in the number line is not a physical requirement given the limits of precision of drawing with a pencil, but a necessity for filling in a hole in the logical structure of the real numbers.

There are different equivalent approaches to defining the real numbers. I have selected the approach due to Dedekind which seems to me to connect most insightfully with our sense of the number line while providing a detailed account of how the real numbers are constructed. Dedekind resolved the problem of defining the real numbers by using cuts in the set of all rational numbers. We can visualize this as a cut in the number line. He defined a cut in the rational numbers as separating all rational numbers into a set, L, or a set R with each member of L less than every member of R. If the cut point happens to be a rational number, say $\mathbb{c}$, and is a member of L then it is the greatest member of L. In mathematical terminology, we say that the set of rational numbers in L is bounded by $\mathbb{c}$, and it is the least upper bound of L (also known as the supremum of L). Note that all members of R are greater than $\mathbb{c}$ so any member of R could be considered to be a bound of L. Another consideration for R is that there is no smallest member in R. The greatest lower bound (infinum) is c. For every member x of R, there is a number w such that $c < w < x$, for example, $w = (c + x)/2$.[xl]

Suppose now that the cut c in the rational numbers is defined by the condition, $c^2 \leqq 2$. We know that this is not a rational number. Moreover, looking at the rational numbers in the set defined by the cut, there is no greatest rational number p, for which $p^2 \leqq 2$ in L (or smallest p in R with $p^2 > 2$). For any number p, no matter how close p^2 is to 2, we can always find a rational number q, with q^2 being closer to 2.[xli] L has no least upper bound in the rational numbers as similarly R does not have a greatest lower bound. For those cuts, for which c is not in L or R, c is called an irrational number and is defined as the least upper bound of L. Dedekind cuts corresponding to rational and irrational numbers are shown schematically below. I have used parentheses to indicate where the cut does not include a point and a bracket where the set includes a point.

$$\longleftarrow \quad\underline{\qquad\qquad c](\qquad}\longrightarrow \longleftarrow\quad\underline{\qquad)c(\qquad}\longrightarrow$$

L R	L R
Rational Cut	Irrational Cut

From this discussion, we see that in order to form the real numbers, the new property that is needed is that for any set of numbers there is a least upper bound. We define the real numbers as the set of all the rational and irrational numbers. We can define all of the operations of addition and multiplication in terms of the cuts. Because they are made up of sets of rational numbers, they will have the properties of the rational numbers.

We will now follow the Dedekind's approach[106] and formally define the real number system and its operations. The theorems establishing the properties of the real numbers will be stated without proof; however, they should be clear from our discussion of cuts.

Definition $\mathcal{R}$1: A Dedekind cut in the rational numbers (A | B) is one in which all rational numbers are either in the set A or B, each

---

xl Dedekind cuts can also be defined with cuts in the set of rational numbers in which the set R may include the rational number c, and L consists of those rational numbers less than c. In this case, L has no greatest member and R has a smallest member; Merzbach and Boyer, p. 537. For simplicity, the discussion here of Dedekind cuts assumes that a rational number defined by the cut is always in L.

xli For the case of $\sqrt{2}$, for any rational number r with $r^2 < 2$, there is another rational number $r + 1/m$, so that $(r + 1/m)^2 < 2$, for m large enough.

containing at least one member and for which every member of A is less than every member of B.

Definition $\mathcal{R}$2: A rational number is a Dedekind cut (A | B) in which the largest member is in A (see footnote xl).

Definition $\mathcal{R}$3: An irrational number is a Dedekind cut (A | B) in which A has no largest member and B has no smallest member.

Examples:
1. The cut of rational numbers corresponding to 1 is: (A | B) with x a member of A if $x \leqq 1$. Note for this cut, B is the set with $x > 1$.
2. The cut of rational numbers corresponding to the irrational number $\sqrt{7}$ is: (A | B) with x a member of A if either $x < 0$, or $0 \leqq x^2 \leqq 7$. Note for this cut, B is the set with $x^2 > 7$.

Definition $\mathcal{R}$4: The set of numbers in $\mathcal{R}$ includes all rational and irrational Dedekind cuts.

Definition $\mathcal{R}$5: For Dedekind cuts of $\mathcal{R}$, (A | B) = (C | D) if and only if set A contains the same members as set C.

Theorem $\mathcal{R}$1: Equality under Definition $\mathcal{R}$5 is an equivalence relation.

Definition $\mathcal{R}$6: For two cuts (A | B) and (C | D) in $\mathcal{R}$, for x a member of A and y a member of C, (A | B) + (C | D) = (E | F) with (E | F) being the cut with every x + y a member of E. This defines the operation of addition.

Theorem $\mathcal{R}$2: Addition in $\mathcal{R}$ is commutative and associative (as the cuts are defined in terms of rational numbers).

Definition $\mathcal{R}$7: For (A | B) in $\mathcal{R}$, (A | B) is called positive if A contains positive rational numbers and (A | B) is called negative if B contains negative rational numbers.

Theorem $\mathcal{R}$3: For (A | B) and (N | P), members of $\mathcal{R}$ with P the set of all positive rational numbers and N, the set of remaining rational numbers, there exists a unique cut $(A^- | B^-)$ so that (A | B) + $(A^- | B^-)$ = (N | P). The cut (N | P) is the identity element for addition in $\mathcal{R}$ and $(A^- | B^-)$ is the additive inverse of the cut (A | B).

Theorem $\mathcal{R}$4: If (A | B) is positive, then $(A^- | B^-)$ is negative: if $(A^- | B^-)$ is positive then (A | B) is negative.

Definition $\mathcal{R}$8: For two cuts in $\mathcal{R}$, for $x > 0$, a member of A and $y > 0$, a member of C, (A | B) $\cdot$ (C | D) = (E | F) with (E | F) being the cut with every $x \cdot y$ a member of E. This defines the operation of multiplication.

We want the rational numbers and their properties to be embedded within the real numbers. We have shown in the integers, from which we developed the rational numbers, that the products of two positive integers and two negative integers are both positive. Also the product of a positive integer and a negative integer is negative. Therefore to maintain this property within the real numbers, we make the following definition for multiplication of cuts in $\mathcal{R}$.

Definition $\mathcal{R}$9: The product of two positive cuts in $\mathcal{R}$ and the product of two negative cuts in $\mathcal{R}$ are positive and the product of a negative cut and positive cut in $\mathcal{R}$ is negative.

Theorem $\mathcal{R}$5: Multiplication in $\mathcal{R}$ is commutative and associative (as the cuts are defined in terms of rational numbers).

Without proof, I note that $\mathcal{R}$ has the properties of an ordered field just like the rational numbers and satisfies analogous canonical postulates. The identification of the real numbers through the Dedekind cuts is called the Dedekind Postulate of Continuity. Considering that every real number can be defined by a Dedekind cut in a set with a least upper bound, it should seem reasonable that alternatively, the real numbers can also be generated by adding the Least Upper Bound Property (Postulate of Continuity) to the Canonical Properties that we associated with the rational numbers.[107]

Dedekind Postulate of Continuity: The Dedekind cuts in the rational numbers form the real numbers, $\mathcal{R}$, with the rational cuts isomorphic with the rational numbers $\mathbb{R}$. The remaining cuts form the irrational real numbers.

Postulate of Continuity: Every nonempty subset of $\mathcal{R}$ with an upper bound has a least upper bound.

The least upper bound property that follows from the Dedekind cuts fills the holes left in the number line by the rational numbers. We can now say that the real numbers are complete forming a complete ordered field in contrast to the rational numbers which only form an ordered field. In the context of geometry, the real numbers can be associated with the length of line segments, and the Dedekind Theorem of Continuity can be expressed entirely in geometrical terms (known as the Cantor-Dedekind Postulate) assuring a one-to-one correspondence between the points on a line and the real numbers.[108]

3.3   The infinity of real numbers

3.3.1   Real numbers as infinite decimals

We have defined a Dedekind cut as one in which all rational numbers are less than or equal to the cut point. From this, it followed that irrational numbers are those cuts for which there is no rational number that is a least upper bound of the cut. Because of the denseness of the rational numbers, there are, however, an infinite number of rational numbers approaching, but never reaching the least upper bound. In the case of the real number that is $\sqrt{2}$, we can envision such a set as $\{1, 1.4, 1.41, 1.414, \ldots\}$. Here the infinite set of rational numbers defines the irrational number $\sqrt{2}$. This is an example of non-terminating, non-repeating sequences of decimals that can in some sense approach and equal the irrational numbers of the real numbers. A full treatment of what is meant by "approach" awaits our discussion of the limit concept in Chapters 5 and 6; however at this point we can illustrate qualitatively what is meant by limit with some examples of the decimal sequences. These should also further our understanding of the least upper bound property and its relation to other properties of the real numbers.

Let us look again at the rational number 3/11. We established previously that the rational number 3/11 can be represented as a repeating infinite sequence:

$3/11 = 0.27272727\ldots$

This may be thought of as the sequence: $\{0.27, 0.2727, 0.272727, 0.27272727\ldots\}$ which has a least upper bound of 3/11. The decimal sequence has the additional property that it is an increasing sequence in that each member of the sequence is greater than previous one.

Similarly in our approximation (Section 2.6) for $\sqrt{2}$, we formed the sequence $\{c_n\}$ in which each c_n was the greatest approximation of $\sqrt{2}$ with n digits in the decimal place:

For $n = 0, 1, 2, 3 \ldots$ $\{c_n\} = 1, 1.4, 1.41, 1.414. 1.4142 \ldots c_n \to \sqrt{2}$

Because of the way we have formed the c_n of the sequence, the difference between it and any subsequent approximation is less than 10^{-n}. For example the third term, c_2 differs from all subsequent terms by less than $10^{-2} = 0.01$. Indeed $c_3 - c_2 = 0.004$. Therefore, we can always find a value of n in our sequence for which c_n and all subsequent terms meet any requirements for accuracy for an approximation of $\sqrt{2}$. To paraphrase Augustin Cauchy (Section 1.2.5.1), we can get as close as we want to the limit of the sequence. We will describe this in precise mathematical terms in Chapters 5 and 6. Here symbolically, $c_n \rightarrow \sqrt{2}$, indicates that the sequence approaches in the limit what we have identified as the least upper bound required by the condition that $c_n^2 \leqq 2$.

We can also form sequences that are decreasing in magnitude and have a greatest lower bound with $d_n^2 \geqq 2$. Again referring to our approximation for $\sqrt{2}$, we have:

For n = 0, 1, 2, 3 ... $\{d_n\}$ = 2, 1.5, 1.42, 1.415, 1.4143 ...

Therefore, $d_n \rightarrow \sqrt{2}$ = greatest lower bound of $\{d_n\}$.

Combining the properties of these two sequences, we can form $\sqrt{2}$ as the point within what is known as a nested sequence of intervals. We say the point x is within the closed interval, [a, b] if a ≤ x ≤b. If the intervals are nested then each interval is within the previous interval. First we find $\sqrt{2}$ in the interval $1 < \sqrt{2} < 2$. We can then refine our estimate of $\sqrt{2}$ on the number line by noting that $1.4 < \sqrt{2} < 1.5$. Continuing, we have $1.41 < \sqrt{2} < 1.42$, and so forth, leading to the nested intervals,

$$[1 \,[1.4[1.41 \ldots \sqrt{2} \ldots 1.42]1.5]2].$$

The above examples are illustrations of important properties of the real numbers that follow from the Property of Continuity or the Dedekind Postulate of the Real Numbers. These include:

1. Every increasing sequence of real numbers that is bounded above has a least upper bound
2. Every decreasing sequence of real numbers that is bounded below has a greatest lower bound
3. Every infinite sequence of nested intervals contains only one real number common to all the intervals.

A practical consequence of these properties, as we shall see in Chapter 6, is that every decimal represents a real number. The infinite decimal represents a least upper bound, that is, it is the smallest number that is greater than or equal to the decimal limited to any finite number of its digits. We may think of all decimal as being an infinite sequence of digits including those normally expressed with a finite number of digits by recalling from the previous chapter that rational numbers such as 1/4 may be equally represented by 0.2500 ... or 0.2499 ....

3.3.2   Cantor counts the real numbers

The addition of the least upper bound property to the properties of the rational numbers generates the real numbers and fills in the holes in the number line left by the rational numbers. Recalling the surprising result that there are no more rational numbers than integers or natural numbers, may lead you to wonder about the comparative size of the real numbers and irrational numbers as related to their ability to fill up the number line. Similar to when we compared the rational numbers with the integers, we might try to find a way to tabulate all the real numbers and match them with the natural numbers. This would be a direct comparison. Cantor, however, established a way to make the comparison through an indirect route, proof by contradiction. He assumed that the real number between 0 and 1 could be listed in their decimal representation to establish the one-to-one correspondence with the natural numbers, that is he assumed the real numbers were countably infinite. He then looked to see if this assumption led to a contradiction.[109]

In Cantor's list of all the real numbers between 0 and 1, let the first decimal number be: $0.a_{11} a_{12} a_{13} a_{14} a_{15} \ldots$, where notation such as a_{12} indicates the second digit in the first row in the listing of all the real numbers. We imagine the list looks like that shown in the next figure. For example if the first decimal number in our listing is $0.1754 \ldots$, then $a_{11} = 1$, $a_{12} = 7$, $a_{13} = 5$, and $a_{14} = 4$.

$$0.a_{11}\, a_{12}\, a_{13}\, a_{14}\, a_{15} \quad \cdot \quad \cdot \quad \cdot$$
$$0.a_{21}\, a_{22}\, a_{23}\, a_{24}\, a_{15} \quad \cdot \quad \cdot \quad \cdot$$
$$0.a_{31}\, a_{32}\, a_{33}\, a_{34}\, a_{35} \quad \cdot \quad \cdot \quad \cdot$$
$$0.a_{41}\, a_{42}\, a_{43}\, a_{44}\, a_{45} \quad \cdot \quad \cdot \quad \cdot$$
$$0.a_{51}\, a_{52}\, a_{53}\, a_{54}\, a_{55} \quad \cdot \quad \cdot \quad \cdot$$

Now we suppose that this list of decimals forms a one-to-one correspondence between the rows of the list (each row being a decimal number) and the natural numbers. Cantor asked if a decimal number between 0 and 1 could be formed that is not on the list. Let this new decimal be $0.b_1 b_2 b_3 b_4 b_5 \ldots$ The first digit b_1 is selected to be any number from 1 to 8 that differs from the digit a_{11}; b_2 is selected to differ from a_{22}. We go down the diagonal of our list as shown by the arrow above continuing to select our b_k's to differ from the value of the a_{kk}'s on the diagonal. Our new decimal, $0.b_1 b_2 b_3 b_4 b_5 \ldots$ cannot be on the list since it is not equal to the first decimal starting with a_{11}, or the second because it differs from a_{22}, and so forth. So if we assume that such a list could be formed of all the real numbers between 0 and 1, we see that this leads us to the contradiction that we can construct a decimal that is not on the list. Therefore our assumption that the real numbers are denumerable is false. The real numbers are said to be uncountable or non-denumerable. This uncountability accounts for the real numbers ability to fill in the number line.

We have only talked about the real numbers between 0 and 1, but it is easy to show that there are as many real numbers between 0 and 1 as any other interval of real numbers. The basis for doing this is Cantor's concept that any sets whose members can be put into a one-to-one correspondence with each other are the same size.

Therefore, all that we need to do is to find a relationship between the interval from 0 to 1 and any other interval. For example the function of a straight line, $y = 20x - 10$ forms a one-to-one correspondence between the real numbers y in the interval from -10 and 10 and the real numbers, x, from 0 and 1. (When $x = 1$, $y = 10$ and when $x = 0$, $y = -10$.) As another example, the function $y = 1/(1 + x^2)$ takes all of the values x on the entire real number line and replaces them with values of y between 0 and 1. It can even be shown that the number of real numbers in the interval from 0 to 1 is the same as the number of points in a square with sides of unit length. If we define the location of every point in a plane with respect to perpendicular x- and y-axes, then every point is defined by a coordinate of real numbers (x, y). For simplicity, the square is positioned in the plane so that it sits on the x-axis from 0 to 1, and its left side coincides with the segment of the y-axis from 0 to 1. Then for any point of the square (x, y), the x-coordinate can be written in decimal form as $x = 0.a_1 a_2 a_3 a_4 \ldots$ and the y-coordinate as $y = 0.b_1 b_2 b_3 b_4 \ldots$. We can then form the number between 0 and 1 as $0.a_1 b_1 a_2 b_2 a_3 b_3 a_{34} b_4 \ldots$ In this way every point in the square would correspond to a point between

0 and 1 on the number line. Similarly, the process could be reversed so that every point between 0 and 1 would correspond to the point in the plane (x, y). Indeed this process could be extended to all of two or three-dimensional space or abstract spaces of as many dimensions as you want, $(x_1, x_2, x_3, x_4 \ldots x_n)$.

The real numbers, like the rational numbers, have the property of denseness. Between any two real numbers, whether irrational or rational, there are an infinite number of real numbers. Since the irrational numbers such as $\sqrt{2}$ are represented as non-repeating, infinite decimals, the product of any rational number and an irrational number is also irrational. For example, if a and b are any two real numbers with b > a, then since $0 < \sqrt{2}/2 < 1$, then $(\sqrt{2}/2)(b - a) + a$, is an irrational number in the interval [a, b].

Because of its historical association with the Pythagoreans, we have focused on $\sqrt{2}$, but we could just as well made the discussion with $\sqrt{5}$, $\sqrt[3]{7}$, etc. These irrational numbers are called algebraic numbers because they are solutions to the algebraic equations such as: $x^2 - 5 = 0$ and $x^3 - 7 = 0$. In general a number is called algebraic if it is the solution of the equation:

$a_n x^n + a_{n-1} x^{n-1} + a_{n-2} x^{n-2} + \ldots + a_1 x^1 + a_0 x^0 = 0$, where the a's are integers and n is a positive integer.

In addition to numbers such as $\sqrt{2}$ or $\sqrt[3]{7}$, every rational number is algebraic as they are solutions to the equation, $a_1 x^1 + a_0 = 0$, that is, $x = -a_0/a_1$. One might suppose that the algebraic numbers are the basis of the uncountability of the real numbers, but that surprisingly (at least to me) is not so. Cantor developed a proof that the algebraic numbers are countably infinite.[110] One can see the plausibility of Cantor's conclusion by noting that the highest power of the equation, n, sets the limit for the number of solutions for the equations (as discussed in Section 5.3). Cantor defined the height, h, of an equation as the sum of the highest power n and the absolute value of the a's.[xlii] Starting with h = 1, the finite number of possible solutions could be listed, followed by h = 2, and so forth. Therefore, one could in

---

xlii The absolute value is the positive value of the number, ignoring the sign. For example, the absolute value of −3, indicated symbolically as |−3| is 3; see also Section 5.2.1.

principle systematically establish a list of all algebraic solutions. Thus, even the algebraic numbers are countably infinite.[xliii]

So if the real numbers are uncountable, there must be other numbers, besides the irrational algebraic numbers that are responsible for filling up the number line. These numbers are called transcendental numbers as they transcend algebraic methods. We are already very familiar with one of these numbers, π, the ratio of the circumference of a circle to its diameter. Archimedes, (287-212 BC), determined approximations to the circumference of a circle using a nested interval approach with calculations of the perimeters of regular polygons of increasing numbers of sides. Polygons inscribed in the circle (inside the circle, with vertices on the circle boundary) would give perimeters which were less than the circumference of the circle while those circumscribed (outside the circle, with sides tangent to the circle) would give approximations greater than the circumference of the circle. As the number of sides of the polygon was increased, both approximations would get closer to the circle's true circumference. The ratio of the circle's circumference to its diameter (i.e., π) would thus be bracketed. Calculations by Archimedes with polygons of ninety six sides resulted in the estimate: $6336/2017\ \frac{1}{4} < \pi < 14688/4673\ \frac{1}{2}$ or $3.14090\ldots < \pi < 3.14282\ldots$. Aside from the remarkable calculation, the approach is a precursor of the reasoning that would lead to the concept of limit.[111] It was not until 1882, however, that Ferdinand Lindemann (1852-1939) proved that π is transcendental.[112]

With the number line "mostly" represented by transcendentals, it behooves us to give examples. But proving that a number is transcendental has often been difficult as attested to by the thirty year effort required to prove that $2^{\sqrt{2}}$ known as the Hilbert number, is transcendental or even irrational.[113] A number of other transcendental numbers were put forth and proved to be transcendental by Joseph Liouville.[114] While parts of the proofs are complex, the numbers themselves provide an intuitive sense of the vastness of their numbers. One such number is:

$L = 0.101001000100001\ldots$

---

xliii For $h = 1$, there are no possible solutions; for $h = 2$, $n = 1$, $a_1 = \pm 1$, and $a_0 = 0$ corresponding to $x = 0$ and $-x = 0$; Breuer, J., *Introduction to the Theory of Sets*, pp. 23-26, [Math References 4].

Clearly the number is non-repetitive and nonterminating. L can be expressed as the limit of a sequence of sums with the terms of the sequence $\{L_n\}$ such as:

$$L_5 = 0.1 + 0.001 + 0.000001 + 0.0000000001 + 0.000000000000001$$

In the sequence of sums $\{L_n\}$, the terms L_n are ever increasing, although the last term of L_n becomes ever smaller as n increases. This is just like the sequence leading to $\sqrt{2}$; however, we have not proved that this sequence is bounded. As it happens this number can be shown to be a real number, but it is more simply discussed in terms of the limit concept, which I have now repeatedly promised to elaborate in Chapters 5 and 6. So I ask for your patience. With this example, you are free to imagine your own transcendental numbers.

3.4   The exponents become real

I close our investigation of the real numbers by looking at the impact of the real numbers on exponents. Recall that it was the Pythagorean's problem of finding square roots that led us to the real numbers. We make the following definitions for real numbers as extensions to definitions for the rational numbers:

Definition $\mathcal{R}10$: $x^a \cdot x^b = x^{a+b}$

Definition $\mathcal{R}11$: $x^a \cdot y^a = (x \cdot y)^a$

Definition $\mathcal{R}12$: $(1/x) = x^{-1}$ $(x \neq 0)$

Definition $\mathcal{R}13$: $x^0 = 1$.

As with the rational numbers, 0^0 is not defined.

Now with irrational numbers defined, we can tentatively extend the exponents to all real numbers, of course including the rational numbers:

Definition $\mathcal{R}14$: $(x^{a/b})^b = x^{(a/b)b} = x^a$

If $x^a = y^b$, then $y = x^{a/b}$.

With the real numbers at our disposal, we can solve the problem that so vexed the Pythagoreans: if the sides of a right triangle are of length x and y, what is the length z of the hypotenuse z. By the Pythagorean Theorem: $z^2 = x^2 + y^2$. Therefore,

$$(z^2)^{1/2} = (x^2 + y^2)^{1/2} \text{ and } z = (x^2 + y^2)^{1/2}.$$

We know that whatever the lengths x and y, the real numbers will provide us with a length for z. But there is still one more problem with the exponents that needs to be resolved.

For all positive real numbers, Definition $\mathcal{R}14$ is valid; however as the product of a negative number and a negative real number is positive, $x^{1/q}$ does not exist in the real numbers for $x < 0$ and q an even integer. As perhaps the most commonly cited example, there is no real number equal to $(-1)^{1/2}$ or $x^2 = -1$. To finally define a set of numbers that will allow us to solve all algebraic equations, we will need to introduce a number whose square is negative. This will lead to the complex numbers. But having traveled this far with infinite sets of numbers, let us first explore that marvelous discovery of Cantor which he called transfinite numbers for sets that contained the entire infinite number of its members.

3.5   Beyond counting; an introduction to the transfinite numbers

Cantor's insight that infinite sets could be compared through the process of matching each member of one set with one of the other led to the possibility that there could be sets containing different orders of infinity. Where once all infinite sets had been thought to be the same, Cantor showed that there were more real numbers than rational numbers, even though both sets were infinite. As we saw in the previous section, the difference between the rational numbers and the real numbers ultimately is crucial to the definition of the real numbers and their completeness. Along with showing that the real numbers are larger in size than the rational numbers, he also showed that the natural numbers are the same size as the integers and rational numbers, a counterintuitive idea. Indeed, as we have seen, portions of the integers such as the positive even numbers are also the same size as all of the integers. In the world of the infinite, Euclid's self-evident truth, that the whole is greater than the part, is not true.

The ability to characterize infinite sets as having different sizes involves a sense in which the entire set exists as an entity rather than simply a set ever increasing in size. With this in mind and with the example of the difference in size of the set of rational numbers and real numbers, it seems natural, in retrospect, to assign a property to the sets which indicates these differences. The property Cantor defined to represent the size of the set is its cardinal number. In developing his concept of the cardinal number, Cantor developed the mathematics of sets which is the natural language for describing these concepts. We will return to this in Chapter 9, but for continuity with our development of the real number, I have included some introductory remarks here.

For finite sets, the cardinal number is simply the number of members of the set. The cardinal number of the set {1, 3, 4, 2, 5} is 5 – order does not matter. He assigned the Hebrew letter, $\aleph_o$, (aleph in the Hebrew alphabet) with the subscript, o, as the cardinal number of the natural numbers. This number, being beyond any finite number is called a transfinite number and is the smallest transfinite number.

Now we know a bit already of the "arithmetic" of this transfinite number. For example since there is a one-to-one correspondence between the positive even and odd numbers and all the natural numbers, each set has a cardinal number of $\aleph_o$. However we also know that the even and odd positive numbers together form the natural numbers. Taking the operation + to mean combining the elements of sets without duplication, we have:

$$\aleph_o + \aleph_o = \aleph_o$$

Note the operation of combining the elements of a set into a single set is known in set theory as the union of sets. You also recall that in our hotel in Section 3.1 with a countably infinite number of rooms (therefore $\aleph_o$), we could always add another guest as for example when we added a set containing the number zero to the natural numbers. However it could be a set of any finite number of members, say 10,000. Considering that the union of the two sets can still be put into a one-to-one correspondence with the natural numbers:

$$\aleph_o + 10{,}000 = \aleph_o$$

More generally, we can always form infinite sets from some portion of a set that is infinite. For example, the various combinations of the infinite sets of even integers, odd integers, negative integers, positive rational numbers, and so forth can be formed from the rational numbers. All the various combinations of these sets can put them into a one-to-one correspondence with the natural numbers, so that:

$$\aleph_0 + \aleph_0 = \aleph_0; \quad \aleph_0 + \aleph_0 + \aleph_0 = \aleph_0; \quad \aleph_0 + \aleph_0 + \aleph_0 + \aleph_0 = \aleph_0 \ldots$$
and so: $\aleph_0 \cdot \aleph_0 = \aleph_0$.

An insightful description of the meaning of $\aleph_0 \cdot \aleph_0$, using Hilbert's Hotel, is given by Stillwell[xliv]. Stillwell imagines $\aleph_0$ buses each carrying $\aleph_0$ passengers to a hotel (the Hilbert Hotel) with $\aleph_0$ rooms. The buses are numbered 1, 2, 3, 4, . . . Each bus has passengers 1, 2, 3, 4, . . . Now from bus 1, the first guest is put in room 1, the second guest from bus 1 is put in room 3, the third in room 6. Each time a room is filled with an additional guest from bus 1, one more room is skipped so the hotel occupancy looks like the table below,

1	2		3			4				5					6						7							...

Bus 2 can begin to unload and puts it passengers shown as encircled numbers in the rooms below followed by bus 3 passengers shown in underlined italics:

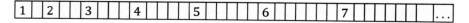

In this way, we show that in the hotel of $\aleph_0$ rooms, we can always find the room for another busload. In other word, the hotel can accommodate $\aleph_0$ buses each with $\aleph_0$ passengers, that is, $\aleph_0 \cdot \aleph_0 = \aleph_0$.

Now in addition to the natural numbers, integers, and rational number and other infinite sets formed from a portion of those sets, we have the real numbers that Cantor has shown to be larger. The cardinal number for the real numbers is often designated as C which stands for the continuum in recognition of the complete nature of the real numbers. Recall that the real numbers in the interval from 0 to 1 can be put into a one-to-one correspondence with any other interval

xliv Stillwell, J., *Roads to Infinity*, pp. 4-6 [Math References 33]. This book brings together for the non-specialist, but non-casual reader of mathematics, details of the complexities of infinite, sets, and logic in the context of developments in twentieth century mathematics.

and even the whole real number line. These considerations and similar arguments as those used for $\aleph_o$ lead to:

$$C + 1 = C; \; C + C = C; \; C + C + C = C, \ldots$$

and

$$C \cdot C = C$$

As the natural number, integers, and rational numbers are embedded within the real numbers:

$$\aleph_o + C = C \text{ and } \aleph_o \cdot C = C$$

It is reasonable to ask if there is a relationship between $\aleph_o$ and C. Also, is C the next transfinite number after $\aleph_o$ or is there a transfinite number, say $\aleph_1$ between them? The first question may be answered informally by considering the numbers between 0 and 1 in their decimal representation. Recall that we found that such a listing was not denumerable. However, we know that for the first digit of the decimals there are 10 possibilities, the second decimal 10 possibilities and so forth to the $\aleph_o{}^{th}$ decimal. So the total number of possible decimals between 0 and 1 is $10^{\aleph_o}$. This means that $10^{\aleph_o} = C$.

We have used the decimal representation of real numbers as decimals in a fundamental way in our mathematical argument which does not seem reasonable since we probably use decimals because we have ten fingers. As noted in Chapter 2, we could also use other bases such as a binary one with only 0 or 1 as digits. Thus using the same arguments as above, we have $2^{\aleph_o} = C$ leading to yet another surprising result in the transfinite world:

$$2^{\aleph_o} = 10^{\aleph_o} = C$$

As to our second question of whether C is the next transfinite number after $\aleph_o$, in 1900, David Hilbert proposed this as the first question in a list of the top twenty three problems for mathematicians.[115] The assumption that there is no transfinite number between $\aleph_o$ and C is known as the Continuum Hypothesis.[xlv]

---

xlv A brief discussion is given in Eves, pp. 228-228 and in much greater detail including the work of Gödel and Cohen in Stillwell, pp. 40-41, 62-65.

The hypothesis turned out to be unprovable. However, Kurt Gödel showed that the hypothesis is consistent with set theory, one of the proposed foundations of mathematics. In 1963, Paul Cohen showed the continuum hypothesis was independent of the postulates of set theory. This situation reminds us of the situation with Euclid's fifth postulate which, as we saw in our history outline, (and will discuss in detail in the next chapter) was discovered to be independent of the other postulates of Euclid and led to a new world of geometries. Thus, the independent status of the Continuum Hypothesis allows different formulations of mathematics.

If the transfinite cardinal numbers were not sufficiently fascinating for you, Cantor introduced another set of transfinite numbers, the ordinals. While the cardinal numbers characterize the size of a set, the order of the members of the set is unimportant. In contrast, the ordinal characterizes the size and order of a set.

If we imagine the following set of numbers in their usual order $\{0, 1, 2, 3, \ldots\}$, one could ask what is the next number after the natural numbers. Cantor designated the ordinal number that is a successor to all denumerable ordinals as ω. So we can visualize the set containing ω as $\{0, 1, 2, 3, 4, \ldots, \omega\}$. Note that the ordinal number for $\{0\}$ is 1, for $\{0, 1\}$ is 2, ... and for $\{0, 1, 2, 3, \ldots\}$ is ω. Beyond ω is $\omega + 1$, $\omega + 2$, ... until we achieve $\omega \cdot 2$. I have specifically chosen to write this as $\omega \cdot 2$ rather than $2 \cdot \omega$ due to number absorbing property of infinite sets. Recall our visit to the hotel of denumerable rooms where we could fit a denumerable number of busloads of denumerable guests. In such a situation we recognize the addition of another guest as $1 + \omega = \omega$. We can fit in one more guest by asking each of our helpful guests to move to the next room. However, the addition of a guest beyond ω results in the successor $\omega + 1$. Hence, $\omega + 1 \neq 1 + \omega$. For example, the ordinal for the set of even natural numbers followed by the odd number, $\{2, 3, 6, \ldots; 1, 3, 5, \ldots\}$ is $\omega + \omega = \omega \cdot 2$.

The ordinal numbers continue:[xlvi]

$\omega \cdot 2 + 1$, $\omega \cdot 2 + 2$, $\omega \cdot 2 + 3$, $\ldots \omega \cdot 3 \ldots \omega \cdot \omega\ (= \omega^2)$, $\omega^2 + 1$, $\ldots \omega^2 + \omega$, $\omega^2 + \omega + 1$, $\ldots$

$\omega^2 \cdot 2$, $\omega^2 \cdot 2 + 1 \ldots \omega^3 \ldots \omega^4 \ldots \omega^\omega \ldots$

The ordinals can continue in this pattern to ever increasing ordinals: $\omega^{\omega^{\omega^{\omega^{\cdot^{\cdot^{\cdot}}}}}}$

---

xlvi As described in more detail by Stillwell, pp. 29-37.

One restriction for the ordinal numbers is that they only apply to what are known as well-ordered sets. A well-ordered set is one with an ordering relation that has a first member. For example if we look at the sets of numbers greater than 3 ordered by magnitude, the smallest natural number and integer is 4; while as we discussed in Chapter 2, there is no smallest real number. If then we look at sets whose members are less than 3, there is no smallest member for either the integers, the rational or the real numbers because of the unending descent of the negative numbers. Sets of real numbers x defined as open intervals such as $0 < x < 1$ do not appear to be capable of being well-ordered. However, this assumes that the ordering principle is the usual one which establishes that c precedes d if $c < d$. In a surprising and contentious proof, Ernst Zermelo showed that consistent with the logic and axioms of set theory, all sets can be arranged to be well-ordered, although a definition for the method of ordering for the real was not shown and remains an open question.

We will return to this point in Chapter 9 when we have developed some of the mathematical language of set theory. Because Cantor developed set theory as the foundation for his transfinite discoveries it is more suited to discussion of this question. We will now finish our travels through the universe of numbers finishing up with the complex numbers.

3.6   When the real meets the imaginary; the complex numbers

We have one more number system after the real numbers to investigate, the complex numbers. These numbers arise from the desire to solve equations such as the quadratic equations that cannot be solved even within the real number system. The simplest example of this is:

$$x^2 = -1.$$

We know going back to the introduction of the negative integers that any positive or negative number squared is positive, so given that the rational and integers are embedded within the real numbers, not even a real number will provide a solution. In this section, a solution to the above equation and indeed to all algebraic equations will be found in the complex numbers.

In the outline of history, I noted that in the sixteenth century, mathematicians such as Cardan were aware that additional solutions to algebraic equations could be found by allowing for numbers whose square was negative. He had found that the square root of negative numbers appeared as preliminary results in the solutions to cubic equations in which the solutions were real.[116] However, in general the use of such solutions was unclear. Terms involving the square root of negative numbers were called imaginary numbers by Descartes.[117] Euler created the now standard notation with $i = \sqrt{-1}$.[118]

Although the simple equation, $x^2 = -1$ certainly illustrates the need for an extension of the real numbers, the solution to the quadratic equation, a staple of your early school mathematics, makes it clear as in Cardan's experience with the solution of cubic equations, that these imaginary numbers are closely bound to solutions with real numbers.

Let us look at the general quadratic equation:

$$ax^2 + bx + c = 0.$$

We wish to solve this equation for x, with the stipulation that a, b, and c are constants that are real numbers. We will use all of our postulates and definitions to put the equation into a form that presents us with a solution. Noting that the variable, x, is raised to the second power suggests that we will have to take a square root, and that this would be most effective if we could form with x a term that was a perfect square. Let us proceed:

First let us simplify the first term by using the multiplicative inverse of a:

$$1/a\ (ax^2 + bx + c) = x^2 + (b/\,a)x + c/a = 1/\,a \cdot 0 = 0$$

Now we move the constant to the right hand side by adding the additive inverse of $c/\,a$:

$$x^2 + (b/\,a)x + c/a + (-c/\,a) = 0 + (-c/\,a)$$

$$x^2 + (b/\,a)x = (-c/\,a)$$

We want the left hand side to be a perfect square, that is, an exact square of some expression. To do this let us take a look at the following example of a perfect square (by the way, this is a good illustration using the distributive, commutative, and associative properties):

$$(y + d)^2 = (y + d) \cdot (y + d) = y \cdot (y + d) + d \cdot (y + d)$$

$$= y^2 + y\,d + d\,y + d^2$$

$$= y^2 + 2y\,d + d^2$$

The example above tells us that in order to form the perfect square $(y + d)^2$, the constant term, d^2, in the sum $y^2 + 2y\,d + d^2$, is the square of half the multiplier of y in the middle term, that is, 2d. In the quadratic equation, we want to turn the left hand side of $x^2 + (b/a)x = (-c/a)$ into a perfect square. Therefore, a constant term equal to $(b/2a)^2$ must be added to both sides of the equation.

$$x^2 + (b/a)x + (b/2a)^2 \qquad = (-c/a) + (b/2a)^2$$

$$(x + b/(2a)) \cdot (x + b/(2a)) \quad = b^2/(4a^2) + (-c/a)$$

$$(x + b/(2a))^2 \qquad\qquad = b^2/(4a^2) + (-c/a)(4a/4a)$$

$$= (b^2 - 4ac)/(4a^2)$$

$$[(x + b/(2a))^2]^{1/2} \qquad\quad = [(b^2 - 4ac)/(4a^2)]^{1/2}$$

Since, for any number, $z \cdot z = (-z) \cdot (-z)$, when we take the square root (the ½ power), $(z^2)^{1/2} = \pm z$.

$$x + b/2a \qquad\qquad = \pm\sqrt{(b^2 - 4ac)/4a^2}$$

$$x + b/2a + (-b/2a) \quad = \pm\sqrt{b^2 - 4ac}\,/2a + (-b/2a)$$

$$x \qquad\qquad\qquad = \frac{-b \pm \sqrt{b^2 - 4ac}}{2a}$$

In this solution it is clear that if $b^2 - 4ac \geqq 0$, x is real. The quantity $D_2 = b^2 - 4ac$ is known as the discriminant for the quadratic equation. If, $D_2 < 0$, then the solution clearly involves imaginary numbers. Using the Euler notation, $i = \sqrt{-1}$, we could write the solution in this case as:

$$x = \frac{-b \pm \sqrt{(-1)(4ac - b^2)}}{2a} = \frac{-b \pm i\sqrt{(4ac - b^2)}}{2a}$$ Thus the solution

is the sum of a real number and an imaginary number, $x = r + i \cdot s$,

where $r = -b/2a$ and $s = \dfrac{\pm\sqrt{(4ac - b^2)}}{2a}$ are real numbers. Such

numbers with real and imaginary parts are known as complex numbers. As an example, let $3x^2 + 2x + 1 = 0$.

Then, $\quad x = \dfrac{-2 \pm \sqrt{(-1)(4 \cdot 3 \cdot 1 - 2^2)}}{2 \cdot 1}$

$x = (-2 \pm \sqrt{-8})/2$

$x = (-2 \pm 2\sqrt{-2})/2 = (-1 \pm \sqrt{-2}) = (-1 \pm \sqrt{2}\ i)$

    With this as motivation, now we want to see how we can once again expand our number system to include a new property while keeping the old properties of the real numbers. In the previous sections when we wanted to expand from the natural numbers to the integers or from the integers to the rational numbers, we looked at the new numbers as pairs of numbers such as [m, n] or [M/ N]. Here we seem to have a natural choice in the ordered pairs of real numbers such as (r, s); however, we found that, all of the numbers, natural, integer, and rational could be interpreted as representing points on a line with the real numbers filling out the entire line. There is no room left on the number line for a new type of number. However, with the introduction of numbers whose square was negative, Wessel, Gauss, and Argand recognized complex numbers could be represented as Cartesian coordinates of real numbers in a plane with the ordinate *(iy axis)*being imaginary (see the following figure).

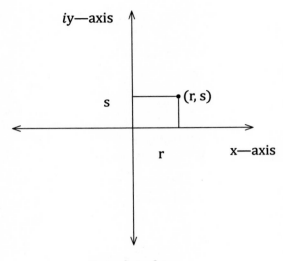

Complex plane

With this representation, the imaginary numbers should seem less mysterious than those numbers that made Cardan so suspicious. The complex numbers can be thought as simply the coordinates of points in what is termed the complex plane.

We will develop the complex numbers from this point of view as it is consistent with our development of the other number systems and as an approach that differs from the traditional introduction of complex numbers in the form, a + b *i*. Once we have interpreted the complex numbers as the ordered pair (a, b), a return to the traditional form a + b*i* will admittedly facilitate calculations.

We begin with definitions for the complex numbers and the operations of addition and subtraction. We are guided in our choices by the desire for the real numbers (and therefore, rational numbers, integers, and natural numbers) to keep all of their properties.

Definition ℂ1: The complex numbers, ℂ, are defined as the ordered pairs of the real numbers, (a, b).

Definition ℂ2: Two integers, (a, b) and (c, d) are equal if and only if a = c and b = d.

Definition ℂ3: The operation of addition between pairs of complex numbers is defined by: (a, b) + (c, d) = [a + c, b + d).

Definition C4: The operation of multiplication between pairs of complex numbers is defined by:$(a, b) \cdot (c, d) = (ac - bd, ad + bc)$.

Of particular importance importance for this definition is the result for $(0, 1) \cdot (0, 1)$.

$$(0, 1) \cdot (0, 1) = (0 \cdot 0 - 1 \cdot 1, 0 \cdot 1 + 1 \cdot 0) = (-1, 0)$$

If we identify $(0, 1)$ with i, and $(-1, 0)$ with -1, then, $i^2 = -1$.

We now check to see if these definitions give us the properties that are desired. It should be clear from Definition C2 that an equivalence relation is formed for the complex numbers.

Theorem C1: (Commutative Property for Addition) For (a, b) and (c, d), complex numbers, with a, b, c, d real numbers, $(a, b) + (c, d) = (c, d) + (a, b)$

$$(a, b) + (c, d) = (a + c, b + d) \qquad \text{Definition C2}$$
$$= (c + a, d + c) \qquad \text{Commutative Property, Theorem } \mathcal{R}2$$
$$= (c, d) + (a, b) \qquad \text{Definition C2}$$
$$\text{Q.E.D.}$$

Theorem C2: (Commutative Property for Multiplication) For (a, b) and (c, d), complex numbers, $(a, b) \cdot (c, d) = (c, d) \cdot (a, b)$.

$$(a, b) \cdot (c, d) = (ac - bd, ad + bc) \qquad \text{Definition C4}$$
$$= (ca - db, da + cb) \qquad \text{Commutative Property, Theorem } \mathcal{R}2$$
$$= (c, d) \cdot (a, b) \qquad \text{Definition C4}$$
$$\text{Q.E.D.}$$

The associative properties for addition and multiplication can be proved following a similar approach.

Theorem C3 (Associative Property for Addition): For (a, b), (c, d), and (e, f), complex numbers, $((a, b) + (c, d)) + (e, f) = (a, b) + ((c, d) + (e, f))$

Theorem C4 (Associative Property for Multiplication): For (a, b), (c, d), and (e, f), complex numbers, $((a, b) \cdot (c, d)) \cdot (e, f) = (a, b) \cdot ((c, d) \cdot (e, f))$

The identity elements and the additive inverse follow from their counterparts in the real numbers.

Theorem ℂ5 (Identity Element for Addition): There exists in ℂ an identity element for addition, (0, 0) such that (a, b) + (0, 0) = (a + 0, b + 0) = (a, b).

Theorem ℂ6 (Identity Element for Multiplication): There exists in ℂ an identity element for multiplication, (1, 0) such that (a, b) · (1, 0) = (a · 1 − b ·0, a · 0 + b · 1) = (a, b).

Theorem ℂ7 (Inverse for Addition): For every complex number, (a, b), there exists an additive inverse, (−a, −b), such that (a, b) + (−a,−b) = (a − a, b − b = (0, 0).

The multiplicative inverse for (a, b) will now be derived by anticipating that the real (and therefore the rational numbers) are expressed in the complex numbers as (a, 0). The desire to maintain the multiplicative inverse for the real numbers suggests the following relationship for complex numbers: if (1, 0)/ (a, 0) = (c, 0), then (a, 0) · (c, 0) = (1, 0). From Definition ℂ4 for multiplication a · c = 1 and c = 1/a, the inverse of a in the real numbers.

With this motivation, we now apply this approach to find the multiplicative inverse in the general case of a complex number (a, b)

If (1, 0)/ (a, b)= (c, d) then (a, b) · (c, d) = (1, 0)

(a, b) · (c, d)= (ac − bd, ad + bc) = (1, 0). Therefore from Definition ℂ2 for equality:

ac − bd = 1 and ad + bc = 0.

Solving for d in the second equation and substituting into the first

d = −bc/a and ac − b(−bc/a) = 1

$c(a + b^2/a) = 1$ or $c = \dfrac{a}{a^2 + b^2}$ and $d = \dfrac{-b}{a^2 + b^2}$ and the multiplicative

inverse of (a, b) is (c, d) = (1, 0)/ (a, b) = $\left(\dfrac{a}{a^2 + b^2}, \dfrac{-b}{a^2 + b^2} \right)$. This result is expressed in the following theorem:

Theorem ℂ8 (Inverse for Multiplication): For every complex number, (a, b) except (0,0), there exists a multiplicative inverse, (1,0)/(a, b) = (a/(a² + b²), −b/ (a² + b²)) such that (a, b) · (a/(a² + b²), −b/(a² + b²)) = (1, 0).

Another approach to the multiplicative inverse is through the use of the complex conjugate. The complex conjugate of (a, b) sometimes denoted as (a, b)* = (a, −b). By multiplying (1, 0)/ (a, b) by (a, −b)/(a, −b) = (1, 0), the inverse is easily obtained.

$$(1,0)/(a, b) = \frac{(a, -b)}{(a, -b)} \cdot \frac{(1,0)}{(a, b)} = \frac{(a, -b)}{(a^2 + b^2, 0)} = \left(\frac{a}{a^2 + b^2}, \frac{-b}{a^2 + b^2} \right)$$

Example:
$$(1, 0)/(2, 3) = \frac{(2, -3)}{(2, -3)} \cdot \frac{(1, 0)}{(2, 3)}$$

$$= \frac{(2, -3)}{(2^2 + 3^2, 0)}$$

$$= \left(\frac{2}{13}, -\frac{3}{13} \right)$$

This result is confirmed below:

$$(2, 3) \cdot (2/13, -3/13) = (2 \cdot 2/13 - (-3 \cdot 3/13), 2 \cdot (-3/13) + 3 \cdot 2/13)$$

$$= (4/13 + 9/13, -6/13 + 6/13)$$

$$= (1, 0)$$

The final property needed for the complex numbers to have the structure of a field is the distributive property.

Theorem ℂ9: (Distributive Property): For complex numbers (a, b), (c, d), (e, f),

(a, b)((c, d) + (e, f)) = (a, b)(c, d) + (a, b)(e, f).

(a, b)((c, d) + (e, f)) = (a, b) · (c + e, d + f)

$$= (a(c + e) - b(d + f), b(c + e) + a(d + f))$$

$$= (ac + ae -bd -bf, bc + be + ad + af)$$

$$= (ac - bd, bc + ad) + (ae - bf, be + af)$$

$$= (a, b)\,(c, d) + (a, b)\,(e, f)$$

Referring to the definitions and theorems above, it is clear that:

Theorem $\mathbb{C}$10: The real numbers, a, in $\mathcal{R}$ are isomorphic with the complex numbers (a, 0) in $\mathbb{C}$. (Numbers such as (0, b) are called pure imaginary numbers.)

At this point, it is worth quoting the mathematician Hamilton on the meaning of complex numbers:

> In the theory of Single Numbers, the symbol $\sqrt{-1}$ is **absurd** (Hamilton's emphasis) and denotes the Impossible Extraction or a merely Imaginary Number; but in the Theory of Couples $\sqrt{-1}$ is **significant** and denotes a Possible Extraction of a Real Couple, namely (as we have just now seen) the principal square root of the couples (-1, 0).[119]

When working within $\mathbb{C}$ then, we can substitute a for the notation (a, 0). As we have already seen, we can identify (0, 1) with $\sqrt{-1} = i$. Thus we see the equivalence of the notation (a, b) with a + bi for the complex numbers.

Reworking our examples from above in this notation, we have:

$$(2, 3) = 2 + 3i$$

$$(1, 0)/\,(2, 3) = \frac{1}{2+3i}$$

$$= \frac{2-3i}{2-3i} \cdot \frac{1}{2+3i}$$

$$= \frac{2-3i}{\left(4+6i-6i-9(i \cdot i)\right)}$$

$$= \frac{2-3i}{13}$$

$$= \left(\frac{2}{13}, -\frac{3}{13}\right)$$

Although the complex numbers have the same first nine properties as the real and rational numbers and form a field, it is not an ordered field as the complex numbers do not have the order property. One way to see this is by applying the Alternate Order Postulate for rational numbers $\mathbb{R}_c$ 10a (Section 2.4.5) which states that if X and Y are members of the positive rational numbers $\mathbb{R}_p$, then $X + Y$ and $X \cdot Y$ are members of $\mathbb{R}_p$. Assume, $i > 0$; then, $i^2 = -1$ which implies $-1 > 0$ to satisfy the order postulate. Disregarding for the moment that actually $-1 < 0$, it would follow that $-1 \cdot i = -i > 0$ which is clearly a contradiction with our initial assumption because if $x > 0$, then $-x < 0$. A similar contradiction occurs if we assume, $i < 0$.

With the extension of the real numbers to the complex numbers, it is now possible to show through the Fundamental Theorem of Algebra that all of the solutions may be found within $\mathbb{C}$ to polynomials with complex coefficients such as:

$$a_n x^n + a_{n-1} x^{n-1} + a_{n-2} x^{n-2} + \ldots + a_2 x^2 + a_1 x + a_0 = 0$$

We will show this in Chapter 5, but now it is time to shift from numbers to geometry, the other foundation of mathematics.

Chapter 4

GEOMETRY SHOWS THE WAY

"There is no royal road to geometry."—attributed to Euclid[120]

". . . the compiler of elements in geometry must give separately the principles of the science, and after that the conclusions from those principles, not giving any account of the principles but only of their consequences. No science proves its own principles; . . . they are treated as self-evident."—Aristotle[121]

"The assumption that the angle sum [of a triangle] is less than 180° leads to a curious geometry, quite different from ours, but thoroughly consistent. . . ."—Karl Friedrich Gauss[122]

4.1   The nature of truth

In the previous two chapters, numerous theorems have been proved, illustrated, or made plausible with some general arguments less rigorous than a proof. So at this point, you may ask in what sense are these theorems true and what do we mean by truth. As an example of a commonly invoked use of the concept of truth, I ask you to recall that the American Declaration of Independence even speaks of self-evident truths. The subject of how we know what is true, known as epistemology goes back as far as ancient Greece and is as current as modern physics.[xlvii] However, without going into these philosophic depths, I will digress a bit and contrast mathematical truth with our more general use of this sometimes contentious word.

---

xlvii An overview of issues from ancient to the present concerning the acquisition of knowledge as related to philosophy, mathematics, and physics forms the themes of Roland Omnès' *Quantum Philosophy, Understanding and Interpreting Contemporary Science* [Other Citation Sources 13]. Of particular interest to topics described here are his discussions on Classical Logic (Chapter I), Classical Mathematics (Chapter III), Formal Mathematics (Chapter V), and the Philosophy of Mathematics (Chapter VI); however, given the close relationship of physics and mathematics described here, the entire book should be one of great interest.

It is reasonable to accept truth as that which has a correspondence within the reality of the universe. Of course there are many different kinds of truth characterizing the realities of the universe. One way to appreciate the different kinds of truth is to consider the means by which a truth is accepted as such. For this purpose, I believe it is useful to categorize the kinds of truth as: personal, social, scientific, mathematical, and that which I call authoritative truth.

Among the widest spread examples of personal truths are those of aesthetics, religious faith, and moral judgments. It is characteristic of such truths that they are arrived at by the individual through complex interactions of experience and introspection. While such truths may be of the utmost importance to the individual, it is characteristic of such truths that they are subjective, that is, the experience of the individual in discovering the truth cannot be transferred to or tested by another individual. For example, religious truths may be arrived at through methods such as contemplation, yoga, prayer, and various behaviors that are thought to enhance the opportunities to have experiences that led others to become believers of the truth. However, the truth as directly experienced by one individual is not open to investigation by others. There are no objective ways to compare the experience of the truth between individuals. The inability to share the experience of such truths is analogous to the inability to know if the color red that I see in my mind is the same as the one you see in yours.[xlviii] Thus, there is no question of proving personal truths since acceptance of truth on this basis excludes shared experiences. This is why personal truths are often described as revealed knowledge, values, or matters of faith. That such truths may not be objectively proved to others, however, does not mean that the truths are invalid only that they are not provable. This distinction will turn out to have a surprising parallel in the realm of mathematical truth.

Scientific truths provide the sharpest contrast with personal truth. Two of the hallmarks of the scientific method are agreed upon

---

xlviii Alfred North Whitehead in *Science and the Modern World* [Other Citation Sources 18, p. 55-56] speaking of John Locke's view of sensations such as color and scent states that, *"But the mind in apprehending also experiences sensations which, properly speaking, are qualities of the mind alone. These sensations are projected by the mind so as to clothe appropriate bodies in external nature. Thus the bodies are perceived as with qualities which in reality do not belong to them, qualities which in fact are purely the offspring of the mind."* Whitehead's collaboration with Russell on the foundations of mathematics will be discussed in Chapter 10.

methodologies for investigating a potential truth and duplication by independent scientists of the investigative experiences, using the agreed upon methodologies. The results of the scientific investigation are reported in objective ways that allow direct comparisons by individuals. The reduction of the phenomena being investigated to measurement, number, and mathematical theory is vital to the objectivity of the scientific method allowing one scientist to confirm the results of another. This is the core of the hundreds of papers that are published yearly in scientific journals. The simplest truths that are reported in scientific papers are the results of experiments with established scientific instruments and under well-defined conditions. These results being confirmed by other scientists are accepted as true and are what we normally call facts. More commonly, facts are those actions which are experienced with our senses or instruments that extend our senses for which in an informal way there is objective acceptance. Even in these cases, however, it is humbling to note the chasm between our naïve appreciation of the physical world and the non-intuitive complex explanation given at the most profound levels of science.

When we speak of fundamental scientific truths, however, we are not usually talking about these types of facts or theoretical implications of accepted theories, but the major theories themselves. Scientific papers may establish theoretical implications of an accepted theory using agreed upon methodologies of mathematics, but these results depend on the truth of the underlying fundamental principles, also known as general laws, The fundamental principles have a universal character from which rules or laws of narrower application may be derived.[123] A fundamental principle, however, can be superseded as when Newton's Law of Gravitation was superseded by Einstein's Theory of General Relativity. Examples of fundamental theories are: Newton's Laws of Motion and Law of Gravitation, Darwin's Theory of Evolution, Maxwell's Equations of Electromagnetism, the Laws of Thermodynamics, Einstein's Special and General Theories of Relativity, and Quantum Mechanics. We ask in what sense can these theories be considered to be proved to be true.

Acceptance of a new scientific theory requires, in addition to the objective presentation of methods and results confirmed by other scientists, that the theory be consistent with previously established facts, explain new facts encountered in developing the theory, and predict new phenomena not previously covered by existing theories. Newton's Laws of Motion and Law of Gravitation are a paradigm for the scientific method in that these theories provided unified explanations for Kepler's Laws of Planetary Motion, observations of motion on the earth by Galileo, and, just as one spectacular example, brought about the discovery of the planet Neptune.[124] If one needed further confirmation of Newton's theories, one need only observe that the navigation of the Apollo spacecraft to the moon was based upon Newton's Laws of Motion. Yet, we have known since Einstein developed his Theories of Special and General Relativity and the triumphant description of the world of the atom by Quantum Mechanics in the first half of the twentieth century that Newton's Laws are not correct. This example sheds light on the meaning and limitations of scientific truth.

The vital point to make in regard to the truth of scientific laws is that they are not proved like the theorems of geometry. Rather they result from generalizations based upon specific facts rather than through a deductive process. The reasoning process from the specific to the general is called inductive reasoning (not to be confused with the method of mathematical induction discussed in Chapter 2). By inductive, here, we mean that the laws are presumed to be correct based on supportive experimental evidence, theoretical consistency and the lack of any significant contradictory evidence. This does not prove that the laws are correct, but as supportive evidence grows, we become increasingly confident in the truth of the laws. It is more accurate to say that the scientific laws are accepted as true rather than that the laws are proved to be true. In the case of Newton's Laws of Motion, scientific discoveries led eventually to the understanding that they did not apply at speeds approaching that of light and at length scales typical of the atom. Thus, despite the overwhelming support of evidence in the most common situations that we encounter, the laws were found to be approximations, which had their range of applicability.

While the fundamental laws of the physical sciences are inductive in nature, the deductive method using the established truths of mathematics plays a major role in development of the implications of the fundamental laws. A good example of the role of mathematics in science is the prediction of the existence of electromagnetic waves from Maxwell's Equations which was then verified experimentally.

To summarize my thoughts on scientific truths, just as in the case of personal truths, we cannot prove them; however unlike personal truths, we can be increasingly confident of their validity and range of applicability through objectively shared experiences of scientists. Even when a scientific law is supplanted by a new one, the new law builds on the old as its conclusions must be consistent with all previous scientific knowledge. If you are asked if you can prove the Law of Conservation of Energy, you should reply that it cannot be proved, but that the basis for its acceptance is available and can be objectively evaluated.[xlix]

I now briefly mention social truths which I feel are intermediate to scientific and personal truths. Social truths to my mind include such areas as those of economics, politics, psychology, historical analysis, and social justice. Attempts are often made to present social truths using the objective methods of science; however, since humans are an integral part of the inquiries, the truths have inherently subjective components. Objective facts may be established (The annual U.S. Federal budget was in surplus in 1999 and 2000.[125]); however, generalization of such facts into laws appears to be virtually impossible. Some social truths have been taken to be self-evident at some time and place, as in "all men are created equal." One might also suggest such statements as, "democracy is the best form of government" or "slavery is wrong" as self-evident truths. Unfortunately, history documents periods in which such statements were not only, not judged to be self-evident truths, but not generally accepted. It is worth recalling that ancient Athens, the community discovering democracy depended upon slavery, as did the man who wrote "all men are created equal." In contrast to scientific truths, it is also quite unclear what the standards are for accepting the validity of a social position.[l] Moreover, unlike scientific truth, history teaches us that social truth does not consistently build upon the past. It is not improbable that many social truths of our time will be viewed with distress in the future. It appears, then that social truth is simply that which is accepted by a social group at some time and place. The

---

xlix In discussing the philosophic views of David Hume (1711-1776) that the validity of the approach of induction cannot be proved, Bertrand Russell notes "that induction is an independent logical principle, incapable of being inferred either from experience or from other logical principles, and without this principle science is impossible;" A History of Western Philosophy, p. 674, [Other Citation Sources 15].

l When speaking of ethical teachings such as those of Jesus, Bertrand Russell noted that "Such ethical innovations obviously imply some standard other than majority opinion, but the standard whatever it is, is not objective fact, as in a scientific question. This problem is a difficult one and I do not profess to be able to solve it;" Russell, p. 118.

contrast between economics with its many contradictory schools and the physical sciences provides a good illustration of the limitations of social truths. Finally, in contrast to the truths of scientific theories, it is characteristic of social theories that acceptance may occur even though they are only suggestive rather than predictive and have unknown ranges of applicability. It should, therefore, go without saying that, like scientific truths, there are no proofs for social truths; however, the empirical support is much, much weaker. With this point I merely comment that given that social and personal truths are arguably the most vital to the decisions of our lives, it would seem prudent to view some of those truths that we do not share with others in a spirit of tolerance and compromise. For those truths that we consider to be "absolute" for our time, we should be highly selective and humble making the broadest use of humanity's long and frequently painful experience.

A major difference between scientific and the mathematical approach to truth is that the scientific approach seeks to describe experimentally verifiable or mathematically inferable truths of the physical universe whereas the truths of mathematics are the relationships that logically follow from abstract systems. The abstract systems are formed from sets of undefined terms, definitions, and basic assumptions, called postulates or axioms. The postulates give meaning to the undefined terms by describing the allowable interactions among the undefined terms. In determining the implications of the abstract system, rules of logic agreed upon by mathematicians are the equivalent of the techniques sanctioned in scientific investigations. This method, called the axiomatic method, was discovered by the Greeks in their development of geometry and was for over two thousand years thought to express absolute truths of the universe rather than simply the logical conclusions of postulates. Just the same, if the postulates are accepted as true then the conclusions are true for a consistent set of postulates. This provides the sense of the possibility of absolute truth in mathematics, setting it apart from other disciplines. However, one must be aware of the severe caveat that the postulates must be consistent, that is, using different portions of a mathematical system we must not come to contradictory conclusions. Theorems established by Gödel in 1931 showed that for mathematical systems such as those encompassing the natural numbers, it is impossible to prove the consistency of such a system within the set of axioms and theorems of the system. Moreover, he also proved that if a system were consistent, there could be mathematical statements expressible in the system for which the truth could not be determined. In other words a mathematical system such as the natural numbers, if consistent, must be incomplete. Thus, Gödel created with his theorems a separation between the concept of truth and that of provability. As in the realm of faith, there may be truths that are undecidable. In the absence of proofs of consistency, the applicability of mathematics would appear then to be similar to that of science in resting on experience showing that no contradictions result. We will explore some of the implications of these limitations in the closing chapter of this book.

While the validity of mathematical conclusions says nothing about their relationship to reality, the use of scientific models based upon mathematical systems has been the greatest source of progress in understanding the universe. From this point-of-view, the assumptions of the mathematical models are like the laws of physics not provable, but their range of applicability may be tested. In additions to scientific modeling, mathematical modeling in quantitative disciplines such as economics is vital as the models may be used to explore the implications of various economic systems; however, the relationship of the conclusions to economic reality depends on the validity of the assumptions.

As a final thought on the nature of truth, I note that overwhelmingly, people (myself included) do not discover their own truths. Rather, most of the truths we accept are passed on to us by our parents, teachers, friends, religious and political leaders, colleagues, the media, experts . . . This is the type of truth that I call authoritative truth. We seek truths from those with demonstrated expertise whom we trust. As we learn with age, sometimes this trust is misplaced. However, we seek the most credible sources for truth— choosing those who should have more knowledge, direct experience, and understanding than we do. For example, that the U.S National Academy of Sciences reports that "strong evidence on climate change underscores need for actions to reduce emissions and begin adapting to impacts,"[126] is good enough for me. The source of any authoritative truth is, however, personal, social, scientific, or mathematical and should be viewed in that light. Ultimately, the acceptance of our most fundamental truths rests upon humanity's ongoing experiences that justify continuing belief in those truths.

I close this section with the sentiment said to have been expressed by Isaac Newton to his nephew, Benjamin Smith. Reflecting on the greatness of Newton, we can only stand in humility before the great mystery that is truth.

*"I do not know what I may appear to the world; but to myself
I seem to have been only like a boy, playing on the sea shore,
and diverting myself, in now and then finding a smoother
pebble or a prettier shell than ordinary, whilst the great ocean
of truth lay all undiscovered before me."*[127]

4.2   Logic, the engine of the axiomatic approach

The axiomatic approach, although first developed historically in establishing the theorems of geometry, has been used first in this book to develop number systems (Chapter 2). I began the use of the axiomatic approach with numbers instead of geometry, on the assumption that your training had made you more familiar and comfortable with numbers and their algebraic manipulation. The development of the properties of the natural numbers from Peano's Postulates (Section 2.1.3) is a perfect example of the axiomatic approach. We have Peano's undefined terms (natural number, successor, and the symbol "1"), five postulates, (the unproven statements that define relationships, hence meaning, to the undefined terms), and definitions. From these elements, all of the theorems of the natural numbers can be developed using the rules of logic as briefly mentioned in Section 2.1.3. In this sense logic is the engine of the axiomatic method.

The rules of logic have a long history, being codified, as mentioned in the history outline, by Aristotle in the fourth century BC. The basics of this logic continued to be used without significant development or question until the nineteenth century. Leibniz imagined a calculus of logic, but it was not realized until symbolic logic was introduced by Augustus De Morgan (1806-1871) and George Boole (1815-1864). Further advancements were made by, among others, Charles Sanders Pierce (1839-1914), Ernst Schöder (1841-1902), and Gottlob Frege (1848-1925). The use of symbolic notation clarified the operations of logic in the same way that symbolic representation in algebra made way for progress in that subject.[128]

In developing the number systems, we made use of a number of logical approaches: the syllogistic proof, proof by contradiction proof by cases, and mathematical induction (mathematical induction was previously discussed in detail in Section 2.1.3 while proof by cases simply exhausts all the possible components of a theorem applying the methods of logic to each). As mathematicians did throughout most of the history, you probably accepted these approaches as reasonable if not obvious. In what follows, I will expand upon my earlier brief discussion in the light of symbolic logic.[li]

The subject of propositional logic deals with statements (also known as propositions) that can be said to be true or false, and the conclusions that may be said to be validly drawn from those statements. The following are hypothetical examples of statements noted as *a*, *b*, and *c* that might be encountered in a hypothetical economics discussion:

a) The Federal Reserve has lowered interest rates.
b) The value of the US currency has fallen with respect to foreign currencies.
c) Exports of US products have increased.

In all of these cases, the statements are either true or false. This is an example of Aristotle's law of the excluded middle.[129] Further Aristotle's law of contradiction states that the statements cannot be both true and false.[130] There are four possible combinations for the state of truthfulness for *a* and *b*. Listings of all of the combinations of logical truth states are called truth tables, and as we shall see are key approaches to establishing the validity of logical arguments. The truth table is shown for *a* and *b* below with T standing for true and F for false.

Truth Table: *a*, *b*

a	*b*
T	T
T	F
F	T
F	F

---

li My purpose here is to give a sense of the significance of symbolic logic for proving theorems of mathematics. However, I will restrict the discussion here to propositional logic which follows from the developments of Boole. An advance known as predicate or first order logic greatly expands the power of logic to allow the evaluation of statements with quantifiers such as "all men are . . ." or "there exists an x such that x has the property that . . ." This is fundamental to mathematical logic, but propositional logic can provide many of the key insights; see, pp. Stillwell, pp. 106-107. Another discussion of propositional logic can be found in Eves, pp. 243-262.

Often statements are joined together by the conjunction "and" (symbolically indicated by $\land$) meaning that the combined statement a and b ($a \land b$) is only true when both a and b are true. Statements are also joined by the logical conjunction "or" (symbolically indicated by $\lor$) meaning that the statement a or b ($a \lor b$) is considered true whenever one of a or b or both a and b are true. Thus, the logical "or" called disjunction, is an inclusive "or", corresponding to the meaning in common usage of "and/or". Another basic of logic operations is negation of a statement. If the statement a is true than not a is false. For example, the negation of the statement, the planets revolve around the sun is: the planets do not revolve around the sun. Negation of statement a is represented symbolically here as $\neg a$. The truth tables for $\neg a$, $a \land b$, and $a \lor b$ are shown below:

Truth Table: a, $\neg a$, $a \land b$, $a \lor b$,

a	$\neg a$	b	$a \land b$	$a \lor b$
T	F	T	T	T
T	F	F	F	T
F	T	T	F	T
F	T	F	F	F

Statements such as a, b, and c in our economic example above are often linked in logical argument by conditional statements also known as implications. For example, a conditional statements linking a with b ($a \Rightarrow b$) and b with c ($b \Rightarrow c$) might be:

$a \Rightarrow b$: If the Federal Reserve lowers interest rates, then the value of the US currency falls with respect to foreign currencies.

$b \Rightarrow c$: If the value of the US currency falls with respect to foreign currencies, then exports of US products increase.

These conditions can then be joined to form one of the most common logical argument forms, syllogistic reasoning; if a, then b, and if b then c, implies if a then c. In our example we conclude: if the Federal Reserve has lowered interest rates, then exports of US have increased. We will show that this is a valid argument; however, the validity of the argument has to do with its form and is independent of its content. Just because the form of an argument is valid does not tell us about the truth of the argument. For example the following syllogism is equally valid, but obviously nonsense:

If $1 + 1 = 3$, then apples are orange.
If apples are orange, then pigs can fly.
Therefore, if $1 + 1 = 3$, then pigs can fly.

An argument is valid if the conclusions follow from the premises. Conclusions are true if we accept the premises of the argument as true and the argument is valid. By using symbolic logic while determining the validity of an argument, we can avoid the distraction of whether the statements are themselves true and remove the ambiguity of verbal presentations. We shall now show the validity of the syllogistic argument.

The determination of the validity of an argument is known as the calculus of propositions. Symbolic logic allows us to easily show that the common form of reasoning from implications is valid. The implication represented symbolically as $a \Rightarrow b$ is expressed verbally as if a, then b or a implies b. Such conditional statements, must also be true or false depending on the truth states of a and b. The mathematical definition of an implication based on the truth states of a and b is shown in the next truth table:[lii]

Truth Table: $a \Rightarrow b$

a	b	$a \Rightarrow b$
T	T	T
T	F	F
F	T	T
F	F	T

Now in some respects the definition of $a \Rightarrow b$ is consistent with usage in common speech. Certainly if a is true and b is true then, we are comfortable with a implies b. Similarly, if a is true, but b is false then a implies b should be considered to be false. When a is false, however, the appropriate truth states for the implication are not as clear. With a being false, we have no information about b. It is not unreasonable to assign the state of the implication as being true if b is true. The most difficult part of the implication truth table to accept is the assignment of true to the implication when both a and b are false. This definition of implication is not accepted by all mathematicians.[131] However, the truth table for implication is consistent with syllogistic

---

lii Another way to think of implication is to note that $a \Rightarrow b$ is logically equivalent to the statement not a or b ($\neg a \lor b$).

reasoning being accepted as a law of logic, as we shall see. Moreover, in using implications in mathematical proofs, we are generally only concerned with those cases in which the premise of the implication is accepted as true as an axiom or known to be true through prior proof. Ultimately, the truth table for implication is a mathematical definition and acceptance by mathematicians is based on its utility.

Using the definitions of implication and the conjunction "and,", we will now determine the truth table for the syllogistic argument, $(a \Rightarrow b \wedge b \Rightarrow c) \Rightarrow a \Rightarrow c$. There are eight possible truth states for all the combination of statements a, b, and c (two truth states for each of the three statements, $2^3 = 8$). From these states and the definition of truth states of implication ($\Rightarrow$) and the conjunction "and" ($\wedge$), the truths states for the syllogistic argument can be worked out as below. The table is completed by working from the left columns to the right to arrive at the truth states of the syllogism.

Truth Table: $(a \Rightarrow b \wedge b \Rightarrow c) \Rightarrow (a \Rightarrow c)$

a	b	c	$a \Rightarrow b$	$b \Rightarrow c$	$(a \Rightarrow b) \wedge (b \Rightarrow c)$	$a \Rightarrow c$	$(a \Rightarrow b \wedge b \Rightarrow c) \Rightarrow (a \Rightarrow c)$
T	T	T	T	T	T	T	T
T	F	T	F	T	F	T	T
F	T	T	T	T	T	T	T
F	F	T	T	T	T	T	T
T	T	F	T	F	F	F	T
T	F	F	F	T	F	F	T
F	T	F	T	F	F	T	T
F	F	F	T	T	T	T	T

The right most column of the truth table indicates that whatever the truth state of a, b, or c, the statement $(a \Rightarrow b \wedge b \Rightarrow c) \Rightarrow (a \Rightarrow c)$ is true. This is what is known as a tautology or a law of logic. The independence of the reasoning from the truth state of statements a, b, and c makes it clear that it is the form of the argument which has been validated. Moreover, its usefulness is also clear in that whenever the premise, $(a \Rightarrow b \wedge b \Rightarrow c)$ is true the conclusion, $(a \Rightarrow c)$ is true.

Syllogistic reasoning is the basis for many of our proofs. For example, in our inductive proofs for the natural numbers, we say if a property for the natural numbers is true for n then through a chain of syllogistic reasoning it is true for its successor n $^+$. When this is accompanied with the proof showing that it is true for n = 1 then the proof is complete. Clearly, the syllogism can be extended to as many implication statements as needed. Most of the theorems proved for the integers and rational numbers are syllogistic in form in that a chain of steps is followed to the final desired conclusion from a premises accepted to be true as axioms, definitions, or previously proven theorems.

Closely related to the syllogism is the statement $(a \wedge (a \Rightarrow b)) \Rightarrow b$. The truth table shown below makes precise our intuitive sense that this is a valid argument:

Truth Table: $(a \wedge (a \Rightarrow b)) \Rightarrow b$

a	b	$a \Rightarrow b$	$(a \wedge a \Rightarrow b)$	$(a \wedge (a \Rightarrow b)) \Rightarrow b$
T	T	T	T	T
T	F	F	F	T
F	T	T	F	T
F	F	T	F	T

Again the right hand column shows this is a valid argument form and, if the premise, $(a \wedge (a \Rightarrow b),)$ is true than the argument is true.

Another classic form of argument that we have encountered is the indirect proof, also known as proof by contradiction or by the Latin name, reductio ad absurdum. We first encountered this method in proving the cancellation property of addition for natural numbers (Theorem ℕ9) and also in the proof that $\sqrt{2}$ is not a rational number (Section 2.6). In a proof by contradiction, we assume that the theorem to be proved is false. If this leads to a contradiction then the theorem is true. In the case of the proof that $\sqrt{2}$ is irrational, we take as our premise that $\sqrt{2}$ is a rational number, that is $\sqrt{2} = p/q$ where p and q have no factors in common. This premise then leads to the contradiction that p and q are both even numbers; hence $\sqrt{2}$ cannot equal p/q and is an irrational number.

Restating the above argument symbolically, if g is the statement that $\sqrt{2}$ is irrational, then a proof by contradiction can be represented in simplest terms as $(\neg g \Rightarrow g) \Rightarrow g$.[liii] The statement $\neg g$ is $\sqrt{2}$ *is not an*

---

liii More generally, a statement g can be proved to be true by contradiction if by assuming $\neg g$ is true the contradiction follows that some statement p and $\neg p$ are both true.

irrational number, that is $\sqrt{2}$ = p/q where p and q have no factors in common. From the assumption that ¬*g* is true, we find that it follows that p is even which in turn implies that q is even. From this the contradiction, it follows that $\sqrt{2}$ cannot be represented as p/q. Thus, (¬*g* ⇒*g*), with the implication (¬*g* ⇒*g*) ⇒ *g*). The truth table shows this is a valid argument.

Truth Table: (¬*g* ⇒*g*) ⇒ *g*

¬*g*	*g*	¬*g* ⇒*g*	(¬*g* ⇒*g*) ⇒ *g*
T	F	F	T
F	T	T	T

Truth tables can be used to facilitate understanding whether two argument forms are the same. For example, you might ask if *a* ⇒ *b* is the same argument as its converse, *b* ⇒ *a*. The truth table below makes it clear that these are not same, that is these arguments are not equivalent since there truth tables are different.

Truth Table: *a* ⇒ *b*, *b* ⇒ *a*,

a	*b*	*a* ⇒*b*	*b* ⇒*a*
T	T	T	T
T	F	F	T
F	T	T	F
F	F	T	T

An equivalent form for *a* ⇒*b* is the contrapositive argument, ¬*b* ⇒¬*a*, which should by now be easily worked out by you in a truth table. You will find that the truth tables for each are identical. Whenever two logical arguments are equivalent, one can be used in place of the other. In general, if we wish to prove that *a* and *b* are equivalent, then we must show that *a* and *b* have the same truth values or *a* ⇒ *b* and *b* ⇒ *a*. This is sometimes expressed as *a* is necessary and sufficient for *b* (or symbolically *a* ⇔ *b*).[liv]

Finally, I note that in relation to *a* ⇒*b*, the statement, ¬*a* ⇒¬*b* is known as the inverse and like the converse (*b* ⇒*a*) is not equivalent

---

liv The symbol ⇔ is also expressed as "iff" for if and only if.

to it. However, the converse $(b \Rightarrow a)$ and inverse statements $(\neg a \Rightarrow \neg b)$ are equivalent arguments.

With this introduction to some of the basics of logic, it is now time to look at Euclid's geometry.

4.3   Euclid's axiomatic approach to geometry

4.3.1   Introduction

The pyramids of ancient Egypt are monuments attesting to the ancient world's knowledge of practical aspects of geometry long before the Greeks of the first millennium BC began their study of geometric principles. In the busy commercial world of the eastern Mediterranean, the Greeks would certainly have become aware of the geometric knowledge of neighboring communities. The revolutionary contribution of the Greeks to geometry and mathematics in general was the shift in focus from the search for solutions to specific problems to an approach that would develop general geometric conclusions. The deduction of propositions from previously proven propositions, in an unbroken chain of reasoning connecting back to only a few basic postulates and definitions, became the basis for deductive mathematics. This method, known as the axiomatic method for its dependence on presumed, self-evident basic postulates called axioms, was thought by the Greeks and mathematicians for two thousand years to provide the only description of space in the universe. We cannot know exactly how this turning point in mathematics came about, but it was consistent with the broad, tenacious search within Greek communities of that period for explanations for everything that was encountered in the world about them. This search would influence art, drama, literature, philosophy, and social organization to this day.

My purpose in this section is not to retrace the geometric system developed in Euclid's *Elements*. For that purpose, the classic translation by Sir Thomas L Heath with historical commentary and many clarifying notes is available (Math References 15-17) as well as modern updates of Euclid's system such as Stahl (Math References 32) which put Euclid's system into the broader context of modern geometry. I recommend them. My main purpose is to present the critical role in Euclid's development of geometry of his fifth postulate (called the Parallel Postulate) to the understanding of the axiomatic method. In focusing on the fifth postulate, I will present some of

Euclid's key propositions while giving a few indications of the modern critique and interpretation of Euclid's system. In Appendix D, I have listed the first twenty eight propositions of Euclid from Heath which do not make use of Euclid's fifth postulate. (I refer to the proofs as propositions in deference to traditional usage when discussing Euclid's *Elements;* however, the meaning of proposition is equivalent to the term theorem used previously.) As noted in the historical outline, Euclid's fifth postulate differed significantly from the first four postulates in being much less acceptable to many as self-evident (see list of postulates below). Many mathematicians tried to prove it from the other postulates, but inevitably only discovered postulates, which while being clearer to some, could be shown to be equivalent to Euclid's Parallel Postulate. Euclid, perhaps having his own concerns about this postulate did not invoke it until after he had given proofs of twenty eighth propositions. I will contrast the limitation of one of the prior proofs with those in which the Parallel Postulate is used. The Pythagorean Theorem relating the length of the sides of a right triangle is perhaps the most famous of those that require the Parallel Postulate. Other key results stemming from the use of this postulate include: the sum of the angles of a triangle being equal to 180°, formulas for the areas of figures and trigonometric functions. In the following sections, we will look at some of the implications of modifying the Parallel Postulate and the resulting non-Euclidean geometries that are generated. The discovery of new consistent geometries would revolutionize mathematicians' views of the axiomatic method, transforming the axioms from self-evident truths corresponding to reality to mathematical abstractions. We begin, however, as Euclid did with definitions and postulates.

4.3.2   Euclid's definitions and postulates

Euclid began in Book I of *Elements* his geometric development on twenty two definitions, five common notions, and five postulates. His common notions are postulates which Euclid has distinguished from the other five postulates as being of broader application than geometry. These definitions, common notions, and postulates are listed below as found in Heath[132] and are a good refresher of the building blocks of geometry.

Definitions

E1.   A point is that which has no part.

E2.   A line is breadthless length.

E3.   The extremities of a line are points.

E4.   A straight line is a line which lies evenly with the points on itself.

E5.   A plane surface is that which has length and breadth only.

E6.   The extremities of a surface are lines.

E7.   A plane surface is a surface which lies evenly with the straight lines on itself.

E8.   A plane angle is the inclination to one another of two lines in a plane which meet one another and do not lie in a straight line.

E9.   And when the lines containing the angle are straight, the angle is called rectilineal.

E10. When a straight line set up on a straight line makes the adjacent angles equal to one another, each of the equal angles is right, and the straight line standing on the other is called perpendicular to that on which it stands.

E11. An obtuse angle is an angle greater than a right angle.

E12. An acute angle is less than a right angle.

E13. A boundary is that which is an extremity of anything.

E14. A figure is that which is contained by any boundary or boundaries.

E15. A circle is a plane figure contained by one line such that all straight lines falling upon it from one point among those lying within the figure are equal to one another.

E16. And the point is called the centre of the circle.

E17. A diameter of the circle is any straight line drawn through the centre and terminated in both directions by the circumference of the circle, and such a straight line also bisects the circle.

E18. A semicircle is the figure contained by the diameter and the circumference cut off by it. And the centre of the semicircle is the same as that of the circle.

E19. Rectilineal figures are those which are contained by straight lines, trilateral figures being those contained by three, quadrilateral those contained by four, and multilateral those contained by more than four straight lines

E20.   Of trilateral figures, an equilateral triangle is that which has its three sides equal, an isosceles triangle that which has two of its sides alone equal, and a scalene triangle that which has its three sides unequal.

E21.   Further, of trilateral figures, a right-angled triangle is that which has a right angle, an obtuse-angled triangle that which has an obtuse angle, and an acute angled triangle that which has its three angles acute.

E22.   Of quadrilateral figures, a square is that which is both equilateral and right angled; an oblong that which is right-angled but not equilateral; a rhombus that which is equilateral but not right-angled; and a rhomboid that which has its opposite sides and angles equal to one another but is neither equilateral nor right-angled. And let quadrilaterals other than these be called trapezia.;

E23.   Parallel straight lines are straight lines which being in the same plane and being produced indefinitely in both directions, do not meet one another in either direction.

Common Notions

E1.   Things which are equal to the same thing are also equal to each other.

E2.   If equals be added to equals, the wholes are equal.

E3.   If equals be subtracted from equals, the remainders are equal.

E4.   Things which coincide with one another are equal to one another.

E5.   The whole is greater than the part.

Postulates

E1.   To draw a straight line from any point to any point.

E2.   To produce a finite straight line continuously in a straight line.

E3.   To describe a circle with any centre and distance.

E4.   That all right angles are equal to one another.

E5.   That if a straight line falling on two straight lines make the interior angles on the same side less than two right angles, the two straight lines, if produced indefinitely, meet on that side on which are the angles less than two right angles.

If we focus first on the definitions, I believe that you will agree that you understand what Euclid means by point, lines, plane, angle, circle, etc., but not because of the clarity of the definition, but because you already have an intuitive notion of what these words mean. If you try to develop your own definitions, I believe that you will see that a fully satisfactory set of definitions cannot be made. The modern view is that there must be a set of undefined terms whose allowed interactions are defined by the axioms of the mathematical system. Hilbert, one of the most significant contributors to this point of view, selected the following undefined terms for plane geometry: point, line, on (indicating the relation of a point and a line), between (indicating the relation between a point and two other points), segment, angle, and congruence (indicating a relation between segments or a relation between angles).[iv] Hilbert's geometric system then continues with fourteen postulates (axioms) which may be grouped as postulates of: connection, order, congruence, parallels, and continuity. From the undefined terms and postulates, all of plane geometry may be deduced. The relation between the undefined terms and postulates is well illustrated and contrasted with Euclid in two of Hilbert's Postulates of Connection:

1. There is one and only one line passing through any two given distinct points.
2. Every line contains at least two distinct points, and for any given line there is at least one point not on the line.

These two postulates clearly define the relationship of the undefined terms point, line, and on without the need for definitions with phrases such as "that which has no part."

Equivalents to the postulates of order and continuity are not included within Euclid's system and represent deficiencies in Euclid's proofs. Eves points out that in the absence of a geometric postulate of order giving meaning to the concept of betweeness, many proofs depend on unrecognized assumptions. For example no grounds exist to assure that a line which enters the vertex of a triangle will intersect the opposite side.[133]

The contrast between Euclid's and Hilbert's understanding of the geometric systems they had created is illustrated by their approaches to congruence of triangles. Euclid concept of congruence is based on superposition (coincidence of figures) as stated in Common Notion

---

iv The discussion of Hilbert's axiomatic system for plane geometry is summarized from Eves, pp. 82-87 in which more details may be found.

E4. He uses this in Proposition 4 of Book I to prove that two triangles are "equal" if the corresponding two sides of each triangle and the angles contained by the two sides are "equal." By "equal" Euclid means here that the figures may be made to coincide by placement of one onto the other—what we designate as congruence.[lvi] Euclid's approach relies upon unstated assumptions about the uniformity of space and on the rigid motion of figures allowing comparisons of figures through their superposition. Thus, his geometry can be thought of as resting on unstated empirical notions of space.[134] In contrast Hilbert specifies a postulate for the congruence of triangles in his system, thereby retaining its abstract nature. Indeed, perhaps the greatest difference between Hilbert's and Euclid's geometric systems is to be found in the abstract nature of Hilbert's system in contrast to the Euclidean system which is meant to represent an idealized geometry of reality. With Hilbert's system, although, we may immediately associate the undefined terms with our common geometric concepts, this is just an interpretation or model of the abstract system. As terms are undefined, any model is legitimate in which the undefined terms satisfy the interactions as given by the postulates. We will see examples of this when we develop non-Euclidean geometries by modifying the postulates. In this regard, the system of Hilbert is Euclidean in that it includes Euclid's Parallel Postulate.

When we compare the form of Euclid's definitions to the postulates, we can feel the tension between concepts which are idealized forms and those that are more closely grounded in experience. For example, we are told in the first two definitions that a point is that which has no part, and a line is breadthless length; whereas, the first postulate assumes as self-evidently true the capability to draw a straight line from any point to any point. This raises the question, how do you draw a breadthless line from that which has no part to that which has no part. A possible resolution of this contradiction for the ancient Greeks may have been found in the philosophy of Plato in which the ultimate realities rested in eternal

---

lvi A discussion of equality of figures as determined by the superposition introduced through Common Notion E4 with further developments by others is given by Heath, Vol. I, pp. 224-231. The proof of Proposition 4 from Book I is given in Heath, Vol. I, pp. 247-248. In Section 4.3.4, we will discuss Euclid's use of equality in which he means equality of area rather than the superposition of one figure onto another.

perfect forms of which their physical counterparts were imperfect representations. Of geometers, Plato said:

> "You know as well that they make use of visible shapes and objects and subject them to analysis. At the same time, however, they consider them only as images of the originals: the square as such or the diagonal as such. In all cases the originals are their concern and not the figures they draw . . . And all the while they seek a reality only the mind can discover."[lvii]

Ultimately, the discovery of non-Euclidean geometries and the resulting realization that the geometric forms were abstractions would make moot the question of whether geometry represented Plato's eternal forms. Let us make the discussion more concrete by taking a look at some of Euclid's proofs.

4.3.3   Propositions without the Parallel Postulate

Euclid's first proposition proves the existence of a geometric figure as a consequence of the postulates with their description of constructions that are permitted for the defined terms of point, line, and circle. Such proofs which establish the existence of geometric figures from the definitions, postulates, and theorems are called construction proofs. Construction proofs are in contrast with other proofs in which relationships of various geometric parts in the established geometric figures are proved. Let us start with the first proposition of Euclid. (I have numbered these, following the order of Euclid's proofs in Heath as for example Theorem IE1 corresponding to Proposition 1 (Book I); the following traditional symbolic notation will be used: $\triangle$ for triangle, $\angle$ for angle, $\cong$ for congruence of figures, and $=$ for equality of magnitudes (angles, lengths of line segments, areas).

Proposition IE1: On a given finite straight line [AB] construct an equilateral triangle.[135]

---

lvii Plato, *The Republic*, Book VI (510 e), p. 200., translated by R. W. Sterling and W. C. Scott, [Other Citation Sources 14]. While quoting from Plato, it is worth noting that he also said, "Further, we know that a man who has studied geometry is a better student across the board than one who has not;" Ibid. (Book VII (527 c), p. 221.

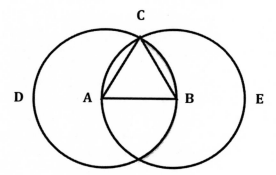

Let AB be the given straight line (see figure above)	By hypothesis
Construct the circle BCD of distance AB, centered at A	Postulate E3
Construct the circle ACE of distance AB, centered at B	Postulate E3
Construct the straight lines AC and BC with C being the point of intersection of the circles	Postulate E1
AC = AB, BC = AB	Definition E15
AC = BC	Common Notion E1
△ABC is an equilateral triangle	Definition E20

Q.E.D.

Proposition IE1 creates the equilateral triangle using only the defined concepts of point, line, and circle and the allowed operations of Postulates E1 and E3. Alternatively, given the line AB and circles of distance (radius) AB to their centers A and B, it is easily proved using the definitions and postulates that △ABC, with C being the intersection of the circles, is equilateral. The proof seems straightforward; however, you should try to understand the proof without reference to the figure above. When you do this, the following question may arise, how do we know that the circles intersect in a point C? Indeed, there is nothing in the definitions and postulates that assure the existence of point C. As mentioned above, Hilbert included a Postulate of Continuity which is equivalent to a geometric version of the Dedekind Theorem of Continuity, (Section 3.2).[lviii] Recalling that, we needed the Dedekind's Postulate to fill out the real number line, it should not be surprising that such a postulate is needed to prove the intersection of the two circles. Such a proof is provided by Heath.[136]

---

lviii A discussion of the equivalence of Dedekind's Postulate and Hilbert's Postulate of Continuity is given by Eves, p. 86.

The next proposition that I have selected to look at, IE16, provides both an example of a proof establishing geometric relationships as well as an example of a proposition that is limited in its conclusion due to Euclid's decision to refrain from using his Parallel Postulate. As a result of not using the Parallel Postulate, this proof, like those prior to Proposition 29, are valid in any non-Euclidean geometry which uses the first four postulates, but modifies the fifth. In the following proof, I refer to propositions that have been proved by Euclid prior to Proposition 16. These are listed in Appendix D. Of particular note is Proposition IE4 which establishes conditions for the congruence of triangles, that is conditions for which the triangles can be made to coincide (can be superimposed on each other). In IE4 this is established when the respective two sides and the included angle of triangles are equal (often abbreviated SAS for side-angle-side). In the proof below (see accompanying figure), the triangles, $\triangle$AEB and $\triangle$CEF are shown to be congruent ($\triangle$AEB $\cong$ $\triangle$CEF). This is proved by establishing that the corresponding two sides of the triangles are equal (AE = CE, BE = EF), and included angles are equal, ($\angle$AEB = $\angle$CEF). Thus by Proposition IE4, the remaining sides and angles of the two triangles are equal. Euclid expresses this as the equality of the triangles; however as noted above, we term the condition in which one figure may be superimposed onto another as congruence. In later propositions which we shall discuss, Euclid would also use the equality of figures such as triangles to mean that the figures were of equal area, underlining the need for unambiguous definitions.

Another frequently used proposition is IE15 in which it is proved that the angles formed by intersecting straight lines are equal (called vertical angles). In the proof below the proposition is invoked to prove $\angle$AEB = $\angle$CEF.

Proposition IE16: In any triangle [($\triangle$ABC], if one of the sides is produced [extended], the exterior angle [$\angle$DCE, see below] is greater than either of the interior and opposite angles [$\angle$BAE, $\angle$ABC].[137]

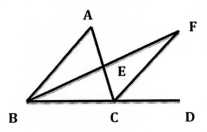

Let △ABC be the given triangle (see figure above)	By hypothesis
Produce base of △ABC to D	Postulate E2
Bisect AC at E	Proposition IE10
Produce BE	Postulate E1
Produce BE to F with BE = FE	Propositions IE2
Produce FC	Postulate E1
∠AEB = ∠CEF	Proposition IE15
∠BAC = ∠FCA	
(△AEB ≅ △CEF; SAS: AE = CE, BE = FE, ∠AEB = ∠CEF)	Proposition IE4
∠FCA < DCE	Common Notion E5
∠BAC < ∠DCE	Common Notion E1

Following the same approach by bisecting BC, it is proved that:
∠ABC < DCE

Q.E.D.

In proposition IE16, the exterior angle (∠DCA) is proved to be greater than either of the interior and opposite angles (∠BAE, and ∠ABC). However, with the use of the Parallel Postulate in Proposition IE32, Euclid was able to show that the exterior angle of a triangle is equal to, the sum of the two interior and opposite angles ((∠DCA = ∠BAC + ∠ABC). Furthermore, in this proposition it is proved that the sum of the angles of the triangle is equal to two right angles (180°). A hallmark of non-Euclidean geometries developed through modifications of Euclid's Parallel Postulate is that the sum of the angles of the triangles of these geometries is not equal to two right angles.

Finally in regard to IE16, I note that as in Proposition IE1, a spatial assumption has been made which is not justified by Euclid's Postulates. In the proof above, line segment EF is produced with F being assumed to be exterior to △ABC. From the figure, this seems intuitively obvious, but it is not established by Euclid's Postulates. This is similar to the situation in Proposition IE1 in which the intersection of the two circles was not established. These are examples illustrating deficiencies in Euclid's approach which would be corrected in Hilbert's System with its Postulates of Connection, Order, and Continuity. We will not pursue these ideas systematically here. Some limitations of Euclid's postulates as related to Proposition IE16 and non-Euclidean geometry are given by Heath.[138] We will return to this subject in the following sections.

The final propositions not using the Parallel Postulate which shall be given in detail are Propositions IE27 and IE28. These propositions give criteria for proving that lines are parallel and are the last propositions of Euclid prior to his use of the Parallel Postulate. Proposition IE28 follows directly from the IE27 extending the criteria for parallel lines.

Proposition IE27: If a straight line [EF] falling on two straight lines [AB and CD] make the alternate angles equal to one another [∠AEF = ∠EFD], the straight lines will be parallel to one another.

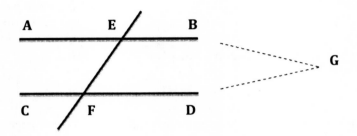

<u>Proof by Contradiction:</u>

Assume AB and CD are not parallel (see figure above)   By hypothesis
AB and CD when produced meet at some point G   Definition E23
EF, EG, FG form straight lines forming △GEF
                              By hypothesis, Postulate E1, Definition E19
∠AEF > ∠EFD   Proposition IE16
∠AEF = ∠EFD   By hypothesis
⇒ a contradiction, AB and CD must therefore be parallel.
                         Q.E.D.

Proposition IE28, the last proposition prior to Euclid's use of the Parallel Postulate extends the previous proposition. It makes use of Proposition IE13 which establishes that a straight line initiated on another straight line will form angles with a sum of two right angles. In the figure accompanying the proof, ∠AEF + ∠BEF = two right angles = 180°.

Proposition IE28: [Part 1.]If a straight line [EF] falling on two straight lines [AB and CD] make the exterior angle [∠GEB]equal to the interior and opposite angle on the same side [∠EFD], or [Part 2.] the interior angles on the same side [∠BEF and ∠EFD] equal to two right angles, the straight lines will be parallel to one another.

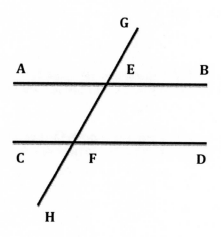

Part 1.

∠GEB = ∠EFD   By hypothesis
∠GEB = ∠AEF   Proposition IE15
∠AEF = ∠EFD (alternate angles)   Common Notion E1
AB is parallel to CD   Proposition IE27

Part 2.

∠BEF + ∠EFD = two right angles   By hypothesis
∠AEF + ∠BEF = two right angles   Proposition IE13
∠BEF + ∠EFD = ∠AEF + ∠BEF   Common Notion E1
∠EFD = ∠AEF (alternate angles)   Common Notion E3
AB is parallel to CD   Proposition IE27

Q.E.D.

Note that the same approach can be used to show that AB is parallel to CD if the exterior angle, ∠AEG equals the interior and opposite angle on the same side, ∠ CFE, or the sum of the interior angles on the same side, ∠AEF and ∠EFC, equal to two right angles.

4.3.4   Propositions with the Parallel Postulate

In this section, some of the implications of the use of the Parallel Postulate are developed. For convenience, I repeat the postulate here.

> *Postulate 5 (Parallel Postulate): That if a straight line falling on two straight lines make the interior angles on the same side less than two right angles, the two straight lines, if produced indefinitely, meet on that side on which are the angles less than two right angles.*

Drawing a figure to illustrate the postulate is helpful; however, this postulate is clearly less obvious than the previous four. In addition, in assuming that lines may be produced "indefinitely," it assumes something that it is beyond direct experience; that is, a line may be extended to exceed any selected length. This is echoed in the second postulate which without restrictions allows one to "produce a finite straight line continuously in a straight line." The denial of the assumption that a line could be extended indefinitely beyond the point of initiation would, as we shall see, be significant for non-Euclidean geometry.

The first proof taking advantage of the Parallel Postulate is Proposition IE29, which is essentially the converse of Proposition IE28. As previously discussed, the converse of a proposition is not necessarily true and in this case requires the use of the Parallel Postulate. Euclid's proof assumes two additional postulates without comment that are closely related to his Common Notions. The first is analogous to our Postulates of Order for the various number systems. Euclid assumes that in comparing two angles, only one of the following can be true: two angles must be either equal, less than, or greater than each other. Also, Euclid extends his Common Notion 2 to include inequalities. He could have stated as did latter geometers: if equals be added (or subtracted) to unequals, the difference between the wholes is equal to the difference between the original unequals. Some geometers evidently felt that such propositions being proved elsewhere were obvious, and thus their inclusion was not warranted.[139] Also, there are situations in which an inequality is modified by multiplying both sides of the inequality with the same constant. Where such an explicit justification has not been supplied by Euclid, I will indicate this with the statement, Common Notion applied to inequalities.

Proposition IE29: [Part 1.] A straight line [EF] falling on parallel straight lines [AB and CD] makes the alternate angles equal to one another (∠AEF = ∠EFD), the exterior angle [∠GEB] equal to the interior and opposite angle on the same side [∠EFD], and [Part 2.] the interior angles on the same side [∠BEF and ∠EFD equal to two right angles.

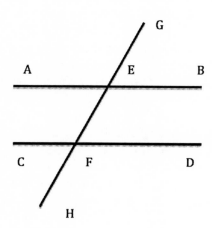

Part 1 (alternate interior angles).

Proof by Contradiction:
Assume ∠AEF ≠ ∠EFD (alternate angles not equal), then   By hypothesis
Assume ∠AEF > ∠EFD   By hypothesis (Order Postulate)
∠AEF + ∠BEF > ∠EFD +∠BEF   Common Notion applied to inequalities
∠AEF + ∠BEF = two right angles   Proposition IE13
∠EFD +∠BEF < two right angles   Common Notion E1
AB and CD are not parallel   **Postulate E5**
AB and CD are parallel   By hypothesis
⇒ a contradiction. Note that the same contradiction occurs in assuming ∠AEF < ∠EFD), therefore, ∠AEF = ∠EFD (alternate angles are equal)

Part 1 (exterior angle and interior opposite angle)
∠AEF = ∠GEB   Proposition IE15
∠GEB = ∠EFD   Common Notion E1

Part 2.
∠GEB = ∠EFD   Shown above
∠GEB + ∠BEF = ∠EFD + ∠BEF   Common Notion E2
∠GEB + ∠BEF = two right angles   Proposition IE13
∠EFD + ∠BEF = two right angles   Common Notion E1
Q.E.D.

Euclid's Parallel Postulate is commonly taught in schools in an equivalent form, known as Playfair's Postulate, (John Playfair (1748-1819)) although it was known to the ancient Greeks.[140] Playfair's Postulate is similar to Euclid's Proposition IE31 which establishes that a straight line parallel to a given straight line may be drawn through a given point. Playfair's Postulate is more restrictive in that it establishes that only one parallel line may be drawn through the given point. We shall prove it from Euclid's Parallel Postulate. As we shall see later on, denials of this postulate are particularly useful for the introduction of non-Euclidean geometries.

In the proof below, Proposition IE23 is invoked which demonstrates that a given angle [∠PQB] may be constructed on a given line [∠PQB on line QG]. Euclid proved this by constructing a triangle with the given angle and then constructing a congruent triangle on the given line. His proof used Proposition IE8 which establishes that triangles are congruent if three sides are equal (abbreviated SSS).

Playfair's Postulate: Through a given point [P] not on a line [AB] **only one** parallel line [CD] can be drawn to a given straight line [AB] in the plane of the point and line.

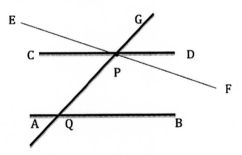

Let AB be the given straight line and P the given point	By hypothesis
Through any point Q on AB, draw the straight line QP	Postulate E1
Produce QP to G	Postulate E2
On line QG construct ∠GPD = ∠PQB(exterior and interior opposite angles)	Proposition IE23
Produce CD	Postulate E2
CD is parallel to AB	Proposition IE28
∠GPD + ∠DPQ = 2 right angles	Proposition IE13
∠PQB + ∠DPQ = 2 right angles	Common Notion E1
Draw any other line EF through P not coincident with CD	Postulate E2

Case 1: $\angle$FPQ < $\angle$DPQ (shown in figure above)   Common Notion E5

$\angle$PQB + $\angle$FPQ < 2 right angles (interior angles)   Common Notion

applied to inequalities

EF is not parallel to AB   Postulate E5

Case 2: Similar arguments apply for $\angle$EPQ < $\angle$CPQ

Q.E.D.

The power of the Parallel Postulate is particularly apparent in Proposition IE32 which can now provide a more precise conclusion than Proposition IE16 due to the use of the Parallel Postulate. Postulate IE16 (see previous section) can only say that the exterior angle of a triangle is greater than either of the opposite interior angles. In Proposition IE32, it is established that the exterior angle of a triangle is equal to the sum of the opposite interior angles. Moreover, it is established that the sum of the three interior angles of a triangle is equal to two right angles. That this latter condition is a key characteristic of Euclidean plane geometry is made clear by noting that the Parallel Postulate may be shown to be equivalent to the proposition of Legendre's that: There exists at least one triangle having the sum of its three angles equal to two right angles. Legendre went on to prove that if the sum of interior angles of one triangle is two right angles then this is true for all triangles. Similarly, the existence of rectangles (quadrilaterals with four right angles) can be shown to be equivalent to the Parallel Postulate. A list of some statements equivalent to the Parallel Postulate is given by Heath[141] and Eves[142]. Of the many statements equivalent to the Parallel Postulate, of particular note for our discussion of non-Euclidean geometry is the equivalent statement that non–congruent, similar triangles (equal interior angles) exist. In non-Euclidean geometries, in which the Parallel Postulate is replaced with another hypothesis, all similar triangles are congruent and the areas of triangles fixed by the sum of the interior angles.

Proposition IE32: In any triangle, [Part 1] if one of the sides be produced, the exterior angle[$\angle$ACD] is equal to the two interior and opposite angles [$\angle$BAC + $\angle$ABC], and [Part 2] the three interior angles are equal to two right angles.

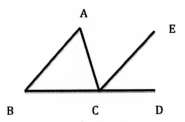

Part 1

Let △ABC be the given triangle (see figure above)	By hypothesis
Produce base of △ABC to D	Postulate E2.
Produce CE parallel to AB	Playfair's Postulate
	(or Proposition IE31)
∠ACE = ∠BAC (interior opposite angles)	Proposition IE29
∠ECD = ∠ABC (exterior and interior opposite angles)	Proposition IE29
∠ACD = ∠ACE + ∠ECD = ∠BAC + ∠ABC	Common Notion E2

Part 2

∠ACD + ∠ACB = ∠BAC + ∠ABC + ∠ACB	Result from
	Part 1, Common Notion E2
∠ACD + ∠ACB = two right angles	Proposition IE13
∠BAC + ∠ABC + ∠ACB = two right angles	Common Notion E1

Q.E.D.

Perhaps the most famous of the propositions resulting from the use of the Parallel Postulate is Proposition IE47 commonly known as the Pythagorean Theorem. In order for Euclid to prove this postulate, it was necessary for him to introduce a new notion of equality between rectilinear figures (triangles, quadrilaterals, and multilaterals—see definitions 19 to 22) based upon area. Critical to proving that the areas of non-congruent figures were equal would be comparisons of figures that were contained between common parallel lines, thus implicitly invoking the Parallel Postulate. In addition to the postulates on parallel lines which I have previously discussed, the propositions are listed below that are needed in the chain of reasoning leading to Euclid's proof of the Pythagorean Theorem. These propositions primarily establish conditions for equal areas based upon demonstrating that the two figures being compared are composites of congruent triangles common to each figure. To aid in the understanding these propositions, the proofs of Proposition IE35 and IE37 are given. Note that parallelograms are first introduced by Euclid in Proposition IE34 and are defined implicitly as a quadrilateral with parallel opposite sides. I shall use symbols such as □ABCD to indicate parallelograms while general quadrilaterals will simply be indicated by the letters of their vertices, ABCD.

Proposition IE34: In parallelogrammic areas the opposite sides and angles are equal to one another. And the diameter [diagonal] bisects the area.

Proposition IE35: Parallelograms which are on the same base and in the same parallels are equal to one another.

Proposition IE37: Triangles which are on the same base and in the same parallels are equal to one another.

Proposition IE41: If a parallelogram have the same base with a triangle and be in the same parallels, the parallelogram is double of the triangle.

Proposition IE46: On a given straight line to describe a square.

Proposition IE35: Parallelograms [□ABCD, □EBCF] which are on the same base [BC] and in the same parallels [AF and BC] are equal to one another.

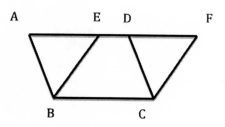

Let □ABCD and □EBCF be the given parallelograms on the base BC between parallel lines BC and AF   By hypothesis

AD = BC (parallelogram □ABCD), EF = BC (parallelogram □EBCF)   Proposition IE34

AD = EF (case with D between E and F)   Common Notion E1

AD − ED = AE = EF − ED = DF   Common Notion E3

AB = DC (parallelogram □ABCD)   Proposition IE34

∠FDC = ∠EAB   Proposition IE29

△EAB ≅ △FDC (SAS)   Proposition IE4

△EAB + EDBC = △FDC + EDBC   Common Notion E2

□ABCD = □EBCF   Common Notion E1

Similar proofs may be constructed if D is between A and E.[lix]
Q.E.D.

Proposition IE37: Triangles (△ABC, △DBC) which are on the same base and in the same parallels are equal to one another.

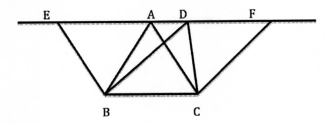

△ABC, △DBC are triangles between the parallel lines AD and the common base, BC	By hypothesis
Produce AD in both directions	Postulate E2
Through B produce BE parallel to C A	Playfair's Postulate (or IE31)
Through C produce CF parallel to BD	Playfair's Postulate (or IE31)
☐EBCA = ☐DBCA	Proposition IE35
△ABC = ½ ☐EBCA, △DBC = ½ ☐DBCA	Proposition IE34
△ABC = △DBC	Common Notion E1

Q.E.D.

We are now ready to follow Euclid's proof of the Pythagorean Theorem. Note that in order to interpret Euclid's proof as most commonly expressed in contemporary terms, it is necessary to take into account that the Greeks used a geometric algebra in which, as seen above, the equality of figures expressed the equality of their areas. So to express that $AB^2 = EF^2$, Euclid would express this as a square of side AB was equal to a square of side EF (for example, ☐ABCD = ☐EFGH).

Proposition IE47 (Pythagorean Theorem): In right-angled triangles [△ABC] the square [☐BCED] on the side subtending the right angle [the hypotenuse, BC] is equal to the squares on the sides containing the right angle [☐ACKH and ☐ABFG; that is $BC^2 = AB^2 + AC^2$]

---

lix Heath discusses the case of D between A and E, noting that CD and BE cross at some point G, for which Euclid gives no proof. In this case the composite figures require subtraction of △DEG, in contrast to the proof given here, Heath, Vol. 1, pp. 327-328.

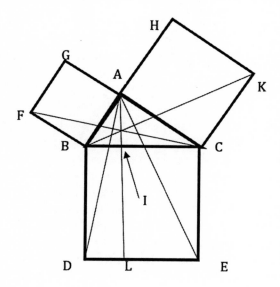

△ABC has a right angle at ∠BAC   By hypothesis

Construct squares:
□BCED, □BAGF, and □ACKH on
BC, BA, and AC, respectively   Proposition IE46
Draw: AD, AE, BK, and CF   Postulate E1
∠BAC, ∠BAG are right angles   By hypothesis, Proposition IE46
∠CAG =2 right angles, CG is a straight line   Proposition IE14
Similarly BH is a straight line   By hypothesis,
                                                Propositions IE46, IE14
∠DBC = ∠FBA   Proposition IE46
∠DBC + ∠ABC = ∠FBA + ∠ABC = ∠DBA = ∠FBC   Common Notion E2
DB = BC, FB = BA   Proposition IE46
△DBA ≅ △FBC, AD = FC (SAS, DB =
BC, FB = BA, ∠DBA = ∠FBC)   Proposition IE4
Through point A,
draw AL parallel to BD, CE   Playfair's Postulate (or IE31)
□BILD = 2△DBA (△DBA and □BILD have
the same base, between parallels BD and AL)   Proposition IE41
□ABFG = 2△FBC (△FBC and □ABFG have
the same base, between parallels FB and GC)   Proposition IE41
□BILD = □ABFG   Common Notion E1

By a similar pattern of arguments:

$\angle ACE = \angle BCK$; $BC = EC$; $CK = AC$; $\triangle KCB = \triangle ACE$; $\square CILE = \square ACKH$

$\square BCED = \square BILD + \square CILE = \square ABFG + \square ACKH$ Common Notion E1

(or $BC^2 = AB^2 + AC^2$)

Q.E.D.

Before leaving Euclid's *Elements*, there are two other themes that relate to parallel lines that I wish to touch upon briefly: formulas for some areas of rectilinear figures and the idea of proportion as related to similar triangles. In regard to areas of rectilinear figures, I ask you to imagine two parallel lines separated by a distance h. On a common base of length b, of the lower parallel line, a rectangle and a parallelogram are formed with the upper parallel line. The area of the rectangle is, of course, b · h. From Proposition IE35, the area of any parallelogram that fits our description is also b · h. Imagine that the parallelogram is divided by a diagonal. Then, from Proposition IE34, the parallelogram is divided by its diagonal into two triangles of equal area, and the area of each of these triangles is ½ b · h. Imagining any other triangle with a base b between the parallel lines, Postulate IE37 says that all of these triangles also have an area of ½ b · h. Thus the propositions on these rectilinear figures between parallel lines provides for the common formulas relating the areas of rectangles, parallelograms, and triangles. This is a consequence of the parallel postulate. The areas of other rectilinear figures, such as trapezoids, can be obtained as composites of these figures.

From Euclid Book VI, similar triangles are those triangles with equal angles, and their corresponding sides are proportional.[143] The propositions of parallel lines provide significant insight into this definition in that straight lines cutting a triangle parallel to any of the sides form similar triangles. For example in the following figure, the straight line DE is parallel to BC, and therefore from Proposition IE29, $\angle ADE = \angle ABC$ and $\angle AED = \angle ACB$. Also, as $\angle BAC$ is common to both $\triangle ABC$ and $\triangle ADE$, the triangles are similar. From the areas of the figure, viewed as a composite of the triangle, $\triangle ADE$ and the trapezoid BCDE, one can then show that $b/a = h_1/h$.[lx] This property of proportionality based upon similarity is not maintained in non-Euclidean geometries

---

lx The area of the trapezoid BCED is equal to the sum of the areas of two triangles:

$\triangle BCE + \triangle BED = 1/2(h - h_1)a + 1/2(h - h_1)b = 1/2 (h - h_1)(a + b)$.

because the Parallel Postulate does not apply. In fact similar triangles for non-Euclidean geometries are congruent.

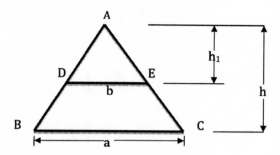

The last subject that I will discuss that falls within the realm of Euclidean geometry is trigonometry. The subject of trigonometry arose from the ancient need to determine the measurements of the sides and angles of general triangles for engineering and astronomical purposes. Although trigonometry is not explicitly covered in the *Elements*, it should not be surprising that the foundations of trigonometry may be found in Euclid's *Elements,* as trigonometry is the discipline that provides a means to determine side and angle relations of triangles. Of particular note, is Euclid's proof of the Law of Cosines given in geometric form in Book II (Proposition IIE12 and IIE13).[144] The Law of Cosines, which is a generalization of the Pythagorean Theorem, allows calculations of triangles that are not right-angled. However, the tabulation of trigonometric functions that facilitate calculations would await the trigonometric tables developed by Hipparchus of Nicaea (ca. 180-ca. 125 B.C)[145] over one hundred years after Euclid.

The following figure shows the relationship of geometric figures that form the basis of trigonometry. A circle of radius r has been centered at the origin of a coordinate system with the x-axis horizontal and y-axis vertical. The trigonometric tables originally took the form of what is known as chords and the arcs of circle subtended by the chords. For example in the figure, the chord AB is associated with the circular arc AB, subtended by ∠ACB.

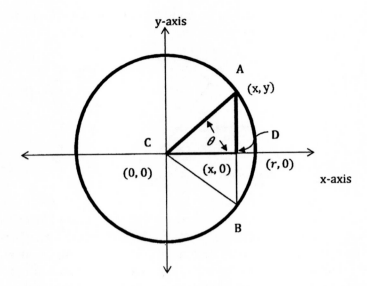

In the modern approach, trigonometric functions are defined in terms of the angle θ which subtends the side AD of the right triangle ∆ADC. The triangle is constructed with its hypotenuse, AC as a radius r of the circle with center at the point (0, 0). In terms of the coordinate system, CD = x, and AD = y. From the Pythagorean Theorem: $AC^2 = CD^2 + AD^2$ or associating the coordinate (x, y) with the general point A on the circle, we have $x^2 + y^2 = r^2$. This is the equation for the circle of radius r. The angle θ is traditionally taken as increasing as the angle moves counterclockwise from the x-axis. A full turn around the circle from the x-axis is taken arbitrarily as 360 degrees (360°) a practice due to the Babylonians with their base 60 number system. Recalling that the circumference of the circle, $C = 2\pi r$, the arc of any circular sector of angle θ degrees may be expressed as $S_\theta = 2\pi r \cdot (\theta/360) = (\pi \cdot \theta /180)$ r. Alternatively, since $C/r = 2\pi$, 2π is an angular measure given the unit name radian which is dimensionless (length per unit length). An angle of 1 radian then subtends an arc of 1 unit in a circle with a radius of 1 unit. With this definition of degrees of a circle, 0° (0 radians) corresponds to the positive x-axis and 90° ($\pi/2$ radians) correspond to the positive y axis. We now define two trigonometric functions of the angle θ, the sine function, abbreviated as sin(θ), and the cosine function, abbreviated as cos(θ).

$$\text{Sin}(\theta) = AD/AC = y/r \text{ and } \cos(\theta) = CD/AC = x/r$$

With the above definitions, you can see from the figure above that, $\sin(90°) = \sin(\pi/2) = 1$, $\cos(90°)=\cos(\pi/2) = 0$, $\sin(0°) = \sin(0) = 0$, $\cos(0°) = \cos(0)=1$. Also, from the equation of the circle, $\sin(\theta)^2 + \cos(\theta)^2 = 1$. Additional trigonometric functions can also be derived from the sine and cosine functions, for example: the tangent function, $\tan(\theta) = y/x = \sin(\theta)/\cos(\theta)$ and its reciprocal, the cotangent, $\cot(\theta) = 1/\tan(\theta) = x/y$.

With these definitions and the geometric relations established in the *Elements*, the Law of Cosines and the Law of Sines can be established allowing the solution of triangles given either two sides and an angle or two angles and a side. I present these laws in terms of the triangle in the accompanying figure (for the moment disregard the line and letters not in bold) using the notation that capital letters refer to the angles at the vertices with the opposite side lengths denoted by the associated lower case letters. Thus: $\angle BAC = \angle A$, and $BC = a$.

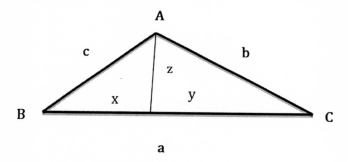

Using the above nomenclature (due to Euler[146]) we have,

Law of Cosines: $c^2 = a^2 + b^2 - 2ab\cos(C)$

Law of Sines: $a/\sin(A) = b/\sin(B) = c/\sin(C)$

We can prove these laws using the geometric approach of Euclid; however an algebraic approach is much simpler and at this stage, I believe the contrast with the geometric algebra of the Greeks is useful. First in the figure above, produce the perpendicular from point A to the line BC. Two right triangles are formed with sides of length c, x, z and b, y, z. Since $BC = a$, $y = a - x$. Now using the Pythagorean Theorem:

$b^2 = y^2 + z^2 = (a - x)^2 + z^2$ or $z^2 = b^2 - (a - x)^2$
$c^2 = x^2 + z^2$, substituting the above expression for z^2 gives,
$c^2 = x^2 + b^2 - (a - x)^2 = x^2 + b^2 - a^2 + 2ax - x^2 = b^2 - a^2 + 2ax$.

Using the definition of $\cos(\theta)$, $y = b \cos$ (C) and, $x = a - y = a - b$ $\cos(C)$, therefore

$c^2 = b^2 - a^2 + 2\,ax = b^2 - a^2 + 2\,a(a - b \cos(C)) = a^2 + b^2 - 2\,ab \cos(C)$. Q.E.D.

The law of sines may easily be proved by noting:

$z = c \sin$ (B) $= b \sin$ (C), therefore, $\sin$ (B) / b $= \sin$ (C)/c.

The law of sines for angle A may similarly be proved by producing a perpendicular from C to the extended line BA and noting that sin $(180° - A) = \sin A$. (See also Appendix H.)

The laws of sine and cosine can be written for all the different possibilities of angles and sides, by cycling the letters a, b, c and A, B, C, for example: $a^2 = b^2 + c^2 - 2bc \cos(A)$. Note that for a triangle with $\angle C = 90°$, the Pythagorean Theorem is recovered, $c^2 = a^2 + b^2$.[lxi] The trigonometric functions will help us to describe many of the new mathematical concepts that we will encounter in the chapters ahead. Now I wish to see what brave new worlds can be created by substituting new postulates for the Parallel Postulate.

4.4   Breaking the rules; the discovery of new geometries

From a relatively early period on, there were many attempts to prove the Parallel Postulate using only the first four of Euclid's Postulate or to replace it with a simpler postulate. Heath provides a commentary on some of these attempts. I note the contributors and their dates in order to give a feeling for the continuing mathematical interest over the centuries: Ptolemy (ca. 150), Proclus (410-485)[lxii], Naṣīraddin aṭ-Ṭūsī (1201-1274), John Wallis (1616-1703), Gerolamo Saccheri (1667-1733), Johann Lambert (1728-1777), and Adrien Marie Legendre (1752-1833).[147] As would only become clear in the nineteenth century, all the proofs necessarily involved circular reasoning as the Parallel Postulate is independent of the first four of Euclid's postulates. Thus the proofs inadvertently involved using the Parallel Postulate itself. However, in hindsight, such efforts

---

lxi Many examples of the use of the Law of Cosines for solving triangles and many other trigonometric identities are given in Ross, D. A., *Master Math: Trigonometry*, pp. 62-77 [Math References 29].

lxii Proclus was a geometer whose commentary on Euclid's *Elements* supplies some of the few known details on the life of Euclid.; Heath, Vol. 1, p. 1.

made valuable contributions by clarifying the nature of the Parallel Postulate and providing equivalent statements that could be used instead.

While none of the mathematicians mentioned above came to understand that the Parallel Postulate was independent, Gerolamo Saccheri made a significant contribution through his attempts to prove the Parallel Postulate by being the first to assume other hypotheses in place of this postulate and looking for contradictions. As we shall see below, the geometric conclusions that he drew for these hypotheses were valid. Only his conviction that Euclidean geometry was uniquely true would lead him to reject the results that followed from what he called the hypothesis of the acute angle and consequently miss the discovery of the new geometry that would come to be called hyperbolic. With Saccheri's failure to see in his results a new geometry, it would take over one hundred years before this insight was revealed in a paper of Nicolai Lobachevsky in 1829 and independently by Johann Bolyai in a work submitted the same year, but not published until 1832.[148] [lxiii] The other hypothesis that Saccheri would investigate(hypothesis of the obtuse angle) would lead, with other modifications of Euclid's postulates, to the geometry called elliptic as part of Riemann's of generalization of concepts of geometry.[149]

4.4.1 The Saccheri Quadrilateral

The main vehicle for Saccheri's work was what has become known as the Saccheri quadrilateral. The Saccheri quadrilateral (see figure below) is formed on a base AB with perpendiculars produced at points A and B of equal length.[lxiv] For comparison recall that in the proof of the Pythagorean Theorem, squares were formed on each side of the right triangle. However, these squares, given a description

---

lxiii Letters and papers of Gauss not published in his lifetime indicate that he may have been the first to realize that the Parallel Postulate was independent of the other postulates of Euclid; Eves, p. 61.

lxiv Saccheri's propositions may be found in *Girolamo Saccheri's Euclides Vindicatus*, edited and translated in English by George Bruce Halsted, [Math References 12]. Descriptions of key propositions in modern terminology are given in McCleary, J., *Geometry from a Differentiable Viewpoint*, pp. 15-16, pp. 34-38, [Math References 22] and Bonola, R., *Non-Euclidean Geometry*, pp. 22-44 [Math References 5]. I have similarly modified the propositions for clarity.

in Euclid's Definition 22 of Book I, are only proved to exist using the Parallel Postulate in Proposition IE46. As previously noted, the existence of rectangles and squares can be shown to be equivalent to the Parallel Postulate.

Let us prove some geometric relations of Saccheri's quadrilateral that only require using Euclid's first four postulates and propositions prior to Proposition IE29. In the figures below, I have drawn the summit of the quadrilateral symbolically as a curve in anticipation that the straight lines drawn in the new geometries are not straight lines in a Euclidean plane when we replace the Parallel Postulate with other hypotheses. (For convenience as nomenclature, ∠1 = ∠DAC, ∠2 = CAB, ∠3 = ∠ABD, ∠4 = DBC, ∠5 = ACB, ∠6 = DCA, ∠7 = ∠BDC, and ∠8 = ADB.)

Saccheri Proposition 1: In the Saccheri Quadrilateral (ABCD) the angles at the summit ∠ADC and ∠ DCB) are equal.

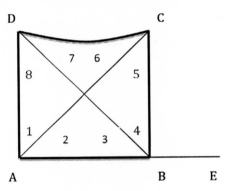

ABCD is a Saccheri quadrilateral (AD = BC,
∠DAB = ∠CBA = right angle)   By hypothesis
Produce DC, AC, BD   Postulate E1
ΔADB ≅ ΔBCA, AC = BD (SAS, AD = BC,
∠DAB = ∠CBA, AB in common)   Proposition IE4
ΔDAC ≅ ΔCBD, ∠ADC = ∠BCD
(SSS, AD = BC, AC = BD, DC in common)   Proposition IE8
                            Q.E.D

In the absence of the Parallel Postulate, we cannot say anything more about ∠ADC and ∠ DCB), other than that the angles are equal.

Before continuing the search for geometric relations in the absence of the Parallel Postulate, let us show that the addition of the Parallel Postulate requires $\angle ADC$ and $\angle DCB$ to form right angles. We will do this through the use of Proposition IE32 (proved with the Parallel Postulate) which states that the sum of the interior angles of a triangle is two right angles (180°). Continuing the proof from above:

Because $\triangle DAC \cong \triangle CBD$, the following corresponding angles are equal: $\angle 6 = \angle 7, \angle 1 = \angle 4$.
Also because $\triangle ADB \cong \triangle BCA$, the following corresponding angles are equal: $\angle 5 = \angle 8, \angle 2 = \angle 3$.

From $\triangle DAC$: $\angle 1 + \angle 6 + \angle 7 + \angle 8 = 2$ right angles.	Proposition IE32
From $\triangle BCA$: $\angle 2 + \angle 3 + \angle 4 + \angle 5 = 2$ right angles.	Proposition IE32
$(\angle 1 + \angle 2) + (\angle 3 + \angle 4) + \angle 5 + \angle 6 +$	
$\angle 7 + \angle 8 = 4$ right angles	Common Notion E2
$(\angle 1 + \angle 2) + (\angle 3 + \angle 4) = 2$ right angles	By hypothesis,
	Common Notions E1, E2
$\angle 5 + \angle 6 + \angle 7 + \angle 8 = 2$ right angles	Common Notion E3
$\angle 6 = \angle 7, \angle 5 = \angle 8$	Shown above
$(\angle 8 + \angle 7) + (\angle 7 + \angle 8) = 2$ right angles	Common Notion E1
$(\angle 7 + \angle 8) = \angle ADC =$ right angle	

Multiplication of both sides of equality by ½, unstated common notion of Euclid
Through similar arguments, $\angle 5 + \angle 6 = \angle BCD =$ right angle
Q.E.D

Continuing now our investigation without using the Parallel Postulate, other important conclusions can be proved:

Saccheri Proposition 2: In the Saccheri Quadrilateral the line [EF} formed by connecting the midpoint of the base and summit is perpendicular to the base and to the summit.

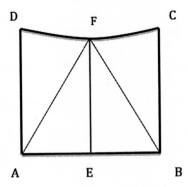

ABCD is a Saccheri quadrilateral, AD = BC	By hypothesis
Produce DC	Postulate IE1
Bisect DC at F, AB at E (DF = FC, AE = EB)	Proposition IE10
Produce AF, BF	Postulate E1
ΔADF ≅ ΔBCF, AF = BF	
(SAS, DF = FC, AD = BC, ∠ADF = BCF)	Saccheri Prop. 1, Prop. IE4
ΔAEF ≅ ΔBEF, ∠AEF = ∠BEF	
(SSS, AF = BF, AE = EB, EF in common)	Proposition IE8
∠AEF = ∠BEF = right angle	Proposition IE13

By producing lines DE and CE, similar arguments show ∠DFE = ∠CFE = right angle.

Q.E.D.

We have created two additional quadrilaterals in the figure above, ADFE and BCFE, each containing three right angles, but as before, without the Parallel Postulate the magnitude of the angles ∠ADF and ∠BCF are unknown.

In searching for a proof of the Parallel Postulate, Saccheri then chose as hypotheses for his indirect proofs that these summit angles are less than a right angle (the hypothesis of the acute angle, HAA) or greater than a right angle (the hypothesis of the obtuse angle, HOA). He then followed the logical consequences of the hypotheses to see if they would lead him to a contradiction. These hypotheses, as we have shown, differ from the right angle result that occurs with the Parallel Postulate. He called that condition the hypothesis of the right angle (HRA). As it turns out, the acute hypothesis leads to the entirely consistent geometry known as hyperbolic, while the obtuse hypothesis with changes to two of Euclid's other postulates leads to elliptic geometry. We will explore Saccheri's findings for these hypotheses.

4.4.2 The Saccheri Hypotheses of the Acute and of the Obtuse Angle

Saccheri Postulate 3: In the Saccheri quadrilateral (ABCD), depending on the assumption of HAA, HOA or HRA, (Part 1), the summit is of greater length than the lower base (DC > AB), less than the lower base (DC < AB), or equal, respectively (DC = AB); and (Part 2) the sum of angles of a triangle are, respectively, less than, greater than, or equal to two right angles.

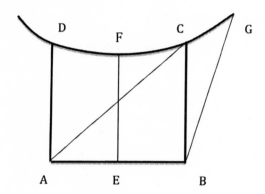

The proof below is for the HAA. The proof for the HOA follows a similar pattern

Part 1

<u>Proof by contradiction</u>

Assume DC < AB	Contradicts HAA
ABCD is a Saccheri quadrilateral	By hypothesis
Bisect DC, AB with DF = FC, AE = EB	Proposition IE10
FE perpendicular to DC and AB	Saccheri Proposition 2
FC < EB	Common Notion applied to inequalities
Extend DC, produce FCG with FG = EB	Postulate E2, Proposition IE3
∠EBG > right angle	Common Notion E5
∠CGB = ∠EBG (EFGB is a Saccheri quadrilateral)	Saccheri Proposition 1
However, ∠CGB < right angle (acute angle of EFGB)	By HAA
⇒ Contradiction, therefore, DC > AB.	

Part 2

Produce AC	Postulate E1
DC > AB	Proven above
∠ABC = right angle (Saccheri quadrilateral)	By hypothesis
∠DAC > ∠ACB (greater side subtends the greater angle)	Proposition IE25
∠CAB + ∠DAC = right angle	Common Notion E4
∠CAB + ∠ACB < right angle	Common Notion applied to inequalities
∠CAB + ∠ACB + ∠ABC < two right angles	Common Notion applied to inequalities
	Q.E.D

Thus, we have proved that for the HAA, the sum of the angles of the right triangle, △ABC is less than two right angles. Saccheri and later Legendre went on to prove that if the sum of the angles of any triangle is less than two right angles then the sum of the angles of all triangles is less than two right angles.[150] Notice that if the sum of the interior angles of a triangle is less than two right angles that the sum of interior angles of any quadrilateral must be less than four right angles as the quadrilateral may be split into two triangles. This is, of course, consistent with the summit angles of the Saccheri quadrilateral being acute.

The proof for the HOA in Saccheri Proposition 3 is quite similar to that above with the proof by contradiction assuming DC > AB producing a point G between F and C so that FG = EB. For the HOA, the sum of the angles of any triangle is proved to be greater than two right angles. Saccheri abandoned the HOA when he correctly proved it contradicted results using Euclid's first four postulates. We will return to the contradiction of the HOA with Euclid's postulates in Section 4.5.

Returning to the HAA and the Saccheri quadrilateral in the figure above, the perpendicular EF forms a quadrilateral having three right angles, EFCB. This is known as a Lambert quadrilateral as it was the starting point for Lambert's investigations of the Parallel Postulate.[151] It can be proved without using the Parallel Postulate that analogous to Proposition IE19 concerning triangles, in a quadrilateral with unequal summit angles, the arm opposite the greater angle is greater. The right angle ∠EFC > ∠BCF which is acute, therefore, BC > EF and furthermore, it can be proved that the perpendicular is the minimum distance between CD and AB. The extensions of line

FC and FD do not intersect AB and points further along these lines recede from AB. Hence lines with a common perpendicular are called diverging parallels. This will be clearer in the next section with the discussion of the geometry discovered by Lobachevsky and Bolyai which is equivalent to the HAA (hyperbolic geometry). Saccheri also investigated the possibility of parallels that do not have a common perpendicular and discovered properties which indicated that such parallels would continuously approach each other in one direction (asymptotically approach) and diverge in the other. Saccheri, however, rejected the validity of his own conclusions as he considered them to be impossible.[lxv] Ironically, these asymptotic or limiting parallels would turn out to be crucial for non-Euclidean geometry. Saccheri never found a legitimate contradiction using the HAA. It took Lobachevsky and Bolyai, starting with a new postulate contradicting the Parallel Postulate to show that Saccheri's conclusions using the HAA were consistent with a new geometry.

4.4.3   The Hyperbolic Geometry of Lobachevsky and Bolyai

The new geometries discovered by Lobachevsky and Bolyai can be developed starting with a postulate that contradicts the Parallel Postulate when expressed in terms of Playfair's Postulate (through a given point P not on a line l only one parallel line can be drawn to the given straight line l in the plane of P and l). This approach which is equivalent to the HAA can be expressed as:

Hyperbolic Parallel Postulate: Through a given point P not on a given line l more than one line may be produced parallel to the given line in the plane of P and l.[152]

---

lxv Saccheri Proposition 33 states, "The hypothesis of acute angle is absolutely false; because repugnant to the nature of the straight line." This is the way Saccheri reacted to his proof in which he found it unacceptable that, "two straights [the parallels] AX, BX, existing in the same plane, which produced *in infinitum* toward the parts of the point X must run together at length into one and the same line, truly receiving at one and the same infinitely distant point a common perpendicular in the same plane with them;" Halsted, p. 173. Allowing for the somewhat obscure nature of Saccheri's description, his findings for the lines that "must run together" was exactly correct and became the limiting asymptotic parallels of hyperbolic geometry.

The meaning of this postulate is illustrated in the figure below

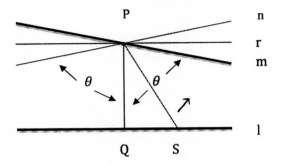

In the figure, the given point and line are respectively, P and l. Line PQ is perpendicular to l. Line r is perpendicular to PQ, hence by Postulate IE28 parallel to l because the alternate interior angles are both right angles. As allowed by the Hyperbolic Parallel Postulate, line m is a second line parallel to l through the point P making the acute angle θ with the perpendicular from PQ. By symmetry, line n is also a parallel. Because r, m, and n are parallel to l, any line through P between m and n is parallel to l.

Now assume the line PS intersects l. Moving S to the right along l, the angle PS makes with the perpendicular PQ increases in a counterclockwise direction until the line PS no longer intersects l. Let us associate the angle θ in the figure with this limiting position. Lobachevsky called θ, the angle of parallelism which he found was a function of the distance between P and Q (d_{PQ}). He denoted the function of the angle of parallelism as Π, in our example, Π (d_{PQ}) = θ. Notice that with this understanding, line m is asymptotic with l on the right side of PQ and n is asymptotic with l on the left hand side of PQ. These are the parallel lines that Saccheri rejected.

I think you may already begin to see the possibility of accommodating the HAA within hyperbolic geometry. To make this correspondence between the HAA and hyperbolic geometry explicit, we now follow the line of reasoning that leads from the Hyperbolic Parallel Postulate to the proposition that the interior angles of a triangle sum to less than two right angles. With the proof of this proposition, the conclusions of Saccheri's HAA are valid in hyperbolic geometry. We will follow Lobachevsky's approach; however, before beginning the proof on the sum of interior angles of a triangle, we will need two other propositions: one which is sometimes known as the Saccheri-Legendre Theorem and a proposition by Lobachevsky on angles. The Saccheri-Legendre Theorem, which does not use the Parallel Postulate, states that the sum of the angles interior to a triangle is less than or equal to two right angles. This theorem is proved in Section 4.5. The proof of Lobachevsky's theorem on angles, given below, is Theorem 21 in his *Theory of Parallels.*[lxvi]

Lobachevsky Angle Proposition: From a given point (A) a straight line can be drawn that can make with a given straight line (l) an angle as small as we choose.

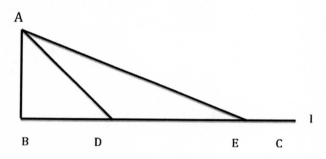

A is a point not on line l	By hypothesis
Produce AB perpendicular to l	Proposition IE 12
Choose D on l, BD = AB	Proposition IE3
∠BAD = ∠ADB	Proposition IE5
∠ADB + ∠BAD + ∠ABD ≦ 180°	Saccheri—Legendre Theorem
∠ADB + ∠BAD ≦ 90° (since ∠ABD = 90°)	Common Notion applied to inequalities
2 · ∠ADB ≦ 90°, ∠ADB ≦ 45°	Common Notion applied to inequalities
Produce on l, DE = AD; produce AE	Proposition IE3
∠DAE = ∠DEA	Proposition IE5
∠ADB + ∠ADE = 180°	Proposition IE13
∠ADE ≧ 135° (since ∠ADB ≦ 45°)	Common Notion applied to inequalities
∠ADE + ∠DAE + ∠DEA ≦ 180°	Saccheri—Legendre Theorem

lxvi Lobachevsky's work in which he developed his new geometry, *Theory of Parallels*, is reprinted as translated by George Bruce Halsted in an Appendix in Bonola's *Non-Euclidean Geometry*. What I have called the Lobachevsky Angle Proposition is Theorem 21 on pp. 18-19 in that Appendix. The work of John Bolyai, *The Science of Absolute Space*, also as translated by Halsted, is reprinted as another Appendix.

∠DAE + ∠DEA ≦ 45°   Common Notion applied to inequalities
∠DEA ≦ 22 ½°   Common Notion applied to inequalities
By similarly extending points along l, angles as small as desired may
be constructed

Q.E.D.

With this preliminary proposition completed, now we can continue
with Lobachevsky's proof:

Lobachevsky Right Triangle Proposition: The sum of the
interior angles of a right triangle [△ABC] is less than two right angles.

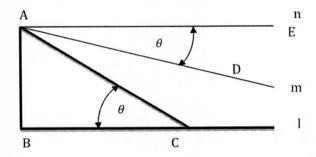

AB is perpendicular to line l at B   Proposition IE11
Line n is perpendicular to AB at A   Proposition IE11
Line m passing through A is parallel to l
(does not intersect l); ∠DAE = θ Hyperbolic Parallel Postulate
Produce ∠ACB = θ with C on line l   Proposition IE23, Lobachevsky
                                                    Angle Proposition

△ABC is a right triangle with base BC
on l and right angle ∠ABC   Definition IE21
∠BAC < 90° − θ (since ∠BAE = 90°)   Common Notion IE5
∠ABC + ∠BAC + ∠ACB < 90° +
(90° − θ) + θ = 180°   Common Notion applied to inequalities
Q.E.D.

Having proved that the sum of the angles in a right triangle is
less than 180°, theorems of Saccheri and Legendre assure us that all
triangles in hyperbolic geometry will have the sum of their interior
angles less than 180°.[lxvii]

---

lxvii This theorem is implied by the propositions of Saccheri, but was not
explicitly stated by him; Bonola, p. 57.

Another of the important and surprising results of hyperbolic geometry is that all similar triangles are congruent. In contrast, recall that in Euclidean geometry, the corresponding sides of similar triangles are proportional, rather than congruent. Thus in Euclidean geometry similar figures can be scaled. With the replacement of Euclid's Parallel Postulate with that of the Hyperbolic Parallel Postulate, this no longer applies. We prove this result below by contradiction by assuming that the similar triangles are not congruent. This assumption will lead to the conclusion that the sum of the interior angles of a quadrilateral equals 360°. As the quadrilateral may be divided into two triangles, this implies that the sum of the interior angles of a triangle is equal to 180°, a contradiction of the Lobachevsky Right Triangle Proposition.

Hyperbolic Similar Triangle Proposition: Similar triangles are congruent.

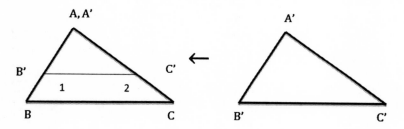

Proof by contradiction

ΔABC and ΔA'B'C' are similar triangles
(∠ABC =∠A'B'C', etc.)   By hypothesis
Assume triangles are not congruent
(AB ≠ A'B', BC ≠ B'C', CA ≠C'A'   By hypothesis
Bring ∠C'A'B' into coincidence with ∠CAB   Proposition IE23

Note that if any one of the sides of the two triangles is equal, the triangles are congruent by Proposition IE26 (AAS). Therefore in one of the triangles, we can select two sides to be shorter than two of the sides of the other triangle; let A'B' < AB and A'C' < AC (see figure above).[lxviii]

---

lxviii The line A'B forms the exterior angle ∠A'B'C' equal to the interior and opposite angle on the same side ∠ABC; thus by Proposition IE28, B'C' does not intersect BC.

∠C'B'B + ∠A'B'C' = 180°; ∠B'C'C + ∠A'C'B' = 180°   Proposition IE13
∠C'B'B + ∠ABC = 180°; ∠B'C'C + ∠ACB = 180°   By hypothesis,
                                                            Common Notion E1

∠C'B'B + ∠ABC + ∠B'C'C + ∠ACB =
360° = interior angles of BB'C'C   Common Notion E2
Interior angles of BB'C'C < 360°   Corollary to Lobachevsky
                                                Right Triangle Proposition

⇒contradiction; therefore
Similar triangles are congruent.

$$\text{Q.E.D.}$$

The importance of the interior angles to hyperbolic geometry is further underlined by noting that the area of a triangle is proportional to the difference between two right angles and the sum of the interior angles of the triangle, called the triangle defect, δ_d. If the three interior angles of a triangle are α, β, and γ, then, $\delta_d = (\pi - \alpha - \beta - \gamma)$. That the area of a triangle in hyperbolic geometry is determined by the angle defect is not entirely surprising considering that similar triangles are congruent. In Euclidean geometry, area may be thought of as adding the number of unit squares in a figure; however, in hyperbolic geometry, there are no squares to add up! It can be shown, however, that the triangle defect has the necessary property for area of being additive; that is, the sum of the defects of a triangle composed of a number of smaller triangles is equal to the sum of the defects of the smaller triangles.

An example of the additivity of triangle defect, δ_d in the HAA is shown below for a triangle which is a composite of two smaller triangles. Let the larger triangle, $\triangle ABC$ consist of two smaller triangles, $\triangle ABD$ and $\triangle ADC$ with angles as shown below.

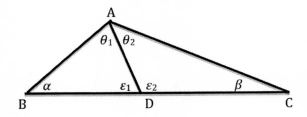

$$\delta_{\triangle ABD} = (\pi - \alpha - \varepsilon_1 - \theta_1); \ \delta_{\triangle ADC} = (\pi - \beta - \varepsilon_2 - \theta_2)$$
$$\delta_{\triangle ABD} + \delta_{\triangle ADC} = (2\pi - \alpha - \beta - (\theta_1 + \theta_2) - (\varepsilon_1 + \varepsilon_2)); \ (\varepsilon_1 + \varepsilon_2) = \pi$$
$$\delta_{\triangle ABD} + \delta_{\triangle ADC} = (\pi - \alpha - \beta - (\theta_1 + \theta_2)) = \delta_{\triangle ABC}$$

Similarly in the case of the HOA, the triangle excess also has the additive property. Of course in Euclidean geometry, the defect is zero for all triangles.

Lambert was the first to recognize the relationship of area and angle defect resulting from the HAA. He also was aware that for the HOA in which the sum of the interior angles is greater than two right angles that the area of a triangle is proportional to the angular excess, $\delta_{ex} = (\alpha + \beta + \gamma - \pi)$. Lambert came very close in this observation to a clear vision of non-Euclidean geometry.[153] Like Saccheri, he could not take the next step and accept his results as forming consistent new geometries. In the next section we will connect the concept of angle defect and excess to curved surfaces.

I close the present discussion by describing one more characteristic that will help us to visualize hyperbolic geometry. The characteristic that I have in mind is the dependence of the angle of parallelism on distance. Recall in the discussion of the Hyperbolic Parallel Postulate that $\Pi(d_{PQ}) = \theta$ represents the limiting angle of a line through the point P that is parallel to a line l with d_{PQ} being the distance of the perpendicular from P meeting the line l at Q (see figure with discussion of the Hyperbolic Parallel Postulate). The angle θ is measured between the parallel line through P and the perpendicular line PQ As d_{PQ} decreases (the point P becoming closer to Q), θ approaches 90°. In other words, the geometry starts to look Euclidean. The angle of parallelism, θ in Euclidean geometry is always 90°. However, as d_{PQ} increases, θ approaches 0°, thus the lines approach a vertical orientation. To help visualize this, recall that in the Saccheri quadrilateral, we proved that the length of the summit was always greater than the base. We can imagine the sides of the Saccheri quadrilateral increasing in length by the addition of adjoining quadrilaterals. It is then not surprising that the parallel lines must diverge and "curve" (if visualized on a Euclidean plane) to maintain this condition. A proof of this characteristic of $\Pi(d_{PQ})$ given by A. D. Aleksandrov [lxix] is summarized in Appendix E.

Continuing with his analysis of the propositions that follow from the Hyperbolic Postulate, Lobachevsky developed an expression for

lxix Aleksandrov, A. D. in Aleksandrov, A.D., Kolmogorov, A.N., Lavrent'ev, M.A. (eds.), *Mathematics, Its Content and Meaning*, [Math References 2], Vol. 3, Chapter XVII, pp. 108-110; this three volume work presents a comprehensive view of mathematics with many conceptual insights to anyone interested in mathematics.

the angle of parallelism as well as expressions analogous to the Laws of Sines and Cosines in Euclidean geometry. We will not develop this involved analysis here.

Lobachevsky and Bolyai created a perfectly consistent geometry by following the path that logic led them as they replaced the Parallel Postulate with those of their own. However, the significance of this new geometry remained unclear. Indeed Lobachevsky initially called it imaginary geometry.[154] An understanding of the new geometry would not be fully clear, until the correspondence of hyperbolic geometry with the surface of a three-dimensional surface was demonstrated by Beltrami in 1868. Ironically, this did not occur until after Riemann had already in 1854 provided the conditions under which the HOA would fit into a consistent and, in fact, a well-known geometry.[155] We will now turn to the HOA and in the process get a better understanding of hyperbolic geometry and the HAA.

4.5   Non-Euclidean geometry and the sphere

In seeking to prove Euclid's Parallel Postulate by contradiction, Saccheri rejected the HOA as incompatible with Euclid's first four postulates.[156] Saccheri may have been the first to follow this path, but not the last. Lambert[157] and Legendre[158] also reformulated this rejection. Recall that Saccheri had shown that if the HOA is accepted, then the sum of the interior angles of a triangle is greater than two right angles. The HOA was abandoned, therefore, when Saccheri, Lambert, and Legendre proved in what is now generally known as the Saccheri—Legendre Theorem that Euclid's first four postulates require the sum of the angles to be less than or equal to two right angles. Legendre presented a number of proofs of what is sometimes called Legendre's First Theorem. One of these proofs is shown next.[159]

Legendre's First Theorem (Saccheri—Legendre): The sum of the angles of any triangle is less than or equal to two right angles.

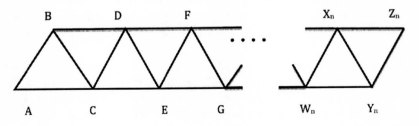

Proof by contradiction

△ABC is a triangle with base AC	By hypothesis
Assume ∠ACB + ∠CBA + ∠BAC > two right angles	By hypothesis
Extend CE = AC on AC	Proposition IE2
Produce ∠DCE = ∠BAC with CD = AB	Proposition IE23, IE2
Produce BD, DE	Postulate E1
∠ACB + ∠BCD + ∠DCE = two right angles	Proposition IE13
∠ACB + ∠BCD + ∠BAC = two right angles	Common Notion E1

Subtracting the above expression from the hypothesis:

∠CBA − ∠BCD > 0, ∠CBA > ∠BCD	Common Notions applied to inequalities
AC > BD (previously, AB= CD and BC is common to △ABC and △BCD)	Proposition IE24
△ABC ≅ △CDE, BC = DE (SAS: CD = AB, CE = AC, ∠DCE = ∠BAC)	Proposition IE4
Construct △EFG as △CDE with EG = CE, ∠FEG = ∠DCE, CD = EF	As above
Produce DF	Postulate E1
△ABC ≅ △CDE ≅ △EFG (SAS: CD = EF, CE = EG, ∠DCE = ∠FEG)	Proposition IE4
∠DEC+ ∠CDE+ ∠DCE > two right angles	By hypothesis
∠DEC+ ∠DEF+ ∠FEG = two right angles	Proposition IE13
∠DEC+ ∠DEF+ ∠DCE = two right angles	Common Notion E1
∠CDE − ∠DEF > 0, ∠CDE > ∠DEF	Common Notions applied to inequalities
CE > DF	Proposition IE24
∠BCD = ∠DEF (∠BCD = two right angles − ∠BCA − ∠DCE = two right angles − ∠DEC − ∠FEG = ∠DEF)	Common Notion 3
△BDC ≅ △DEF, BD = DF (SAS: BC = DE, CD = EF, ∠BCD = ∠DEF)	Proposition IE4

We can continue to construct as many congruent triangles as we wish such that:

AC = CE = EG = . . . $W_n Y_n$; BD = DF = . . . $X_n Z_n$ with AC > BD. If we construct enough triangles, say n of them, then n · (AC−BD) will be greater than any length we choose.[lxx] We choose $n \cdot (AC - BD) > AB + Y_n Z_n$. Therefore we find that $n \cdot AC > n \cdot BD + AB + Y_n Z_n$. Now, $n \cdot AC = AY_n > n \cdot BD + AB + Y_n Z_n$. This says that AY_n is not the shortest path between A and Y_n. This can be proved to be a contradiction of Proposition IE20 which states that in any triangle two sides taken together in any manner are greater than the remaining one. Therefore, $\angle ACB + \angle CBA + \angle BAC \leqq$ two right angles.

Q.E.D.

The contradiction that results in proving the Saccheri—Legendre Theorem is based on the shortest distance between two points being the straight line joining the points. This is not stated as a proposition by Euclid, but follows, as noted above, from Proposition IE20. The line on any surface that is the shortest distance between two points is known as a geodesic. On a plane surface, a geodesic is Euclid's straight line; however, on curved surfaces on which a Euclidean straight line cannot be formed, a geodesic, as we will see, is interpreted as a straight line of a non-Euclidean geometry.

Because of the importance of the shortest line concept, I will illustrate the use of Proposition IE20 to prove that the base of a quadrilateral is shorter than the sum of the connecting sides.[lxxi]

Proposition: In the quadrilateral ABCD, AB < AD + DC + CB.

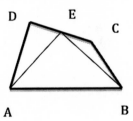

lxx This is the Archimedean Property that we discussed in relation to the denseness of the rational numbers (Section 3.1, fn. xxxviii). This principle included in modern axiomatic systems of plane geometry such as that of Hilbert was not included by Euclid.

lxxi Perhaps you find such a proof to be so obvious as to be a waste of time. If so you are in good company, Epicureans said of Proposition IE20 that it was so obvious as to be evident even to an ass. The Epicureans stated as proof that "If fodder is placed at one angular point and the ass at another, he does not in order to get to his food, traverse the two sides of the triangle but only the one side separating them." Heath, Vol. 1, p. 287.

ABCD is a quadrilateral	By hypothesis
E is a point on line DC	Definition E4
Produce AE, BE	Postulate E1
AE + EB > AB	Proposition IE20
AD + DE > AE, EC + CB > EB	Proposition IE20
AD +DE+ EC + CB > AB	Common Notion applied to inequalities

Q.E.D.

Returning now to the HOA, it would seem that the Saccheri—Legendre Theorem shows that there is no place for this hypothesis in the world of geometry. However, a clue as to how the HOA could be used to create a consistent geometry is found at the very end of Legendre's proof. Legendre asks that as many triangles be constructed as necessary to meet the needs of his proof. This is the same as asking to extend the base of his quadrilateral indefinitely. Euclid had done the same thing in his Parallel Postulate. But how do we know that a line can be extended indefinitely. Perhaps it will return to its initial position. In 1854, as part of a generalization of geometry to abstract surfaces, Riemann recognized that a line could be boundless yet finite.[160] The example that satisfies this condition is one that we live with every day as we travel on the earth—it is the geometry of the surface of a sphere. The circumference of the earth is a finite length, but we can go around as many times as we want which is to say that it is boundless. Thus, on a sphere, we cannot reason as Legendre did that we can extend lines indefinitely without returning to the initial position.

In addition to accepting that lines could be boundless, Riemann proposed two other modifications of Euclid's postulates to form a new consistent geometry. Riemann proposed that two distinct points determine at least one straight line as a replacement for Euclid's first postulate, and that there are no lines that are parallel as a replacement to the Parallel Postulate. Just as the geometry of a sphere gives us an example of boundlessness, the intersection of all meridians at the North and South Pole of the earth gives a concrete example for two points determining more than one line. Riemann's postulate on parallel lines provides an interesting contrast to the geometry of Lobachevsky and Bolyai in which there are at least two lines through a point parallel to a given line and Euclidean geometry in which there is only one.

Our next task is to reveal the consistent non-Euclidean geometry that follows from the insights of Riemann, but let us first take a step back and compare results for the HAA, HRA, and HOA. Below is a table summarizing results for the three hypotheses: the sum of interior angles of a triangle and of a quadrilateral, the ratio of the length of the summit to the base in a Saccheri quadrilateral, the number of lines that may be drawn through a point parallel to given line, and the existence of non-congruent similar triangles.

	HAA	HRA	HOA
Sum of ∠'s in △	< 180°	= 180°	>180°
Sum of ∠'s in □	< 360°	= 360°	> 360°
CD (summit)/AB (base)	>1	= 1	< 1
# parallel lines	∞	1	0
Non-congruent, similar triangles ?	NO	YES	NO

Let us now turn to the geometry of the surface of a sphere to confirm its correspondence to Riemann's postulates and the conclusions from the HOA.[lxxii] The surface of a sphere consists of those points which are equidistant from a given point in three dimensional space. On this surface, the shortest distance between two points (the geodesic) is the curve formed by the intersection with the surface of the plane containing the two points and the center of the sphere. The geodesic or the arc of a great circle will be what we mean by a line on the surface of a sphere. The intersection of any extensive plane containing the center and the surface of the sphere forms a circle. Thus any line that is extended indefinitely will return to its beginning. Such a line will cut the surface of the sphere into two regions, thus any other line will intersect this line if extended far enough, and there can therefore be no parallel lines in this geometry.

Our familiarity with the geometry of the earth as a globe makes the effects of the HOA quite apparent. In the following figure of a sphere, I have shown the great circle that is formed on the surface by the intersection of a horizontal plane with the center of the sphere O. The short arc formed by the points BC is part of this great circle. In terms of our globe, the great circle corresponds to the equator. A line

_____

lxxii An excellent source on spherical geometry may be found at www. gutenberg.org/ebooks/19770Cached Nov 12, 2006, Todhunter, I., *Spherical Trigonometry for the Use of Colleges and Schools with Numerous Examples*, [Math References 35].

perpendicular to the equatorial plane from the center of the sphere meets the surface at point A, the pole of the equatorial great circle. A plane passing through points A, B, and the sphere center produces the line AB. Extending AB to the opposite pole would produce the traditional meridian of maps. The position of point B on the equatorial circle is defined by its angular position around the circle with 0° starting at an arbitrary position. Our maps of the earth traditionally select the meridian going through Greenwich, UK as that starting point. In regard to ∠ABC, it should be clear that this is a right angle as the plane forming the line AB is perpendicular to the equatorial plane. Another way to see this is to note that the tangents of the lines AB and BC at point B are perpendicular.

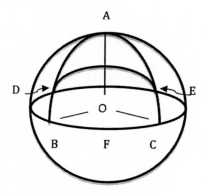

In the figure above, I also show another line AC forming with AB and BC a triangle, △ABC. If we locate point C a quarter of the way around the great circle from point B, then ∠BOC is 90°. This would correspond to the meridian just east of Calcutta, India. The line AC is formed by a plane through points A, C, and the sphere center and is perpendicular to the equatorial plane forming the line BC. Hence ∠ACB is also a right angle. To determine ∠BAC, we look at the planes forming AB and AC, (or the tangents to AB and AC at A; so ∠BAC is also a right angle. The sum of the angles of △ABC is therefore three right angles. It should be clear that by moving point C towards B along the equatorial great circle, triangles could be formed in which the sum of the angles is any value between two and three right angles as ∠BAC can take on any value between 0°. and 90°. With the assurance of the proofs of Saccheri and Legendre, we now know that any triangle on the surface of the sphere will have angles summing to more than two right angles. By continuing to form triangles by moving C further away from B along the equatorial great circle, we can see that triangles with angle sums between two and six right angles can be formed.

From the knowledge that the surface area of a sphere is $4\pi r^2$ with r the radius of the sphere, we can determine the area of $\triangle ABC$. As I have chosen C to be a quarter of the way around the equatorial circle, $\triangle ABC$ is a quarter of the hemisphere or an eighth of the surface area of the sphere, $A_{\triangle ABC} = 4\pi r^2/8 = \pi r^2/2$. Lambert first discovered that under conditions in which the HOA is true, the area of a triangle is proportional to the difference between the sum of the angles of the triangle and two right angles. In our case this gives:

$$A_{\triangle ABC} = r^2\,(\angle BAC + \angle CBA + \angle ACB - \pi) = r^2\,(\pi/2 + \pi/2 + \pi/2 - \pi) = \pi \cdot r^2/2.$$

Notice that if $\angle BAC$ is any angle θ formed by moving the point C along the equatorial circle then: $\triangle ABC = \theta \cdot r^2$ where θ is given in radians. Similar techniques[lxxiii] may be used to prove that for the general triangle with interior angles α, β, and γ, the area is given as:

$$A_{\triangle ABC} = r^2\,(\alpha + \beta + \gamma - \pi).$$

Thus, we can see the correspondence of spherical geometry with the requirements of the HOA as discovered by Lambert.

Now we can also form quadrilaterals by passing a plane containing the center O at an angle to the equatorial plane to cut lines AB and AC symmetrically forming points D and E at the intersection. This would form the line DE in the above figure and the quadrilateral BDEC. The angles $\angle BDE$ and $\angle CED$ being obtuse are examples of Saccheri's requirements for a quadrilateral with the HOA. A Lambert quadrilateral can be created by connecting on the sphere's surface point A with point F taken as the midpoint of BC. Because of the symmetry of the resulting figures, the intersection of AF with DE and with BC would form right angles, and we would have a quadrilateral having three right angles and one obtuse angle.

Another comparison with Euclidean geometry is provided by the relationships between sides and angles of triangles. In Euclidean geometry, we have the Law of Cosines as a generalization of the Pythagorean Theorem. We can use the geometry of the sphere as a model of the HOA to see its equivalent. The derivation is given in

---

lxxiii See Todhunter online, pp. 71-73.

Appendix F. Let us look at an arbitrary triangle △ABC, on the surface of a sphere of radius r

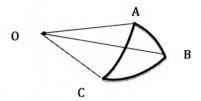

From the center of the sphere, O, radii of length r are drawn to points A, B, and C of the triangle. We use the notation: ∠A = ∠CAB, ∠B = ∠ABC and ∠C = ∠ACB, and a = BC (opposite vertex A), b = AC (opposite vertex B), c = AB (opposite vertex C,). Also,. Note that a = r · ∠COB, b= r · ∠AOC, and c = r · ∠AOB. This notation leads to the more easily recalled formulas for the law of cosines for spherical geometry:

$$\cos (a/r) = \cos(b/r) \cdot \cos(c/r) + \sin(b/r) \cdot \sin(c/r) \cdot \cos(A),$$
$$\cos (b/r) = \cos(c/r) \cdot \cos(a/r) + \sin(c/r) \cdot \sin(a/r) \cdot \cos(B),$$
$$\cos (c/r) = \cos(a/r) \cdot \cos(b/r) + \sin(a/r) \cdot \sin(b/r) \cdot \cos(C).$$

These formulas are the equivalent to the Law of Cosines in Euclidean geometry. For example, given two sides and the included angle, the third side may be obtained.[lxxiv] If r is large compared to the triangle sides, a, b, c, then the formulas can be approximated by the Law of Cosines as shown in Chapter 6 in which infinite series are introduced.

The cosine laws for spherical geometry may be used to determine distances between two locations on the earth surface. I will illustrate their use by determining the distance along a geodesic (great circle path) between two cities approximately at the same latitude and compare it with the distance following instead the path of constant latitude. We so often see maps of the earth projected on a plane surface that it is easy to forget that the shortest distance between two locations of the same latitude does not follow the path of constant latitude. Rather the path for the crow and jets to fly is the great circle connecting the two points. Let us calculate the distance between Boston, Massachusetts and Rome, Italy which are both at a latitude of approximately 42°. The approximate longitude for Boston is 71.1°

___

lxxiv Examples of solutions for spherical triangles are given in Ross, D. A., *Master Math: Trigonometry*, pp. 395-408.

west of the Greenwich meridian and for Rome it is 12.5° east of Greenwich. Let us convert these coordinates to the spherical geometry coordinates r, θ, and φ shown in the figure below. In terms of the Cartesian coordinate x, y, and z, $x = r \sin \theta \cos \varphi$, $y = r \sin \theta \sin \varphi$, and $z = r \cos \theta$.

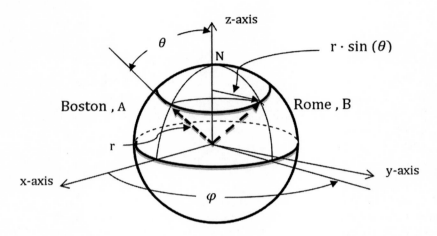

For our purpose, we only need the differences in longitude, so φ = 71.1° + 12.5° = 83.6° or 83.6 (π/180) = 1.46 radians. Latitude is measured from the plane of the equator, so $\theta = 90° - 42° = 48°$ or 48 (π/180) = 0.838 radians. Let us first calculate the distance between Boston and Rome along the constant latitude line of 42°. The path will be part of a circle of radius r $\cdot$ sin (θ) where r is the radius of the earth taken as approximately 4,000 miles. The distance along the path of constant latitude is therefore

$$d_{Lat.} = r \cdot \sin(\theta) \cdot \varphi = 4000 \sin(48°) \cdot 1.46 = 4{,}340 \text{ miles.}$$

Now let us look at the great circle from Boston (point A) to Rome (point B) by forming the triangle ABN on the earth's surface with N being the North Pole. Let the arc AN = b, BN = a, and the arc between Boston and Rome, AB = c. Furthermore, let the spherical angle, $\angle$ANB = $\angle$C. Then from the law of cosines for spherical geometry:

$$\cos(c/r) = \cos(a/r) \cdot \cos(b/r) + \sin(a/r) \cdot \sin(b/r) \cdot \cos(C).$$

Since Boston and Rome are at the same latitude, $a = b = r\theta$.
$\cos(c/r) = \cos^2(\theta) + \sin^2(\theta) \cdot \cos(C)$ with $\theta = 48°$ and $\angle C = \varphi = 83.6°$.
Therefore,

$\cos(c/r) = 0.448 + 0.552\ (0.111)$
$\cos(c/r) = 0.509$. Using a calculator with the inverse cosine function, we can find the angle c/r in radians for which the cosine equals 0.509.
$c/r = 59.4°$ or $59.4\ (\pi/180) = 1.037$ radians
$c = 1.037 \cdot r = 4{,}148$ miles, and indeed the great circle route is shorter.

We have seen that a consistent geometry for the HOA is possible by applying it to the curved surface of a sphere. Our final task in this chapter will be to relate the curvature of surfaces to the HAA. To begin, let us look at curvature as represented by movement around the circumference of a circle of radius r. In the figure below, the direction of the curve is shown by the arrow perpendicular to the radius at point S_1. The direction arrow is tangent to the circle in that it only touches the circle at this point. After moving clockwise around the circle by an angle ϕ, the tangent line as shown by the direction arrow has moved to S_2.[lxxv]

S_1

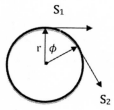

S_2

The curvature of the circle can be characterized by determining the change of direction ϕ of the curve per unit change of distance along the path of the curve ΔS. Because in this case, the tangents are perpendicular to radii which are separated by an angle ϕ, the tangent's direction also changes by an angle ϕ. The path length corresponding to a change in position from S_1 to S_2 is the arc length from S_2 to S_1. The curvature, k, is defined as an expression determined as the limiting result of the position S_2 approaching S_1:

$$k = \lim_{S_2 - S_1 \to 0} \phi/\Delta S$$

For the case of a circle of radius r, $\Delta S = r \cdot \phi$ or $k = 1/r$.

---

lxxv I note that to properly discuss the tangent, the concept of vectors, entities that have both magnitude and direction, needs to be introduced which we will do in the next chapter, but here a simplified discussion should suffice.

The surface curvature that we just obtained may represent the curvature of any great circle formed by cutting a sphere with any extensive plane containing the sphere's center. Not surprisingly, the surface curvature is the same at every point on the sphere. This is a special case and, of course, not true for all surfaces of three dimensional objects. In general the curvature at a point of a surface is characterized by a maximum, $k_{max,}$ and a minimum, $k_{min.}$ The curvature is defined for curves at the surface formed by planes cutting the surface in a manner similar to the example of planes cutting the surface of a sphere. The planes associated with the maximum and minimum curvature may be shown to be perpendicular to each other. The Gaussian curvature, κ, at a point on a surface is defined as: $\kappa = k_{max,} \cdot k_{min.}$[161] In the case of the sphere, $k_{max,} = k_{min} = 1/r$; so, $\kappa = 1/r^2$. Gauss discovered a profound connection between the area of a triangle on a surface $A_{\triangle}$, the curvature of the surface κ, and the excess of the interior angles α, β, and γ. For the special case of a surface with constant Gaussian curvature:

$$\kappa \cdot A_{\triangle} = (\alpha + \beta + \gamma - \pi)$$

In the case of a spherical triangle formed by two right angles on the equatorial circle and an angle θ at the pole, we have: $1/r^2 \, (A_{\triangle}) = (\theta + \pi/2 + \pi/2 - \pi)$ or $A_{\triangle} = r^2 \, \theta$ in agreement with the previous discussion. Under the HOA, the excess of the interior angles must be greater than zero. Since the area of a triangle must be greater than zero, this means that the Gaussian curvature must also be greater than 0.

Now in Euclidean plane geometry, the excess of the interior angles equals zero. Again since $A_{\triangle}$ must be greater than zero, this means that the Gaussian curvature is zero. This suggests that the geometry of spheres of large radius r will look Euclidean since $\kappa = 1/r^2$ which approaches zero for large r. For many purposes, we are quite happy to think of the earth as flat.

The Gaussian curvature, κ also has implications for length as well as area. We can use the model of spherical geometry for the HOA to investigate some of these implications. On a sphere of radius R with $\kappa = 1/R^2$, we draw a circle with its center at the North Pole N (see next figure). The angle between the circumference of the circle and the normal, NO to the equatorial plane is $\angle AON = \theta$. Point A is on the circle, therefore AO = R and the distance from N to A is R $\cdot$ θ.

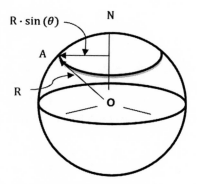

Now those living on the sphere might assume that it is a Euclidean flat world and measure the radius $\mathcal{R} = R \cdot \theta$. Then assuming Euclidean geometry, they calculate that the apparent circumference of the circle, $C' = 2\pi \mathcal{R} = 2\pi R \cdot \theta$ (since they measure the radius to be $\mathcal{R} = R \cdot \theta$). We, however, know better. The actual radius is $R \sin(\theta)$ and $C = 2\pi R \sin(\theta)$. As will be discussed in Chapter 6, $\sin(\theta)$ may be expressed as an infinite series in the variable θ so that:

$$C = 2\pi R \sin(\theta) = 2\pi R \left(\theta - \frac{\theta^3}{3 \cdot 2 \cdot 1} + \frac{\theta^5}{5 \cdot 4 \cdot 3 \cdot 2 \cdot 1} - \ldots\right)$$

With $\kappa = 1/R^2$ and $\mathcal{R} = R \cdot \theta$, this becomes

$$C = 2\pi \mathcal{R} - \frac{\pi}{3} \cdot \kappa \mathcal{R}^3 + \frac{\pi}{60} \cdot \kappa^2 \mathcal{R}^5 + \ldots$$

$$= C' - \frac{\pi}{3} \cdot \kappa \cdot \mathcal{R}^3 + \frac{\pi}{60} \cdot \kappa^2 \mathcal{R}^5 + \ldots$$

So for small values of the Gaussian curvature, κ the apparent circumference, C' will approach the value, C expected for Euclidean geometry in which $\kappa = 0$. The Gaussian curvature may be considered to be a measure of a surface's deviation from Euclidean space. For $\kappa > 0$, the actual circumference C is smaller than the circumference C'. We can see this also by rewriting the above equations in the following form:

$$\frac{3}{\pi} \cdot (C' - C)/\mathcal{R}^3 = \kappa - \kappa^2 \mathcal{R}^2 /20 + \ldots$$

For circles of small radius $\mathcal{R}$, $\kappa \approx \frac{3}{\pi} \cdot (C'-C)/\mathcal{R}^3$. In the mathematical language of limits (Chapter 6), $\kappa = \lim_{\mathcal{R} \to 0} \frac{3}{\pi} \cdot (C'-C)/\mathcal{R}^3$.

We have derived this for the case of a sphere, but the definition and its geometric interpretation are general.[162]

Let us see if the ideas of surface curvature can help us make sense of the HAA or equivalently hyperbolic geometry. Unlike the HOA, the hyperbolic geometry requires no changes in Euclid's first four postulates. We would like to find a model for hyperbolic geometry as satisfying as spherical geometry is for the HOA. From Saccheri's propositions for the HAA, we know that in the case of a triangle formed within hyperbolic geometry, the sum of the interior angles is less than two right angles and $(\alpha + \beta + \gamma - \pi) < 0$. Because $\kappa \cdot A_{\triangle} = (\alpha + \beta + \gamma - \pi)$, the Gaussian curvature $\kappa < 0$, and $k_{max,}$ and k_{min} must be of opposite signs. With this insight, the possibility of surfaces of negative curvature playing the same role in hyperbolic geometry as that of the spherical surface in elliptic geometry becomes apparent.

In 1868, Eugenio Beltrami (1835-1900) made the connection between a surface of negative curvature and hyperbolic geometry. The surface, known as a pseudosphere, has constant negative curvature and is formed by the revolution of a curve known as a tractrix about its axis.[163] The tractrix has the property that the line formed by the tangent to the curve and its intersection with the y axis is of constant length. The y-axis is the curve's asymptote (the curve approaches the y-axis). The form of the curve is illustrated in the accompanying figure. The tractrix has been described as the curve in the x-y plane followed by a weight initially on the x-axis (see below) and dragged by a line of fixed length l by someone starting at the origin walking along the y-axis.[164] The surface of the pseudosphere is formed by rotating the curve about the y-axis (see below).

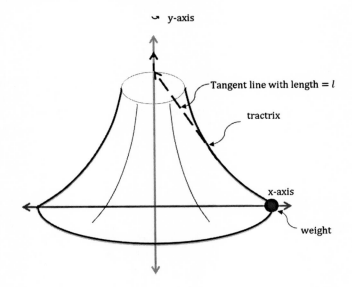

Expressions for the geometry of this surface similar to those for spherical geometry may be obtained; however the development and expressions are more complicated than for spherical geometry and will not be developed here. Qualitatively however, the tractrix curve, in the plane of the x and y axes, is concave and its radius of curvature increases with increasing y. In contrast, if we take a plane cutting the pseudosphere perpendicular to the x-y plane, then circles (which are convex) are formed of decreasing radius for planes cutting the pseudosphere at increasing y. Informally, the contrasting curvature in these two cases, gives the sense that the Gaussian curvature is negative. If the length of the fixed length tangent line is l, it may be shown that the Gaussian curvature, $\kappa = -1/l^2$.[lxxvi] Thus, triangles formed by geodesics on the surface have interior angles which sum to less than two right angles. The circumference of a circle drawn on the pseudosphere grows more rapidly than its radius. From the definition of Gaussian curvature with $\kappa < 0$, the actual circumference C is greater than the apparent circumference C'. However, once again for small κ and/or small circles, the circumference approaches the Euclidean value.[165] With Beltrami's discovery, hyperbolic geometry was clearly no longer an imaginary abstraction.

As noted in Chapter 8, our normal conception of space has been superseded by the space-time of Einstein's General Relativity in which the geometry of space-time is determined by the distribution of mass in the universe. However, approximations of the theory suggest that significant deviations from Euclidean geometry only occur at cosmic length scales or near massive objects such as stars. With the approximation that the distribution of mass in the universe is uniform, some theories have proposed that the large scale geometry of the universe is hyperbolic.[166] Thus in this viewpoint, Euclidean geometry can be viewed as a limiting case of hyperbolic geometry.[lxxvii]

What is most important for our purposes here is that the discovery of Beltrami made it clear that Euclid's Parallel Postulate

---

lxxvi The equation for the tractrix curve is: $y = l \cdot \ln\left(\frac{l+\sqrt{l^2-x^2}}{x}\right) + \sqrt{l^2-x^2}$ in which $ln(x)$ is the log of x with a base e, that is, $ln(e^2) = 2$. The length of the tangent line is l; at y =0, x = l; see Bonola, p. 132 fn. 1; also for a general discussion of Gaussian curvature, pp. 132-137.

lxxvii A discussion of the relationship of abstract geometry to real space is provided by Aleksandrov in Aleksandrov, Kolmogorov, and Lavrent'ev, Vol. 3, pp. 178-189.

is independent of the first four postulates and that consistent geometries could be established by replacing this postulate with another as in the case of the hyperbolic geometry of Lobachevsky and Bolyai or by modifying the Parallel Postulate along with some of the first four postulates as inspired by the insights of Riemann. An understanding of these geometries in terms of surface curvature would lead to the possibility of geometries that would vary continuously over the surface. This was proposed by Riemann and led to new geometrical formulations that will be introduced in subsequent chapters. These concepts would be essential to the mathematical foundations of Einstein's Theory of General Relativity.

The pseudosphere, a surface in three-dimensional space, is only one model for the hyperbolic geometry; however, other models applied in the Euclidean plane would be found that would also be consistent with hyperbolic geometry. Klein in 1870 discovered a model in which the hyperbolic geometry was described by defining expressions for magnitudes of line segments and angles within a circular region applicable to the entire hyperbolic plane. With his definitions, his model was consistent with all of the postulates of Lobachevsky and Bolyai.[167] Indeed it was Klein who coined the name hyperbolic geometry for the non-Euclidean geometry of Lobachevsky and Bolyai and the name elliptic for that corresponding to spherical geometry.[168]

We have now looked at three of the pillars of mathematics: the axiomatic method and its consequences for those other two pillars, number systems and geometry. Although a deductive system of geometry had been created in the fourth century BC, it was not truly understood until the passage of over 2000 years. The discovery of non-Euclidean geometries showed that in an axiomatic system the propositions are the logical conclusions that follow from a set of postulates rather than self-evident truths. The development of systematic understanding for number systems and algebra would remain in even a more unsatisfactory state throughout this same period. However, major new developments in algebra would begin with the presentation of geometric concepts in algebraic forms. Due to the intuitive understanding granted by geometry, this would lead to enormous breakthroughs in such mathematical concepts as function, continuity, and limits. These are some of the key subjects of the next chapter.

Chapter 5

THE BRIDGE BETWEEN ALGEBRA AND GEOMETRY

"The solution of any one of these problems of loci is nothing more than the finding of a point for whose complete determination one condition is wanting . . . . In every such case an equation can be obtained containing two unknown quantities."—Rene Descartes[lxxviii]

5.1 From figures to equations; Descartes and analytic geometry

Just as our first acquaintance with numbers and geometric figures can be a steppingstone to some of the most significant concepts in mathematics, so our first acquaintance with the equation for a straight line offers a similar opportunity. Traditionally in school, the equation for a straight line in a plane is expressed as $y = mx + b$, with y and x being variables, and m and b representing constants. With this simple equation, we are introduced to the idea of coordinate systems, algebraic interpretations of geometric concepts such as slope, geometric interpretations for the solution of equations, and the concept of a mathematical function expressing the relationship between variables.

The idea of coordinate systems envisioned somewhat obscurely by Descartes in the seventeenth century seems rather obvious to us now. We are used to it not only as a means of plotting the relationship of two variables on a flat piece of paper in school, but in our experience of expressing the location of a place on a map of the world through the coordinates of latitude and longitude. In both cases we notice that to express the location of a point on a surface we need two variables such as x and y or on the globe latitude and longitude.

---

lxxviii Descartes in his *La Géométrie* refers to the loci (paths) of points forming curves such as the parabola, ellipse, or hyperbola; cited in Merzbach and Boyer, p. 317.

As discussed in the history outline, much of the effort through the sixteenth century in the development of algebraic methods was related to finding methods for solving equations, for example, Tartaglia's and Cardan's work in the sixteenth century on cubic equations such as $x^3 + qx = r$. Descartes and Fermat recognized that such equations could be made visual as curves on a coordinate system, with the benefit of providing insight into their solution (for example, by representing them as $y = x^3 + qx - r$). This insight is the beginning of the subject known as analytic geometry. Following Descartes, we routinely make use of a coordinate system with one variable referred to an axis called the abscissa and with the other variable referred to an axis perpendicular to the abscissa called the ordinate. In honor of Descartes, we call such a coordinate system Cartesian. In the case of the straight line, $y = mx + b$, the abscissa is conveniently taken as the x axis and the ordinate as the y axis. A point in the plane of the x and y axes is noted as (x, y). The two axes are representations of the number line; however, neither Descartes nor Fermat would be aware of the logical deficiencies associated with a number line which must include the irrational numbers that were not well-defined or understood. Indeed, Descartes did not even include negative numbers.[169] The familiar graph of the straight line, $y = mx + b$ is shown below.

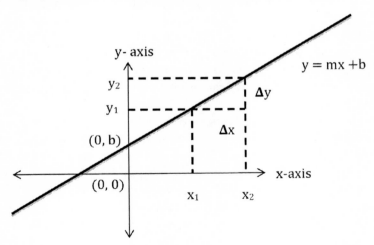

In the figure above, the curve $y = mx + b$, shown in bold, is referenced to x and y axes. The origin $(0, 0)$ is the intersection of these axes. The straight line intersects the y-axis where x is equal to 0 at the point $(0, b)$. This point is known as the y-intercept. Two general points on the curve, (x_1, y_1) and (x_2, y_2) are selected to remind you how the points are referred to the axes. The slope of the line can be calculated from these two points and is defined as the change in the y coordinate compared to the x coordinate, sometimes described as the rise over the run.

Slope $= (y_2 - y_1) / (x_2 - x_1) = \Delta y / \Delta x$ where Δy and Δx refers symbolically to the change in y and x, respectively.

Because the curve is a straight line, the slope is the same for every pair of points (x, y) and (x_1, y_1) on the line. Therefore:

$$(y - y_1) / (x - x_1) = \text{constant} = k \text{ or solving for y,}$$

$$y = k(x - x_1) + y_1 = kx + (y_1 - kx_1).$$

Now, comparing this result with the equation, $y = mx + b$, we see that $m = k$, thus m is just the slope and $b = (y_1 - kx_1)$. We have recovered the usual school result that a straight line can be defined by its slope and the y-intercept or equivalently by any two points.

While the Cartesian coordinate system is being introduced, I note that the use of axes perpendicular to one another allows the Pythagorean Theorem to be readily used to define distances in terms of the coordinates. In the figure above the projections of the coordinates to the x and y axes forms a right triangle with the hypotenuse formed by the line connecting (x_1, y_1) and (x_2, y_2). The square of the distance between the two points is therefore, $(x_2 - x_1)^2 + (y_2 - y_1)^2$ with the distance being $\sqrt{(x_2 - x_1)^2 + (y_2 - y_1)^2}$.

The power of a coordinate representation of geometric objects such as a straight line is that we can use all of our algebraic properties of the number system to determine geometric properties. We have seen an example of this already in the derivation of the Laws of Cosines and Sines (Section 4.3.4). The equivalence of an algebraic description of geometry and Euclidean geometry may be made clear from a list of algebraic interpretations of Euclid's definitions and postulates. I will not be comprehensive in pointing out this correspondence, but I hope to make it plausible and to draw your attention to some of the main features. (Eves discusses the correspondence of the analytic geometry approach to Hilbert's system in which the deficiencies of Euclid's geometry have been removed.[170])

The first eight definitions in Euclid's geometric system refer to points, lines, surfaces, and angles. I will give algebraic interpretations for these, as well as, the circle (the fourteenth definition) because of its prominence in Euclid's third postulate and its use in the proof of the first proposition.

We have already identified a point as the coordinate (x, y) on the plane formed by the x-y axes. I will further take the unhistorical leap of identifying the points x and y with the real number system. Euclid's first Postulate (IE1) states that in his geometric system, it is always possible to draw a straight line from any point to any point. Given two point (x_1, y_1) and (x_2, y_2), we have shown that we can identify the straight line, $y = m(x - x_1) + y_1$ with the slope $m = (y_2 - y_1) / (x_2 - x_1)$. Moreover, the equation of the straight line being made up of the real numbers can be drawn continuously as required by the second postulate and indeed indefinitely as allowed in the fifth postulate.

In regard to surfaces, the Cartesian plane formed by the x and y axes can be considered to be within a three dimensional space with a third z-axis perpendicular to the Cartesian plane and intersecting the origin. In this sense all closed curves described by a algebraic relation between the variables y and x are surfaces in the plane defined by z =0. Such an interpretation helps to illuminate Euclid's more obscure view that "A plane surface is that which has length and breadth only."

The third postulate states that a circle can be described with any centre and distance (radius, r). For a circle centered at the origin of the x-y axis, we have already used the Pythagorean Theorem in Section 4.3.4 to show that the equation of the circle is given by $x^2 + y^2 = r^2$. With a little reflection, I believe you can see that if the circle is centered at the point (x_1, y_1), then the equation becomes $(x - x_1)^2 + (y - y_1)^2 = r^2$, satisfying the requirements of the postulate.

The final algebraic interpretation of a definition that I wish to present here is that of an angle. Euclid, in definition IE8, defines an angle as the inclination to one another of two lines in a plane which meet one another and do not lie in a straight line. Having algebraic interpretations for points and lines should allow us to provide a consistent algebraic interpretation for an angle. In the following figure, an angle θ is formed by the points (x_1, y_1), (x_2, y_2) and the origin (0, 0). I have used the origin as the vertex of the angle to simplify the algebra. Also, I have noted the triangle formed in the figure ($\triangle ABC$) with the angles A, B, and C and sides a, b, and c in the Euler notation to facilitate the comparison with the Law of Cosines.

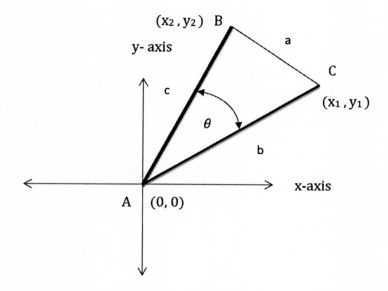

From the Pythagorean Theorem, the square of the distances between the points (x_1, y_1), (x_2, y_2) and the origin, $(0, 0)$ are respectively, $b^2 = (x_1^2 + y_1^2)$ and $c^2 = (x_2^2 + y_2^2)$. The square of the distance between the points (x_1, y_1) and (x_2, y_2) is $a^2 = (x_2 - x_1)^2 + (y_2 - y_1)^2$. Therefore, from the Law of Cosines:

$$a^2 = b^2 + c^2 - 2bc \cdot \cos(A)$$
$$(x_2 - x_1)^2 + (y_2 - y_1)^2 = (x_1^2 + y_1^2) + (x_2^2 + y_2^2) - 2 \cdot (\sqrt{x_1^2 + y_1^2} \cdot \sqrt{x_2^2 + y_2^2}) \cdot \cos(\theta)$$

or after simplification,

$$\cos(\theta) = (x_1 \cdot x_2 + y_1 \cdot y_2) / (\sqrt{x_1^2 + y_1^2} \cdot \sqrt{x_2^2 + y_2^2}).$$

In words, the cosine is the product of the components of length of AC and AB along the horizontal axis plus the product of their component lengths along the vertical axis, all divided by the product of the lengths of AC and AB. If instead of using the origin as the third point, we choose the general point (x_3, y_3) as the vertex of the angle, the equations becomes:

$$\cos(\theta) =$$
$$((x_1 - x_3) \cdot (x_2 - x_3) + (y_1 - y_3) \cdot (y_2 - y_3)) / \sqrt{(x_1 - x_3)^2 + (y_1 - y_3)^2} \cdot \sqrt{(x_2 - x_3)^2 + (y_2 - y_3)^2}$$

In this case the definition in words remains the same except the lengths are measured with respect to (x_3, y_3) rather than the origin. This will be useful when we discuss vectors in Section 7.2.

We therefore have an algebraic description for any angle in terms of the coordinates which define the straight lines of the angle. As it is based on the Law of Cosines, it is consistent with Euclidean geometry and in particular the fourth postulate about the equivalence of right angles.

The algebraic interpretations of the Euclidean definitions are consistent with the first four postulates—what about the fifth, the Parallel Postulate. First we must give an algebraic interpretation of parallel lines. We have shown that a straight line is defined by a slope, m and a point, (x_1, y_1). This straight line is given by, $y = mx + (y_1 - mx_1) = mx + b_1$. If we choose another point not on the line, (x_2, y_2), then a line passing through it with a slope of m will result in another line of the form $y = mx + (y_2 - mx_2) = mx + b_2$. We can look for a point of intersection between the two lines by setting $mx + b_1 = mx + b_2$. From this, we see that there are no common points unless $b_1 = b_2$. Thus, the lines are either identical or do not intersect and are parallel.

Now that we have interpreted parallel lines algebraically, we would like to know that the algebraic interpretation of parallel lines is consistent with the Parallel Postulate or its equivalent, Playfair's Postulate. Recall that Playfair's Postulate says that only one line can be drawn through a point not on a line which is parallel to the line. Now we ask, can another line pass through (x_2, y_2) with a different slope, say $m + \varepsilon$, and still be parallel to the line passing through (x_1, y_1). Let this other line be $y = (m + \varepsilon)x + (y_2 - (m + \varepsilon)x_2)$ where ε is any number as small as we like. Solving for a possible intersection by setting $mx + (y_1 - mx_1) = (m + \varepsilon)x + (y_2 - (m + \varepsilon)x_2)$, a point of intersection is found no matter the magnitude of ε.[lxxix] Thus the algebraic interpretation is consistent with Parallel Postulate along with the other four postulates.

In addition to the five postulates, Euclid also included as part of his geometric system five common notions. These are really just additional postulates. You should recognize from Chapters 2 and 3 that these are a subset of the properties of the real numbers. So, once we identify the coordinates with the real numbers, the algebraic interpretation is consistent with Euclid.

The algebraic interpretation of Euclid's definitions and postulates makes it possible to establish the propositions through algebraic

---

lxxix The point of intersection is given by: $\varepsilon x = y_1 - y_2 - m(x_1 - x_2) + \varepsilon x_2$.

methods. As an example, let us look at Proposition IE11 from an algebraic point-of-view. Proposition IE11 states: To draw a straight line at right angles to a given straight line from a given point on it.

In the figure below, the given straight line is represented algebraically as $y = mx$. (I have again simplified the algebra by having the line pass through the origin.) Let the given point on the line be (x_1, y_1) so $y_1 = mx_1$. A perpendicular is produced at (x_1, y_1) extending to the point (x_2, y_2). A right triangle is thus formed by the three points: $(0, 0)$, (x_1, y_1), and (x_2, y_2) with the line from the origin to (x_2, y_2) being the hypotenuse in which the square of its length is $(x_2{}^2 + y_2{}^2)$.

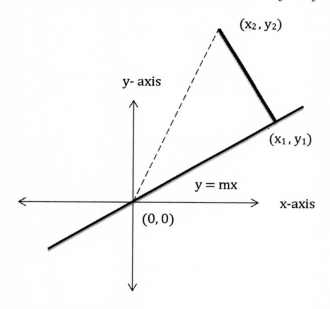

From the Pythagorean Theorem:
$$(x_2{}^2 + y_2{}^2) = (x_1{}^2 + y_1{}^2) + ((x_2 - x_1)^2 + (y_2 - y_1)^2).$$

Let the slope of the perpendicular be: $(y_2 - y_1) / (x_2 - x_1) = n$, or $y_2 = n(x_2 - x_1) + y_1$. Substituting for y_2 and $y_1 = mx_1$ into the expression for the square of the length of the hypotenuse and simplifying:

$x_1{}^2 (1 + nm) - x_1 x_2 (1 + nm) = 0$. This can only be true if $n = -1/m$. Therefore the perpendicular at (x_1, y_1) to the line $y = mx$ is: $(y - y_1) / (x - x_1) = -1 / m$.

Thus, the algebraic equivalent of Proposition IE11 has been demonstrated.

In addition to the geometry formed from straight lines and circles, the Greeks were also aware of the curved figures known as conics. Conics as described geometrically by Menaechmus (375-325 BC) were the curves that were formed on the surfaces of cones cut at different angles by planes.[171] Their names, the parabola, ellipse, and hyperbola, were given to them by Apollonius (260-200 BC)[172] in reference to the Pythagoreans' names for their geometrical solution to geometric interpretations of quadratic equations.[173] Apollonius in his book, *Conics,* derived many of their properties, but the algebraic interpretation greatly facilitated and expanded the understanding of these properties beyond the capabilities of geometric algebra available to Apollonius. The algebraic approach is shown below for the three conics.

Definition of an ellipse: the locus (path) of the points P(x, y) such that the sum of the distances of the point P from two fixed points (the foci) is constant.

In order to simplify the algebra, we will place the two fixed points on the x-axis with the y-axis located at the midpoint between the fixed points. The fixed points are therefore taken as $(-c, 0)$ and $(c, 0)$. The sum of the distances from these two points, we designate as 2a.

$$2a = \sqrt{\left(x-\left(-c\right)\right)^2 + \left(y\right)^2} + \sqrt{\left(x-c\right)^2 + \left(y\right)^2}$$

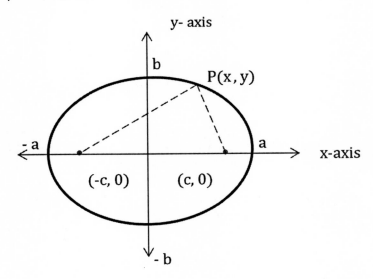

A more accessible algebraic form for the ellipse may be obtained by squaring both sides of the equation, $2a - \sqrt{(x-(-c))^2 + (y)^2} = \sqrt{(x-c)^2 + (y)^2}$ and simplifying. The resulting equation may be further simplified, by transferring the remaining square root to one side of the equation and then again squaring. Terms of the resulting equation may be algebraically grouped to form the equation:

$x^2/a^2 + y^2/(a^2 - c^2) = 1$

For y =0, the solution is x = ± a. We can show that a > c. Along the x-axis (y = 0), if a < c, then, the sum of the distances is, (c − a) + (a − (− c)) = 2c, not 2a as required. The sum gives the correct result for a > c, that is, (a − c) + (a − (−c) = 2a. It is convenient to introduce $b^2 = a^2 - c^2$. The equation for the ellipse then takes on its standard form:

$x^2 / a^2 + y^2 / b^2 = 1$

The constants a and b, shown on the figure above, are the lengths of the semi-major, and semi-minor axes of the ellipse, respectively. In order to rotate the ellipse 90°, you merely switch the x and y variables. An ellipse translated horizontally a distance h_1 and vertically v_1 is represented as:

$(x − h_1)^2/a^2 + (y − v_1)^2/b^2 = 1$

Algebraic expressions for the parabola and the hyperbola may be derived from their definitions following the same approach. The results are given below.

Definition of a parabola: the locus of points P (x, y) that are equal distances from a fixed point (the focus) and a line (the directrix).

As in the derivation of the ellipse, a coordinate system and location of the focus and directrix are selected to simplify the resulting algebra. The origin of the coordinate system is the midpoint of the perpendicular from the focus to the directrix, and the perpendicular is taken as the y-axis. Hence the coordinates of focus may be taken as (0, p) and the directrix is the line y= −p. The coordinate system and resulting parabola are shown in the next figure.

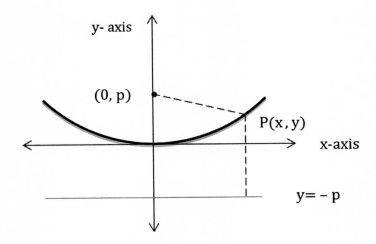

$\sqrt{x^2+(y-p)^2}=y+p$ or after simplification $x^2=4py$.

Definition of a hyperbola: the locus of the points P(x, y) such that the difference of the distances of the point P from two fixed points (the foci) is constant.

We follow the same approach as in the case of the ellipse; however, there are two conditions because it is the difference in distances that must be constant, therefore:

$$\pm 2a = \sqrt{\left(x-(-c)\right)^2+(y)^2}-\sqrt{(x-c)^2+(y)^2}$$

Using the same simplification techniques as in the case of the ellipse, we get the same result: $x^2/a^2 + y^2/(a^2 - c^2) = 1$

For y = 0, x = ± a. The two solutions correspond to the two different branches of the hyperbola (see the following figure). We now show that unlike the ellipse, c > a. If c < a, then on the positive x-axis, the difference, a − (−c) − (a − c) = 2c, not 2a as required. For c > a, 2a = a − (−c) − (c − a). With the consideration that c > a, let $b^2 = c^2 - a^2$. The equation for the hyperbola then takes on the standard form:

$x^2 / a^2 - y^2 / b^2 = 1$

Focusing on the solutions at x = ±a, as the point on the hyperbola moves from the x-axis and y increases or decreases, x must also increase since $y^2/b^2 \geq 0$. From this consideration, there are no solutions for x and y between the points (a, 0) and (−a, 0). Finally, as x^2 and y^2 become increasingly large, x^2/a^2 is approximately equal to y^2/b^2 and therefore the branches of the hyperbola approach the straight lines, $y = b\,x/a$ and $y = -b\,x/a$.

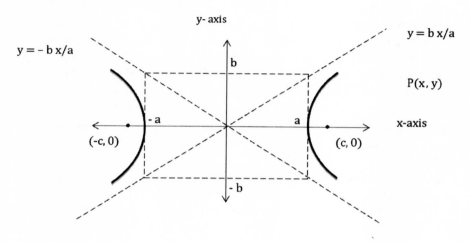

5.2   Equations as functions

5.2.1   Functions and curves

The equation, $y = mx + b$ provided us with the opportunity to illustrate the marvelous insight of Descartes and Fermat that equations could be represented as curves in a coordinate plane. It also is an example of a function, an equally important concept in mathematics. The simplest view of a function is that it is a rule that associates members of one collection with another. For example, a list of guests at a party along with their seating locations can be viewed as a discrete function. From this point-of-view, the concept of a function is very ancient as it may be seen in the mathematical tablets of the Babylonians including listings of numbers and their squares, cubes, square and cube roots, and reciprocals.[174] Similarly the tables in the Ptolemy's *Almagest*, equivalent to trigonometric results, are an example of discrete functions.[175] Despite such examples, the full importance of the function concept does not seem to have become apparent until the eighteenth century. Contributing factors to this delay in recognition are the dominance of geometric forms of algebra, the associated lack of an effective symbolic algebraic notation, and the emphasis on developing methods to solve polynomials such as Tartaglia's cubic equation, $x^3 + qx = r$. Descartes insight that equations could be viewed on a coordinate plane as curves in two unknowns, could have provided the necessary insight to develop the function as a key mathematical concept, but this was not apparent to Descartes.[176]

As with many of the other developments of mathematics, the contributions of Euler were vital to the general understanding and acceptance of the function concept. Euler, who introduced or through his various treatises standardized much of modern mathematical notation, introduced the common notation for a function of the variable x as f(x). In regard to our straight line, this notation finds employment as $y = f(x) = mx + b$. Euler appears to have viewed functions narrowly compared to the modern approach as he restricted them to such expressions as those involving polynomials, exponentials, and trigonometric functions.[177] A more expansive view of functions is Dirichlet's view in the nineteenth century that a function was simply a rule that assigns a unique value y to the variable x.[178] The assignments can therefore be through algebraic expressions, tables, or graphs. Let us look at the characteristics of functions as illustrated by the equation for a straight line.

The function, $f(x) = mx + b$, has x as its independent variable. The variable x, the argument of the function, may take on any value of the real numbers. We say therefore that the domain of the independent variable is the real numbers. As the input x varies over the real numbers, f(x) provides the rule by which the dependent variable $y = f(x)$ is assigned. In this case, given the properties of the real numbers, the dependent variable also takes on all the real numbers. Thus, the range of the function is also said to be the real numbers, and the function is described as mapping the real numbers into the real numbers. Some functions which map into the real numbers are not mappings into all the real numbers. In that case the real numbers are sometimes specified as the codomain with the specific real numbers mapped by the function being known as the range of the function.

An important characteristic of the function $f(x) = mx + b$ is that it generates a unique result for any input x. This is easily seen from the graph of $y = f(x) = mx + b$. For any value x, a vertical line intercepts the function at only one point. This characteristic is the requirement for all function (also called single-valued). Similarly, for any value of the dependent variable, a horizontal line also only intercepts the function at one point. Under these conditions, if $f(x_1) = f(x_2)$, then $x_1 = x_2$. The straight line function, $f(x) = mx + b$, is an example of functions which are described as having a one-to-one correspondence.[179] Furthermore, as the function maps all the real numbers into all the real numbers, it is possible to define an inverse function $f^{-1}(x)$ mapping the dependent variable back to the independent variable. In our case, the function is easily inverted, namely $x = (y - b)/m$, so $f^{-1}(x) = (x - b)/m$. We can form the composite function $f^{-1}(f(x))$ considering $f(x)$ to be the argument of the inverse function f^{-1}. Therefore $f^{-1}(f(x)) = f^{-1}(mx +b)=((mx +b) - b)/m = x$. All functions $f(x)$ forming a one-to-one correspondence have an inverse function.[lxxx]

In addition to the straight line function, we have just had occasion to look at the conics which provide some contrasting characteristics. First let's look at the ellipse defined by $x^2 / a^2 + y^2 / b^2 = 1$. In this example, if we take y as the dependent variable, the functional relation is not explicit as in $y = mx +b$. Such a relation is called an implicit function. Further, looking at the graph of the ellipse, the following observations are clear: the domain of the function is limited to the interval, $-a \leqq x \leqq a$, the range of the function is limited to $-b \leqq x \leqq b$, the function is not single-valued, and an inverse function cannot be formed. However, by solving explicitly for the dependent variable, and limiting the domain and range appropriately, single-valued functions can be defined along with their associated inverse functions. The following function $y = f(x) = (b/a)\sqrt{a^2 - x^2}$ forms a one-to-one correspondence over the domain $0 \leqq x \leqq a$ and the range $0 \leqq y \leqq b$ and an inverse function may be defined. Other functions can similarly be defined to cover the entire ellipse.

Unlike the ellipse, the standard form for the parabola allows the functional dependence to be explicit: $y = f(x) = x^2/4p$. However, the function also does not form a one-to-one correspondence since for

---

lxxx Functions are commonly described by a number of different names depending on their characteristics. Another name for a one-to-one correspondence is a bijective function. An injective function is one for which each element of the domain is also mapped uniquely to an element of its range, but not necessarily covering the whole codomain in contrast to a bijective function. Thus an injective function may not have an inverse function. In a surjective function, the entire codomain is mapped, but each member is not necessarily mapped from a single member of the domain. Therefore, a surjective function may also not have an inverse. Examples of these various types of functions are given in Appendix G. (Note that the inverse function f^{-1} is not the reciprocal of f.)

example $f(2) = f(-2) = 1/p$. Forming two functions with domains $x <$ 0 and $x \geqq 0$ allows inverse functions to be defined.

Similar observations as those for ellipses may be made for hyperbolas in the standard form, $x^2/ a^2 - y^2 / b^2 = 1$. However, if we take the hyperbola, $x^2 / 2 - y^2 / 2 = 1$, and rotate clockwise the coordinate system by 45°, a new issue of importance to functions becomes somewhat more apparent. The equation for the rotated hyperbola takes the simple form, $x'y' = 1$. (The transformation of coordinates is discussed in Chapter 7.) The rotated hyperbola is shown in the figue below.

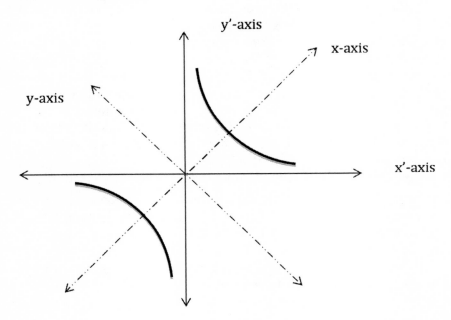

As transformed, the function associated with the hyperbola is quite simple, $y' = f(x') = 1/x'$. The domain of the function covers all of the real numbers except $x' = 0$, since there is no real number equal to 1/0. We say that the function has a discontinuity at $x' = 0$, or it is discontinuous at $x' = 0$. Notice that for $x' > 0$ or $x' < 0$, the function is quite ordinary. As x' increases beyond 0, the function is positive, continually decreases, and approaches 0. However it does not attain 0 for any finite value of x'. We say that the function asymptotically approaches 0 for large x'. A similar description of the function can be made for the portion of the function for which $x' < 0$. In this case the function is negative and increasing as x' decreases (x' becomes more negative). Intuitively, we think of a function representing a curve in two dimensions as continuous, if we can draw it without lifting our pencil off the paper, In this view, the two branches of the hyperbola separated at x' = 0 are continuous. To give a precise definition of continuity, however, we will need to define the idea of a limit. As discussed in the history outline, this was one of the great contributions of Cauchy, which would lead to a precise understanding of infinite sequences and series and in the calculus, derivatives and integrals. Before we define limit mathematically, it will be useful to look at the single-valued function, the absolute value.

The absolute value of x, denoted symbolically as |x| has the following definition:

$$|x| = \begin{cases} -x, & x < 0 \\ x, & x \geq 0 \end{cases}$$

The graph of f(x) = |x| is shown below:

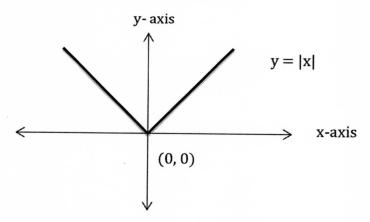

From the definition and figure, |3| = 3 and |−3| = 3. Thus, for any x, ±x ≦ |x|.

The absolute value is useful for designating symmetric intervals about a given number. For example If we want to designate all numbers, x, in the range of 3 ± 7, then this is easily expressed as, |x−3| ≦ 7.

For x ≧ 3, |x − 3| = x − 3 ≦ 7 or x ≦ 10.

For x < 3, |x − 3| = − (x − 3) = 3 − x ≦ 7 or x ≧ −4.

From the definition of absolute value, a frequently used relation can be proved called the Triangle Inequality. Several steps in the proof below follow from the definition of absolute value.

Triangle Inequality:[180] If x and y are real numbers then, $|x - z| \leqq |x - y| + |y - z|$

Proof:
For a and b real numbers,

$\pm a \leqq |a|, \pm b \leqq |b|$ Definition of absolute value
$\pm(a + b) \leqq |a| + |b|$ Properties of real numbers

Considering the cases for the various magnitudes and signs of a and b, then either $(a + b) = |a + b|$ or $-(a+b) = |a+b|$, therefore,

$|a + b| \leqq |a| + |b|$
Let: $x - y = a, y - z = b$
$|x - y + y - z| = |x - z| \leqq |x - y| + |y - z|$ Equivalence relation
                        Q.E.D.

Descriptions of intervals, such as $|x - c| \leqq d$, will allow us to concisely define a region around the point c where we want to explore the behavior of $f(x)$.

5.2.2   Limits and continuity

The concepts of a limit and a continuous function were made precise by Cauchy in response to the need to understand the process of determining the derivative and integral of a function in the calculus of Newton and Leibniz. However, the seeds for Cauchy's idea of limit were very ancient. Archimedes' estimate of the numerical value of π as the ratio of the circumference of a circle to its diameter implied π as a limit of his estimation technique. Archimedes estimated π from the sequence of perimeters of circumscribed and inscribed polygons with an increasing numbers of sides (Section 3.3.2). This technique depends on the estimate for the circumference of the circle becoming increasingly accurate as n increases.

Another example that we have encountered of a limit is the process by which we determined the sum of a repeating sequence of decimal numbers to represent a rational number. In this case, like Archimedes, we formed a sequence of estimates, $S_1, S_2, S_3, \ldots S_n$. We found that we could represent a rational number as the limit of the sequence of non-terminating, repeating decimals. The rational number could be expressed as a decimal number to any accuracy we wished by simply taking enough terms in the decimal. This should remind you of our similar experience with the estimate for the irrational number $\sqrt{2}$ as a non-repeating, non-terminating decimal number.

We shall make these ideas for the limit of sequences precise in Section 6.2. Here, our goal is to describe the limit process for a function of a single variable $f(x)$ as a means of determining whether a function is continuous. However, limits of sequences and functions are related in that the limit process for a function $f(x)$ or the sequence S_n will involve determining if each remains arbitrarily close to a given value (called the limit) for any small region about x in the case of a function or for all S_n beyond any selected n. In both cases, this process can only be logically rigorous because there are no holes in the real number line. From this perspective, a different way of describing the real numbers, but equivalent to Dedekind cuts, is to define the real numbers through limits of sequences (called Cauchy sequences) of rational numbers. We can look at the variation of a function as it approaches its limit as a sequence. At this point, I mention this simply so that you will be aware that the subject of limits for functions and sequences are not unrelated.

Given our intuitive notion of a continuous function as one we can plot without picking up our pencil, it makes sense to require that in order for a function to be continuous, it must change very little if the independent variable changes very little. This insight is given meaning by Cauchy's qualitative conditions for a limit to exist (Section 2.5.1):

> *"When the successive values attributed to a variable approach indefinitely a fixed value so as to end by differing from it by as little as one wishes, this last is called the limit of all others."*

Now, how do we express this mathematically? Cauchy's concept (made precise by Weierstrass) for the limit of $f(x)$ as x approaches c requires that the difference between $f(x)$ and the limit L must be "as little as one wishes" for some region of x around c. In other words, if we choose the difference one wishes to be ε, then, $|f(x) - L| < \varepsilon$ for some $|x - c| < \delta$, no matter how small we choose ε to be. The next figure shows the relationship between c, L, δ and ε.

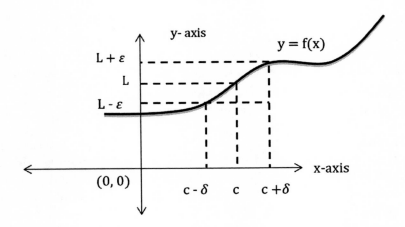

With this background, a formal definition of the limit of the function f(x) as x approaches c is given below.

Definition, Limit of a function: For a function of the real numbers f (x) with domain, $a < x < b$, and for c within the domain, the limit of f(x) as x approaches c is L ($\lim_{x \to c} f(x) = L$) if for every $\varepsilon > 0$, there exists a $\delta > 0$ such that $|f(x) - L| < \varepsilon$, whenever $|x - c| < \delta$.

Let us try this definition for a function that appears to be discontinuous at x = 1, f(x) = $(x^2 - 3x + 2) / (x - 1)$. The function is clearly not defined at x = 1. In fact, evaluating f(x) at x = 1 results in 0/0 which is meaningless. However, since the limit process does not require us to set x = 1, we can perform the algebraic operations in the usual way. Notice that everywhere but x = 1, f(x) may be written as,(x − 2) (x − 1)/(x − 1) = x − 2. At x = 1, f(x) looks like it should have a limit of −1. Let us see if this is consistent with the definition of a limit. We require in a region around x = 1 and excluding x= 1 that:

$|(x^2 - 3x + 2) / (x - 1) - (-1)| < \varepsilon$, for $|x - 1| < \delta$. We simplify the relationship for ε as

$|((x^2 - 3x + 2) + (x - 1) \cdot 1)/ (x - 1)| = |(x^2 - 2x + 1)/(x - 1)| = |(x-1) \cdot (x - 1)/ (x - 1)|.$

Therefore, $|x - 1)| < \varepsilon$.

This is exactly the requirement for δ. So for any ε we choose, if $\delta = \varepsilon$, the requirements for the limit to be − 1 at x = 1 are met, and $\lim_{x \to 1}$

$(x^2 + 3x + 2)/(x - 1) = -1$. The discontinuity at x =1 is called a removable discontinuity. To create a continuous function, we therefore remove the discontinuity at $x = 1$, by redefining f(x) as,

$$F(x) = \begin{cases} (x^2 + 3x + 2)/(x-1), x < 1 \text{ or } x > 1 \\ -1, \ x = 1 \end{cases}$$

I emphasize that in proving the existence of the limit, it was not necessary to substitute x =1 into the function $f(x) = (x^2 + 3x + 2)/(x-1)$. This will turn out to be vital when we define the concept of a derivative in Chapter 8.

Now the requirements can be given for a function, f(x) to be continuous at a point c. Clearly the function must be defined at c, and in order to apply the limit principle, it must be defined in some interval containing c such as a < c < b. The definition of limit assures us that the function follows a connected path. Therefore it is required that $\lim_{x \to c} f(x) = f(c)$. If f(x) is continuous at every point in the interval a < x < c, then the function is said to be continuous in that interval. These points are summarized in the following definition.

Definition, Continuity of a function: A function, f(x) defined over an interval a < c < b is continuous at a point c if $\lim_{x \to c} f(x) = f(c)$. The function is continuous over the interval if it is continuous at every point in the interval.

If $\lim_{x \to c} f(x)$ does not exist, then the function is said to have a discontinuity at x = c. If $\lim_{x \to c} f(x)$ exists, but $\lim_{x \to c} f(x) \neq f(c)$, or f(c) is undefined, then, as we have seen, the function has a removable discontinuity at x = c. Different right and left limits may also be defined as x approaches c from the left, $x \to c^-$ and right, $x \to c^+$, respectively. In those cases in which the function is continuous at x = c, $\lim_{x \to c-} f(x) = \lim_{x \to c+} f(x) = f(c)$. As an example of a discontinuity, the following function has a right limit that does not equal the left limit.

$$f(x) = \begin{cases} x^2 \text{ for } x < 2 \\ x \text{ for } x \geq 2 \end{cases}$$

In this case, $\lim_{x \to 2+} f(x) = 2$, and $\lim_{x \to 2-} f(x) = 4$, so there is a jump discontinuity at x =2.

With these ideas in mind, let us look again at the hyperbola in the form $y = f(x) = 1/x$. The function is defined everywhere except at $x = 0$. What can we say about the limit as x approaches 0^+.

Suppose that $\lim_{x \to 0+} 1/x = L$ and we choose $1/x - L = \varepsilon$ for $x = \delta$. Then, $1/\delta = L + \varepsilon$ or $\delta = 1/(L + \varepsilon)$. If $x < \delta$, then $1/x - L > \varepsilon$. No matter how great L, a region $x < \delta$ cannot exist and $1/x$ does not have a limit. More simply, for any L, $1/x > L$, if $0 < x < 1/L$. The function $1/x$ is unbounded as x approaches 0 from the right. Symbolically this is expressed as

$$\lim_{x \to 0+} 1/x = \infty.$$

Similar observations apply for the left limit of $1/x$ as x approaches zero. In this case for negative numbers, x and $- L$, $1/x < - L$ if $- 1/L < x < 0$, or

$$\lim_{x \to 0-} 1/x = -\infty.$$

For $f(x) = 1/x$ the left and right limits at $x = 0$ are different. However, there are functions such as $1/x^2$ or $-(1/x^4)$ which are unbounded but have the same left and right limits: $\lim_{x \to 0} 1/x^2 = \infty$ and $\lim_{x \to 0} -1/x^4 = -\infty$.

The determination of limits is greatly aided by laws for limits which can be proved from the fundamental definition. These laws which should seem quite plausible are listed below without proof (an approach to proving the laws is given by Meserve[181]):

Laws of Limits: If $\lim_{x \to c} f(x)$ and $\lim_{x \to c} g(x)$ exist and k is a constant then:

1. $\lim_{x \to c}(f(x) \pm g(x)) = \lim_{x \to c}f(x) \pm \lim_{x \to c}g(x)$
2. $\lim_{x \to c} k \cdot f(x) = k \cdot \lim_{x \to c}f(x)$
3. $\lim_{x \to c} f(x) \cdot g(x) = \lim_{x \to c} f(x) \cdot \lim_{x \to c} g(x)$
4. $\lim_{x \to c} f(x)/g(x) = \lim_{x \to c}f(x)/\lim_{x \to c}g(x)$ for $g(c) \neq 0$.

Using these laws, it can be proved that all polynomials, and ratios of rational polynomials, $f(x)/ g(x)$, called rational polynomials, are continuous except at $g(x) = 0$.

With this understanding of continuity, we will now look at finding the solutions of polynomials, a central historical objective of mathematics that was clarified through the identification of polynomials as curves and a more precise understanding of continuity.

5.3   Getting to the root of the problem; the Fundamental Theorem of Algebra

From the time of the Babylonians, the search for methods for determining solutions to equations has been one of the activities advancing mathematics. As mentioned in the history outline, Babylonians knew methods to solve what we call linear and quadratic equations, but the absence of an effective symbolic notation made it virtually impossible to perceive general principles of equations. The solutions of the equations are traditionally called roots, from Islamic custom going back to the ninth century (as in roots of plants, from which perhaps the equations grow)[182] or are called zeroes as values for which the polynomial equals zero. The first major advancement in solving polynomial equations beyond the knowledge of ancient civilizations came with the development of general methods for solving cubic and quartic equations (polynomials of the third and fourth power) in the sixteenth century. However, the discovery of these solutions owed more to heroic and ingenious efforts rather than the discovery of underlying principles. Indeed with the solution to quartic equations came a three hundred year search for general solutions of polynomials of higher powers. In 1824 Niels Henrik Abel (1802-1829) showed that general solutions were impossible for polynomials of degree greater than four.[183] Coming in the same time period as the development of non-Euclidean geometry, the experience is reminiscent of the end of the search for a proof of the Parallel Postulate.

The equations and solutions for the linear, quadratic, and cubic equations with constant coefficients are shown below. The leading coefficient is taken as 1 for the linear and quadratic equations, assuming that if otherwise we have divided the polynomial by the leading coefficient. The general cubic equation $aX^3 + bX^2 + cX + d = 0$ with a, b, c, and d real constants can be reduced to the form given below by letting $X = x - b/(3a)$. A solution to the cubic equation is known as Cardan's formula.[184] The method for solving quartic equations was discovered by Ludovico Ferrari (1522-1565); Ferrari's approach to solving the quartic is given by Merzbach and Boyer.[185]

Equation: **Solution:**

Linear: $x + c = 0$ $x = -c$

Quadratic: $x^2 + ax + b = 0$ $x = (-a \pm \sqrt{a^2 - 4b})/2$

Cubic: $x^3 + p\,x + q = 0$
$$x = \sqrt[3]{-\frac{q}{2} + \sqrt{\frac{q^2}{4} + \frac{p^3}{27}}} + \sqrt[3]{-\frac{q}{2} - \sqrt{\frac{q^2}{4} + \frac{p^3}{27}}}$$

The three equations and their solutions illustrate some of the characteristics of the solutions of polynomials with real coefficients. In the case of the linear and quadratic equations, the number of solutions is clearly the same as the highest power of the equation. This is also true for the cubic equation as three solutions result from taking the cube root.[lxxxi] However, in order to see this we will need to expand our view beyond the real number system and interpret taking the cube root within the system of complex numbers. This will be more convenient to explain in the next chapter after we show that $e^{i\theta} = \cos(\theta) + i\sin(\theta)$ and introduce another method to express complex numbers. That complex numbers are useful for the solution of the cubic equation, should not be surprising as we have already encountered them in solutions for the quadratic equation. For the quadratic equation above, if the discriminant, $D_2 = a^2 - 4b < 0$, then there are two complex solutions, as described in Section 3.6. If one of the complex solutions is of the form $r + si$, then, as apparent from the quadratic solutions, the other solution is its complex conjugate, $r - s\,i$, For $D_2 \geqq 0$, there are two real solutions with the two solutions being equal (called a multiple root) if $D_2 = 0$.[lxxxii]

Because of the presence of a square root, the solution of the cubic equation, also involves a discriminant, $D_3 = \dfrac{q^2}{4} + \dfrac{p^3}{27}$. If $D_3 > 0$, there is one real and two conjugate roots; if $D_3 = 0$, there are three real roots, of which at least two are equal; and if $D_3 < 0$, there are three distinct real roots.[186] The case in which $D_3 < 0$, is somewhat ironic in that Cardan found that to get to the solutions of the cubic equation, it was necessary to employ the square roots of negative numbers even though he did not believe in their existence as actual numbers.

The insight that a polynomial of degree n has n roots was understood although not proved by Albert Girard (1595-1632).[187] His

---

lxxxi The cube root of x is denoted in Cardan's formula as: $\sqrt[3]{x} = x^{1/3}$. Recall that in general, $\sqrt[q]{x^p} = x^{p/q}$.

lxxxii To see the relationship for $D_2 = 0$ between the quadratic equation and the two equal solutions, $x = -a/2$, note that for $a^2 - 4b = 0$, $b = a^2/4$. The quadratic equation becomes: $x^2 + a\,x + b = x^2 + a\,x + a^2/4 = (x + a/2)^2 = 0$.

work advanced beyond Viète's results for roots of equations since he included negative and imaginary numbers in his analysis. The insight of Girard may be expressed in the following theorem.

Theorem of Polynomial Roots: If $f(x)$ is a polynomial of degree $n > 0$ with complex coefficients, then it has n complex roots (including multiple roots).

This theorem can be proved using the following theorem first proved by Gauss.

Fundamental Theorem of Algebra: Every polynomial, $f(x)$ of degree $n > 0$ with complex coefficients has at least one root.

The Fundamental Theorem of Algebra has been proved a variety of ways; however, a particularly elegant result that will be given at the end of this section is based upon complex variable theory. For the moment, let us concentrate on the proof that the existence of one root for a polynomial of degree n requires that there be a total of n roots. Let us suppose that the polynomial of degree n is $p_1(x) = a_n x^n + a_{n-1} x^{n-1} + \ldots + a_1 x + a_0 = 0$. If the single root required by the Fundamental Theorem of Algebra is α_1, then using the division algorithm, there is a polynomial $p_2(x)$ such that $p_1(x) = (x - \alpha_1) \cdot p_2(x)$, or $p_2(x) = p_1(x) / (x - \alpha_1)$.

The division algorithm for polynomials works in a manner similar to that for the natural numbers. For example, because 1 is a root of $x^3 - 2x^2 - x + 2$, $(x - 1)$ is a divisor without a remainder:

$$
\begin{array}{r}
x^2 - x - 2 \\
x-1 \overline{)\, x^3 - 2x^2 - x + 2} \\
\underline{x^3 - x^2} \\
-x^2 - x \\
\underline{-x^2 + x} \\
-2x + 2 \\
\underline{-2x + 2}
\end{array}
$$

Therefore, $x^3 - 2x^2 - x + 2 = (x - 1) \cdot (x^2 - x + 2)$ or $(x^3 - 2x^2 - x + 2)/(x - 1) = (x^2 - x - 2)$. Dividing $x^3 - 2x^2 - x + 2$ by $(x - 1)$ results in the degree of the resulting polynomial being lowered from 3 to 2. In the general case of a polynomial of degree n, dividing by $(x - \alpha_1)$ reduces $p_1(x)$ to the polynomial $p_2(x)$ of degree $n - 1$. Now $p_2(x)$ is also a polynomial, so the Fundamental Theorem of Algebra requires that $p_2(x)$ also have at least one root, α_2. Therefore, $p_2(x) = (x - \alpha_2) \cdot$ $p_3(x)$ with $p_3(x)$ of degree $n - 2$. We continue in this manner until we have reduced the final polynomial, $p_n(x)$ to $(x - \alpha_n)$ with α_n being the nth and final root. The various terms $(x - \alpha_i)$ where α_i represents any of the roots, are known as factors of $p(x)$.

The knowledge that there are n roots to a polynomial of degree n is the basis for considerable understanding of the relationship between the roots and the coefficients of the various powers of the polynomial. Girard was aware that for a polynomial with a leading coefficient of unity that the coefficient of the $n - 1$ power is the negative of the sum of the roots; the coefficient of the $n - 2$ power is the positive sum of all the combinations of the products of two roots followed by the coefficient of the $n - 3$ power being the negative of all combinations of the product of three roots, and so on until the final term, a constant was the product of $(-1)^n$ and all the roots. This is illustrated below for polynomials up to the fourth degree with roots, $\alpha_1, \alpha_2, \alpha_3,$ and α_4:

$$(x - \alpha_1) = 0$$

$$(x - \alpha_2) \cdot (x - \alpha_1) = x^2 - (\alpha_1 + \alpha_2) x + \alpha_1 \cdot \alpha_2 = 0$$

$$(x - \alpha_3) \cdot (x^2 - (\alpha_1 + \alpha_2) x + \alpha_1 \cdot \alpha_2) = x^3 - (\alpha_1 + \alpha_2 + \alpha_3) x^2 + (\alpha_1 \cdot \alpha_2 + \alpha_1 \cdot \alpha_3 + \alpha_2 \cdot \alpha_3)x - \alpha_1 . \alpha_2 . \alpha_3 = 0.$$

$$(x - \alpha_4) \cdot (x^3 - (\alpha_1 + \alpha_2 + \alpha_3) x^2 + (\alpha_1 \cdot \alpha_2 + \alpha_1 \cdot \alpha_3 + \alpha_2 \cdot \alpha_3)x - \alpha_1 \cdot \alpha_2 \cdot \alpha_3) =$$
$$x^4 - (\alpha_1 + \alpha_2 + \alpha_3 + \alpha_4)x^3 + (\alpha_1 \cdot \alpha_2 + \alpha_1 \cdot \alpha_3 + \alpha_1 \cdot \alpha_4 + \alpha_2 \cdot \alpha_3 + \alpha_2 \cdot \alpha_4 + \alpha_3 \cdot \alpha_4)x^2$$
$$- (\alpha_1 \cdot \alpha_2 \cdot \alpha_3 + \alpha_1 \cdot \alpha_2 \cdot \alpha_4 + \alpha_1 \cdot \alpha_3 \cdot \alpha_4 + \alpha_2 \cdot \alpha_3 \cdot \alpha_4)x + \alpha_1 \cdot \alpha_2 \cdot \alpha_3 \cdot \alpha_4.$$

In the case of polynomial in which all the coefficients are real, it may be proved, using a similar approach, that if one of the roots is complex then its complex conjugate is also a root.[188]

While insight into the roots of polynomials may be gained from the above considerations, undoubtedly the quickest route to understanding the behavior of any function of the real numbers of a single variable is to be gained by interpreting the function as the curve $y = f(x)$ and plotting it. Below in the leftmost graph, a cubic, $p(x)$ is plotted which crosses the x-axis at three points, therefore we know that all the roots are real. The cubic is of the form, $(x - \alpha_2) \cdot (x - \alpha_2)$ $\cdot (x - \alpha_3) = 0$. A cubic, $q(x)$, is also shown in which there are two real roots, one of which, β_2 is a multiple root. The third plot below shows a cubic, r(x) with a single real root, γ, the other two roots being complex conjugates, $a + bi$ and $a - bi$. From graphical estimates of the points and the relations of the coefficients of a polynomial, it is sometimes possible to factor polynomials exactly.

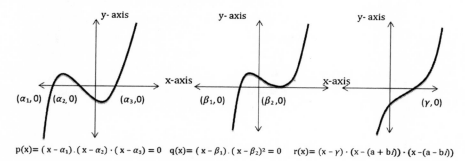

$p(x)= (x - \alpha_1).(x - \alpha_2) \cdot (x - \alpha_3) = 0$ $q(x)= (x - \beta_1).(x - \beta_2)^2 = 0$ $r(x)= (x - \gamma) \cdot (x - (a + bi)) \cdot (x - (a - bi))$

An additional insight into polynomials comes from the knowledge that the curves are continuous. As a consequence of this condition along with the property of the real numbers being complete, the theorem below follows:

Intermediate Value Theorem: If $f(x)$ is a continuous function of the real numbers with $f(a) < f(b)$ [or $f(a) > f(b)$], and $a < b$, then there exists c with $a < c < b$ such that $f(a) < f(c) < f(b)$ [or $f(a) > f(c) > f(b)$].

The Intermediate Value Theorem gives immediate information on all polynomials $p(x)$ of degree n if n is an odd number. For sufficiently large positive x, $p(x) > 0$; while for sufficiently negative x, $p(x) < 0$. This is because the term with x^n will dominate all other terms for sufficiently positive or negative x. Since for some number $a < 0$, $p(a) < 0$ and for $b > 0$, $p(b) > 0$, by the Intermediate Value Theorem, there is a value c with $a < c < b$, where $p(c) = 0$. Thus, all polynomials of degree n with n odd have at least one real root.

This completes our introduction to the subject known as the theory of equations. The promised proof of the Fundamental Theorem of Algebra will now be given using a result from complex variable theory known as Liouville's Theorem. It is beyond the scope of this book to prove this theorem which comes from the properties of complex variables; however, its use leads to a simple proof of the Fundamental Theorem of Algebra and is an example of the power that frequently comes when one mathematical system is embedded within another one. New interpretations and properties may appear that are not apparent in the embedded system. In our case it is the real numbers within the complex numbers. As noted by Churchill, the proof by purely algebraic methods is otherwise quite difficult.[lxxxiii]

To discuss Liouville's Theorem and the proof of the Fundamental Theorem of Algebra, the complex variable z must be introduced. The variable z is defined as the ordered pair of real numbers (x, y) or alternatively as we have shown $z = x + yi$ (see Section 3.6). The properties of z follow from those of the complex numbers (x, y) with x and y real numbers. For example,

$$z_1 + z_2 = (x_1, y_1) + (x_2, y_2) = (x_1 + x_2, y_1 + y_2);$$
$$z_1 \cdot z_2 = (x_1, y_1) \cdot (x_2, y_2) = (x_1 x_2 - y_1 y_2, y_1 x_2 - x_1 y_2)$$

The magnitude or modulus of z is defined as: $|z| = \sqrt{x^2 + y^2}$.

If we imagine the x and y axes forming the complex plane, then the function F(z) defines a surface above the plane as illustrated in the next figure.

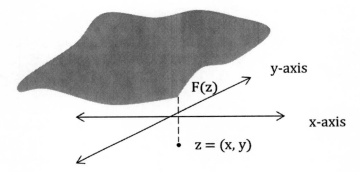

Liouville's Theorem characterizes functions of the complex variable z, known as entire functions. An entire function is one in which the surface formed by the function F(z) has a tangent defined at every point of the surface. If F(z) is a polynomial then it can be shown that F(z) is an entire function. With this background, Liouville's Theorem may now be stated.

---

lxxxiii Proof of Liouville's Theorem and the Fundamental Theorem of Algebra are given in Churchill, R., V., *Complex Variables and Applications*, [Math References 7], p. 123-126.

Liouville's Theorem: If $F(z)$ is an entire function and $|F(z)|$ is bounded for all values of z in the complex plane, then $F(z)$ is a constant.

We wish to use this to prove that the polynomial $P(z)$ forms an equation that has least one root, that is $P(z) = a_n z^n + a_{n-1} z^{n-1} + a_{n-2} z^{n-2} + \ldots + a_2 z^2 + a_1 z + a_0 = 0$. We proceed using a proof by contradiction. Let us assume that $P(z) \neq 0$. Then the function, $F(z) = 1 / P(z)$ is defined everywhere and is an entire function. Now $\lim_{z \to \infty} |F(z)| = 0$ as $F(z) = 1/(a_n z^n + a_{n-1} z^{n-1} + a_{n-2} z^{n-2} + \ldots + a_2 z^2 + a_1 z + a_0)$. Furthermore, by the assumption that $P(z) \neq 0$, $F(z)$ is finite for all z. Thus, $F(z)$ is bounded for all z (assumes some maximum value for finite z and equals 0 as $z \to \infty$). Therefore, by Liouville's Theorem $F(z)$ must be constant, but clearly, $F(z)$ is not a constant, The hypothesis that $P(z) \neq 0$ must be untrue, and therefore $P(z) = 0$ for at least one z.

Chapter 6

ONE DARN THING AFTER ANOTHER; INFINITE SEQUENCES AND THE REAL NUMBERS

"Whatever the common Analysis performs by Means of Equations of a finite Number of Terms (provided this can be done) this can always perform the same by Means of Infinite Equations so that I have not made any question of giving this the name of Analysis likewise. For the reasonings in this are no less certain than in the other, nor the equations less exact . . . ."—Isaac Newton[lxxxiv]

"The divergent series are the invention of the devil, and it is a shame to base on them any demonstration whatever. By using them one may draw any conclusion he pleases . . . ."—Niels Henrick Abel[lxxxv]

6.1   Introduction; sequences and series revisited

In the history outline and in the chapters that have followed, we have explored a number of topics that have been major themes in the development of mathematics. One that we only touched on informally, however, has been that of sequences and series. The concepts of sequences and series were of particular importance when we discussed in Chapter 2 the representation of rational numbers as decimals and the approximation of the irrational number $\sqrt{2}$. This led to the conclusion that the irrationals were non-repeating, non-terminating decimals. In approximating $\sqrt{2}$, we formed an infinite sequence $\{a_n\}$ with $a_{n+1} > a_n$ and $a_n^2 < 2$. The first four terms of sequence were: $\{1.\ 1.4,\ 1.41,\ 1.414 \ldots\}$ Because of the least upper bound property of the real numbers, we said that in the limit as n

---

lxxxiv From a paper of Newton's in 1699, cited in Kline's discussion of the early uncertainties surrounding infinite series; Kline, pp. 141-142.
lxxxv From a letter in 1826 indicating the evolution from a naïve view of infinite sequences and series, cited in Kline, p. 170.

becomes large, the sequence approaches $\sqrt{2}$ or in symbolism of the previous section, $\lim_{n \to \infty} a_n = \sqrt{2}$.

The Babylonians were also able to approximate irrational numbers like $\sqrt{2}$ in their sexagesimal system, although they did not have the concept of taking a sequence to a limit. The Babylonian procedure to estimate $\sqrt{2}$ may be expressed in modern notation through a definition of the terms of the sequence $\{a_n\}$:[189]

$$a_{n+1} = (a_n + 2/a_n)/2$$

Taking $a_1 = 2$, then $a_2 = (2 + 2/2)/2 = 1.5$. Continuing, we get the following four terms of the sequence: $\{2, 1.5, 1.4166\ldots, 1.4142\ldots\}$. We will see that this sequence may be shown to approach $\sqrt{2}$ as a limit for any initial guess greater than zero. This raises the general questions, what do we precisely mean by the limit of a sequence, and how do we know whether a sequence converges to a limit.

A similar discussion accompanied the description of the decimal representation of rational numbers. Here, I will summarize the results of that discussion with a more explicit reference to sequences. The rational number $3/11$ was expressed as the non-terminating, but repeating decimal, $0.2727272727\ldots$ This repeating decimal may be constructed to any finite number of terms from the sequence $\{a_n\}$ $= \{0.27, 0.0027, 0.000027, \ldots\}$ by summing n terms with $a_n = 0.27 \cdot 0.01^{(n-1)}$. The resulting finite sums $S_n = 0.27 + 0.0027 + 0.000027 + \ldots + 0.27 \cdot 0.01^{(n-1)}$ form another sequence $\{S_n\}$ known as a series in this case, $\{0.27, 0.2727, 0.272727, \ldots\}$. In general, the series formed from the sequence $\{a_n\}$ is the sequence of partial sums $\{S_n\}$ with $S_n = a_1 + a_2 + a_3 + \ldots + a_n$. A series is known as a geometric series when the ratio $r = \dfrac{a_{n+1}}{a_n}$ of the terms of the sequence forming the series is a constant. In the case of the decimal representation of $3/11$, $r = 0.01$. The geometric nature of the series may be made explicit by expressing the nth partial sum, S_n, as:

$$S_n = 0.27(1 + 10^{-2} + (10^{-2})^2 + (10^{-2})^3 + \ldots + (10^{-2})^{n-1}).$$

In Section 2.5.2, we generalized this result by letting c be the common multiplier of the series and r, the ratio of successive terms in the sum. The general expression for the partial sum was shown to be:

$$S_n = c (1 + r + r^2 + r^3 + \ldots + r^{n-1}) = c(1 - r^n)/(1-r)$$

A method for determining the partial sums of a geometric series was known in the ancient Egyptian civilization as indicated in the Rhind papyrus of about 1650 BC.[190] Couched in geometric form, the formula for partial sums is expressed by Euclid in his Proposition 35 of Book IX.[191] But just as in the case of the Babylonians, the concept of a limit and convergent series would remain unknown to them.

As in the case of the sequence approximating the irrational number $\sqrt{2}$, we ask, what are the general conditions for a geometric series to represent a definite result as n becomes indefinitely large, that is converge to a limit? In the case of the geometric series, I said that,

for $-1 < r < 1$, $\lim_{n\to\infty} r^n = 0$. Therefore in this range of r,

$$S = c(1 + r + r^2 + r^3 + \ldots) = \lim_{n\to\infty} S_n = c/1-r.$$

Our task will be to more generally define the concept of a limit for sequences and series and in the process to prove this specific result.

Another way to look at the infinite geometric series is to look at r as a variable of the function, $S(r) = c/(1 - r)$ and ask what are the necessary conditions for which $S(r) = c/(1 - r) = c (1 + r + r^2 + r^3 + \ldots)$. Newton and later mathematicians such as Euler would make extensive use of the expression of functions as infinite series to explore relations between functions and verify the results of the new mathematical approaches provided by the calculus. They did not have the advantage of the concept of limit and along with much progress, much confusion resulted over a period of more than a hundred years.

As a way of emphasizing the importance of the concept of the limit of a sequence or series and illustrating possible pitfalls, it is instructive to note the following examples encountered by mathematicians in the absence of the limit concept. [192]

Assume $S(r) = c/1-r = c (1 + r + r^2 + r^3 + \ldots)$ and let $r = -1$ and $c = 1$: In the case of the function $S(r) = c/1-r$, the result is quite ordinary in that $S(-1) = \dfrac{1}{\left(1-(-1)\right)} = 1/2$. However, the relation of the infinite series to this result seems quite mysterious with $S(-1) = 1 + (-1) + (-1)^2 + (-1)^3 + (-1)^4 + \ldots = 1 - 1 + 1 - 1 + 1 - 1 + \ldots$

This seemed to imply before there was an understanding of the concept of limits that $1/2 = 1 - 1 + 1 - 1 + 1 - 1 + \ldots$

Saccheri's student Guido Grandi (1671-1742) argued that the infinite series was indeed equal to 1/2. However, by grouping terms as S(−1) = (1−1) + (1−1) + (1−1) + . . . , we seem to obtain S(−1) = 0.[193] Leibniz interpreted the series by looking at the sequence of partial sums, {1, 1 − 1, 1 − 1 + 1, 1 −1 + 1 −1 . . .} = {1, 0, 1, 0 . . .}. He reasoned that Grandi's result was correct in that on average the sum was 1/2. Perhaps even more bizarrely, arguments by Euler with S(2) led to considering −1 = 1 + 2 + 4 + 8 + ... Euler even interpreted this to mean that negative numbers were larger than infinity.[194]

Despite the obvious need for some guiding principles to lead the mathematicians of the day out of such chaos, great advances continued to be made using infinite sequences and series even though mathematicians like Euler moved forward somewhat on faith and ingenuity. Fortunately, we are in a good position to give a precise mathematical description of sequences and their limits and avoid paradoxes such as those mentioned above.

6.2.   Limits of sequences—some add up, others don't

As we have seen in several examples, an infinite sequence is just an ordered infinite collection, for example the even numbers {2, 4, 6 . . .}. To summarize from the previous section, a short hand for a sequence is for example, $\{a_n\}$ = {2n} with n understood to be the sequence of natural numbers, {1, 2, 3 . . .}. If a sequence of partial sums is formed from the sequence, then it is called a series. The infinite series formed from the sequence $\{a_n\}$ would be $\{S_n\}$ = {a_1, a_1 + a_2, a_1 + a_2 + a_3 . . .} with n indefinitely large. Let us without further ado look at the definition of the limit of a sequence that comes from the approach inspired by concepts of Cauchy with the rigorous details supplied by Weierstrass. You will notice the close relation between what we will call the standard limit of a sequence (to distinguish it from what is known as a Cauchy sequence) and the definition for the limit of a function.

Definition of the Standard Limit of a Sequence: A sequence $\{a_n\}$ has a limit, L, ($\lim_{n \to \infty} a_n = L$) if for any number ε, there exists a number N such that for all n > N, $|a_n - L| < \varepsilon$.

As in the discussion of the meaning of limits for functions, Cauchy's qualitative description[lxxxvi] is made precise through identification of ε with the quantity which is "as little as one wishes," and the "successive values" with all n > N.

Using the definition of limit of a sequence, let us now look at some examples that should clarify the strange results from the previous section.

Example 1: $\{a_n\} = \{(-1)^{n-1}\} = \{1, -1, 1, -1 \ldots\}$

For any L that might be a limit, it is easy to choose an ε such that no N exists which satisfies the condition that for all n > N, $|a_n - L| < \varepsilon$. This is because as n increases, $|a_n - L|$ will oscillate from $|1 - L|$ to $|-1 - L|$ no matter what N we choose. Let us look at 1/2 as a possible limit. In this case for any n, $|a_n - 1/2| = 1/2$ or 3/2. Thus we can easily choose an ε, say $\varepsilon = 1/4$, for which our definition fails. If we choose 0 as our limit, then since $|a_n - 0| = 1$ for all n, the requirements for a limit fail for any $\varepsilon < 1$.

Similar arguments can be made for the infinite series $\{S_n\}$ obtained from the sequence $\{a_n\}$,

$\{a_n\} = \{1, -1, 1, -1 \ldots\}$ and $\{S_n\} = \{1, 1 - 1, 1 - 1 + 1, 1 - 1 + 1 - 1, \ldots\}$
$\{S_n\} = \{1, 0, 1, 0, \ldots\}$.

Thus, the limit of the series also does not exist. Under these conditions, the sequence is said to oscillate and is therefore without meaning.

Now let us use the definition of limit to look at the conditions for which the infinite geometric series has the limit, $S(x) = c/(1 - x)$.

Example 2: Let $S_n = c(1 + x + x^2 + x^3 + \ldots + x^{n-1})$

We want to know the condition for which $\lim_{n \to \infty} S_n = L = c/(1-x)$. From our discussion of repeating decimals in Chapter 2, we found that for any finite n:

$S_n = c(1 - x^n)/(1-x)$, therefore,
$|S_n - L| = |(c(1 - x^n)/(1-x)) - (c/(1-x))| = |-x^n/(1-x)|$

---

lxxxvi *"When the successive values attributed to a variable approach indefinitely a fixed value so as to end by differing from it by as little as one wishes, this last is called the limit of all others;"* see Sections 1.2.5.1 and 5.2.2.

If the limit exists, we can choose an ε and find an N, such that for all n > N, $|S_n - L| = |- x^n / (1-x)| < \varepsilon$. First note that the limit does not exist for x = 1, because $|- x^n / (1-x)|$ is undefined. For fixed x > 1, $|-x^n|$ increases with increasing n and no matter what ε we choose, $|- x^n / (1-x)|$ can be made greater than ε by increasing n. However, for $|x| < 1$, $|-x^n|$ decreases with increasing n. Therefore, by picking an N so that $|-x^N / (1-x)| \leqq \varepsilon$, $|S_n - L| < \varepsilon$ for all n > N. We have therefore confirmed that for $|x| < 1$, the series converges and $\lim_{n \to \infty} S_n = c/(1-x) = S(x)$.

We now will look at a series which diverges. But first, it is a convenient moment to introduce the notation used by Euler for series.[195] Let the infinite series formed from the sequence $\{a_n\}$ be $\{S_n\}$ $=\{a_1, a_1 + a_2, a_1 + a_2 + a_3, \ldots\}$. Euler introduced the following notation for the terms of a sequence of partial sums using an abbreviation for summation:

$$S_n = a_1 + a_2 + a_3 + \ldots + a_n = \sum_{k=1}^{n} a_k$$

Here the Greek capital letter sigma, Σ stands for summation with the sum going from k = 1 to k = n. Therefore, $S_1 = a_1 = \sum_{k=1}^{1} a_k$, $S_2 = a_1 + a_2 = \sum_{k=1}^{2} a_k$, $S_3 = a_1 + a_2 + a_3 = \sum_{k=1}^{3} a_k$ and so forth. Now let us look at the series known as the harmonic series.

Example 3: We will begin by looking at the sequence $\{h_n\} = \{1/n\} = \{1/1, 1/2, 1/3 \ldots\}$. Let us suppose that the limit of the sequence is 0, then we want to show that $|h_n - 0| = |1/n - 0| < \varepsilon$ for all n > N. If we choose an N so that $1/N \leqq \varepsilon$, then for n > N $\geqq 1/\varepsilon$, $1/n < 1/N \leqq \varepsilon$. Therefore, $\lim_{n \to \infty} 1/n = 0$. The harmonic series $\{H_n\}$ is formed from the sequence $\{h_n\}$:

$$H_n = \frac{1}{1} + \frac{1}{2} + \frac{1}{3} + \frac{1}{4} + \ldots + \frac{1}{n} = \sum_{k=1}^{n} \frac{1}{k} = \sum_{k=1}^{n} h_k.$$

With the last term in the sum forming H_n approaching 0, one might expect that $\{H_n\}$ will have a limit. However, as we shall see and as demonstrated by Nicole Oresme in the fourteenth century, the harmonic series can be shown to exceed any number.[196] To show this Oresme, grouped the terms of H_n after $\frac{1}{2}$ into sums of 2 terms, 4 terms, 8 terms, and so forth:

$$H_n = \frac{1}{1} + \frac{1}{2} + \left(\frac{1}{3} + \frac{1}{4}\right) + \left(\frac{1}{5} + \frac{1}{6} + \frac{1}{7} + \frac{1}{8}\right) + \left(\frac{1}{9} + \frac{1}{10} + \frac{1}{11} + \frac{1}{12} + \frac{1}{13} + \frac{1}{14} + \frac{1}{15} + \frac{1}{16}\right) + \cdots$$

$$+ \left(\cdots + \frac{1}{n-1} + \frac{1}{n}\right)$$

A new series, $\{\mathcal{H}_n\}$ is defined using the last term of each grouping:

$$\mathcal{H}_n = \frac{1}{1} + \frac{1}{2} + \left(\frac{1}{4} + \frac{1}{4}\right) + \left(\frac{1}{8} + \frac{1}{8} + \frac{1}{8} + \frac{1}{8}\right) + \left(\frac{1}{16} + \frac{1}{16} + \frac{1}{16} + \frac{1}{16} + \frac{1}{16} + \frac{1}{16} + \frac{1}{16} + \frac{1}{16}\right) + \cdots$$

$$+ \left(+ \frac{1}{n} + \frac{1}{n}\right)$$

Therefore, $\mathcal{H}_n = 1 + 1/2 + 1/2 + 1/2 + 1/2 + \ldots$

By taking larger and larger n, $\mathcal{H}_n$ can exceed any number we choose, that is, it is unbounded. Now by comparing the terms in the two series, we see that $\mathcal{H}_n < H_n$ because the grouped terms of $\mathcal{H}_n$ are less than those of H_n except for the first two terms which are equal. Because $\mathcal{H}_n$ is unbounded, the harmonic series H_n must also be unbounded and the series diverges or $\lim_{n \to \infty} H_n = \lim_{n \to \infty} \sum_{k=1}^{n} \frac{1}{k} \to \infty$.

We have now seen three possibilities for a sequences and series. The sequence may oscillate and not approach a limit, it may converge, or the sequence may diverge. The definition that we have been using requires an assumption of the limit for its application. However, in cases where the limit is unknown, it would be useful to be able to determine if a limit even exists. Such an evaluation of sequences can be accomplished through the use of what is known as a Cauchy sequence. The definition of a Cauchy sequence is given below[197]. Whenever a Cauchy sequence converges, a standard sequence also converges.[lxxxvii] The converse of this is true also. Thus, there is equivalence between the Cauchy convergence definition and the standard definition of convergence. I have designated this equivalence as the Cauchy Principle.

Definition of a Cauchy Sequence: A sequence $\{a_n\}$ is called a Cauchy sequence if for any number ε, there exists a number N such that for all $m > N$ and all n, $|a_{m+n} - a_m| < \varepsilon$.

---

lxxxvii A proof of the Cauchy Principle is given by Labarre, Jr., p. 138-141.

In other words, a sequence is a Cauchy sequence if we can find an N such that for all m > N, the difference between any two numbers in the sequence is less than our chosen ε.

Cauchy Principle: A sequence $\{a_n\}$ converges if and only if $\{a_n\}$ is a Cauchy sequence.

The proof that a convergent sequence is a Cauchy sequence is given below. Recall from the section on logic in Chapter 4 that "if and only if" means that the Cauchy Principle may also be expressed as: The sequence $\{a_n\}$ converges implies $\{a_n\}$ is a Cauchy sequence, **and** $\{a_n\}$ is a Cauchy sequence implies the sequence $\{a_n\}$ converges. The proof below is for the first implication.

Proof: If $\{a_n\}$ converges, then $\{a_n\}$ is a Cauchy sequence.

$\{a_n\}$ has a limit L	By hypothesis
$\|a_{m+n} - a_m\| \le \|a_{m+n} - L\| + \|L - a_m\|$	Triangle inequality[lxxxviii]
$\|L - a_m\| = \|a_m - L\|$	Property of absolute value
$\|a_{m+n} - a_m\| \le \|a_{m+n} - L\| + \|a_m - L\|$	Equivalence relation

We select $\varepsilon/2$ as the allowed difference between a_m and L.

For m > N, $\|a_m - L\| < \varepsilon/2$	Definition of convergence
$\|a_{m+n} - L\| < \varepsilon/2$	Order property (m + n > N)
$\|a_{m+n} - a_m\| < \varepsilon/2 + \varepsilon/2 = \varepsilon$	Properties of real numbers

Q.E.D.

To get a feel for how the Cauchy Sequence Definition works, let us apply it to the geometric series, $S_m = 1 + x^1 + x^2 + x^3 + \ldots + x^{m-1} = (1 - x^m)/(1 - x)$ for the case x > 0.

$$S_{m+n} - S_m = (1 - x^{m+n})/(1 - x) - (1 - x^m)/(1 - x)$$

$$= (x^m - x^{m+n})/(1 - x)$$

$$= (x^{m+n} - x^m)/(x - 1)$$

$$= x^m (x^n - 1)/(x - 1)$$

Therefore, we want $\| x^m (x^n - 1)/(x - 1)\| < \varepsilon$ for m > N and all $n \ge 1$

---

lxxxviii See Section 5.2.1.

First for $x = 1$, the Cauchy Sequence definition is not satisfied as $|x^m (x^n - 1)/(x - 1)|$ is not defined. Also, for $x > 1$, x^m and x^n increase without bound with increasing m and n. Therefore, $| x^m (x^n-1)/(x-1)|$ is greater than any selected number for some m and n. Consequently, the Cauchy Sequence definition cannot be satisfied for $x \geqq 1$.

Finally, if $0 < x < 1$, for any given ε, we can choose an N such that:

$|x^N / (x - 1)| \leqq \varepsilon$. For any $m > N$ with $m = N + p$,
$|x^m(x^n-1)/(x-1)| = |\varepsilon \cdot x^p (x^n-1)| < \varepsilon$ since $0 < |x^p(x^n-1)| < 1$ for $0 < x < 1$.

Thus, following the Cauchy Sequence Definition and Principle, the geometric series converges for $0 < x < 1$ which was previously established using the standard definition of limit. However, notice that using the Cauchy Sequence approach did not require knowledge of the limit of the sequence. The Cauchy sequence may also be used to show that the sequence diverges for $x \leqq -1$ and converges over the entire range $-1 < x < 1$.

In our discussions of the real numbers, we encountered sequences of estimates leading to the irrational number $\sqrt{2}$, as well as a number which clearly did not represent a rational number which is called a Liouville number,

$L = 0.10100100010000100000\ldots$

L could also be expressed as a series obtained from the sequence $\{l_n\}$ $= \{10^{-n(n+1)/2}\}$ by noting that the nth term of the sequence $\{L_n\}$ is given as $L_n = \sum_1^n l_n$. For example,

$L_4 = 0.1 + 0.001 + 0.000001 + 0.0000000001$. This suggests that

$L \overset{?}{=} \lim_{n \to \infty} L_n$.

With our background in sequences and series, it is now time to look at the relationship between sequences and the real numbers and show that L is a real number. We will find that the Cauchy sequence and the Cauchy Principle can be used as an alternate method to the Dedekind cuts for defining the real numbers.

6.3   Cauchy sequences and the real numbers

In Chapter 2, when we discussed the presentation of numbers as decimals, we found that all rational numbers could be represented as decimals with a finite number of digits or infinite decimals with a repeating sequence of digits. Noting that rational numbers with a finite number of decimal digits, such as 1/4, can be represented either as 0.25000 . . . or as 0.24999 . . . , all rational number can be represented as infinite decimals with a repeating sequence. The irrational numbers in the decimal representation were infinite non-repeating decimals. Focusing on decimals between 0 and 10, we can represent a decimal as a sequence $\{a_n\}$ where any particular number can be represented as $a_0. a_1 \, a_2 \, a_3 \, a_4 \ldots$, that is, for the specific number 1.4142 . . . , $a_0 = 1$, $a_1 = 4$, $a_2 = 1$, $a_3 = 4$, $a_4 = 2$, and so forth. One approach to the decimals is to ask if the sequence $\{A_n\}$ formed as below converges for infinite decimals either repeating or non-repeating.

$$A_n = a_0 \cdot 10^0 + a_1 \cdot 10^{-1} + a_2 \cdot 10^{-2} + \ldots + a_n^{-n} = \sum_{k=0}^{n} a_k \cdot 10^{-k}$$

The definition of a Cauchy sequence gives us an approach to determine whether every infinite decimal converges to a limit. As required by the definition of a Cauchy sequence, for any number ε that we choose, there must be a number N such that for all m > N and all n, $|A_{m+n} - A_m| < \varepsilon$.

$$|A_{m+n} - A_m| = \left| \sum_{k=0}^{m+n} a_k \cdot 10^{-k} - \sum_{k=0}^{m} a_k \cdot 10^{-k} \right|$$

$$= \left| \sum_{k=m+1}^{m+n} a_k \cdot 10^{-k} \right|$$

$$= \left| \sum_{k=1}^{n} a_{m+k} \cdot 10^{-(m+k)} \right|$$

Each digit $a_{m+k} \leqq 9$, and any factor not dependent on k is common to all the terms of the sum, therefore

$$= \left| \sum_{k=1}^{n} a_{m+k} \cdot 10^{-m} \cdot 10^{-k} \right| \leqq \left| \sum_{k=1}^{n} 9 \cdot 10^{-m} \cdot 10^{-k} \right|$$

$$= 9 \cdot 10^{-m} \left| \sum_{k=1}^{n} 10^{-k} \right|$$

Now for fixed m, the sum is a geometric series with:

$$|\sum_{k=1}^{n} 10^{-k}| = 1/10 + (1/10)^2 + (1/10)^3 + \ldots + (1/10)^n$$

For any finite n, $|\sum_{k=1}^{n} 10^{-k}| < \lim_{n\to\infty} |\sum_{k=1}^{n} 10^{-k}| = 0.1/(1 - 1/10) = 1/9$, therefore,

$$|A_{m+n} - A_m| < 9 \cdot 10^{-m} \lim_{n\to\infty} |\sum_{k=1}^{n} 10^{-k}| = 9 \cdot 10^{-m} (1/9) = 10^{-m}$$

For a given ε, let N be chosen such that $10^{-N} \leqq \varepsilon$, then

for $m = N + p$ and all n, $|A_{m+n} - A_m| < 10^{-m} \leqq 10^{-(N+p)} \leqq \varepsilon$.

Thus, all infinite decimals converge to a limit as Cauchy sequences and thereby define the real numbers. Any prescription for an infinite sequence of non-repeating decimal numbers such as the Liouville number must therefore converge to an irrational number as part of the real numbers. If we restricted ourselves to rational numbers there would be nothing to converge to!

In Chapter 3, the real numbers were defined in terms of the Dedekind cuts which I said were equivalent to an ordered field having the least upper bound property. We may equivalently define real numbers as the set of numbers of an ordered field in which all Cauchy sequences converge. Many different Cauchy sequences can be defined which converge to the same real number. Just as the integers are formed from the equivalent classes defined through equivalent pairs of natural numbers [m, n], the real numbers are determined by the equivalent classes of Cauchy sequences converging to the same limit. It is worth repeating that although the rational numbers form an ordered field, the Cauchy sequence of rational numbers approaching irrational numbers such as $\sqrt{2}$ does not converge if we are limited to rational numbers.[lxxxix]

The field and order properties of the real numbers (Theorems $\mathcal{R}1$ through $\mathcal{R}5$—see Section 3.2) can be established through laws of limits of sequences similar to those of Section 5.2.2. Furthermore, that all Cauchy sequences are bound may be easily seen from the requirement of a Cauchy sequence that for any number ε, there

lxxxix Full details on building the real numbers from the rational numbers using Cauchy sequences is given in Hamilton, pp. 26-50 and Thurston, pp. 28-35, pp. 96-119.

exists a number N such that for all m > N and all n, $|a_{m+n} - a_m| < \varepsilon$. In other words, for all m > N and all n, $a_{N+1} - \varepsilon < a_{m+n} < a_{N+1} + \varepsilon$. If we compare the terms in this interval with the finite number of terms in the sequence ending with a_N, then an upper bound can be selected. If every Cauchy sequence converges (that is we have the real numbers) then, there is a least upper bound. Thus, Dedekind's Cuts, the Least Upper Bound Property, and Cauchy Sequences of Rational Numbers all provide equivalent definitions of the real numbers. (A discussion of this point is given by Stečkin in Aleksandrov, Kolmogorov, and Lavrent'ev.[198])

With the equivalence of the various definitions of the real numbers in mind, it is convenient to repeat here some of the related properties of the real numbers from Chapter 3:

1. Every increasing sequence of real numbers that is bounded above has a least upper bound
2. Every decreasing sequence of real numbers that is bounded below has a greatest lower bound
3. Every infinite sequence of nested intervals contains only one real number common to all the intervals.

We will use the second property to show that the Babylonian sequence to determine the square root of a number provides a convergent sequence. In the general case, the Babylonian algorithm to find $\sqrt{b}$ is:

$$a_{n+1} = (a_n + b/a_n)/2. \text{ (If } a_1 > 0, \text{ all } a_n > 0.)$$

$$a_{n+1} - b/a_{n+1} = (a_n + b/a_n)/2 - b/a_{n+1}$$

$$= \frac{(a_{n+1})\left(a_n + \dfrac{b}{a_n}\right) - 2b}{2a_{n+1}}$$

$$= \frac{1/2\left(a_n + b/a_n\right)^2 - 2b}{2a_{n+1}}$$

$$= \frac{\left(a_n + b/a_n\right)^2 - 4b}{4a_{n+1}}$$

$$= \frac{a_n^2 + 2b + \left(b/a_n\right)^2 - 4b}{4a_{n+1}}$$

$$= \frac{(a_n - b/a_n)^2}{4a_{n+1}} > 0, \text{ as any number squared is positive.}$$

Therefore, $a_{n+1} - b/a_{n+1} > 0$, implying $a_{n+1} > b/a_{n+1,}$ and $a_{n+1}^2 > b$
This is true for any n, therefore, $a_n > b/a_n$ and $a_n^2 > b$.
It follows that, $a_n + a_n = 2 a_n > a_n + b/a_n$ or $a_n > \frac{1}{2}(a_n + b/a_n) = a_{n+1}$.

We have therefore shown that $\{a_n\}$ is a decreasing sequence ($a_n > a_{n+1}$) and that it is bounded below ($a_n^2 > b$) therefore, the sequence converges. That the limit of the sequence is $\sqrt{b}$ is suggested by noting that if $a_n \to a$ in the limit then, $a = \frac{1}{2}(a + b/a)$ with the solution $a = \sqrt{b}$. More formally, using a sequence of nested intervals, it can be shown that $\lim_{n\to\infty} a_n = \sqrt{b}$.

With the real numbers capable of being defined through Cauchy sequences, it seems natural to look for a relationship between sequences and limits of functions. The notion of the limit of a function $f(x_n)$ as the sequence $\{x_n\}$ approaches some number, say c defined in terms of sequences is perhaps closer to the intuitive idea of limit than the $\varepsilon - \delta$ definition given in the previous chapter. The two approaches may be shown to be equivalent.[199] The definition of the limit of a function in terms of sequences is given below.

Definition of Sequential Limit of Function: For a function $f(x)$ with c defined within the domain of the function, $\lim_{x\to c} f(x) = d$ if and only if every sequence $\{x_n\}$ with $\lim_{n\to\infty} x_n = c$ and $x_n \neq c$ implies $\lim_{n\to\infty} f(x_n) = d$.[200]

Example: $f(x) = \frac{x^2-1}{x-1}$, then for the sequence $\{x_n\}$ with $\lim_{n\to\infty} x_n = 1$,

$$\lim_{x\to 1} f(x) = \lim_{n\to\infty} f(x_n) = \lim_{n\to\infty} \frac{x_n^2-1}{x_n-1} = \lim_{n\to\infty} \frac{(x_n+1)(x_n-1)}{x_n-1} = \lim_{n\to\infty}(x_n+1) = 2$$

We conclude this section by listing several interesting infinite series that represent functions and converge for all x. A method to derive these results known as the Taylor series will be given when calculus is introduced in Chapter 8.

$\sin x = x - x^3/3! + x^5/5! - x^7/7! + \ldots + (-1)^n x^{2n+1}/(2n+1)! + \ldots$
with $n = 0, 1, 2, \ldots$

$$= \lim_{n\to\infty} \sum_{k=0}^{n} (-1)^k x^{2k+1}/(2k+1)!$$

with k! =k (k − 1)(k − 2) . . . 2 · 1; for example, 3! = 3 · 2 · 1.

$\cos x = 1 - x^2/2! + x^4/4! - x^6/6! + \ldots + (-1)^n x^{2n}/(2n)! + \ldots$

$\quad = \lim_{n \to \infty} \sum_{k=0}^{n} (-1)^k x^{2k}/(2k)!$ with 0! = 1.

$e^x = 1 + x/1! + x^2/2! + x^3/3! + \ldots + x^n/n! + \ldots$

$\quad = \lim_{n \to \infty} \sum_{k=0}^{n} x^k/k!$

Recall from the history outline that e is the transcendental number identified by Euler as $e = \lim_{n \to \infty} \left(1 + \dfrac{1}{n}\right)^n$

As an example of the utility of representing functions as infinite series, the relationship between the Law Of Cosines and its analog for spherical geometry is shown below. From Section 4.5 and Appendix F, the relations for a sphere of radius r between triangle sides (a, b, and c) and angles (∠A, ∠B, and ∠C)are given by:

$\cos(a/r) = \cos(b/r) \cdot \cos(c/r) + \sin(b/r) \cdot \sin(c/r) \cdot \cos(A),$
$\cos(b/r) = \cos(c/r) \cdot \cos(a/r) + \sin(c/r) \cdot \sin(a/r) \cdot \cos(B),$
$\cos(c/r) = \cos(a/r) \cdot \cos(b/r) + \sin(a/r) \cdot \sin(b/r) \cdot \cos(C).$

If the sides of the spherical triangle are small compared to the radius of the sphere, then a/r << 1, b/r <<1, and c/r <<1 (that is, a/r is much less than 1, etc.). Expanding the cosine and sine functions as infinite series in terms of a/r, b/r, and c/r, we will only need to keep the terms like $(a/r)^2$ since higher powers will be much smaller. Let us look at the equation for cos(a/r) using the infinite series given above.

$\cos(a/r) = 1 - (a/r)^2/2 + (a/r)^4/24 + \ldots$
$\cos(b/r) \cdot \cos(c/r) = (1 - (b/r)^2/2 + (b/r)^4/24 + \ldots) \cdot (1 - (c/r)^2/2 + (c/r)^4/24 + \ldots)$
$\sin(b/r) \cdot \sin(c/r) \cdot \cos(A) = ((b/r) - (b/r)^3/6 + \ldots) \cdot ((c/r) - (c/r)^3/6 + \ldots) \cdot \cos(A)$
Keeping only the terms no smaller than those like $(a/r)^2$, we have after multiplication term by term in cos(b/r) · cos(c/r) and sin(b/r) · sin(c/r) · cos (A):

$\cos(a/r) \approx 1 - (a/r)^2/2$

$\cos(b/r) \cdot \cos(c/r) \approx 1 - (b/r)^2 /2 - (c/r)^2 /2$
$\sin(b/r) \cdot \sin(c/r) \cdot \cos(A) \approx (b/r) \cdot (c/r) \cdot \cos(A)$
and we can approximate $\cos(a/r)$ as:
$1 - (a/r)^2 /2 = 1 - (b/r)^2 /2 - (c/r)^2 /2 + (b/r) \cdot (c/r) \cdot \cos(A)$
After multiplying by $-2r^2$ and simplifying, we have:
$a^2 = b^2 + c^2 - 2bc \cdot \cos(A)$

We have recovered the Law of Cosines. As noted in Chapter 4, for small triangles (sides small compared to the radius of the sphere), the results for spherical geometry approach those of Euclidean geometry. The same technique can obviously be used for the other two relationships with $\cos(b/r)$ and $\cos(c/r)$.

Another result suggested by these infinite series is the relationship between the exponential function, e^x and the trigonometric sine and cosine functions. If you stare at the series for $\sin x$, $\cos x$, and e^x, you will see that the series for e^x includes both the even and odd power types of terms that are found in $\sin x$ and $\cos x$. If you make the substitution $x = i\, y$ (with $i = \sqrt{-1}$) into the series for e^x and then compare the result with the series for sine and cosine functions, you will get what is sometimes referred to as the Euler identity:

$e^{i\,y} = \cos y + i \sin y$

This relation greatly facilitates finding solutions to polynomials such as the cubic equation we discussed previously in Section 5.3. We shall revisit the cubic equation in the next section. Returning to the Euler identity and recalling that $\sin \pi = 0$, $\cos \pi = -1$, we have

$e^{i\pi} = \cos\pi + i\sin\pi = -1$ or $e^{i\pi} + 1 = 0$

This is known as the Euler equation which encompasses some of the most fundamental numbers of mathematics.

6.4   Revisiting cubic equations in the complex plane

The Fundamental Theorem of Algebra ultimately assures us that a polynomial of degree n has n roots, but it doesn't tell us how to find them. In the case of a cubic equation with real coefficients, we saw in Section 5.3 that the discriminant of the equation tells us whether the roots are all real or whether two of the roots are complex conjugates, but even using Cardan's formula, it is not so clear how to find all three roots. Just as the use of complex variables resulted in a simple proof of the Fundamental Theorem of Algebra, the use of complex variables will gives us a straight forward way to determine the cube roots and square roots that show up in Cardan's formula. Before, we get there, however, we will need to see how to use the relationship, $e^{Iy} = \cos y + i \sin y$, to express complex numbers.

Recall in Chapter 3, some of the mystery of complex numbers, and in particular, imaginary numbers was hopefully removed by interpreting them as simply the points in a plane, with the x coordinate being the real part of the complex number and the y coordinate the imaginary part. We showed this graphically in Chapter 3, and it is shown again below. If z is taken as the complex variable, then in the figure below, $z = x + i\,y$.

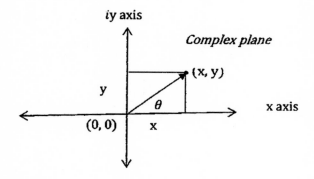

We have identified the point in the complex plane by the Cartesian coordinates (x, y), but we could just as well have identified the location of the point in the plane with its distance from the origin, $\rho = \sqrt{x^2 + y^2}$, and the angle, θ, between the x-axis and the line formed by (x, y) and the origin (0, 0). This method of locating the point, known as the polar form, is indicated in the figure by the arrow of length ρ inclined at an angle θ. Now from the definition of sine and cosine functions, $x = \rho\cos\theta$ and $y = \rho\sin\theta$ or $z = \rho\,(\cos\theta + i \sin\theta)$ which as we learned in the previous section can be written $z = \rho e^{I\,\theta}$. In this manner of expressing the complex variable, ρ is known as the modulus and θ, the argument. Since ρ is a distance, a positive number, it is frequently written as $|\rho|$. As examples of the polar form, along the positive x-axis, if $\rho = 1$, $\theta = 0$ or 360°, then $z = 1 = e^{I\,2\pi}$. At $\theta = 90°$, $z = i = e^{i\,\pi/2}$; at $\theta = 180°$, $z = -1 = e^{i\,\pi}$; and at $\theta = 270°$, $z = -i = e^{I\,3\pi/2}$.

The convenience of the exponential expression is apparent when we want to raise the variable z to a power. For example, let us look at $z^{1/3}$. We use the normal rule for exponentiation to find that:

$$z^{1/3} = (\rho e^{i\theta})^{1/3} = \rho^{1/3} e^{(i\theta)/3} = \rho^{1/3}(\cos\theta/3 + i\sin\theta/3).$$

The sine and cosine functions can be defined in terms of the points (x, y) on the circumference of a circle of radius ρ, centered at the origin, that is $\sin(\theta) = y/\rho$ and $\cos(\theta) = x/\rho$. Therefore, if in going around the circle, θ is increased by 360° or 2π radians, the sine and cosine functions return to the same value. Another way of indicating this is to note that $\sin\theta = \sin(\theta + n \cdot 2\pi)$ for integer values of n. Therefore,

$z^{1/m} = \rho^{1/m}(\cos((\theta + n \cdot 2\pi)/m) + i\sin((\theta + n \cdot 2\pi)/m)$ for n = 0, 1, 2 ... m−1

Correct values for $z^{1/m}$ are also found for all other integer values of n, but give the same results as n = 0, 1, 2 ... m − 1.[xc]

Let us look at how this works for a simple case where the answer is now well known to you:

$z^2 + 1 = 0$
$z^2 = -1 = e^{i(\pi + n \cdot 2\pi)}$ for n =0, 1,
(n = 0) $z_1 = e^{i(\pi + n \cdot 2\pi)/2} = e^{i(\pi)/2} = i,$
(n = 1) $z_2 = e^{i(\pi + n \cdot 2\pi)/2} = e^{i(\pi + 2\pi)/2} = e^{i3\pi/2} = -i.$

Thus, the two roots are found in a straightforward manner.

We will now use this approach in solving a cubic equation. Before taking advantage of the complex variables to obtain roots; however, we will introduce two ingenious transformations of Viète that simplify the solution of the cubic.[201]

The general cubic equation can be expressed as: $ay^3 + by^2 + cy + d = 0$. If you make the substitution, $y = x - b/3a$,[202] the following simpler equation results:

xc Abraham De Moivre (1667-1754) discovered this relation, known as De Moivre's Theorem, as $(\cos\theta + i\sin\theta)^{1/m} = \cos((\theta + n \cdot 2\pi)/m) + i\sin((\theta + n \cdot 2\pi)/m)$—see Merzbach and Boyer, pp. 372-375.

$x^3 + px + q = 0$, with $p = (3ac-b^2)/3a^2$ and $q = d/a + 2b^3/27a^3 - bc/3a^2$

The cubic equation that we will use as an example is: $y^3 + 2y^2 - y - 2 = 0$.

In this case with $b/3a = 2/3$, let $y = x - 2/3$, then, $x^3 - 7/3 \, x - 20/27 = 0$. (So $p = -7/3$ and $q = -20/27$. You should check out this result by direct substitution, a tedious but useful exercise.)

In the second substitution, let $x = w - p/(3w)$ or in our specific case, $x = w + 7/(9w)$ since $p = -7/3$. This substitution results in: $w^3 - p^3/(3w)^3 + q = 0$. Multiplying the equation by w^3, we obtain: $w^6 + qw^3 - (p/3)^3 = 0$. The advantage of this substitution is that if we identify a variable $v = w^3$, then a quadratic equation in v results, which we can easily solve with the quadratic formula:

$v^2 + qv - (p/3)^3 = 0$ or, $v^2 - 20/27 \, v - (-7/3)^3/3^3 = v^2 - 20/27 \, v + (7/9)^3 = 0$

From the quadratic formula:

$$v = \frac{20/27 \pm \sqrt{\left(\dfrac{-20}{27}\right)^2 - 4 \cdot \left(\dfrac{7}{9}\right)^3}}{2}$$

With a solution for v, we can now reverse our transformations and determine w, then, x, and finally the solutions for y.

$$v = w^3, \text{ therefore } w = v^{1/3} = \sqrt[3]{\frac{20/27 \pm \sqrt{\left(\dfrac{20}{27}\right)^2 - 4 \cdot \left(\dfrac{7}{9}\right)^3}}{2}}$$

Looking back to Section 5.3 and Cardan's formula, I think you will be begin to see its origins. The quantity under the square root is what we called the discriminant. After simplification of the discriminant, we obtain:

$$w = \sqrt[3]{\frac{20/27 \pm \dfrac{\sqrt{-972}}{27}}{2}} = \sqrt[3]{\frac{20/27 \pm \dfrac{\sqrt{972}}{27}\,i}{2}} = \sqrt[3]{(10/27) \pm \left(\sqrt{3}/3\right)i}$$

Because the discriminant is negative, there will be three distinct real roots when we take the cube root. We need only look at the cube root of $\left(\frac{10}{27}\right)+\left(\sqrt{3}/3\right)\ i$ as the other solutions from $\left(\frac{10}{27}\right)-\left(\sqrt{3}/3\right)\ i$ will be the same. Also with this solution, we can see where Cardan's concerns came from. In order to get a real solution he had to work with numbers such as $\sqrt{-972}$.

In order to take the cube root, we will write $(10/27)+\left(\sqrt{3}/3\right)\ i$ in polar form, $v = \rho e^{i\theta}$. (Please use your calculator to determine θ as the inverse of the cosine function and approximate the results to three significant figures.) I express the results for the arguments in radians and in degrees.

$$v = \left(10/27\right)+\left(\sqrt{3}/3\right)\ i = \rho e^{i\theta}$$

$$\rho = ((10/27)^2 + (\sqrt{3}/3)^2)^{1/2} = ((\tfrac{10}{27})^2 + (\tfrac{3}{9})(\tfrac{3\cdot 27}{3\cdot 27}))^{1/2}$$

$$= \sqrt{343}/27 = \sqrt{7^3}/27 \approx 0.686$$

$$\cos\theta = \frac{10/27}{\sqrt{7^3}/27} \approx 0.540 \Rightarrow \theta \approx 57.3° \approx 1 \text{ (radian)}$$

$$v = \left(10/27\right)+\left(\sqrt{3}/3\right)\ i = \sqrt{7^3}/27 e^{i\cdot 1}$$

$$w = v^{1/3} = (\sqrt{7^3}/27 e^{i\cdot 1})^{1/3} = \sqrt{7}/3 e^{i(1+n\cdot 2\pi)/3}, \text{ for } n = 0, 1, 2$$

The solution for $n = 0$ is given below.

$$w_1 = \sqrt{7}/3 e^{i\left(\frac{1}{3}\right)} \approx 0.882\ (\cos\ (57.3/3)° + i\ \sin(57.3/3)°) \approx 0.882$$
$$(0.945 + 0.327\ i)$$

$$w_1 \approx 0.833 + 0.288\ i$$

The next step is to determine x from w:

$$x = w_1 - p/(3w_1) = w_1 + 7/(9w_1) = 0.833 + 0.288\ i + 7/(9\ (0.833 + 0.288\ i))$$

The denominator of the second term, $7/(9w_1)$, can be simplified by using the complex conjugate of $0.833 + 0.288\ i$.

$$x = 0.833 + 0.288\ i + \frac{7}{\left(9\left(0.833 + 0.288\ i\right)\right)} \cdot \frac{\left(0.833 - 0.288\ i\right)}{\left(0.833 - 0.288\ i\right)}$$

$$= 0.833 + 0.288\ i + \frac{7\left(0.833 - 0.288\ i\right)}{9\left(0.833^2 + .288^2\right)}$$

$$= 0.833 + 0.288\ i + 0.833 - 0.288\ i$$

$$x \approx 1.666 \approx 5/3$$

The final step is to determine $y = x - 2/3 = 5/3 - 2/3 = 1$. A check with the original equation, $y^3 + 2\,y^2 - y - 2 = 0$, shows this is correct. We can continue by solving for w_2, and w_3; however with one root known, it is easier to solve the quadratic equation resulting from dividing the cubic equation by the factor $(y - 1)$.

$$
\begin{array}{r}
y^2 + 3y + 2 \\
\hline
y-1\overline{)\,y^3 + 2y^2 - y - 2} \\
\underline{y^3 - y^2} \qquad\quad \\
3y^2 - y \quad\; \\
\underline{3y^2 - 3y} \quad\; \\
2y - 2 \\
\underline{2y - 2}
\end{array}
$$

The roots of the equation, $y^2 + 3y + 2 = 0$, may easily be determined by the quadratic equation or by factoring to be, -1 and -2. Therefore the original cubic may be written as $(y - 1)(y + 1)(y + 2) = 0$. Clearly if one root can be found, it is easier to proceed in this way; however, in the more general case, the solution with complex variables provides a straight forward solution. Perhaps more importantly for our purposes, the solution to the cubic equation has given us the opportunity to have a better understanding of operations with complex variables.

CHAPTER 7

THE NUMBERS MOVE IN SPACE; ROTATIONS, CONICS, VECTORS, TENSORS, AND MATRICES

"For a firm and secure rule, then, when one must designate the quantity of impetus resulting from two given impetuses, one horizontal and the other vertical, both being equable, one must take the squares of both, add these together and extract the square root of their combination; this will give us the quantity of the impetus compounded from both . . . Now let us see what happens in compounding equable horizontal motion with vertical [downward] motion starting from rest and naturally accelerating. It is already manifest that the diagonal which is the line of motion compounded from those two is not a straight line, but a semiparabola, as has been shown in which the impetus goes always growing, thanks to the continual growth of speed in the vertical motion."—Galileo Galilei[xci]

7.1   Moving on and beyond the plane

Up to this point, we have looked almost exclusively at situations in which there is only one independent variable, and functions could be represented as curves on a plane surface. The sole exception is our proof of the Fundamental Theorem of Algebra where we took advantage of functions of the complex variable, $F(z) = F(x + i\,y)$ which we interpreted as a surface above the complex plane. A natural extension of functions in the plane is to consider a coordinate axis perpendicular to the plane of the x and y axes. The three coordinates, taken as (x, y, z) then represent the space of our familiar three-dimensional world. Indeed when considering the straight line, $y = mx + b$, we noted this could be considered to be a line in the plane $z = 0$ cut out of this space. We now want to consider mathematical

---

xci Galileo, G., *Two New Sciences*, translated with new introduction, notes, and, *History of Free Fall: Aristotle to Galileo* by S. Drake; quotation concerning a projectile with initial horizontal velocity from *Two New Sciences*, pp. 238-239.

concepts developed for three-dimensional space, but before we leave the plane, let us look at the effect of rotation in the plane. As we have seen with the hyperbola, rotation of the coordinate axes can result in a change of functional form to standard forms that facilitate the identification of the resulting curves. Another motivation for looking at rotations of functions or equivalently rotation of coordinate axes is to give an algebraic interpretation to rotation of figures which was implied by Euclid (along with translation of figures) in his proofs of congruence by superposition.

7.1.1   Rotation in the plane

Suppose we wish to show that the function $y = 1/x$ is the same as the hyperbola in its standard form if the coordinate system x-y is rotated an angle θ as shown in the figure below to form new x'-y' axes. We will need to know how the coordinates (x, y) are transformed into (x', y') by this rotation.

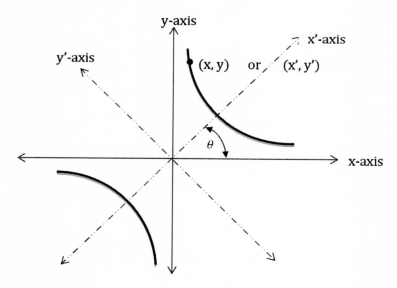

Below, we have redrawn the figure looking only at the point (x, y) on the hyperbola. Let us assume that the line from the point (x, y) to the origin makes an angle α with respect to the new x'-axis. The distance, ρ of the point (x, y) from the origin is, $\rho = \sqrt{x^2 + y^2}$.

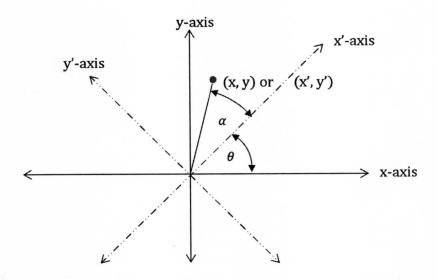

Using the definitions of the sine and cosine functions, the components of the point (x, y) can be expressed in terms of ρ, α, and θ as:

$x = \rho \cos(\alpha + \theta)$
$y = \rho \sin(\alpha + \theta)$

Also from the Euler identity, it is shown in Appendix H that,

$\cos(\alpha + \theta) = \cos \alpha \cos \theta - \sin \alpha \sin \theta$ and $\sin(\alpha + \theta) = \sin \alpha \cos \theta + \sin \theta \cos \alpha$

Therefore,

$x = \rho\cos \alpha \cos \theta - \rho\sin \alpha \sin \theta$
$y = \rho\sin \alpha \cos \theta + \rho\sin \theta \cos \alpha$

Similarly, the components of the point on the rotated x'-y' axis may be expressed as:

$x' = \rho \cos \alpha$
$y' = \rho \sin \alpha$

Therefore, the relation between the coordinates (x, y) and (x', y') due to a rotation through and angle θ is:

$x = x' \cos \theta - y' \sin \theta$

$y = x' \sin \theta + y' \cos \theta$

We now apply this to any point of the curve, $xy = 1$

$xy = (x' \cos \theta - y' \sin \theta) \cdot (x' \sin \theta + y' \cos \theta) = 1$. Therefore,
$x'^2 \cos \theta \cdot \sin \theta + x'y' \cos^2 \theta - x'y' \sin^2 \theta - y'^2 \sin \theta \cos \theta = 1$, and
$(x'^2 - y'^2) \cos \theta \cdot \sin \theta + x'y' (\cos^2 \theta - \sin^2 \theta) = 1$.

In the standard form for a hyperbola, there is no xy term. The equation above, implies that the angle of rotation, θ must be such that $\cos^2 \theta - \sin^2 \theta = 0$ or $\cos \theta = \sin \theta$. In this case $\tan \theta = \sin \theta / \cos \theta = 1$ and the angle of rotation is $45° = \pi/4$ (radians). If θ is the angle of a right triangle, then $\tan \theta = 1$ means the adjacent sides are equal as shown in the figure below, and the hypotenuse must be $\sqrt{2}$. Therefore $\sin \theta = \cos \theta = 1/\sqrt{2}$ which can be substituted into above equations.

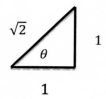

$(x'^2 - y'^2) (1/\sqrt{2}) \cdot (1/\sqrt{2}) + x'y' (1/2 - 1/2) = 1$ resulting in the standard form, $x'^2/2 - y'^2/2 = 1$.

An important feature of the transformation of coordinates by rotation is that lengths (as we assumed above) are preserved. We will show this by transforming $\rho^2 = (x^2 + y^2)$ to the rotated coordinate system (x', y').

$\rho^2 = (x^2 + y^2) = (x' \cos \theta - y' \sin \theta)^2 + (x' \sin \theta + y' \cos \theta)^2$
$= (x'^2 + y'^2) (\cos^2 \theta + \sin^2 \theta) - 2x'y' (\cos \theta \sin \theta - \sin \theta \cos \theta)$

Since as we have shown previously that $\cos^2 \theta + \sin^2 \theta = 1$,

$\rho^2 = (x^2 + y^2) = (x'^2 + y'^2) = \rho'^2$, and length is not changed by rotation.

Thus the algebraic interpretation of rotation is consistent with Euclidean geometry.

Rotation of axes may be used to transform the general equation of second degree in x and y into the standard form for a conic. The general second degree equation is:

$$Ax^2 + 2Bxy + Cy^2 + 2Dx + 2Ey + F = 0$$

Using the transformation for rotation of coordinates through an angle θ, the term in xy may be eliminated if,

$1/\tan 2\theta = \cot 2\theta = (A - C)/2B$ with $\cot \theta$ being the cotangent function.[xcii]

In the case of the curve $xy = 1$, $A = 0$, $2B = 1/2$, and $C = 0$. Therefore, $\cot 2\theta = 0$ and $2\theta = 90° = \pi/2$ (radians). The angle of rotation θ is 45° as we have previously shown.

In the general case, by eliminating, the term in xy, the equation of the conic becomes:

$$A'x'^2 + C'y'^2 + 2D'x' + 2E'y' + F' = 0.$$

This can then be put into standard form by completing the square where necessary in the variables x and y to remove the terms in D and E. An example of this is the functional form for the ellipse, $\dfrac{(x-c)^2}{a^2} + \dfrac{(y-d)^2}{b^2} = 1$ formed by completing the square. The resulting equation in the example indicates an ellipse translated from the origin a distance c in the positive x direction and d in the positive y direction.

Rotation of axes can be shown to leave the value, $AC - B^2 = \Gamma$ unchanged (invariant) after rotation of coordinates. If $\Gamma > 0$, the curve is an ellipse; $\Gamma = 0$, a parabola; and $\Gamma < 0$, a hyperbola.[xciii] Just as we expect that lengths of lines will remain unchanged by rotation, an ellipse must also remain an ellipse. (Another example of the transformation of an equation by rotation is given in Appendix I.) Now it is time to move off the plane.

---

xcii Details leading to this result are given by B. N. Delone in Aleksandrov, Kolmogorov, and Lavrent'ev, Vol. 1, pp. 210-213; see also Meserve, pp. 256-257.
xciii A discussion of the characterization of conic invariants is given by B. N. Delone in Aleksandrov, Kolmogorov, and Lavrent'ev, Vol. 1, pp. 238-242 [Math References 2].

7.1.2 Conics in three dimensions

The simplest examples of conics forming three dimensional surfaces are those surfaces known as cylinders. A common example is the circular cylinder. If a circle is formed with its center at the origin of the x-y plane, then the surface of the cylinder is generated by lines parallel to the z-axis passing through the points of the circle. All of the planes perpendicular to the z axis will therefore form circles congruent to the circle generating the surface. Any closed path in the x-y plane can similarly form a cylindrical surface. If the closed path is a conic then, any plane cutting the z-axis will form the same conic.[xciv] A bit more complex is the ellipsoid (defined below for simplicity in standard orientation) for which any plane perpendicular to the x, y, or z axis forms an ellipse. The equation of the ellipsoid is shown with the figure on the left below. A different example of a three-dimensional surface, formed by a parabola and an ellipse, is the elliptic paraboloid shown to the right.

ellipsoid: $\dfrac{x^2}{a^2} + \dfrac{y^2}{b^2} + \dfrac{z^2}{c^2} = 1$ elliptic paraboloid: $\dfrac{x^2}{a^2} + \dfrac{y^2}{b^2} - 2cz = 0$

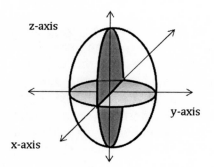

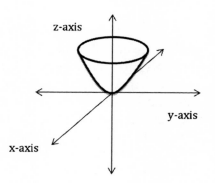

In either figure it is easy to imagine the form of the surfaces when the equations are in these standard forms. The general shape should be apparent by simply considering the curves formed on three planes: the y-z plane with x = c (x equal to some constant); the x-z plane, y = c; or the x-y plane, z = c. The general second degree equation in x, y, and z may be put in such a standard form through rotation of coordinates; however since rotation may occur about the x, y, and z

---

xciv More generally, a cylinder can be formed by the path around the closed curve of a generating line parallel to any straight line.

axes, the procedure is more complicated and will not be given here.[xcv] Equations for other second degree surfaces formed with hyperbolas are shown below:

Hyperbolic paraboloid: $\dfrac{x^2}{a^2} - \dfrac{y^2}{b^2} - 2cz = 0$

Hyperboloid of one sheet: $\dfrac{x^2}{a^2} + \dfrac{y^2}{b^2} - \dfrac{z^2}{c^2} = 1$

Hyperboloid of two sheets: $\dfrac{x^2}{a^2} + \dfrac{y^2}{b^2} - \dfrac{z^2}{c^2} = -1$

The discussion of surfaces in three dimensions so far has been a relatively simple extension of what we did in the plane. In our next sections, however, new mathematical entities called vectors and tensors will be introduced which turn out to have an algebra that differs from that of the real numbers.

7.2   Vectors[xcvi]

One of the most prevalent and significant features of human history from virtually the beginning of civilization has been commercial trading by ship. One might imagine that the resulting need for methods of navigation taking into account wind, current and ship speeds and associated directions might have led early on to the discovery of vectors as a natural means to describe entities such as velocity having direction and magnitude. Some early premonitions of vectors related to the resultants of combinations of forces were anticipated by Aristotle in the fourth century BC and Simon Stevin in the sixteenth century. [203] However, it was only in the seventeenth century that Galileo would give some precision to the concept of a vector. The vector concept, allowing motions to be analyzed in

---

xcv A discussion of this general case is given by B. N. Delone in Aleksandrov, Kolmogorov, and Lavrent'ev, along with illustrations of general quadratic surfaces, Vol. 1, pp.220-227.

xcvi A summary of the historical background of vectors and tensors is given by Wrede, R. C., *Introduction to Vector and Tensor Analysis*, [Math References 37] pp. 1 - 7. Introductory definitions of vectors and vector operations given in Chapter 1, pp. 7 - 21, lead to an advanced treatment of vectors and tensors.

terms of their horizontal and vertical components was crucial to Galileo's description of projectile motion as a parabolic path when air resistance was neglected.[204] Examples of vectors in physics are force, velocity, acceleration, and the electric and magnetic field. Thus, the vector concept, along with its generalization, tensors, would turn out to be central to the description of the physics of the universe.

We have already encountered a mathematical entity which describes magnitude and direction, the complex variable z in the complex plane. Although, the variable $z = x + i\,y$, as expressed in Cartesian coordinates is restricted to the plane, it will provide us with a place to begin our development of vectors. Ultimately the algebra for vectors and complex variables differ, as in for example the operation of multiplication.

That the complex variable, z encompasses our need for something which describes both magnitude and direction is most clearly seen when it is expressed in its polar form, $z = \rho e^{i\,\theta}$. We have also established that this is consistent with complex numbers expressed as the ordered pair (x, y). From Section 3.6, $z_1 + z_2 = (x_1 + x_2, y_1 + y_2) = (x_1 + x_2) + i\,(y_1 + y_2)$ which can be expressed as $\rho e^{i\,\theta}$ with $\rho = \sqrt{(x_1 + x_2)^2 + (y_1 + y_2)^2}$ and $\cos\theta = (x_1 + x_2)/\rho$ and $\sin\theta = (y_1 + y_2)/\rho$. We will extend this approach to vectors having three dimensions, analogously defining magnitude and direction and in the process define what is known as a vector space.

Vectors will be designated as variables in bold, for example, **v** and be designated as an ordered triple, $\mathbf{v} = (a, b, c)$. Note that if in the ordered triple, the third component of the triple is zero, then the definitions for a vector space have counterparts in the complex numbers. The vector space, defined below, is designated as Euclidean as the expression for distance will be dictated by the Pythagorean Theorem.

Euclidean Vector Space[xcvii]

Definition V1: A Cartesian vector is defined with respect to Cartesian axes as the coordinate triple of real numbers, $\mathbf{v} = (a, b, c)$.

---

xcvii The definitions and properties are an example of a linear vector space which can be extended from the three dimensional space of our experience to abstract spaces of n dimensions. B. N. Delone in Aleksandrov, Kolmogorov, and Lavrent'ev gives a geometrical interpretation of vectors, Vol. I, pp. 213 - 218, and S. B. Stečkin discusses abstract spaces, Vol. III, pp. 45 - 59, 136-143.

Definition V2: Two Cartesian vectors, $\mathbf{v}$ = (a, b, c) and $\mathbf{w}$ = (d, e, f) are equal if and only if a = d, b = e, and c = f.

Definition V3: The operation of addition between two Cartesian vectors, $\mathbf{v}$ = (a, b, c) and $\mathbf{w}$ = (d, e, f) is defined by: $\mathbf{v}$ + $\mathbf{w}$ = (a, b, c) + (d, e, f) = (a + d, b + e, c +f).

Definition V4: If d is a real number and $\mathbf{v}$ = (a, b, c), then scalar multiplication is defined as: d $\mathbf{v}$ = (d · a, d · b, d · c).

Note that multiplication by two vectors, $\mathbf{v}$ $\mathbf{w}$ is not defined. From the properties of the real numbers, vectors satisfy the closure, associative, and commutative properties with respect to addition. The vector space also contains the identity element $\mathbf{z}$ = (0, 0, 0) and each vector $\mathbf{v}$ = (a, b, c) has an additive inverse, $-\mathbf{v}$ = (−a, −b, −c).

In addition to these properties familiar from the real numbers, the following additional properties are satisfied by scalar multiplication:

Associativity of scalar multiplication: $a(b\mathbf{v}) = (ab)\mathbf{v}$
Distributive property of scalar sums: $(a + b)\mathbf{v} = a\mathbf{v} + b\mathbf{v}$
Distributive property of vector sums: $a(\mathbf{v} + \mathbf{w}) = a\mathbf{v} + a\mathbf{w}$
Identity element for scalar multiplication: $1\mathbf{v} = \mathbf{v}$

We now look at the geometric interpretation of vector addition which we shall illustrate in the plane. The next figure shows the geometrical interpretation of the addition of $\mathbf{v}$ = (a, b, 0), and $\mathbf{w}$ = (c, d, 0) to form the resultant vector, $\mathbf{r}$ = (a + c, b + d, 0),. The resultant vector $\mathbf{r}$ is the diagonal of the parallelogram formed with sides equal to $\mathbf{v}$ and $\mathbf{w}$. The length of the resultant $|\mathbf{r}| = \sqrt{(a+c)^2 + (b+d)^2}$. The angle that $\mathbf{r}$ makes with the x-axis θ_r is such that $\cos \theta_r = (a + c)/|\mathbf{r}|$. Scalar multiplication can be considered as stretching the length of the vector while maintaining its direction. Scalar multiplication by a negative number indicates a stretching in which the vector is now directed in the opposite sense as illustrated by $-\mathbf{r}$.

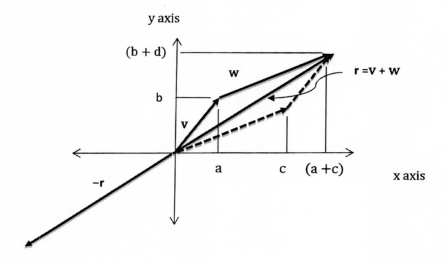

The concept of representing a vector sum as the diagonal of a parallelogram goes back as early as dimly perceived ideas of Aristotle on the direction of forces. This geometrical definition, however, becomes explicit in Corollary 1 of Newton's *Principia*. Newton states that:

> *"A body acted on by [two] forces acting jointly describes the diagonal of a parallelogram in the same time in which it would describe the sides if the forces were acting separately."*[xcviii]

Further geometric interpretations can be established for vectors, Let $\mathbf{v} = (v_1, v_2, v_3)$ and $\mathbf{w} = (w_1, w_2, w_3)$. The figure below shows the two vectors $\mathbf{v}$ and $\mathbf{w}$ and the angle, θ between them.

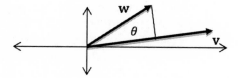

---

xcviii The *Principia* of Isaac Newton inaugurated modern physics; however, it is as obscure for modern readers as it was for Newton's contemporaries. An excellent translation and guide to the *Principia* is given by Cohen, I. B. and Whitman, A., *Isaac Newton, The Principia, A New Translation*, preceded by *A Guide to Newton's Principia* (I.B. Cohen, [Other Citation 2]. The quote is from the p. 417.

Recalling the discussion on the algebraic definition of the cosine function in Section 5.1, the angle θ between the vectors v and w is:

$$\cos \theta = (v_1 w_1 + v_2 w_2 + v_3 w_3)/(\sqrt{(v_1^2 + v_2^2 + v_3^2)} \cdot \sqrt{(w_1^2 + w_2^2 + w_3^2)})$$

$$= (v_1 w_1 + v_2 w_2 + v_3 w_3)/(|v| \cdot |w|)$$

We now introduce a new operation with vectors.

Definition of the scalar product: $v \bullet w = |v| \cdot |w| \cos \theta$

A comparison of the definition of the scalar product with the expression for $\cos \theta$, results in the following definition for Cartesian vectors. (The scalar product is also frequently called the dot product for obvious reasons.)

Theorem of scalar product for Cartesian vectors: For Cartesian vectors with $\mathbf{v} = (v_1, v_2, v_3)$ and $\mathbf{w} = (w_1, w_2, w_3)$, the scalar product $\mathbf{v} \bullet \mathbf{w} = v_1 w_1 + v_2 w_2 + v_3 w_3 = \sum_{i=1}^{3} v_i \cdot w_i$.

This is a good time to note that while we have arrived at our notion of a vector in Cartesian coordinates, the vector and vector concepts such as the scalar product have an independent existence that does not depend on the coordinate system. There are many different coordinate systems, for example spherical and polar coordinates in which the relationship of the components are different than that of Cartesian vectors; however fundamental definitions such as, $\mathbf{v} \bullet \mathbf{w} = |v| \cdot |w| \cos \theta$, remain true in other coordinate systems.

The geometric interpretation of the scalar product is that $|w| \cdot \cos \theta$ is the length of the projection of the vector w onto v and $\mathbf{v} \bullet \mathbf{w}$ is the length $|v|$ times this projection. In Cartesian vectors, $\mathbf{v} \bullet \mathbf{w} = (v_1 w_1 + v_2 w_2 + v_3 w_3)$ and clearly from the definition, $\mathbf{v} \bullet \mathbf{w} = \mathbf{w} \bullet \mathbf{v}$. Also, the magnitude of a vector can be easily expressed in terms of the scalar product: $|v|^2 = \mathbf{v} \bullet \mathbf{v}$. From the definition of Cartesian scalar products in component form, one may prove the following,

Scalar Product Properties:

Commutative Property: $u \bullet v = v \bullet u$
Associative Property: $u \bullet (v \bullet w) = (u \bullet v) \bullet w$
Distributive Property: $u \bullet (v + w) = (u \bullet v) + (u \bullet w)$

The scalar product provides a simple guide to whether vectors are perpendicular to each other. If $\mathbf{v} \cdot \mathbf{w} = 0$ (v and w $\neq$ 0), then $\cos\theta = 0$ and $\theta = 90°$. In many physical situations a scalar product such as $\mathbf{u} \cdot \mathbf{A}$ represents the flow of some quantity through an area. For example, if $\mathbf{u}$ represents the velocity of a fluid and $\mathbf{A}$ is an area through which the fluid can flow with the vector $\mathbf{A}$ representing the magnitude of the area and its orientation, then $\mathbf{u} \cdot \mathbf{A}$ is the volumetric flow rate, say in meter^3/second.

Vectors provide another means of interpreting and demonstrating geometric relationships. A simple proof of the Law of Cosines using vectors is shown below. The figure below is the same as that used in Chapter 4 updated for vectors. Let $\mathbf{a} + \mathbf{b} = \mathbf{c}$ as shown in the next figure. Note that the angle between $\mathbf{a}$ and $\mathbf{b}$ is θ as shown so with $\angle ACB = \angle C$, $\theta = 180° - \angle C$.

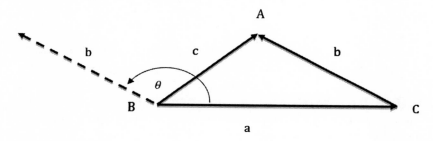

$\mathbf{a} + \mathbf{b} = \mathbf{c}$, therefore:

$\mathbf{a} \cdot \mathbf{a} + \mathbf{a} \cdot \mathbf{b} = \mathbf{a} \cdot \mathbf{c}$
$\mathbf{b} \cdot \mathbf{a} + \mathbf{b} \cdot \mathbf{b} = \mathbf{b} \cdot \mathbf{c}$
$\mathbf{c} \cdot \mathbf{a} + \mathbf{c} \cdot \mathbf{b} = \mathbf{c} \cdot \mathbf{c}$

Summing the three equation, simplifying and noting that $\mathbf{a} \cdot \mathbf{c} = \mathbf{c} \cdot \mathbf{a}$, $a^2 = |a|^2 = \mathbf{a} \cdot \mathbf{a}$ and so forth for terms with b and c, we have:

$a^2 + b^2 + 2\,\mathbf{a} \cdot \mathbf{b} = c^2$, or
$a^2 + b^2 + 2\,a \cdot b \cos\theta = c^2$
$a^2 + b^2 + 2\,a \cdot b \cos(180° - \angle C) = c^2$

Using Appendix H,
$\cos(180° - \angle C) = \cos(180°)\cos(\angle C) + \sin(180°)\sin(\angle C)$
$\qquad\qquad = -1 \cdot \cos(\angle C) + 0 \cdot \sin(\angle C)$

Thus, using vectors, we arrive at our destination, the Law of Cosines.

$$a^2 + b^2 - 2\,a \cdot b \cos(C) = c^2$$

Let us now look at vectors as a means of describing lines and planes in three dimensional space. Suppose we want to describe a line in the direction of the vector $\mathbf{v} = (a, b, c)$ with the point $x_0,\, y_0,\, z_0$ on the line. Any other point, (x, y, z) will form a line with $(x_0,\, y_0,\, z_0)$ and the direction of that line is the vector $\mathbf{w} = (x - x_0, y - y_0, z - z_0)$. The vector $\mathbf{w}$ is in the direction of $\mathbf{v}$ if $\mathbf{w} = s\mathbf{v}$ for some constant s. Equating components of the vectors $\mathbf{v}$ and $\mathbf{w}$, we have:

$x - x_0 = s \cdot a,\, y - y_0 = s \cdot b,$ and $z - z_0 = s \cdot c$
or solving for s,
$(x - x_0)/\,a = (y - y_0)/\,b = (z - z_0)/\,c = s,$ and we have the equation for the desired line.

Now suppose instead, we wish to describe a plane perpendicular to $\mathbf{v} = (a, b, c)$ and containing the point $x_0,\, y_0,\, z_0$. The vector, $\mathbf{w} = (x - x_0,\, y - y_0,\, z - z_0)$ forms a family of vectors describing all possible directions. We now select those points perpendicular to v by requiring $\mathbf{v} \cdot \mathbf{w} = 0 = a\,(x - x_0) + b\,(y - y_0) + c(z - z_0)$. Collecting all constant terms this may also be written as $ax + by + cz + d = 0$, which is the general equation of a plane perpendicular to the direction $\mathbf{v} = (a, b, c)$.

Another notation for Cartesian vectors uses unit vectors aligned with each of the Cartesian axes. Traditionally, $\mathbf{i}$, $\mathbf{j}$, and $\mathbf{k}$ are the unit vectors associated with the x, y, and z axes. As unit vectors, $|\mathbf{i}| = |\mathbf{j}| = |\mathbf{k}| = 1$. In this notation, $v = (a, b, c) = a\,\mathbf{i} + b\,\mathbf{j} + c\,\mathbf{k}$.

We will now introduce the vector product, illustrating it in this new notation.

Definition vector product: $\mathbf{v} \times \mathbf{w} = \mathbf{n}\,|v|\,|w| \sin\theta$ with $\mathbf{n}$ a vector (called the normal) perpendicular to the plane formed by the vectors $\mathbf{v}$ and $\mathbf{w}$, and θ the angle between the vectors.

There are two possibilities for the direction of the normal $\mathbf{n}$ to the plane formed by $\mathbf{v}$ and $\mathbf{w}$. By convention, the normal is oriented as in the following figure. If your palm and fingers of your right hand are aligned with the direction of $\mathbf{v}$ and then rotated counterclockwise to the position of **w**, your thumb will point in the direction of **v x w**. This is called the right hand rule.[xcix]

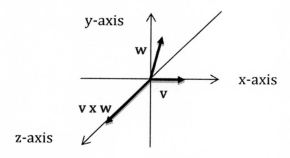

We can use the right hand rule to evaluate the vector product of the unit vectors. Since the unit vector are perpendicular, we have **i** x **j** = **k**, **j** x **k** = **i**, and **k** x **i** = **j**. Similarly, **j** x **i** = −**k**, **k** x **j** = −**i**, and **i** x **k** = −**j**. Also, for parallel vectors, the angle θ between the vectors is 0°, therefore. **i** x **i** = **j** x **j** = **k** x **k** = 0.

Using the unit vectors, one can show the following properties,

Vector Product Properties:

Anti-Commutative Property: **u** x **v** = − **v** x **u**
Distributive Properties: **u** x (**v** + **w**) = **u** x **v** + **v** x **w**
(**u** + **v**) x **w** = **u** x **w** + **v** x **w**

The associative property for the vector product is not generally valid. For example:
(**i** x **i**) x **k** = 0 x **k** = 0 ≠ **i** x (**i** x **k**) = **i** x (−**j**) = −**k**. However, there is an associative property with scalars:

Scalar Associative Property: a(**u** x **v**) = (a**u**) x **v** = **u** x (a**v**)

An example of the use of the vector product is the Lorentz force, F_L which gives the force on a particle of charge q, moving at a velocity **v** in a magnetic field **B** as F_L = q**v** x **B**. A geometric example of the vector product is that **v** x **w** is the area of the parallelogram formed by the vectors **v** and **w**.

---

xcix Another popular way to determine the direction of the normal **n** is by noting that it is the direction a normally threaded screw would move if turned in the same direction as the rotation of **v** towards **w**.

We can now evaluate the vector product in Cartesian form using the unit vectors.

Let $\mathbf{a} = (a_1, a_2, a_3) = a_1 \mathbf{i} + a_2 \mathbf{j} + a_3 \mathbf{k}$ and $\mathbf{b} = (b_1, b_2, b_3) = b_1 \mathbf{i} + b_2 \mathbf{j} + b_3 \mathbf{k}$. Then using, the distributive property of the vector product, for example, $\mathbf{a} \times (\mathbf{b} + \mathbf{c} + \mathbf{d}) = \mathbf{a} \times \mathbf{b} + \mathbf{a} \times \mathbf{c} + \mathbf{a} \times \mathbf{d}$, you will find the following result:

Theorem of the vector product for Cartesian vectors: For Cartesian vectors $\mathbf{a}$ and $\mathbf{b}$, $\mathbf{a} \times \mathbf{b} = (a_2 b_3 - a_3 b_2) \mathbf{i} + (a_3 b_1 - a_1 b_3) \mathbf{j} + (a_1 b_2 - a_2 b_1) \mathbf{k}$

Returning to our geometric example of the parallelogram, the vectors $\mathbf{v} = b\,\mathbf{i}$ and $\mathbf{w} = c\,\mathbf{i} + h\,\mathbf{j}$ can form the sides of a parallelogram with base b and height h. The vector product $\mathbf{v} \times \mathbf{w} = b\,\mathbf{i} \times (c\,\mathbf{i} + h\,\mathbf{j}) = b\,h\,\mathbf{k}$ gives the formula for the area of the parallelogram with the orientation of the resulting area vector normal to the plane of $\mathbf{v}$ and $\mathbf{w}$.

Using the definitions of scalar and vector products along with the unit vectors, you can show that the volume, V of a parallelepiped formed by vectors $\mathbf{a}$, $\mathbf{b}$, and $\mathbf{c}$, seen in the figure below, can be calculated as: $V = \mathbf{a} \cdot (\mathbf{b} \times \mathbf{c})$. This is known as the triple scalar product. That the triple product is equal to the volume V may be seen by noting that $\mathbf{b} \times \mathbf{c}$ is a vector with magnitude equal to the area A of the parallelogram and direction $\mathbf{n}$ normal to the area that is the base of the parallelepiped ($\mathbf{b} \times \mathbf{c} = A\mathbf{n}$). Thus, the height h of the parallelepiped normal to the base is $\mathbf{a} \cdot \mathbf{n}$. Therefore, $\mathbf{a} \cdot (\mathbf{b} \times \mathbf{c}) = \mathbf{a} \cdot A\mathbf{n} = Ah = V$

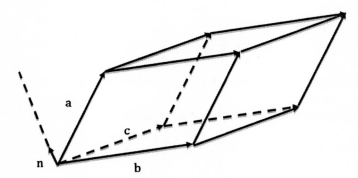

Using the unit vector definitions $(\mathbf{i}, \mathbf{j}, \mathbf{k})$ with $\mathbf{a}$, $\mathbf{b}$, and $\mathbf{c}$ gives the following result for the triple scalar product:

$$\mathbf{a} \cdot (\mathbf{b} \times \mathbf{c}) = a_1 b_2 c_3 + a_2 b_3 c_1 + a_3 b_1 c_2 - a_3 b_2 c_1 - a_1 b_3 c_2 - a_2 b_1 c_3$$

This result is also known as the determinant of a, b, and c and is of great importance in the solution of systems of three simultaneous equations. We will see this again at the end of the chapter.

Our last subject relating to vectors is the transformation of their components due to rotation of coordinate systems in three dimensions. For convenience in what follows the traditional x, y, and z coordinates are designated as x_1, x_2, and x_3. If the position vector is $\mathbf{r}$ = $(x_1, x_2, 0)$ then we have already seen the results in terms of rotating the x_1- x_2 axes in Section 7.1.1 by an angle θ to form new x'_1 - x'_2 axes. Restricting our rotations to those about the third axis x_3, we have then in three dimensions:

$$x_1 = x'_1 \cos \theta - x'_2 \sin \theta$$
$$x_2 = x'_1 \sin \theta + x'_2 \cos \theta$$
$$x_3 = x'_3$$

Without doing a detailed derivation for the general rotation in three dimensions, I will try to give a plausible explanation for the final result. In the equation above relating x_1 to the rotated coordinates x'_1 and x'_2, cos θ is the cosine of the angle between the x_1 and x'_1 axis. Similarly, in the equation for x_2, cos θ is the cosine of the angle between the x_2 and x'_2 axis. The terms with the sine function give the impact of x'_2 on the transformation to x_1 in the first equation and x'_1 on x_2 in the second equation. I note that the angle between the x_1-axis and the x'_2-axis is 90° + θ (see the figure showing rotated axes in Section 7.1.1). From Appendix H,

$$\cos (90° + \theta) = \cos (90°) \cos \theta - \sin 90° \sin \theta = - \sin \theta.$$

Similarly, the angle between the x_2-axis and the x'_1-axis equals $(90-\theta)$ and cos $(90-\theta)$ = cos $(90°)$ cos θ + sin 90° sin θ = sin θ.

Therefore, the sine functions in the transformation are just cosines of the angles between associated axes. This result can be generalized by defining a_{ij} as the cosine between the x_i and the x'_j axis. The a_{ij} are known as direction cosines. In general we may write for any orientation of axes:

$$x_1 = a_{11} \cdot x'_1 + a_{12} \cdot x'_2 + a_{13} \cdot x'_3$$
$$x_2 = a_{21} \cdot x'_1 + a_{22} \cdot x'_2 + a_{23} \cdot x'_3$$
$$x_3 = a_{31} \cdot x'_1 + a_{32} \cdot x'_2 + a_{33} \cdot x'_3$$

We could similarly form an explicit relation between the primed and unprimed coordinates:[c]

$$x'_1 = a_{11} \cdot x_1 + a_{21} \cdot x_2 + a_{31} \cdot x_3$$
$$x'_2 = a_{12} \cdot x_1 + a_{22} \cdot x_2 + a_{32} \cdot x_3$$
$$x'_3 = a_{13} \cdot x_1 + a_{23} \cdot x_2 + a_{33} \cdot x_3$$

Here again, a_{ij} is the cosine between the x_i and the x'_j axis. You should examine closely the difference between these expressions and the previous ones. The difference results from the definition of the direction cosine a_{ij}. For example in the first equation above, there is the term $a_{21} \cdot x_2$ because a_{21} is the cosine of the angle between the x_2-axis and the x'_1-axis.

From the relations between the direction cosines in a Euclidean space, one can show the following relation is an invariant: $x_1^2 + x_2^2 + x_3^2 = x'^2_1 + x'^2_2 + x'^2_3$. Another way to define a vector in Euclidean space is the requirement that a vector satisfy the general transformation shown above.

There are transformations that are not Euclidean as should be apparent from the discussion of hyperbolic geometry. A particularly famous one is the Lorentz transformation of Einstein's Special Relativity.[ci] Special relativity deals with coordinate systems that are moving at a fixed velocity with respect to each other. Einstein postulated, however, that no matter which coordinate system one is in, the speed of light c is the same. This contradicts our normal perception that if two people are running at the same velocity, but one is on the ground and the other is on a moving train, their velocities will be different with the runner on the train having a velocity augmented by the addition of the train's velocity.

---

c In the plane, the result is: $x'_1 = x_1 \cos \theta + x_2 \sin \theta$, and $x'_2 = -x_1 \sin \theta + x_2 \cos \theta$. This result can be simply seen by switching the roles of the axes in our previous result and assuming a clockwise rotation of $-\theta$ from the $x'_1 - x'_2$ axes to the $x_1 - x_2$ axes. Note using Appendix H, $\sin(-\theta) = \sin(0 - \theta) = -\sin \theta$, and $\cos(-\theta) = \cos(0 - \theta) = \cos \theta$.

ci The Lorentz Transformation is derived by B. N. Delone in Aleksandrov, Kolmogorov, and Lavrent'ev, Vol. I, pp. 249 - 253. Einstein provided a presentation with minimal mathematics in *Relativity, The Special and General Theory*, [Other Citation Sources 7]. A simple derivation of the Lorentz transformation is given in Appendix 1, pp. 117- 123. Also, we are privileged to have the qualitative discussion of the development of Relativity and its relation to classical physics by its creator, Albert Einstein with his co-author and co-worker Leopold Infeld, *The Evolution of Physics, from Early Concepts to Relativity and Quanta*, pp. 153 - 208, [Other Citation Sources 8].

One way to look at the impact of the constancy of the speed of light is to look at the distance moved by a light wave initiated at the origin of each of two coordinate systems at time zero as they pass each other. In one of the coordinate systems, which we consider to be at rest, the location of the spherical light wave is such that $x^2 + y^2 + z^2 = (ct)^2$ or $(ct)^2 - x^2 - y^2 - z^2 = 0$. This is an application of nothing more than distance $\sqrt{x^2 + y^2 + z^2}$ equals the speed c times the time t. The second system moves at a velocity v with respect to the first. What is shocking in Einstein's theory is that in the other coordinate system (x', y', z') moving with velocity v compared to the unprimed system, it is also true that, $(ct')^2 - x'^2 - y'^2 - z'^2 = 0$ with t' being time measured in the moving frame. In other words, it is an invariant. The velocity of the primed frame has no impact on the speed of light! Because the invariant includes time, we must have a space-time geometry rather than separate realms for space and time as imagined since the time before Einstein's revelation.

The Lorentz transformation gives the relationship between different coordinate systems that maintains the space-time invariant for all systems. For simplicity, I choose the example where the primed system moves with a positive velocity, v parallel to the unprimed systems x-axis. We have then:

$$x' = (x - v\,t)/\sqrt{1 - \frac{v^2}{c^2}}$$
$$y' = y$$
$$z' = z$$
$$c\,t' = (c\,t - v\,x/c)/\sqrt{1 - \frac{v^2}{c^2}}$$

You should check that the space-time invariant is maintained. Also note that if two events occur at (x_1, y_1, z_1, t_1) and (x_2, y_2, z_2, t_2) in the unprimed frame with $x_2 - x_1 = \Delta x$, $y_2 - y_1 = \Delta y$, and $t_2 - t_1 = \Delta t$, then using the Lorentz transformation,

$$\Delta x' = (\Delta x - v\,\Delta t)/\sqrt{1 - \frac{v^2}{c^2}}$$
$$\Delta y' = \Delta y'$$
$$\Delta z' = \Delta z$$
$$c\,\Delta t' = (c\,\Delta t - v\,\Delta x/c)/\sqrt{1 - \frac{v^2}{c^2}}$$

Also, the event interval, Δs is invariant in all frames:

$$\Delta s = (c\Delta t)^2 - \Delta x^2 - \Delta y^2 - \Delta z^2 = (c\Delta t')^2 - \Delta x'^2 - \Delta y'^2 - \Delta z'^2.$$

A quick look at the Lorentz transformation tells us that if someone in the primed frame measures a time change $\Delta t'$ while observing you in the unprimed frame, then your wristwatch ($\Delta x = 0$) will see only a time change of, $\Delta t = \Delta t' \sqrt{1-v^2/c^2}$. In other words your time has slowed down. As your velocity approaches the speed of light, time for you will become slower and slower. Experimentally we see this in the longer lifetimes of accelerated atomic particles.

Other fascinating consequences of the transformation are that lengths contract in moving systems and that events are not simultaneous in all systems. To see how the phenomenon of length contraction is predicted by the Lorentz transformation, let there be a bar in the moving frame of length $l' = x_2'-x_1'$. In the stationary frame, the bar length is measured by marking simultaneously the location of its ends at a time t as it moves by the unprimed frame and $l = x_2-x_1$. Using the first of the Lorentz transformation equations, $l' = l/\sqrt{1-v^2/c^2}$, or from the point-of-view of the stationary (unprimed frame), the bar is contracted compared to the measurement in the moving frame, $l = l' \cdot \sqrt{1-v^2/c^2}$. However, the transformation equations indicate that the contraction only occurs in the direction of motion. No contraction occurs in the directions perpendicular to motion.

In regard to events that are simultaneous in one frame, notice that when the bar is marked simultaneously at time t, at its ends, x_1 and x_2, the Lorentz transformation for time tells us that an observer in the moving frame will tell us the marks were made at two difference times, $t_1' = (t - v\,x_1/c)/\sqrt{1-v^2/c^2}$ and $t_2' = (t - v\,x_2/c)/\sqrt{1-v^2/c^2}$,

Our main purpose here, however, is to give an example of a transformation that leads to a new geometry. One way to look at space-time geometry is to think of it in terms of geometry with four coordinates instead of the usual three. If we let the fourth coordinate, x_4 be ct, then the invariant becomes: $-x_1^2 - x_2^2 - x_3^2 + x_4^2 = 0$. This is an example of a non-Euclidean geometry with more than 3 dimensions. Long before Einstein, Riemann had already generalized geometry to abstract spaces of n dimensions.[205] The generalized spaces included Euclidean n-dimensional vectors or n—tuples with $\mathbf{v} = (v_1, v_2, v_3, \ldots, v_n)$, $\mathbf{u} \bullet \mathbf{v} = u_1 \cdot v_1 + u_2 \cdot v_2 + \ldots + u_n \cdot v_n$, $\cos \theta = \mathbf{u} \bullet \mathbf{v}/\sqrt{\mathbf{u} \cdot \mathbf{u}} \cdot \sqrt{\mathbf{v} \cdot \mathbf{v}}$, and invariants such as $x_1^2 + x_2^2 + \ldots + x_{n-1}^2 + x_n^2$. However, Riemannian geometry introduced even more general non-Euclidean geometries. These new geometries were introduced through an entity called the metric tensor. These tensors defined the characteristics of the space, including among many other things, relationships of the coordinates to the invariants such as $(ct)^2 - x^2 - y^2 - z^2 = 0$. We will introduce the concept of a tensor in the next section where we will also see that a vector is just a special case of a tensor.

The concept of a tensor would also be vital to satisfying Einstein's requirement in Special Relativity that the laws of physics be consistent with the Lorentz transformation. The laws of electromagnetism meet this requirement; however Newton's laws of dynamics do not. The new formulation of the dynamics, introducing four component vectors of space and time to replace the three components of Euclidean space, would result in one of the most famous equations of physics, $E = mc^2$. We will discuss this when we have gained some insight into the calculus of Newton and Leibniz in the next chapter. The requirement of Einstein in General Relativity that the laws of physics be the same for reference frames moving arbitrarily with respect to each other would similarly lead to the use of tensors.

7.3 Tensors

The concept of a vector follows naturally from the need to define basic physical concepts such as velocity and acceleration which require the specification of a magnitude and direction. Other physical entities require more than a single direction, resulting in the concept of a tensor. Perhaps the most commonly known tensor quantity is that of mechanical stress, a concept in solid and fluid mechanics. For example, if a steel bar of cross sectional area, A is pulled by an axial force, F, (as shown in the next figure) the bar is in a state of tension with a stress, $\sigma = F/A$.

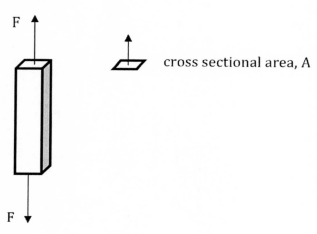

F

cross sectional area, A

F

The stress in this case has the value F/A approximately uniformly throughout the bar. As the bar is under tension, it will begin to deform and when the stress exceeds a characteristic value for the steel material (the maximum tensile stress), the bar will break. If the force is in the opposite direction, a compressive stress will result. The tensile and compressive stresses discussed above are examples in which elements of the steel material respond to forces that are perpendicular to the cross sectional area. Recalling that area is described as the vector perpendicular (normal) to the cross sectional area, another description of the tensile stress is that it is characterized by a force parallel to the surface area vector. In fluid mechanics, the normal stress is the pressure of the fluid which acts normal to the surface area of any element of fluid.

Because force is a vector with three components (F_1, F_2, F_3) it is not hard to imagine other types of stresses. If the resultant force on the bar is at any angle with respect to the cross-sectional area, then other types of stresses occur. These stresses which form the components of a stress tensor are characterized by the direction of the force and the direction (orientation) of the area over which the force acts. As the stresses are distributed throughout the material, the stresses at a particular point in the bar can be thought of as the limit of stresses in elemental cubes of material as the cube size approaches zero. Such an element is shown below with just the components of the stress tensor on the cube face normal to the x_1 direction, (see coordinate system, to the right). In our illustration of the tensile stress in the steel bar above, the normal stress, σ corresponds to the stress $\tau_{11} = \sigma = F_1/A_1$ because the direction of the force component and the surface area vector are both in the x_1 direction. The stress, $\tau_{12} = F_2/A_1$, known as a shear stress, has the force in the x_2 direction parallel to the surface area. A_1. Such a stress would occur in a fluid due to viscous forces as it flows over a solid surface.

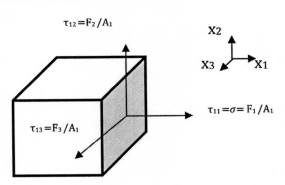

The stress at a point within a material is defined by the limit as the cube's surface areas approach zero. For example, $\tau_{11} = \lim_{A_1 \to 0} \frac{F_1}{A_1}$, $\tau_{12} = \lim_{A_1 \to 0} \frac{F_2}{A_1}$, and $\tau_{13} = \lim_{A_1 \to 0} \frac{F_3}{A_1}$. Taking into account all three directions for force and surface area, the stress tensor $\bar{\bar{\tau}}$ has nine components, which are often listed in what is known as a matrix (much more about this in the next section).

$$\bar{\bar{\tau}} = \begin{pmatrix} \tau_{11} & \tau_{12} & \tau_{13} \\ \tau_{21} & \tau_{22} & \tau_{23} \\ \tau_{31} & \tau_{32} & \tau_{33} \end{pmatrix}$$

Another means of designating a tensor is by a general indication of the indices which form the individual components. In this notation, $\bar{\bar{\tau}}$ is represented as τ_{ij} with the understanding that the range of i and j is 1 to 3. The tensor τ_{ij} having two indices is known as a second order tensor. With this notation, it is natural to designate the vector **v** with three components as v_i. Thus a vector is a first order tensor. This notation greatly simplifies the use of tensor and vectors as individual components need not be expressed.

We are now in a position to form a simple expression for a vector **v'** in a Cartesian coordinate system rotated with respect to the system in which the coordinates for **v** are given. From the previous section, recall that the direction cosine, a_{ij} is defined as the cosine between the x_i and the x_j' axis. A Cartesian vector is transformed rotationally from one Cartesian coordinate system to another just as the coordinate are transformed, therefore:

$v'_1 = a_{11} \cdot v_1 + a_{21} \cdot v_2 + a_{31} \cdot v_3$
$v'_2 = a_{12} \cdot v_1 + a_{22} \cdot v_2 + a_{32} \cdot v_3$
$v'_3 = a_{13} \cdot v_1 + a_{23} \cdot v_2 + a_{33} \cdot v_3.$

In our new notation, this becomes:

$$v'_j = \sum_{i=1}^{3} a_{ij} \cdot v_i$$

This may be further simplified by noting that when an index, such as i is repeated as in $a_{ij} \cdot v_i$, then summation is implied (this is known as the Einstein convention). So we have:

$$v'_j = a_{ij} \cdot v_i$$

It is clear that both sides of the equality represent a vector since there is only one non-summed (free) index on either side, j. Also, in this notation, $u \bullet v = \sum_{i=1}^{3} u_i v_i = u_i v_i$, is clearly a scalar since there is no free index.

Analogous to the transformation of a vector, the transformation of a second order tensor, τ_{ij}, to a new rotated Cartesian coordinate system is given by:

$$\tau'_{mn} = \sum_{i=1}^{3} a_{im} \sum_{j=1}^{3} a_{jn} \cdot \tau_{ij} = a_{im} a_{jn} \tau_{ij}.$$

If this relationship holds between τ_{ij} and τ'_{mn}, then the definition of a second order Cartesian tensor is satisfied. The definition can be extended to tensors of any order. A powerful characteristic of tensors is that any invariant in one coordinate system will be an invariant in all coordinate systems. For example, $u_i' v_i' = u_i v_i$.

The stress tensor representing a physical concept has hopefully provided you with a model of what a tensor is; however another tensor, the metric tensor, $\bar{\bar{g}} = g_{ij}$ is closer to the central themes of our story. The details of the development of the metric tensor are beyond the scope of our introductory story, but a general discussion can provide insight into the breadth of modern geometry and its relation to General Relativity.[cii]

The metric tensor was introduced by Riemann as a means of generalizing geometry. In Euclidean geometry of three dimensions, the metric tensor is particularly simple. I represent it in its matrix form below:

$$\bar{\bar{g}} = g_{ij} = \begin{pmatrix} g_{11} & g_{12} & g_{13} \\ g_{21} & g_{22} & g_{23} \\ g_{31} & g_{32} & g_{33} \end{pmatrix} = \begin{pmatrix} 1 & 0 & 0 \\ 0 & 1 & 0 \\ 0 & 0 & 1 \end{pmatrix}$$

The metric tensor takes its name from its use in the determination of distance in its associated geometry. Thus, in Euclidean geometry, if

---

cii Wrede begins with Cartesian vectors and tensors leading to the theory of general tensors including introductions to Special and General Relativity. D. F. Lawden, *Introduction to Tensor Calculus, Relativity, and Cosmology* [Math References 21] provides a development of vectors and tensors with an emphasis on their application to Special and General Relativity.

Δx_i is the difference between the coordinates of two points, then the distance, Δs is given by:

$$\Delta s^2 = \Delta x_1{}^2 + \Delta x_2{}^2 + \Delta x_3{}^2 = \sum_{i=1}^{3} \sum_{j=1}^{3} g_{ij} \Delta x_i \Delta x_j \,.$$

Because $g_{ij} = 1$ if $i = j$, and is 0 otherwise, with the Einstein convention:

$$\Delta s^2 = g_{ij} \Delta x_i \Delta x_j = \Delta x_i \Delta x_i.$$

In other coordinate systems such as cylindrical or spherical coordinates the metric tensor is more complicated, but if the geometric space is Euclidean, a transformation to a Cartesian coordinate system may always be accomplished to give the simple diagonal metric tensor shown above. Moreover, it can be applied everywhere in the Euclidean space (g_{ij} is independent of the coordinates). Such a simplification is not possible on the surfaces of hyperbolic and elliptic geometries discussed in Chapter 4. This is not surprising considering the deviations we have seen from Euclidean geometry such as in the ratio of a circle's circumferences to its diameter and the sum of the interior angles of triangles. However, we have seen that for small circles and triangles, the geometric relationships approach those found in Euclidean geometry. For example on the surface of a sphere with a non-Cartesian coordinate system, ξ_i, a local Cartesian system could be set up at a point on the sphere with $x_i = f(\xi_i)$, so that $\Delta s^2 \approx \Delta x_1^2 + \Delta x_2^2 = \Delta x_i \Delta x_i$. As $\Delta s \to 0$, in the language of the calculus, $ds^2 = dx_i{}^2$. Such local Cartesian systems are illustrated in the next figure at two points on the surface of the sphere. However, unlike the situation on a plane Euclidean surface, the local Cartesian system orientation clearly varies with location. We are very comfortable with our local coordinate systems on the earth's surface and seldom, if ever, give a thought that our local plane differs from those at different latitudes and longitudes. Therefore, as on the earth's surface, the metric tensor for non-Euclidean geometries is a function of the coordinates.

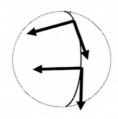

Non-Euclidean geometric spaces in which distance can be expressed locally using a metric tensor are known as Riemannian geometries. In these geometries distance is expressed as: $ds^2 = g_{ij} d\xi_i d\xi_j$. Straight lines between two points are defined as being geodesics, the lines forming the shortest distance between the points. For example, in Chapter 4, we showed that the distance between two cities, Boston and Rome, following a line of constant latitude was longer than the geodesic formed by the great circle route between the cities. The metric tensor provides the means for determining distance, hence the form of the geodesic. Another quantity dependent upon the metric tensor is the curvature tensor, a fourth order tensor. If a surface is flat, the curvature tensor is zero and for a two dimensional surface, an invariant of the tensor is closely related to the Gaussian curvature; the fundamental properties of a space are determined by g_{ij}.[ciii]

The dependence of the metric tensor on location is associated with the introduction of more general expressions for vectors and tensors known as covariant and contravariant tensors. This greater generality would be necessary for Einstein to express his Theory of General Relativity for arbitrarily moving frames of reference. The Cartesian vectors and tensors that I have introduced do not need the concepts of covariant and contravariant tensors since for a Cartesian tensor, their covariant and contravariant forms are the same. This is because the Cartesian coordinate systems can be translated in Euclidean space without their orientation changing.[civ]

The considerations discussed above for non-Euclidean geometries and the metric tensor also apply to Einstein's space-time geometry. However, in this geometry, there are three spatial coordinates, corresponding to our usual space coordinates plus a time coordinate. As in the case of Riemannian geometries, a coordinate system can be set up in space-time coordinates, $(\xi_1, \xi_2, \xi_3, \xi_4)$ with $ds^2 = g_{\mu\nu} d\xi_\mu d\xi_\nu$. Here the indices, μ and ν go from 1 to 4. Similar to non-Euclidean space geometries, at any particular event, a local coordinate system

---

ciii As an example, on the surface of a sphere using the spherical coordinates (r, θ, φ) introduced in Section 4.5, $\Delta s^2 \approx r^2 (\Delta\theta^2) + r^2\sin^2\theta (\Delta\varphi^2)$. Hence, $g_{ij} = \begin{pmatrix} r^2 & 0 \\ 0 & r^2\sin^2\theta \end{pmatrix}$ and from the metric tensor, the curvature tensor and the Gaussian curvature of $\frac{1}{r^2}$ may be obtained (Wrede, p. 367).

civ The development of the concepts of covariant and contravariant tensors is a major theme of the references of Wrede and of Lawden.

may be set up with $ds^2 = (cdt)^2 - dx^2 - dy^2 - dz^2$, similar to the local Euclidean coordinate system at a point on a sphere.

Special Relativity dealt with frames of reference moving at a uniform velocity with respect to each other. The postulate that the speed of light is constant in all frames of reference moving at constant velocity led to the merging of space and time. General Relativity extended the range of frames of reference to include accelerating frames. The central postulate of General Relativity is the Equivalence Principle which may be summarized as postulating that the laws of physics in a frame of reference in a gravitational field are equivalent to those in an accelerating frame. The experience of a downward force in an upward accelerating elevator gives a sense of this principle.[cv]

Numerous authors have described a thought experiment showing the impact of the Equivalence Principle on our concepts of the geometry of space through measurements taken on a rotating frame of reference.[cvi] In D.F. Lawden's version as adapted here, there is a space station in deep space in the form of a torus with spokes to its center. [206] The space station spins around its central axis as shown in the next figure.

---

cv More than two decades before Einstein, a sense of the equivalence of accelerating and gravitational frames was given by Lewis Carrol (of *Alice in Wonderland* fame whose real name is Charles Dodgson) in *Sylvie and Bruno*: "Well, now, if I take this book, and hold it out at arm's length, of course I feel its *weight*. It is trying to fall, and I prevent it. And, if I let go, it falls to the floor. But, if we were all falling together, it couldn't be *trying* to fall any quicker, you know: for, if I let go, what more could it do than fall? And, as my hand is falling too—at the same rate—it would never leave it, for that would be to get ahead of it in the race. And it could never over take the falling floor!" Citation from p. 341, *The Complete Works of Lewis Carrol*, [Other Citation Sources 2]. A description of General Relativistic effects using an elevator as a frame of reference is given by Einstein and Infeld, pp. 209 - 222.

cvi A similar discussion is given by Einstein and Infeld, pp. 226 - 228 as part of a qualitative description of General Relativity, pp. 209 - 240. Other similar descriptions are given by Gamow of imagined measurements on a rotating disc in which in addition to measuring the circumference and radius, Gamow's physicists also measure the sum of the angles of a triangle and find it to be less than 180°, *The Great Physicists from Galileo to Einstein*, pp. 201 - 203. The discussion is part of a qualitative discussion of General Relativity and the curvature of space, pp. 195 -206, [Other Citation Sources 11].

An astronaut on the space station measures the radius of the space station as r' and the circumference of the station as C'. A stationary observer (with respect to the space station) outside the station agrees with the radius measurement (the spoke is moving perpendicular to the direction of motion as viewed by the stationary observer and does not undergo contraction). However, she sees that the measurements around the rim of the torus need to be corrected as the rods used for measurement on the space station are placed parallel to the direction of motion. Our observing astronaut computes the circumference in her frame as $C = 2\pi r'$ and compares it to the measurement C' made around the rim of the space station in the rotating frame. She corrects for length contraction of the moving measuring rods finding that $C'\sqrt{1-\frac{v^2}{c^2}} = 2\pi r'$ with v being the speed the rod passes by the observer. Therefore, the astronaut on the spaces station makes the measurement $C' = 2\pi r'/\sqrt{1-\frac{v^2}{c^2}}$. In other words, the astronaut on the space station finds the result $C'/2r' > \pi$. Because he considers himself to be stationary, he is adamant that the forces that he feels are due to a gravitational field; hence he observes that the space is not Euclidean in the presence of a gravitational field. The Equivalence Principle says that whether a frame of reference is accelerating or in a gravitational field, the laws of physics will be the same, so ironically, the astronaut on the space station is correct to conclude that Euclidean geometry is also not satisfied in frames of reference in a gravitational field.

The metric tensor, $g_{\mu\nu}$ is determined from Einstein's Field Equation relating the metric and curvature tensor to mass distribution. Objects only subjected to gravitational forces follow the geodesic lines that are determined by the metric tensor. Hence, Newton's gravitational forces and the resulting orbits of the planets are replaced by motion along geodesics in space-time. The deviation of the planet Mercury's orbit from that predicted by Newtonian mechanics has been found to support General Relativity.[207] The first support for General Relativity occurred in 1919 only four years after Einstein's publication. Taking advantage of a solar eclipse to study the effect of the sun's presence on the location of stars, an astronomical expedition measured the bending of the light path by the sun to be consistent with General Relativity.[cvii]

Although Riemann could not have foreseen the use of his generalized geometries by Einstein, the framework that he developed was crucial to Einstein's development of General Relativity. For me, the extraordinary connection between the imaginative efforts of these two men reveals the mystery that the structure of the universe is reflected in our consciousness of mathematics.

I close this section on tensors with some relations between Cartesian vectors and tensors as a way to give further insight into their use. (Recall that repeated indices implies summation). To begin, I introduce two tensors, the Kronecker delta tensor, δ_{ij} and the alternating tensor, ε_{ijk}. The second order tensor, δ_{ij} is defined as:

$$\delta_{ij} = \begin{cases} 1, & i = j \\ 0, & i \neq j \end{cases} \text{ or } \delta_{ij} = \begin{pmatrix} \delta_{11} & \delta_{12} & \delta_{13} \\ \delta_{21} & \delta_{22} & \delta_{23} \\ \delta_{31} & \delta_{32} & \delta_{33} \end{pmatrix} = \begin{pmatrix} 1 & 0 & 0 \\ 0 & 1 & 0 \\ 0 & 0 & 1 \end{pmatrix}$$

Therefore, $\delta_{ij}\,\delta_{ij} = \delta_{ii} = \delta_{jj} = 3$.

The third order tensor, ε_{ijk} is defined as:

$$\varepsilon_{ijk} = \begin{cases} 1, & \text{for i, j, k cyclic} \\ -1, & \text{for i, j, k anti-cyclic} \\ 0, & \text{for two or more indices equal} \end{cases}$$

By cyclic, I mean indices in the order: 123, 231, or 312. Anti-cyclic refers to indices in the order: 132, 213, or 321.

We have already seen that the scalar product, $\mathbf{u} \bullet \mathbf{v} = u_i v_i$. The vector product may also be expressed by tensors: $\mathbf{w} = \mathbf{u} \times \mathbf{v} = \varepsilon_{ijk} u_j v_k = w_i$. Notice in the tensor definition, there is only one free index, i so it represents a vector. If you work through the various products with the

---

cvii Einstein, pp. 129 - 132. The bending of light in an accelerating laboratory is also discussed in Einstein and Infeld, pp. 218 - 221 and in Gamow's *The Great Physicists from Galileo to Einstein*, pp. 195 - 198.

alternating tensor you will find for example that, $w_1 = \varepsilon_{1jk} u_j v_k = (u_2 v_3 - u_3 v_2)$.

In the previous section we saw that:
the triple scalar product $\mathbf{a} \cdot (\mathbf{b \times c}) = a_1 b_2 c_3 + a_2 b_3 c_1 + a_3 b_1 c_2 - a_3 b_2 c_1 - a_1 b_3 c_2 - a_2 b_1 c_3$.
In tensor form, this is written as: $\mathbf{a} \cdot (\mathbf{b \times c}) = a_i \varepsilon_{ijk} b_j c_k = \varepsilon_{ijk} a_i b_j c_k$.
Notice that there are no free indices, so it is a scalar. On comparing the results with the expression with vector components shown above, the role of the alternating tensor should be apparent. For example, $\varepsilon_{123} = 1$, therefore, $\varepsilon_{123} a_1 b_2 c_3 = a_1 b_2 c_3$; $\varepsilon_{321} = -1$, and $\varepsilon_{321} a_3 b_2 c_1 = -a_3 b_2 c_1$.

The following relation between the Kronecker and alternating tensors is useful for vector identities. It may be established by using the definitions of δ_{ij} and ε_{ijk} then, evaluating the various possible combinations of indices.

$$\varepsilon_{ijk} \varepsilon_{imn} = (\delta_{jm} \delta_{kn} - \delta_{jn} \delta_{km})$$

It is also useful to note that the effect of multiplying a tensor quantity such as v_i or b_{mi} by δ_{ij} is to change an index.
For example, $v_j = v_i \delta_{ij}$ and $b_{mj} = b_{mi} \delta_{ij}$.

These relations will be used to evaluate the vector: $\mathbf{a \times (b \times c)}$.

Let $\mathbf{w} = \mathbf{b \times c} = \varepsilon_{imn} b_m c_n = w_i$ Definition of the vector product

$\mathbf{a \times (b \times c)} = \mathbf{a \times w} = \varepsilon_{jki} a_k w_i = \varepsilon_{jki} a_k \varepsilon_{imn} b_m c_n$.

$\varepsilon_{jki} a_k \varepsilon_{imn} b_m c_n = \varepsilon_{jki} \varepsilon_{imn} a_k b_m c_n$ ε_{imn} does not involve the index k

$\varepsilon_{jki} = \varepsilon_{ijk}$, therefore   Indices are cyclically transposed

$\varepsilon_{jki} \varepsilon_{imn} a_k b_m c_n = \varepsilon_{ijk} \varepsilon_{imn} a_k b_m c_n = (\delta_{jm} \delta_{kn} - \delta_{jn} \delta_{km}) a_k b_m c_n$

$\delta_{jm} \delta_{kn} a_k b_m c_n = a_n b_j c_n$ $\delta_{kn} a_k = a_n$, etc., since $\delta_{kn} a_k = 0$ unless k = n.

and

$-\delta_{jn} \delta_{km} a_k b_m c_n = -a_m b_m c_j$, therefore,

$(\delta_{jm} \delta_{kn} - \delta_{jn} \delta_{km}) a_k b_m c_n = a_n b_j c_n - a_m b_m c_j$, or

$\mathbf{a \times (b \times c)} = \mathbf{b}(\mathbf{a \cdot c}) - \mathbf{c}(\mathbf{a \cdot b})$

With this demonstration, let us now move on to the interpretation of arrays such as A_{ij} as matrices.

7.4   Matrices

We have looked at arrays such as τ_{ij} and g_{ij} as tensors which are defined in terms of coordinate transformations; however, arrays need not be so defined. In what follows, the algebra of arrays called matrices will be discussed in terms of systems known as linear equations.[cviii] An example is shown below with three unknowns, x_1, x_2, and x_3 related through three linear equations:

$$x_1 + x_2 + x_3 = 2 \tag{7.1}$$
$$2x_1 + x_2 + x_3 = 3 \tag{7.2}$$
$$x_1 + x_2 + 3x_3 = 0 \tag{7.3}$$

The equations are considered to be linear because the unknowns appear only to the first power. Note also that their coefficients are constant. Such a system of equations may be solved by introducing matrix algebra; however, before defining the example problem in this way, I will briefly discuss approaches to its solution using the algebra of the real numbers with which we are already acquainted. This will give some insight into matrix algebra.

Perhaps the most straight forward approach is to solve equation 7.1 for x_1 in terms of x_2 and x_3, substitute the result into 7.2. Then solve for x_2 in terms of x_3 in 7.2, which allows x_1 also to be expressed in terms of x_3. With these expressions for x_1 and x_2, x_3 may be found from 7.3 allowing x_2 and x_1 to be determined. In detail:

From 7.1,
$x_1 = 2 - x_2 - x_3$.
From 7.2,
$2(2 - x_2 - x_3) + x_2 + x_3 = 3$ or $x_2 = 1 - x_3$.
From 7.3,
$(2 - x_2 - x_3) + (1 - x_3) + 3x_3 = 0$ or $(2 - (1 - x_3) - x_3) + (1 - x_3) + 3x_3 = 0$.
Therefore, $x_3 = -1$,
$x_2 = 1 - x_3 = 2$,
$x_1 = 2 - x_2 - x_3 = 1$.

---

cviii An introduction to matrices, linear algebra, and their relation to vectors is given by Davis, P. J., *The Mathematics of Matrices*, [Math References 9]. An advanced discussion is given by S. B. Stečkin in Aleksandrov, Kolmogorov, and Lavrent'ev, Vol. 3, 37 - 74. Highlights of the matrix algebra are given in what follows here.

Although this solution is straightforward, it obviously becomes increasingly tedious as the number of unknowns and equations increase. This approach must also be repeated if we change the constants on the right hand side of the equations. Another approach is to algebraically manipulate the equations as a whole in a method called Gauss-Jordan elimination. This method could be illustrated without using matrices, but it is convenient way to picture the method while introducing matrix notation.

We introduce the matrix, $\overline{A} = \overline{A}_{ij}$ of the coefficients of the unknowns in our example problem. Rows 1, 2, and 3 of the matrix correspond to the coefficients on the left hand side of equations 7.1, 7.2, 7.3, respectively.

$$\overline{A} = \overline{A}_{ij} = \begin{pmatrix} a_{11} & a_{12} & a_{13} \\ a_{21} & a_{22} & a_{23} \\ a_{31} & a_{32} & a_{33} \end{pmatrix} = \begin{pmatrix} 1 & 1 & 1 \\ 2 & 1 & 1 \\ 1 & 1 & 3 \end{pmatrix}$$

We will associate the constants on the right hand side of equations 7.1, 7.2, and 7.3 with the column, $\overline{b} = \overline{b}_i$:

$$\overline{b} = \overline{b}_i = \begin{pmatrix} b_1 \\ b_2 \\ b_3 \end{pmatrix} = \begin{pmatrix} 2 \\ 3 \\ 0 \end{pmatrix}$$

So all of the information we have for our three equations is in $\overline{A}$ and $\overline{b}$. The three equations could be shown as below with each row representing one of equations 7.1, 7.2, and 7.3:

$$\begin{pmatrix} 1 & 1 & 1 \\ 2 & 1 & 1 \\ 1 & 1 & 2 \end{pmatrix} \begin{pmatrix} 2 \\ 3 \\ 0 \end{pmatrix}$$

Our goal in the Gauss-Jordan method is to manipulate the three equations so that when we are finished the result looks like:

$$\begin{pmatrix} 1 & 0 & 0 \\ 0 & 1 & 0 \\ 0 & 0 & 1 \end{pmatrix} \begin{pmatrix} a \\ b \\ c \end{pmatrix}$$ which will mean $x_1 = a$, $x_2 = b$, and $x_3 = c$, for some constants, a, b, c.

Let us begin this process. First we know that the order of the equations does not make any difference, so let's exchange the first two rows to bring the largest coefficient into the first row:

$$\begin{pmatrix} 1 & 1 & 1 \\ 2 & 1 & 1 \\ 1 & 1 & 3 \end{pmatrix} \begin{pmatrix} 2 \\ 3 \\ 0 \end{pmatrix} \rightarrow \begin{pmatrix} 2 & 1 & 1 \\ 1 & 1 & 1 \\ 1 & 1 & 2 \end{pmatrix} \begin{pmatrix} 3 \\ 2 \\ 0 \end{pmatrix}$$

Now let's multiply the top row by 1/2 which is the same as multiplying the original 7.2 by 1/2.

$$\begin{pmatrix} 2 & 1 & 1 \\ 1 & 1 & 1 \\ 1 & 1 & 3 \end{pmatrix} \begin{pmatrix} 3 \\ 2 \\ 0 \end{pmatrix} \rightarrow \begin{pmatrix} 1 & 1/2 & 1/2 \\ 1 & 1 & 1 \\ 1 & 1 & 3 \end{pmatrix} \begin{pmatrix} 3/2 \\ 2 \\ 0 \end{pmatrix}$$

Subtract the top row from the second row (the same as subtracting two equations).

$$\begin{pmatrix} 1 & 1/2 & 1/2 \\ 1 & 1 & 1 \\ 1 & 1 & 3 \end{pmatrix} \begin{pmatrix} 3/2 \\ 2 \\ 0 \end{pmatrix} \rightarrow \begin{pmatrix} 1 & 1/2 & 1/2 \\ 0 & 1/2 & 1/2 \\ 1 & 1 & 3 \end{pmatrix} \begin{pmatrix} 3/2 \\ 1/2 \\ 0 \end{pmatrix}$$

Subtract row 2 from row 1. $\begin{pmatrix} 1 & 1/2 & 1/2 \\ 0 & 1/2 & 1/2 \\ 1 & 1 & 3 \end{pmatrix} \begin{pmatrix} 3/2 \\ 1/2 \\ 0 \end{pmatrix} \rightarrow \begin{pmatrix} 1 & 0 & 0 \\ 0 & 1/2 & 1/2 \\ 1 & 1 & 3 \end{pmatrix} \begin{pmatrix} 1 \\ 1/2 \\ 0 \end{pmatrix}$

Multiply row 2 by 2. $\begin{pmatrix} 1 & 0 & 0 \\ 0 & 1/2 & 1/2 \\ 1 & 1 & 3 \end{pmatrix} \begin{pmatrix} 1 \\ 1/2 \\ 0 \end{pmatrix} \rightarrow \begin{pmatrix} 1 & 0 & 0 \\ 0 & 1 & 1 \\ 1 & 1 & 3 \end{pmatrix} \begin{pmatrix} 1 \\ 1 \\ 0 \end{pmatrix}$

Subtract row 1 from row 3. $\begin{pmatrix} 1 & 0 & 0 \\ 0 & 1 & 1 \\ 1 & 1 & 3 \end{pmatrix} \begin{pmatrix} 1 \\ 1 \\ 0 \end{pmatrix} \rightarrow \begin{pmatrix} 1 & 0 & 0 \\ 0 & 1 & 1 \\ 0 & 1 & 3 \end{pmatrix} \begin{pmatrix} 1 \\ 1 \\ -1 \end{pmatrix}$

Subtract row 2 from row 3. $\begin{pmatrix} 1 & 0 & 0 \\ 0 & 1 & 1 \\ 0 & 1 & 3 \end{pmatrix} \begin{pmatrix} 1 \\ 1 \\ -1 \end{pmatrix} \rightarrow \begin{pmatrix} 1 & 0 & 0 \\ 0 & 1 & 1 \\ 0 & 0 & 2 \end{pmatrix} \begin{pmatrix} 1 \\ 1 \\ -2 \end{pmatrix}$

Multiply row 3 by 1/2. $\begin{pmatrix} 1 & 0 & 0 \\ 0 & 1 & 1 \\ 0 & 0 & 2 \end{pmatrix}$ $\begin{pmatrix} 1 \\ 1 \\ -2 \end{pmatrix} \rightarrow \begin{pmatrix} 1 & 0 & 0 \\ 0 & 1 & 1 \\ 0 & 0 & 1 \end{pmatrix}$ $\begin{pmatrix} 1 \\ 1 \\ -1 \end{pmatrix}$

Subtracting row 3 from row 2, gives the desired form. $\begin{pmatrix} 1 & 0 & 0 \\ 0 & 1 & 1 \\ 0 & 0 & 1 \end{pmatrix}$ $\begin{pmatrix} 1 \\ 1 \\ -1 \end{pmatrix} \rightarrow \begin{pmatrix} 1 & 0 & 0 \\ 0 & 1 & 0 \\ 0 & 0 & 1 \end{pmatrix}$ $\begin{pmatrix} 1 \\ 2 \\ -1 \end{pmatrix}$

Therefore, as before $x_1 = 1$, $x_2 = 2$, and $x_3 = -1$. The important matrix, $\bar{I} = \begin{pmatrix} 1 & 0 & 0 \\ 0 & 1 & 0 \\ 0 & 0 & 1 \end{pmatrix}$ is known as the identity matrix and has the same

definition as the Kronecker delta, δ_{ij}.

The Gauss-Jordan elimination procedure, in addition to providing a more general solution method also should give you a feel for the kinds of operations on rows and columns that lead to matrix algebra.

The system of equations just solved by Gauss-Jordan elimination can be written succinctly using summation and indicial notation: $\sum_{j=1}^{3} \bar{A}_{ij} X_j = \bar{b}_i$ or $\bar{A}_{ij} X_j = \bar{b}_i$ with the Einstein convention. Using the matrix notation with the x_i considered as a single column, the equations are written as:

$$\begin{pmatrix} 1 & 1 & 1 \\ 2 & 1 & 1 \\ 1 & 1 & 3 \end{pmatrix} \begin{pmatrix} x_1 \\ x_2 \\ x_3 \end{pmatrix} = \begin{pmatrix} 2 \\ 3 \\ 0 \end{pmatrix}$$

Here, as before, $\bar{A} = \bar{A}_{ij} = \begin{pmatrix} 1 & 1 & 1 \\ 2 & 1 & 1 \\ 1 & 1 & 3 \end{pmatrix}$, $\bar{b} = \bar{b}_i = \begin{pmatrix} 2 \\ 3 \\ 0 \end{pmatrix}$, and the unknowns

are defined as the column, $\bar{X} = \bar{X}_i = \begin{pmatrix} x_1 \\ x_2 \\ x_2 \end{pmatrix}$ The system of equations can

be expressed therefore as $\bar{A}\,\bar{X} = \bar{b}$.

Comparing this form of the system of equations with the original algebraic equations, it should be clear that in the matrix multiplication, $\overline{A}\,\overline{X}$ we go across each row in $\overline{A}$ and down the column $\overline{X}$. This is described by $a_{ij}x_j = b_i$, if we associate the index i with a row and the j index with a column. So for i = 1 (row 1), $1 \cdot x_1 + 1 \cdot x_2 + 1 \cdot x_3 = 2$,; for i =2 (row 2), $2 \cdot x_1 + 1 \cdot x_2 + 1 \cdot x_3 = 3$; and for i = 3 (row 3), $1 \cdot x_1 + 1 \cdot x_2 + 3 \cdot x_3 = 0$.

In this this example, I have multiplied a 3 row by 1 column matrix by a 3 row by 3 column matrix. Matrices of other dimensions can similarly be multiplied; however, it should be clear that if we have a matrix with m rows and n columns, it can only multiply a matrix of n rows and p columns. The result after matrix multiplication would be a matrix with m rows and p columns. We will assume from here on that all matrices will be square matrices with n rows and n columns except for single column matrices with n rows.

With this introduction to matrix notation, the form, $\overline{A}\,\overline{X} = \overline{b}$ suggests that if the matrix $\overline{A}$ had an inverse, $\overline{A}^{-1}$ such that $\overline{A}^{-1}\,\overline{A} = \overline{I}$, then we could obtain a solution through matrix multiplication: $\overline{A}^{-1}\,\overline{A}\,\overline{X} = \overline{I}\,\overline{X} = \overline{X} = \overline{A}^{-1}\,\overline{b}$. Once we had determined the inverse matrix: $\overline{A}^{-1}$ solutions could easily be obtained for any $\overline{b}$.

It should be clear that $\overline{I}\,\overline{X} = \overline{X}$, from either indicial notation, $\delta_{ij}\,x_j = x_i$ or from matrix multiplication:

$$\begin{pmatrix} 1 & 0 & 0 \\ 0 & 1 & 0 \\ 0 & 0 & 1 \end{pmatrix} \begin{pmatrix} x_1 \\ x_2 \\ x_2 \end{pmatrix} = \begin{pmatrix} x_1 \\ x_2 \\ x_2 \end{pmatrix}.$$

Now how can we find $\overline{A}^{-1}$. A clue comes from the Gauss-Jordan elimination method. Because the matrices are associated with linear equations, all of the operations that we performed in the Gauss-Jordan method on $\overline{A} = \begin{pmatrix} 1 & 1 & 1 \\ 2 & 1 & 1 \\ 1 & 1 & 3 \end{pmatrix}$ can be performed by multiplying $\overline{A}$ by a matrix $\overline{C}$. By a proper choice of $\overline{C}$, multiplication such as $\overline{C}\,\overline{A}$ will result in a new matrix $\overline{A}'$ with $a'_{ij} = c_{ik}\,a_{kj}$ being the same as the element obtained by Gauss-Jordan elimination operations. The new elements a'_{ij} are formed by summing the products of the ith row of $\overline{C}$ and j^{th} column of $\overline{A}$. For example, $a'_{11} = c_{11}\,a_{11} + c_{12}\,a_{21} + c_{13}\,a_{31}$ and $a'_{12} = c_{11}\,a_{12} + c_{12}\,a_{22} + c_{13}\,a_{32}$

Robert G. Bill

Let's look at the first three steps in our Gauss-Jordan elimination
of the matrix $\begin{pmatrix} 1 & 1 & 1 \\ 2 & 1 & 1 \\ 1 & 1 & 3 \end{pmatrix}$. As you go through the matrix multiplications

below, you should be able to see the pattern by which the various operations in the Gauss-Jordan method are duplicated.

The first matrix multiplication duplicates exchanging rows 1 and 2. Moving the element 2 to the first row and column from the second row results from the multiplication of $0(1) + 1(2) + 0(1) = 2$ with the involved elements shown in the matrices in bold. Similarly, moving 1 from the second row and column to the first row and second column results from $0(1) + 1(1) + 0(1) = 1$. The matrix multiplications to multiply the first row by ½ and to subtract the first row from the second are also shown.

Exchanging rows1 and 2: $\begin{pmatrix} \mathbf{0} & \mathbf{1} & \mathbf{0} \\ 1 & 0 & 0 \\ 0 & 0 & 1 \end{pmatrix} \begin{pmatrix} \mathbf{1} & 1 & 1 \\ \mathbf{2} & 1 & 1 \\ \mathbf{1} & 1 & 3 \end{pmatrix} = \begin{pmatrix} \mathbf{2} & 1 & 1 \\ 1 & 1 & 1 \\ 1 & 1 & 3 \end{pmatrix}$

Multiply the first row by 1/2: $\begin{pmatrix} 1/2 & 0 & 0 \\ 0 & 1 & 0 \\ 0 & 0 & 1 \end{pmatrix} \begin{pmatrix} 2 & 1 & 1 \\ 1 & 1 & 1 \\ 1 & 1 & 3 \end{pmatrix} = \begin{pmatrix} 1 & 1/2 & 1/2 \\ 1 & 1 & 1 \\ 1 & 1 & 3 \end{pmatrix}$

Subtract the first row from the second: $\begin{pmatrix} 1 & 0 & 0 \\ -1 & 1 & 0 \\ 0 & 0 & 1 \end{pmatrix} \begin{pmatrix} 1 & 1/2 & 1/2 \\ 1 & 1 & 1 \\ 1 & 1 & 3 \end{pmatrix} = \begin{pmatrix} 1 & 1/2 & 1/2 \\ 0 & 1/2 & 1/2 \\ 1 & 1 & 3 \end{pmatrix}$

The steps in the Gauss-Jordan elimination method for $\overline{A}$ can therefore be considered as a set of sequential matrix multiplications, one for each of the nine operations in the example above leading to the identity matrix, $\overline{I}$. These matrices can be combined through matrix multiplication into a single matrix, $\overline{C}$.

$\overline{C_9}\ \overline{C_8}\ \overline{C_7}\ \overline{C_6}\ \overline{C_5}\ \overline{C_4}\ \overline{C_3}\ \overline{C_2}\ \overline{C_1}\ \overline{A} = \overline{C}\ \overline{A} = \overline{I}$, therefore $\overline{C} = \overline{A}^{-1}$.

If at the same time, we perform the same Gauss-Jordan operations on $\overline{I}$ that we perform on $\overline{A}$ (equivalent to $\overline{C}\ \overline{I} = \overline{C}$), we obtain $\overline{A^{-1}}$.

If the matrix, $\overline{A}$ has an inverse, $\overline{A}^{-1}$, then $\overline{A}^{-1}\ \overline{A} = \overline{A}\ \overline{A}^{-1} = \overline{I}$. This can be shown as follows:

$$\overline{A^{-1}}\ \overline{A} = \overline{I}$$

$$\overline{A}\ \overline{A^{-1}}\ \overline{A} = \overline{A}\ \overline{I} = \overline{A}$$

Since, $\overline{I}\ \overline{A} = \overline{A}$, $\overline{A}\ \overline{A^{-1}} = \overline{I}$.

In our example problem, if at the same time that the Gauss-Jordan elimination method is applied to $\overline{A} = \begin{pmatrix} 1 & 1 & 1 \\ 2 & 1 & 1 \\ 1 & 1 & 3 \end{pmatrix}$, we apply it to

$\overline{I} = \begin{pmatrix} 1 & 0 & 0 \\ 0 & 1 & 0 \\ 0 & 0 & 1 \end{pmatrix}$, we find that $\overline{A^{-1}} = \begin{pmatrix} -1 & 1 & 0 \\ 5/2 & -1 & -1/2 \\ -1/2 & 0 & 1/2 \end{pmatrix}$

You can easily check by matrix multiplication that $\overline{A^{-1}}\ \overline{A} = \overline{A}\ \overline{A^{-1}} = \overline{I}$.

With the identification of the inverse matrix, $\overline{A^{-1}}$, we are now in a position to solve the general set of equations, $\overline{A}\ \overline{X} = \overline{b}$. For any general $\overline{b}$, $\overline{X} = \overline{A^{-1}}\ \overline{b}$.

Please note that I have been careful to consistently multiply matrices on the right or on the left, because matrix multiplication does not in general commute, $\overline{A}\ \overline{B} \neq \overline{B}\ \overline{A}$. A single example is sufficient to show this:

$$\begin{pmatrix} 1 & 2 \\ 3 & 4 \end{pmatrix}\begin{pmatrix} 5 & 6 \\ 7 & 8 \end{pmatrix} = \begin{pmatrix} 19 & 22 \\ 43 & 50 \end{pmatrix} \text{ while } \begin{pmatrix} 5 & 6 \\ 7 & 8 \end{pmatrix}\begin{pmatrix} 1 & 2 \\ 3 & 4 \end{pmatrix} = \begin{pmatrix} 23 & 34 \\ 31 & 46 \end{pmatrix}$$

If $\overline{A}$ and $\overline{B}$ have inverses, then $(\overline{A}\overline{B})^{-1} = \overline{B^{-1}}\ \overline{A^{-1}}$. This can be proved noting that:

$(\overline{A}\overline{B})(\overline{B^{-1}}\ \overline{A^{-1}}) = \overline{A}(\overline{B}\ \overline{B^{-1}})\overline{A^{-1}} = \overline{A}\ \overline{I}\ \overline{A^{-1}} = \overline{A}\ \overline{A^{-1}} = \overline{I}$ and similarly,

$(\overline{B^{-1}}\ \overline{A^{-1}})\overline{A}\overline{B} = \overline{B^{-1}}(\overline{A^{-1}}\ \overline{A})\overline{B} = \overline{B^{-1}}\ \overline{I}\ \overline{B} = \overline{B^{-1}}\ \overline{B} = \overline{I}$, therefore, $(\overline{A}\overline{B})^{-1} = (\overline{B^{-1}}\ \overline{A^{-1}})$.

You might wonder whether all n x n matrices have an inverse. The obvious example of one that does not is $\overline{0}$ shown here as a 3 by 3 matrix, $\begin{pmatrix} 0 & 0 & 0 \\ 0 & 0 & 0 \\ 0 & 0 & 0 \end{pmatrix}$. Other cases, however, are less obvious. I will illustrate the requirement necessary for an inverse matrix to exist with 3 by 3 matrices.

Let us return to linear equations in x_j with constants a_{ij}, b_i ($i, j = 1$ to 3), and $\sum_{j=1}^{3} a_{ij} x_j = b_i$.

$$a_{11} \cdot x_1 + a_{12} \cdot x_2 + a_{13} \cdot x_3 = b_1$$
$$a_{21} \cdot x_1 + a_{22} \cdot x_2 + a_{23} \cdot x_3 = b_2$$
$$a_{31} \cdot x_1 + a_{32} \cdot x_2 + a_{33} \cdot x_3 = b_3$$

The general solution for x_1, x_2, and x_3 can be conveniently expressed with the following constants:

$$\Delta = a_{11} a_{22} a_{33} + a_{12} a_{23} a_{31} + a_{13} a_{21} a_{32} - a_{13} a_{22} a_{31} - a_{11} a_{23} a_{32} - a_{12} a_{21} a_{33}.$$
$$\Delta_1 = b_1 a_{22} a_{33} + a_{12} a_{23} b_3 + a_{13} b_2 a_{32} - a_{13} a_{22} b_3 - b_1 a_{23} a_{32} - a_{12} b_2 a_{33}$$
$$\Delta_2 = a_{11} b_2 a_{33} + b_1 a_{23} a_{31} + a_{13} a_{21} b_3 - a_{13} b_2 a_{31} - a_{11} a_{23} b_3 - b_1 a_{21} a_{33}$$
$$\Delta_3 = a_{11} a_{22} b_3 + a_{12} b_2 a_{31} + b_1 a_{21} a_{32} - b_1 a_{22} a_{31} - a_{11} b_2 a_{32} - a_{12} a_{21} b_3$$
$$x_1 = \Delta_1 / \Delta; \; x_2 = \Delta_2 / \Delta; \; x_3 = \Delta_3 / \Delta$$

Clearly if $\Delta = 0$, then the system of equations has no general solution for all b_i. Under these conditions, the matrix is said to be singular. We can gain some insight into the meaning of this condition if we think of the coefficients in our system of equations as the following vectors: $\mathbf{a}_1 = (a_{11}, a_{12}, a_{13})$, $\mathbf{a}_2 = (a_{21}, a_{22}, a_{23})$, and $\mathbf{a}_3 = (a_{31}, a_{32}, a_{33})$. From the sections on vectors and tensors:

$$\mathbf{a}_1 \bullet (\mathbf{a}_2 \mathbf{x} \, \mathbf{a}_3) = \varepsilon_{ijk} a_{1i} a_{2j} a_{3k} = a_{11} a_{22} a_{33} + a_{12} a_{23} a_{31} + a_{13} a_{21} a_{32} - a_{13} a_{22} a_{31}$$
$$- a_{11} a_{23} a_{32} - a_{12} a_{21} a_{33} = \Delta.$$

A geometric interpretation of Δ is that it represents the volume of the parallelepiped formed from the vectors $\mathbf{a}_1$, $\mathbf{a}_2$, and, $\mathbf{a}_3$. If $\Delta = 0$, then $\mathbf{a}_1$, $\mathbf{a}_2$, and $\mathbf{a}_3$ must all be in the same plane. Since two vectors determine the plane, the third vector represented by one of the equations must be expressed as a combination of the other two equations and therefore is capable of being eliminated by Gauss-Jordan type operations. Mathematically, we say that the equations are not independent. This reasoning may be extended to equations of n-tuples. Therefore, the condition that an inverse exists is that the equations be independent. This discussion is suggestive of the close links between vector spaces and linear and matrix algebra.

In our example, the condition of independence is evaluated through the quantity, Δ, which is known as the determinant of the 3 by 3 matrix $\mathbf{a}_1$, $\mathbf{a}_2$, and $\mathbf{a}_3$ and is indicated symbolically as:

$$\Delta = \det|a_{ij}| = \begin{vmatrix} a_{11} & a_{12} & a_{13} \\ a_{21} & a_{22} & a_{23} \\ a_{31} & a_{32} & a_{33} \end{vmatrix}$$

The theory of determinants can be extended to n-tuples and is discussed in the context of linear equations by Faddeev in Aleksandrov, Kolmogorov, and Lavrent'ev.[208] The solution of the three linear equations is an application of determinants using Cramer's rule.[209] Note that in the solution of three linear equations for $x_j = \Delta_j / \Delta$, that the Δ_j are formed by replacing a_{ij} in the expression for Δ with b_i. For example, in the expression for Δ_1, a_{11} is replaced by b_1; a_{21} by b_2; and a_{31} by b_3. This is a specific result for three linear equations that can be generalized using determinants.

I close this introduction of matrices by listing the postulates that make up the matrix algebra. Matrix algebra was developed by Arthur Cayley in 1857.[210] Lacking the commutative property, it played a key role in the recognition of the axiomatic nature of algebra.

With the identification of matrices symbolized as $\overline{A}$ with a_{ij}, $\overline{A}\ \overline{B} = \sum_{k=1}^{3} a_{ik} b_{kj}$, and quantities such as c without indices as scalars, the postulates should now be clear.

Matrix Algebra[211]

$$\overline{A} + \overline{B} = \overline{B} + \overline{A}$$

$$(\overline{A} + \overline{B}) + \overline{C} = \overline{A} + (\overline{B} + \overline{C})$$

$$\overline{A} + \overline{0} = \overline{A}$$

$$\overline{0}\ \overline{A} = \overline{0}$$

$$(\overline{A} + \overline{B})\overline{C} = \overline{A}\ \overline{C} + \overline{B}\ \overline{C}$$

$$\overline{C}(\overline{A} + \overline{B}) = \overline{C}\ \overline{A} + \overline{C}\ \overline{B}$$

$$(\overline{A}\ \overline{B})\overline{C} = \overline{A}(\overline{B}\ \overline{C})$$

$$c(\overline{\mathbf{A}} + \overline{\mathbf{B}}) = c\,\overline{\mathbf{A}} + {}_c\overline{\mathbf{B}}$$

$$(c + d)\,\overline{\mathbf{A}} = c\,\overline{\mathbf{A}} + d\,\overline{\mathbf{A}}$$

$$(cd)\,\overline{\mathbf{A}} = c(d\,\overline{\mathbf{A}})$$

For every $\overline{\mathbf{A}}$, there exists a matrix $-\overline{\mathbf{A}}$ such that $\overline{\mathbf{A}} + (\overline{-\mathbf{A}}) = \mathbf{0}$

Chapter 8

MAKING A LOT OUT OF THE INFINITESIMAL

"This is one particular, or rather a corollary, of a general method which extends, without any troublesome calculation, not only to the drawing of tangents to all curve lines, whether geometric or mechanical or having respect in any way to straight lines or other curves, but also to resolving other more abstruse kinds of problems concerning curvature, areas, lengths centers of gravity of curves, ..."—Isaac Newton[cix]

8.1 Overview

The discovery of the calculus by Isaac Newton and Gottfried Leibniz must be numbered among the great turning points in civilization. Not only did it inspire an explosive growth in mathematics, but it also provided the basis for the language that would describe the physics of Mechanics, Electromagnetism, General Relativity, and Quantum Mechanics. Moreover, the mathematical language, brought to life in the discovery of the calculus, remains central to science and engineering to this day.

Despite the far reaching consequences of the applications of the calculus, its concepts may be illustrated by Galileo's famous and simple experiment of the free fall of an object. Galileo stated that under the conditions of uniform acceleration of free fall that *"the spaces run through in any times are to each other as . . . the squares of those times."*[cx]

---

cix Newton quotes in his *Principia* from a letter in which he describes the generality of his method of fluxions and fluents, implying thereby the Fundamental Theorem of Calculus, Cohen and Whitman, pp. 649 - 650.

cx Galileo, G., *Two New Sciences*, translated with new introduction, notes, and, *History of Free Fall: Aristotle to Galileo* by S. Drake, ([Other Citation Sources 9]; quotation from *Two New Sciences*, p. 166. The laws associated with a falling body along with ideas of coordinates were anticipated by Nicole Oresme in the fourteenth century; Merzbach and Boyer, pp.239-241. However, these ideas being isolated by the general understanding of the times would not be exploited.

Galileo did not have available the algebraic concepts that would have simplified the expression of his ideas. He used the ideas of proportion from Euclid (Book V). With the advantages of algebraic notation and additional physical insight, this can be expressed more precisely as: $s = \frac{1}{2} gt^2$, $v = gt$ and $a = g$ in which s is the distance an object has fallen, v the object's velocity, a, acceleration due to gravity which is equal to g near the earth'surface, and t the time. These relations are shown graphically in the next figue.

Differential Calculus →

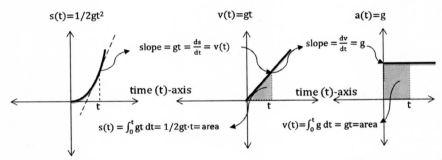

← Integral Calculus

Starting with the graph on the left hand side, plotting distance s that the object has fallen versus time t, a parabolic curve is shown, consistent with Galileo's square of the times relation and $s(t)=1/2gt^2$. If we wanted to estimate speeds of the falling object at a given time t it would be natural to compute a change in distance Δs divided by the change in time Δt near the time of interest. In addition, to being an estimate of the speed, a bit of reflection should lead to the understanding that Δs/Δt is also an estimate of the slope of the curve in the graph. One might expect that as the time differences in the estimates got smaller, we would approach the instantaneous speed and the exact local slope of the distance versus time curve. The differential calculus provides the means for making such an exact determination which in the notation of Leibniz would be indicated as the derivative ds/dt. Using the results of the differential calculus, the slope of the distance curve or speed of the falling object at any time t is computed to be gt. In the next section, the methodology of determining the derivative will be explained.

The second graph from the left shows a plot of velocity versus time as a straight line because at any time the speed or velocity is equal to gt.[cxi] This is consistent with Galileo's statement that under conditions of constant acceleration *". . . motion is equably or uniformly accelerated which, abandoning rest, adds onto itself equal momenta of swiftness [Δv] in equal times [Δt]."*[212] The average time rate of change in velocity Δv over a time change Δt is Δv/Δt which is the average acceleration. Because the velocity versus time curve is the straight line v= gt, the slope which is equal to the acceleration is constant. The constant acceleration g is identified with the acceleration of gravity g. In other words the slope or derivative of the velocity-time curve is the acceleration as shown in the final graph on the right.

Although the method to determine derivatives has not yet been discussed, the relation of the derivatives to slopes of the time dependent curves of distance, velocity, and their meaning for acceleration is straightforward. Probably less clear, however, are the concepts that will allow us to retrace our path from acceleration to the velocity and distance curves using the integral calculus. Starting with the rightmost graph of acceleration versus time, the key insight in this process is to notice that for any time, t, the area under the acceleration versus time curve is equal to gt. This is precisely the velocity at time, t.

Finding the area in the case in which the acceleration is constant, $a(t) = g$, is particularly easy. However, if the acceleration curve were more complex, we could divide the time interval from 0 to t into small increments, Δt and estimate the area under the curve by adding up the rectangles with Δt as their base and their height equal to the ordinates of the acceleration curve. In our simple case, the ordinate is always g. As with the derivatives, we will find that the estimates become exact as Δt approaches 0. We will show this in Section 8.3. For the moment, I only note that this determination of area under a curve by the summation of rectangles with ever smaller bases is, following Leibniz's notation, indicated as $\int_0^t g\, dt$. The symbol $\int$, that looks a bit like an S, stands for the summation from 0 to t of rectangles with (to be momentarily imprecise) infinitesimal bases dt. The velocity is said to be the integral of the acceleration.

Having recovered the velocity as a function of time from acceleration, let us look to see if the same trick works for velocity and

---

cxi Here, I am being careless as velocity is a vector and speed is a scalar calculated independent of direction. However, because the current discussion involves only the motion of an object in one direction (its fall due to gravity), I will in this context use the terms interchangeably and will not bring in vector notation.

distance. As v = gt, the area under the curve forms a triangle with base t and height gt. Therefore, the area under the curve is again easily computed and equal to ½ gt · t = $1/2gt^2$, our original expression for distance versus time. Thus, distance is the integral of velocity.

As v = ds/dt and a = dv/dt, we have just seen an example showing that the operation of integration (computing the area under a curve) is the inverse operation of taking a derivative (finding a slope), for

$$\int_0^t a \, dt = \int_0^t \frac{dv}{dt} \, dt = v \quad \text{and} \quad \int_0^t v \, dt = \int_0^t \frac{ds}{dt} \, dt = s(t).$$ Moreover, the

reverse is also true: $\dfrac{dv}{dt} = a = \dfrac{d}{dt}\int_0^t a \, dt$ and $\dfrac{ds}{dt} = v = \dfrac{d}{dt}\int_0^t v \, dt$. It is a

remarkable and surprising result that the problem of determining the slopes of curves should be so closely related to the problem of finding the area under a curve. The relationship between integration and taking derivatives is proved in the Fundamental Theorem of Calculus which we will examine in Section 8.4.

For over one hundred years after Newton and Leibniz, mathematicians would argue over the precise justification and methods for integrals and derivatives, but since correct answers were (often) found, the lack of precision in the logic of the subject was overlooked. Since physics deals with change in the material world in either time, Δt or space, Δx, the approach of differential and integral calculus became part of the natural language of that subject. In the next two sections, precise definitions of the derivative and integral will be given with examples.

8.2   The slope of a curve; differential calculus

8.2.1   Definition and some consequences

Now that we have established the definition of a limit in Section 5.2.2, the definition of derivative can be stated in a straightforward manner along with its relationship to the slope or tangent to a curve:

Definition of Derivative: For a function f(x) defined over the interval $a \lessgtr x \lessgtr b$, the derivative at x = c with a < c < b is defined as $\dfrac{df}{dx}\big|_{x=c} = \lim_{x \to c} \dfrac{f(x) - f(c)}{x - c}$ if the limit exists. Identifying x − c with Δx, this may also be expressed as: $\dfrac{df(x)}{dx} = \lim_{\Delta x \to 0} \dfrac{f(x + \Delta x) - f(x)}{\Delta x}$.

The notation $f'(c)$ is frequently used for $\frac{df}{dx}|_{x=c}$ or in general for any x, $f'(x)$. The limit concept is crucial to the definition of the derivative for if $\Delta x = 0$, $\frac{f(x+\Delta x)-f(x)}{\Delta x} = 0/0$ which is meaningless. This was the source of much of the criticism of the calculus in the eighteenth century before the concept of a limit was defined. Recall the definition of limit means that for any ε, there exists a neighborhood $|\Delta x| < \delta$ for which $|\frac{f(x+\Delta x)-f(x)}{\Delta x} - \frac{df}{dx}| < \varepsilon$. In this definition, Δx is not set equal to 0. The result of letting $\Delta x \to 0$ often will seem obvious and will not be shown explicitly, but behind each limit expressed in the form $\Delta x \to 0$ is the ε, δ process. By identifying $y = f(x)$ with a curve in Cartesian coordinates, $\frac{f(x+\Delta x)-f(x)}{\Delta x} = \frac{\Delta y}{\Delta x}$

is an estimate of the slope of the curve at the point (x, y). Thus, $\frac{dy}{dx}$, obtained as $\Delta x \to 0$ is the slope of the curve at the point (x, y).

The definition of the derivatives leads to a number of immediate conclusions about a function when the derivative of a function exists. If the derivative of a function exists at a point, then the function is continuous at that point. For if $\frac{df}{dx}$ exists at $x = c$, then

$$\lim_{\Delta x \to 0} f(c+\Delta x) - f(c) = \lim_{\Delta x \to 0} \frac{df}{dx}|_{x=c} \cdot \Delta x = 0 \text{ and } \lim_{\Delta x \to 0} f(c+\Delta x) = f(c).$$

The converse is not true. For example, $f(x) = |x|$ is continuous, but the derivative does not exist at $x = 0$.

Another consequence of the definition is that if $\frac{df}{dx} = 0$ at $x = c$, then the continuous function f has a local maximum or minimum at that point. This is easy to see for if $f(c)$ is a maximum, then with $\Delta x > 0$, $\frac{f(c+\Delta x)-f(c)}{\Delta x} < 0$ and for $\Delta x < 0$, $\frac{f(c+\Delta x)-f(c)}{\Delta x} > 0$ which leads to the condition that at c, $\frac{df}{dx}|_{x=c} = 0$. Analogous comments can be made for a local minimum. Let's now look at some simple examples of derivatives of functions.

Example 1: $y = f(x) = c$. Here, y does not vary with x and $\frac{f(x+\Delta x)-f(x)}{\Delta x} = 0$ for any δ, therefore, $\frac{dy}{dx} = 0$.

Example 2: $y = f(x) = mx + b$. $\dfrac{f(x+\Delta x)-f(x)}{\Delta x} = \dfrac{m(x+\Delta x)+b-(mx+b)}{\Delta x} = \dfrac{m\Delta x}{\Delta x} = m$

which does not vary with x, similar to the above example, therefore, $\dfrac{dy}{dx} = m$. This confirms the relationship between the derivative and the slope of a straight line.

Example 3: Let us confirm the result used in the overview that if $s = 1/2gt^2$, $v = \dfrac{ds}{dt} = gt$.

$$\frac{s(t+\Delta t)-s(t)}{\Delta t} = \frac{\frac{1}{2}g(t+\Delta t)^2 - \frac{1}{2}gt^2}{\Delta t} = \frac{\frac{1}{2}g(t^2+2t\Delta t+\Delta t^2 - t^2)}{\Delta t} = \frac{\frac{1}{2}g(2t\Delta t+\Delta t^2)}{\Delta t} = gt + \frac{\Delta t}{2}$$

Then, $\dfrac{ds}{dt} = \lim_{\Delta t \to 0} \dfrac{s(t+\Delta t)-s(t)}{\Delta t} = \lim_{\Delta t \to 0}(gt + \dfrac{\Delta t}{2}) = gt$.

More formally for any ε, if $|\Delta t| < \delta = 2\varepsilon$, then,

$$\left|\frac{s(t+\Delta t)-s(t)}{\Delta t} - \frac{ds}{dt}\right| = \left|\frac{\frac{1}{2}g(t+\Delta t)^2 - \frac{1}{2}gt^2}{\Delta t} - \frac{ds}{dt}\right| = \left|gt + \frac{\Delta t}{2} - \frac{ds}{dt}\right| < \varepsilon \text{ for } \frac{ds}{dt} = \frac{d(\frac{1}{2}gt^2)}{dt}) = gt.$$

Having confirmed the result stated in the overview that $v = gt$, let us now calculate the acceleration $a = \dfrac{dv}{dt} = \dfrac{d(gt)}{dt}$. Using the result of Example 2, we indeed find that $a = g$. As acceleration is obtained from the derivative of velocity which is itself the derivative of distance, we can also speak of acceleration as the second derivative of distance, or

$a = \dfrac{dv}{dt} = \dfrac{d}{dt}\left(\dfrac{ds}{dt}\right) = \dfrac{d^2s}{dt^2}$.

Example 4: $y = f(x) = x^r$ (r being any real number)

$$\frac{f(x+\Delta x)-f(x)}{\Delta x} = \frac{(x+\Delta x)^r - x^r}{\Delta x}$$

In order to evaluate $(x + \Delta x)^r$, we apply the binomial theorem first stated by Newton for all r.[213]

$$(x + \Delta x)^r = x^r + \frac{r}{1}x^{r-1}\Delta x + \frac{r(r-1)}{2\cdot 1}x^{r-2}\Delta x^2 + \frac{r(r-1)(r-2)}{3\cdot 2\cdot 1}x^{r-3}\Delta x^3 + \dots$$

$$+ \frac{r(r-1)(r-2)\cdots(r-k+1)}{k!}x^{r-k}\Delta x^k + \dots (k = 1, 2, 3\dots)$$

If r is a natural number, then the result has the expected finite number of terms obtained by multiplying the terms in the usual way as for example with r = 4:

$(x + \Delta x)^4 = x^4 + 4x^3 \Delta x + 6x^2 \Delta x^2 + 4x\Delta x^3 + \Delta x^4$ in which the last term corresponds to k = 4, (All of the terms following Δx^4 equal 0 as their coefficients include (r − k).)

If r is not a natural number, then an infinite series is formed, as for example:

$$(x + \Delta x)^{1/2} = x^{1/2} + \frac{1}{2}x^{-1/2}\Delta x + \frac{\left(\frac{1}{2}\right)\left(-\frac{1}{2}\right)}{2}x^{-3/2}\Delta x^2 + \frac{\left(\frac{1}{2}\right)\left(-\frac{1}{2}\right)\left(-\frac{3}{2}\right)}{3\cdot2\cdot1}x^{-5/2}\Delta x^3 + \frac{\left(\frac{1}{2}\right)\left(-\frac{1}{2}\right)\left(-\frac{3}{2}\right)\left(-\frac{5}{2}\right)}{4\cdot3\cdot2\cdot1}x^{-7/2}\Delta x^4 + \cdots .$$

$$= x^{1/2} + \frac{1}{2}x^{-1/2}\Delta x - \frac{1}{8}x^{-3/2}\Delta x^2 + \frac{1}{16}x^{-5/2}\Delta x^3 - \frac{5}{2^7}x^{-7/2}\Delta x^4 + \cdots$$

In either case, $\dfrac{(x+\Delta x)^r - x^r}{\Delta x} = \dfrac{rx^{r-1}\Delta x + \dfrac{r(r-1)}{2\cdot1}x^{r-2}\Delta x^2 + \dfrac{r(r-1)(r-2)}{3\cdot2\cdot1}x^{r-3}\Delta x^3 + \ldots}{\Delta x}$

$$= rx^{r-1} + \frac{r(r-1)}{2\cdot1}x^{r-2}\Delta x + \frac{r(r-1)(r-2)}{3\cdot2\cdot1}x^{r-3}\Delta x^2 + \ldots$$

The term with Δx and those of higher powers are known as higher order terms which vanish as $\Delta x \to 0$. One can show formally that in the limit as $\Delta x \to 0$, $\dfrac{d(x^r)}{dx} = rx^{r-1}$

Example 5: $y = x^{-2/3}$, then $\dfrac{dy}{dx} = \left(\dfrac{-2}{3}\right)x^{-\frac{2}{3}-1} = -\dfrac{2}{3}x^{-5/3}$

Derivatives of other elementary functions are determined in conceptually the same way, although some ingenious insights may be necessary in obtaining the limits to get to the final form. For example, along with some trigonometric identities, the demonstration that $\lim_{x\to0}\dfrac{\sin x}{x} = 1$ is frequently used in the proof that $\dfrac{d(\sin x)}{dx} = \cos x.$[214] A few other commonly encountered derivatives are given below:

$$\frac{d(\cos x)}{dx} = -\sin x$$

$$\frac{d(\tan x)}{dx} = \frac{1}{\cos^2 x}$$

$$\frac{d(\cot x)}{dx} = -\frac{1}{\sin^2 x}$$

$$\frac{de^x}{dx} = e^x$$

Of some importance later on will be the result from above that

$$\frac{d}{dx}\frac{d}{dx}(e^x) = e^x, \ \frac{d}{dx}\frac{d}{dx}(\sin x) = -\sin x, \text{ and } \frac{d}{dx}\frac{d}{dx}(\cos x) = -\cos x.$$

In addition to derivatives of elementary functions such as those discussed above, derivatives of more complex functions can be easily obtained through the rules of taking derivatives that follow from its definition and limit laws.

Derivative of sums of functions:

From the definition of the derivative, it should be clear that if g(x) = u(x) + v(x), then,

$$\frac{dg}{dx} = \frac{du}{dx} + \frac{dv}{dx} \text{ as } \frac{g(x+\Delta x)-g(x)}{\Delta x} = \frac{u(x+\Delta x)-u(x)}{\Delta x} + \frac{v(x+\Delta x)-v(x)}{\Delta x} \text{ and}$$

$$\lim_{\Delta x \to 0} \frac{g(x+\Delta x)-g(x)}{\Delta x} = \lim_{\Delta x \to 0} \left[\frac{u(x+\Delta x)-u(x)}{\Delta x} + \frac{v(x+\Delta x)-v(x)}{\Delta x} \right]$$

$$= \lim_{\Delta x \to 0} \frac{u(x+\Delta x)-u(x)}{\Delta x} + \lim_{\Delta x \to 0} \frac{v(x+\Delta x)-v(x)}{\Delta x} = \frac{du}{dx} + \frac{dv}{dx}$$

This result applies to sums of any length.

Example 6: $g(x) = x^{1/2} + x^{-1} + \sin x$

$$\frac{dg}{dx} = \frac{d(x^{1/2})}{dx} + \frac{d(x^{-1})}{dx} + \frac{d(\sin x)}{dx}$$

$$\frac{dg}{dx} = \frac{1}{2}x^{-\frac{1}{2}} - x^{-2} + \cos x$$

Derivative of products of functions:

$g(x) = u(x)v(x)$, then:

$$\frac{g(x+\Delta x)-g(x)}{\Delta x}=\frac{(u+\Delta u)(v+\Delta v)-uv}{\Delta x}=\frac{uv+u\Delta v+v\Delta u+\Delta u\Delta v-uv}{\Delta x}=\frac{u\Delta v+v\Delta u+\Delta u\Delta v}{\Delta x}$$

$$\lim_{\Delta x\to 0}\frac{u\Delta v+v\Delta u+\Delta u\Delta v}{\Delta x}=\lim_{\Delta x\to 0}\frac{u\Delta v}{\Delta x}+\lim_{\Delta x\to 0}\frac{v\Delta u}{\Delta x}+\lim_{\Delta x\to 0}\frac{\Delta u\Delta v}{\Delta x}$$

As $\Delta x\to 0$, $\Delta u\to 0$ and $\Delta v\to 0$, $\lim_{\Delta u\to 0}\Delta u\cdot\lim_{\Delta x\to 0}\dfrac{\Delta v}{\Delta x}=0$

therefore, $\dfrac{d(uv)}{dx}=u\dfrac{dv}{dx}+v\dfrac{du}{dx}$.

As a consequence of the properties that $\dfrac{d(f(x)+g(x))}{dx}=\dfrac{df}{dx}+\dfrac{dg}{dx}$ and $\dfrac{d(cf(x))}{dx}=c\dfrac{df}{dx}$, the derivative is what is known as a linear operator.

Example 7: $g = u(x)v(x) = x^{2/3}\sin x$

$$\frac{d(uv)}{dx}=\frac{d(x^{\frac{2}{3}}\sin x)}{dx}=x^{2/3}\frac{d\sin x}{dx}+\sin x\frac{dx^{2/3}}{dx}=x^{2/3}\cos x+\frac{2}{3}x^{-1/3}\sin x$$

Example 8: $g(x) = u(x)/v(x) = uv^{-1}$
Using the rule for derivatives of products of functions and the result of example 4,

$$\frac{d\left(\frac{u}{v}\right)}{dx}=\frac{d(uv^{-1})}{dx}=u\frac{dv^{-1}}{dx}+v^{-1}\frac{du}{dx}=-u\frac{\frac{dv}{dx}}{v^2}+v^{-1}\frac{du}{dx}=\frac{v\frac{du}{dx}-u\frac{dv}{dx}}{v^2}$$

Derivative of functions of functions, the chain rule:

Suppose we wish to take the derivative of a function such as $y = (x^2 + 1)^{1/3}$. This does not fall into any of our rules for differentiation; however, if we let $y = y(u) = u^{1/3}$ and $u = x^2 + 1$, we can use a procedure called the chain rule to obtain the derivative without developing any other new method. We can get insight into the chain rule by noting that:

$\dfrac{\Delta y}{\Delta x}=\dfrac{\Delta y}{\Delta u}\cdot\dfrac{\Delta u}{\Delta x}$ and letting $\Delta x\to 0$, $\Delta u\to 0$ suggests that through the limit

process, $\dfrac{dy}{dx}=\dfrac{dy}{du}\cdot\dfrac{du}{dx}$.

As discussed by Courant and Robbins, [215] this result is valid although the argument has some subtle elements, which we will not elaborate on here.

Example 9: $y = (x^2 + 1)^{1/3}$,

Let $y = y(u) = u^{1/3}$, $u = x^2 + 1$.

$$\frac{dy}{dx} = \frac{dy}{du} \cdot \frac{du}{dx} = \frac{1}{3} u^{-\frac{2}{3}} \frac{du}{dx} = \frac{1}{3} (x^2 + 1)^{-\frac{2}{3}} \frac{d(x^2 + 1)}{dx} = \frac{1}{3} (x^2 + 1)^{-\frac{2}{3}} (2x) = \frac{2x}{3} (x^2 + 1)^{-2/3}$$

8.2.2   One derivative after another; Taylor's series

If the derivative of functions exists at a point, then the function is continuous at that point. As we have seen with functions such as distance as a function of time $s(t)$, the operation of taking derivatives can be continued. In the case of the distance function we saw that the acceleration was the second derivative, $a = \frac{d}{dt}\left(\frac{ds}{dt}\right) = \frac{d^2s}{dt^2}$. A function such as $y = \sin x$ can be differentiated indefinitely; $\frac{d\sin x}{dx} = \cos x$ and $\frac{d\cos x}{dx} = -\sin x$. Designating the nth derivative as $\frac{d^n \sin x}{dx^n}$, for $n = 1, 3, 5 \ldots, \frac{d^n \sin x}{dx^n} = (-1)^{\frac{(n+1)}{2}+1} \cos x$. For $n = 2, 4, 6, \ldots \frac{d^n \sin x}{dx^n} = (-1)^{\frac{n}{2}} \sin x$.

Just as the first derivative provides the slope from the change of the function with changes in the independent variable, the second derivative gives the change in the slope with the change in the independent variable and so forth for the next derivatives. From knowledge of all of the derivatives of a function, it seems reasonable to be able to reconstruct the function. This is in essence what the Taylor series does by using the derivatives to generate an infinite series.[cxii] For convenience in the discussion that follows, I will use another

---

cxii The series is generally named after the British mathematician Brook Taylor (1685-1731) despite being known by previous mathematicians, Merzbach and Boyer, pp. 377-378.

traditional notation for derivatives, at any x, $\dfrac{df}{dx} = f'(x)$, $\dfrac{d^2f}{dx^2} = f''(x)$, or in general for the nth derivative $\dfrac{d^n f}{dx^n} = f^n(x)$.

Let us assume that f(x) can be represented as an infinite series and is continuous and differentiable at x = b:

$$f(x) = f(b) + a_1(x-b) + a_2(x-b)^2 + a_3(x-b)^3 + \ldots + a_n(x-b)^n + \ldots$$

Notice that at x = b, the infinite series gives f(x) = f(b). To find a_1, we take the derivative, $f'(x) = 0 + a_1 + 2 \cdot a_2(x-b) + 3 \cdot a_3(x-b)^2 + \ldots$. And at x = b, f'(b) = a_1. Taking the next derivative,

$$f''(x) = 2 \cdot a_2 + 3 \cdot 2 \cdot a_3(x-b) + \ldots; \text{ at } x = b, \ a_2 = \frac{f''(b)}{2}.$$

By continuing the process, we get the general coefficient, $a_n = \dfrac{f^n(b)}{n!}$ (with $n! = n \cdot (n-1) \cdot (n-2) \ldots 3 \cdot 2 \cdot 1$). Therefore, the Taylor series is:

$$f(x) = f(b) + f'(b)(x-b) + \frac{f''(b)}{2!}(x-b)^2 + \frac{f'''(b)}{3!}(x-b)^3 + \ldots + \frac{f^n(b)}{n!}(x-b)^n + \ldots$$

The Taylor series can be used to generate the infinite series given in Section 6.3. However, in general the range of x over which the series converges must be established. As an example, the infinite series for sin x can be generated about x = 0 with the derivatives for sin x and cos x previously given and by noting that sin (0) = 0, cos (0) = 1.

sin x = sin(0) + cos(0) (x − 0) + (−sin (0) (x − 0)² /2! + (−cos(0)) (x − 0)³ /3! + sin(0) (x − 0)⁴ /4! + cos(0) (x − 0)⁵ /5! + ...

$\sin x = x - x^3/3! + x^5/5! + \ldots$

Similarly,

$\cos x = x^2/2! - x^4/4! + x^6/6! - \ldots$

With $\dfrac{de^x}{dx} = e^x$, $f^n e^x = e^x$ and $e^0 = 1$, it should be clear that the Taylor series gives:

$$e^x = 1 + x + \frac{x^2}{2!} + \frac{x^3}{3!} + \cdots$$

As noted in Section 1.2.4, and 6.3, letting $x = i\theta$, informally we can see that:

$$e^{i\theta} = \cos\theta + i\sin\theta$$

8.2.3   An application from Special Relativity

In Section 7.2 on coordinate rotations, I introduced the Lorentz transformation for coordinate frames moving parallel to the x direction at a constant velocity v. This transformation results from the constancy of the speed of light in all frames and creates a four coordinate space-time geometry with $x_1 = x$, $x_2 = y$, $x_3 = z$, and $x_4 = ct$.

$$x_1' = (x_1 - v\,x_4/c)/\sqrt{1 - \frac{v^2}{c^2}}$$
$$x_2' = x_2$$
$$x_3' = x_3$$
$$x_4' = (x_4 - v\,x_1/c)/\sqrt{1 - \frac{v^2}{c^2}} \text{ with } x_4'^2 - x_1'^2 - x_2'^2 - x_3'^2 \text{ invariant.}$$

Given the importance that we saw in the overview of time derivatives in Galileo's work on uniformly accelerated motion, it is natural to ask how the intermingling of space and time affects definitions such as velocity. To approach this question, we need to consider the vector representation of velocity as there are now four coordinates instead of three.

The velocity vector must also be a four-vector and must be related to other coordinate frames through the Lorentz transformation.[216] If the four-vector velocity is $u = (u_1, u_2, u_3, u_4)$ then it transforms as $x = (x_1, x_2, x_3, x_4)$ by simply replacing x_v with u_v (v ranges from 1 to 4) in the Lorentz transformation:

$$u_1' = (u_1 - v\,u_4/c)/\sqrt{1 - \frac{v^2}{c^2}}$$
$$u_2' = u_2$$
$$u_3' = u_3$$
$$u_4' = (u_4 - v\,u_1/c)/\sqrt{1 - \frac{v^2}{c^2}} \text{ with } u_4'^2 - u_1'^2 - u_2'^2 - u_3'^2 \text{ invariant.}$$

The usual velocity $u_1 = \dfrac{dx_1}{dt}$, does not transform properly in the primed frame to $u'_1 = \dfrac{dx'_1}{dt'}$ because of the complex relationship between the coordinates of the primed frame (including time) and unprimed coordinates. For example, after some algebraic manipulation, the relationship between the velocities u'_1 and u_1 is found to be:[217]

$$u'_1 = \frac{u_1 - v}{1 - \dfrac{u_1 v}{c^2}}.$$

To obtain a four-vector of velocity we need to take the derivative of the x_i with respect to a time-like coordinate that does not change with the frame of reference. Such an invariant can be formed with the event interval, $\Delta s^2 = (c\Delta t)^2 - \Delta x^2 - \Delta y^2 - \Delta z^2 = (c\Delta t')^2 - \Delta x'^2 - \Delta y'^2 - \Delta z'^2$. Let $\Delta \tau$ be the time change of a stationary clock that is a clock attached to the moving object, then in any other frame:

$$(\Delta \tau)^2 = \Delta t^2_{\text{moving object}} = \Delta s^2 / c^2 = \Delta t^2 - (\Delta x^2 - \Delta y^2 - \Delta z^2)/c^2.$$

We want to form derivatives such as $\dfrac{dx_1}{d\tau}$. However, through the chain rule we can relate this to our familiar velocity, $u_1 = \dfrac{dx_1}{dt}$ as $\dfrac{dx_1}{d\tau} = \dfrac{dx_1}{dt} \cdot \dfrac{dt}{d\tau} = u_1 \cdot \dfrac{dt}{d\tau}$.

Now, we need $\dfrac{dt}{d\tau}$.

$$(\Delta \tau / \Delta t)^2 = \Delta s^2 / (c\Delta t)^2 = 1 - (\Delta x^2 + \Delta y^2 + \Delta z^2)/(c\Delta t)^2 = 1 - \frac{u^2}{c^2}$$ where u is the velocity of the moving object since $(\Delta x^2 + \Delta y^2 + \Delta z^2)$ is distance moved in time Δt in a frame not attached to the moving object. Therefore,

$$(\Delta t / \Delta \tau) = 1 / \sqrt{1 - \frac{u^2}{c^2}}$$ and taking the limit as $\Delta \tau \to 0$,

$$\frac{dt}{d\tau} = 1 / \sqrt{1 - \frac{u^2}{c^2}}$$. Therefore, the four-vector of velocity is:

$$\boldsymbol{u} = \frac{d(x_1, x_2, x_3, x_4)}{d\tau} = \frac{d(x_1, x_2, x_3, x_4)}{dt} \cdot \frac{dt}{d\tau} = \frac{1}{\sqrt{1 - \dfrac{u^2}{c^2}}} \cdot \frac{d(x_1, x_2, x_3, x_4)}{dt}.$$

The usual velocity vector in Euclidean space is $\mathbf{u} = (u_1, u_2, u_3) =$ $\dfrac{d(x_1, x_2, x_3)}{dt}$ and $\mathbf{u} \cdot \mathbf{u} = u^2$.

The derivative. $\dfrac{dx_4}{dt} = \dfrac{d(ct)}{dt} = c$, so finally we may concisely represent

the four velocity as $\boldsymbol{u} = \dfrac{1}{\sqrt{1 - \dfrac{u^2}{c^2}}}$ $(\mathbf{u}, c)$. The scalar product of

the four-velocity is invariant since it is governed by the Lorentz

transformation, that is $\boldsymbol{u} \cdot \boldsymbol{u} = u_4{}^2 - u_1{}^2 - u_2{}^2 - u_3{}^2 = \dfrac{c^2 - u^2}{\left(\sqrt{1 - \dfrac{u^2}{c^2}}\right)^2} = c^2$.

The expression of physical laws using four-vectors and their extension to tensors has many implications for relativistic physics. We will just explore one of the implications. In classical Newtonian physics, one of the key laws is conservation of momentum. The classical momentum of a particle of mass m and velocity $\mathbf{v}$ is the

vector, $\mathbf{p} = m\mathbf{v}$. The four vector equivalent is $\boldsymbol{p} = m_0\, \boldsymbol{v} = \dfrac{m_0(\mathbf{v}, c)}{\sqrt{1 - \dfrac{v^2}{c^2}}}$.

Here I have used the notation m_0 for the mass of the particle at rest. By defining m_0 as the mass in the frame where the particle is at rest, its value does not change with reference frame. Therefore, $m_0\boldsymbol{v}$ is a four-vector and satisfies the Lorentz transformation. This is similar to the reasoning that led us to use τ for time derivatives.

In classical physics, mass is not affected by coordinate transformation. However, this is not true in Special Relativity. In the particle's rest frame, $\boldsymbol{p} = m_0\, \boldsymbol{v} = (0, m_0\, c)$. In a frame in which the particle is moving at a velocity v, the Lorentz transformation gives,

$\boldsymbol{p}'_4 = m'c = \dfrac{m_0 c + 0}{\sqrt{1 - \dfrac{v^2}{c^2}}}$. Thus in the moving frame mass, m' is greater

than the rest mass. The four-vector of momentum can be simply

expressed as $\boldsymbol{p} = m_0\, \boldsymbol{v} = (mv, mc)$ with $m = \dfrac{m_0}{\sqrt{1 - \dfrac{v^2}{c^2}}}$.

An interpretation for the mass can be made using the binomial theorem[cxiii] or equivalently a Taylor series to look more closely at the implications of relativistic mass.

$$m = \frac{m_0}{\sqrt{1 - \frac{v^2}{c^2}}} = m_0 \left(1 + \left(-\frac{v^2}{c^2}\right)\right)^{-\frac{1}{2}}$$

$$= m_0 \left(1 + (-1/2)\,(1)^{-1/2}\left(-\frac{v^2}{c^2}\right) + \frac{\left(-\frac{1}{2}\right)\left(-\frac{1}{2}-1\right)}{2}\left(-\frac{v^2}{c^2}\right)^2 + \cdots\right)$$

$$m \approx m_0 + \frac{\frac{1}{2}m_0 v^2}{c^2} + \ldots .$$

You may recognize the term $\frac{1}{2}m_0 v^2$ as the classical kinetic energy of a particle. So mass in the frame of the moving particle is increased by $1/c^2$ times the kinetic energy. We identify the rest energy of the particle as $m_0 c^2$. The remaining terms add to form the total energy, E. Thus we arrive at Einstein's famous equation, $E = mc^2$.

It is important to remember that this extraordinary result comes essentially from the constancy of the speed of light and the requirement that the physical laws transform consistently as expressed mathematically by vectors and the calculus.

8.3 Adding up the little pieces; integral calculus

Let us now return to classical physics of Newton to motivate us for the next subject, integral calculus. Newton's Second Law of Motion is the vector equation, $\mathbf{F} = m\mathbf{a}$ in which $\mathbf{F}$ is the net vector force on a body, m is its mass, and $\mathbf{a}$ is the resulting acceleration. In coordinate form in which the subscript indicates components in the direction of the Cartesian axes, x, y or z, the equation represents three differential equations determining motion in the x, y, and z direction as a function of time t or x(t), y(t), and z(t):

$$F_x = ma_x = m\frac{dv_x}{dt} = \frac{d^2x}{dt^2}, \; F_y = ma_y = m\frac{dv_y}{dt} = \frac{d^2y}{dt^2}, \text{ and } F_z = ma_z = m\frac{dv_z}{dt} = \frac{d^2z}{dt^2}.$$

---

cxiii Recall from example 4 in Section 8.2.1: $(x + \Delta x)^r = x^r + \frac{r}{1}x^{r-1}\Delta x + \frac{r(r-1)}{2\cdot 1}x^{r-2}\Delta x^2 + \frac{r(r-1)(r-2)}{3\cdot 2\cdot 1}x^{r-3}\Delta x^3 + \ldots .$

Given a known force $\mathbf{F} = (F_x, F_y, F_z)$, the acceleration $\mathbf{a}$ is determined by Newton's Second Law. To determine the velocity $\mathbf{v}(t)$, we must find a function whose derivative is $\mathbf{a}$. Similarly, we determine $\mathbf{s}=(x(t), y(t), z(t))$ as a function whose derivative is $\mathbf{v}(t)$. In the example in the overview, we did this by finding the area under curves. It is not obvious how in general this approach relates to solving Newton's problem, but we will start by looking once more at the problem of an object falling under the force of the earth's gravity in which velocity and acceleration are in a single direction.

For $v(t) = gt$, the area under the curve $v(t)$ gave us the expression for distance, $s(t)=1/2gt^2$. In this case, finding the area at any time t was easy because the curve formed a triangle of base t and height, gt. However, if $v(t)$ was a complicated curve, I said that we could estimate the result by breaking up the area under the curve into a series of rectangles and then add their areas up. Since we know the answer for the triangle, let's see how this works before tackling a more difficult case. The approach is illustrated in the figure below.

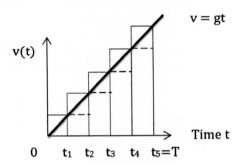

In the figure, I have shown how to estimate the area under the curve $v = gt$ from time 0 to T by two sets of five rectangles. In both cases the bases of the rectangles on the time axis are equal to T/5. The heights of rectangles are determined by their intersection with the straight line $v =gt$. The upper rectangles, shown completely with solid lines, overestimate the area as the height is set by the right edge of the rectangle. Lower rectangles, with their height set by the left edge indicated by a dashed line, underestimate the area. Thus the two sets of rectangles bracket the area under the curve.

If we increase the number of rectangles and the width of their bases decrease, our estimates should get better, and perhaps we can show that in the limit as the base width approaches 0, we get the right answer. Let N be the number of rectangles, then the base width is

$\Delta t = T/N$. The time associated with any particular rectangles can be indicated as $k \cdot \Delta t$ in which k goes from 1 to N for the upper rectangles and 0 to $N - 1$ for the lower rectangles. At time $k \cdot \Delta t$, the height of the rectangle is g $k \cdot \Delta t$. Let ${}_0^T A_{U_N}$ be the area of the upper N rectangles from time 0 to T and ${}_0^T A_{L_N}$ be the corresponding area for the lower triangles, then:

$${}_0^T A_{U_N} = [(g \cdot 1 \cdot \Delta t)\Delta t + (g \cdot 2 \cdot \Delta t)\Delta t + \cdots + (g \cdot N \cdot \Delta t)\Delta t]$$

$$= \sum_{k=1}^{N} (g k \cdot \Delta t)\Delta t = \sum_{k=1}^{N} (g k \cdot \tfrac{T}{N})\tfrac{T}{N}$$

$$= g \frac{T^2}{N^2} \sum_{k=1}^{N} k$$

Similarly, ${}_0^T A_{L_N} = g \dfrac{T^2}{N^2} \sum_{k=0}^{N-1} k$

In Chapter 2, we proved by mathematical induction that, $\sum_{k=1}^{N} k = N(N+1)/2$, therefore

$${}_0^T A_{U_N} = g \frac{T^2}{N^2} \sum_{k=1}^{N} k = g \frac{T^2}{N^2} \cdot \frac{N(N+1)}{2} = gT^2 \left(\frac{1}{2} + \frac{1}{2N} \right).$$

and, ${}_0^T A_{L_N} = g \dfrac{T^2}{N^2} \sum_{k=0}^{N-1} k = g \dfrac{T^2}{N^2} \cdot \dfrac{(N-1)N}{2} = gT^2 \left(\dfrac{1}{2} - \dfrac{1}{2N} \right).$

Now we want to find the limit as $\Delta t = T/N \to 0$ or equivalently, $N \to \infty$.

The limit as $N \to \infty$ of $\dfrac{1}{2N} = 0$ as $\dfrac{1}{2N} < \varepsilon$ for all $N > \dfrac{1}{2\varepsilon}$.

$${}_0^T A_{v=gt} = \lim_{N \to \infty} {}_0^T A_{U_N} = \lim_{N \to \infty} gT^2(\frac{1}{2} + \frac{1}{2N}) = \frac{1}{2}gT^2$$

Also, ${}_0^T A_{v=gt} = \lim_{N \to \infty} {}_0^T A_{L_N} = \lim_{N \to \infty} gT^2(\frac{1}{2} - \frac{1}{2N}) = \frac{1}{2}gT^2$. Thus our procedure works for this simple case and the upper or lower estimates converge to the same limit.

Now let's follow exactly the same procedure to find the area under the curve $y = x^2$ from $x = 0$ to $x = X$. Let $\Delta x = X/N$. The coordinate $k \cdot \Delta x$ is associated with rectangle height of $(k \Delta x)^2$.

$$_0^T A_{U_N} = [(1 \cdot \Delta x)^2 \Delta x + (2 \cdot \Delta x)^2 \Delta x + \cdots + (N \cdot \Delta x)^2 \Delta x]$$

$$= \sum_{k=1}^{N} (k \cdot \Delta x)^2 \Delta x = \sum_{k=1}^{N} (k \cdot \frac{X}{N})^2 \frac{X}{N}$$

$$= \frac{X^3}{N^3} \sum_{k=1}^{N} k^2$$

By mathematical induction, you should be able to prove that $\sum_{k=1}^{N} k^2 = \dfrac{N(N+1)(2N+1)}{6}$. Therefore,

$$_0^X A_{y=x^2} = \lim_{N \to \infty} {_0^X A_{U_N}} = \lim_{N \to \infty} \frac{X^3}{N^3} \sum_{k=1}^{N} k^2 = \frac{X^3}{N^3} \cdot \frac{(2N^3 + 3N^2 + N)}{6}$$

$$= \lim_{N \to \infty} \frac{X^3}{6} \left(2 + \frac{3}{N} + \frac{1}{N^2} \right) = \frac{X^3}{3}$$

Following the same approach, we would find that the estimate of the lower rectangles gives the same answer. This is equivalent to the result discovered by Archimedes with geometric arguments.[218] With these examples for guidance, the following definition of an integral of a function should seem reasonable:[cxiv]

The Definite Riemann Integral: If $f(x)$ is a bounded function on the closed interval $a \leqq x \leqq b$, and the interval $a \leqq b$ is divided into intervals $\Delta x_i = x_i - x_{i-1}$ with $a = x_1 \leqq x_2 \ldots$ $x_{n-1} \leqq x_n = b$, with c_i such that $x_{i-1} \leqq c_i \leqq x_i$, then the integral,

$$\int_a^b f(x)dx = \lim_{max.\Delta x_i \to 0} \sum_a^b f(c_i)\Delta x_i$$ if the limit exists.

The above definition is consistent with the examples given above and is known as Riemann integration. If $\lim_{max.\Delta x_i \to 0} \sum_a^b f(c_i)\Delta x_i$ exists then the function $f(x)$ is said to be Riemann integrable. Unlike the examples, the definition does not require that the intervals Δx_i be

---

cxiv More details are given Lavrent'ev and Nikolskiĭ in Aleksandrov, Kolmogorov, and Lavrent'ev, Vol. 1, pp. 128 - 130; see also Labarre, Jr., pp. 144-148.

equal. Any division is fine as long as the limit is taken with the largest of the Δx_i approaching 0.

In our examples, the integrands $f(x)$ are bounded and continuous over the limits of integration, and we showed that their integrals existed. This may also be shown to be true for all continuous bounded functions resulting in the following theorem.[cxv]

Theorem on Riemann Integrability: If $f(x)$ is a continuous bounded function over the interval $a \leqq x \leqq b$, then the function is Riemann integrable over that interval.

However, the two following integrals also exist as Riemann integrals over the limits shown despite discontinuities in $f(x)$.

$$\int_0^5 f(x)dx \text{ with } f(x) = \begin{cases} 3, \text{ for } x<3 \\ 10, \text{ for } x=3 \\ 4, \text{ for } x>3 \end{cases} \text{ and } \int_0^2 \frac{dx}{x^{1/2}}$$

The integrand $f(x)$, in the first integral is discontinuous at $x = 3$; in the second integral, $f(x) = \frac{1}{x^{1/2}}$ is undefined at $x = 0$. Other functions, sometimes described as pathological function, require a more general procedure known as Lebesgue integration. An example given below of such a function, is a Dirichlet function $f(x)$, which is discontinuous everywhere and not Riemann integrable.

$$f(x) = \begin{cases} 1, \text{ for x irrational} \\ 0, \text{ for x rational} \end{cases}$$

I will return to the issues of integrability as related to the Riemann and Lebesgue integrals after we have proved the Fundamental Theorem of Calculus in the next section. This theorem, known to Newton and Leibniz, links the derivative and the integral and provides a much easier method to calculate integrals than the method we have introduced here.

Some general properties of integrals will be needed to prove the Fundamental Theorem of Calculus. These properties are based upon the definition of the integral with an assist from our understanding of the integral as the area under the curve.

---

cxv A proof is given in Labarre, Jr., pp. 160 - 161.

In the example of finding the area from x = 0 to X under the curve $y = x^2$, suppose we also wanted to know the area from x = 0 to b with b < X. Using the additivity of area we know that,

$$_0^X A_{y=x^2} = {_0^b}A_{y=x^2} + {_b^X}A_{y=x^2} = \frac{X^3}{3}$$ or using the symbols for integration:

$$\int_0^X x^2 dx = \int_0^b x^2 dx + \int_b^X x^2 dx$$. Also note that this implies,

$$\int_b^X x^2 dx = \int_0^X x^2 dx - \int_0^b x^2 dx = \frac{X^3}{3} - \frac{b^3}{3}.$$

With this as motivation, I will state the following properties of the integral:

$$\int_a^c f(x)dx = \int_a^b f(x)dx + \int_b^c f(x)dx$$

$$\int_a^a f(x)dx = 0$$

Furthermore, considering the definition of the integral, if we reverse the order of integration with the intervals $\Delta x_i = x_{i-1} - x_i$ instead of $x_i - x_{i-1}$, you should see that this implies, $\int_a^b f(x)dx = -\int_b^a f(x)dx$ which is consistent with $\int_a^a f(x)dx = 0$.

Two other properties which should be apparent from the definition and which establish the integral as a linear operator are:

$$\int_a^b (f(x)+g(x))dx = \int_a^b f(x)dx + \int_a^b g(x)dx \text{ and } \int_a^b cf(x)dx = c\int_a^b f(x)dx.$$

8.4   A surprising relationship; the Fundamental Theorem of Calculus

We now have the background to understand the linkage between the derivative and the integral established in the Fundamental Theorem of Calculus. The theorem can be illustrated by results obtained in a previous example. We have shown that the area under the curve from x = b to x = X is given by:

$$\int_{b}^{x} x^2 dx = \int_{0}^{x} x^2 dx - \int_{0}^{b} x^2 dx = \frac{X^3}{3} - \frac{b^3}{3}$$

If we think of X as just any general point x then, we can express this as $\int_{b}^{x} t^2 dt = \frac{x^3}{3} - \frac{b^3}{3}$. Here, I have also substituted t for x in the integral to avoid confusion since we are integrating (summing) over this variable and it doesn't make any difference what we call it as long as it has the right functional form.[cxvi] The integral can therefore be seen as a function of x.

$$\int_{b}^{x} t^2 dt = \frac{x^3}{3} - \frac{b^3}{3} = F(x) - F(b), \text{ also often written as } \frac{x^3}{3}\Big|_{b}^{x}$$

From our work on derivatives we know that $\dfrac{dx^r}{dx} = rx^{r-1}$ and for any constant c, $\dfrac{dc}{dx} = 0$. Therefore, $\dfrac{d}{dx}\left[\int_{b}^{x} t^2 dt\right] = \dfrac{d}{dx}\left[\dfrac{x^3}{3} - \dfrac{b^3}{3}\right] = \dfrac{3x^2}{3} - 0 = x^2$,

So we see in this example that the derivative of the integral gives us back the integrand.

$$\frac{dF}{dx} = \frac{d}{dx} \int_{b}^{x} f(t) dt = f(x) \text{ with } f(x) = x^2 \text{ and } F(x) = \frac{x^3}{3}$$

And since in our example above with $f(t) = t^2$, $F(x) - F(b) = \int_{b}^{x} f(t) dt = \int_{b}^{x} \dfrac{dF}{dt} dt$, the integral and the derivative are also inverse operations. The integral is also called the anti-derivative.

I will now formally state the Fundamental Theorem and its proof for continuous functions. The theorem has two parts which can be proved in a number of different ways. My proof follows the order given in Courant and Robbins.[219]

The Fundamental Theorem of Calculus: Part 1, If $f(x)$ is a continuous function over the interval $a \leqq x \leqq b$ and $\int_{a}^{x} f(t) dt = F(x)$,

---

cxvi This is similar to the situation with the scalar product of vectors with $\mathbf{v} \bullet \mathbf{v} = \sum_{i=1}^{3} v_i \cdot v_i = \sum_{k=1}^{3} v_k \cdot v_k$ in which it makes no difference whether the subscript is i or k.

then $\dfrac{dF}{dx} = f(x)$; Part 2, if $\dfrac{dF}{dx} = f(x)$ is continuous over the interval a $\leqq$

x $\leqq$ b, then $\displaystyle\int_a^x \dfrac{dF}{dt}dt = \int_a^x f(t)dt = F(x) - F(a)$.

<u>Part 1</u>: Given $F(x) = \displaystyle\int_a^x f(t)dt$ then, $\dfrac{dF}{dx} = \dfrac{d}{dx}\int_a^x f(t)dt = f(x)$.

<u>Proof</u>

From the definition of the derivative,

$$\frac{d}{dx}\int_a^x f(t)dt = \lim_{\Delta x \to 0}\frac{\int_a^{x+\Delta x}f(t)dt - \int_a^x f(t)dt}{\Delta x} = \lim_{\Delta x \to 0}\frac{\int_a^x f(t)dt + \int_x^{x+\Delta x}f(t)dt - \int_a^x f(t)dt}{\Delta x}$$

$$= \lim_{\Delta x \to 0}\frac{\int_x^{x+\Delta x}f(t)dt}{\Delta x}, \text{ therefore}$$

$$\frac{dF}{dx} = \lim_{\Delta x \to 0}\frac{\int_x^{x+\Delta x}f(t)dt}{\Delta x}$$

Let m be the minimum of $f(x)$ over the interval Δx and M be the maximum. Then from the definition of the integral,

$$m\Delta x \leqq \int_x^{x+\Delta x}f(t)dt \leqq M\Delta x \text{ or } m \leqq \int_x^{x+\Delta x}\frac{f(t)}{\Delta x}dt \leqq M$$

Since $f(x)$ is continuous as $\Delta x \to 0$, m = M = $f(x)$, and therefore,

$$\frac{dF}{dx} = \frac{d}{dx}\int_a^x f(t)dt = \lim_{\Delta x \to 0}\frac{\int_x^{x+\Delta x}f(t)dt}{\Delta x} = f(x).$$

<u>Part 2</u>: Given $\dfrac{dF}{dx} = f(x)$, then $F(x) - F(a) = \displaystyle\int_a^x f(t)dt$

<u>Proof</u>

Let $G(x) = \displaystyle\int_a^x \dfrac{dF}{dt}dt = \int_a^x f(t)dt$

Then from Part 1,

$$\frac{dG}{dx} = \frac{dF}{dx}$$

Therefore, $F(x) = G(x) + c$ with c being any constant since,

$$\frac{dF}{dx} = \frac{dG}{dx} + \frac{dc}{dx} = \frac{dG}{dx}.$$

$G(x) = F(x) - c = \int_a^x f(t)dt$. At $x = a$, $F(a) - c = \int_a^a f(t)dt = 0$, therefore

$c = F(a)$ and $F(x) - F(a) = \int_a^x f(t)dt$.[cxvii]

Q.E.D.

Thus, the Fundamental Theorem of Calculus tells us that if we want to determine $\int_a^x f(t)dt$, we just need to find a function $F(x)$ such that $f(t) = \frac{dF}{dx}$ Notice that any function $F(x) + c$ also works. Ignoring the constant, the indefinite integral or ant-derivative is defined as

$F(x) = \int f(t)dt$, for example $\int x^2 dx = \frac{x^3}{3}$ since $\frac{d\frac{x^3}{3}}{dx} = \frac{3x^2}{3} = x^2$. From the derivative relations that have already been established, integrals that otherwise would be more difficult to determine from the basic definition with an infinite sum are readily obtained. A short list is given below:

$$\frac{d(c \cdot x)}{dx} = c \qquad\qquad \int c\,dx = c \cdot x$$

$$\frac{d(x^2)}{dx} = 2x \qquad\qquad \int 2x\,dx = x^2 \text{ or } \int x\,dx = \frac{x^2}{2}$$

---

cxvii Note that Part 1 is implied by Part 2 which says $F(x) - F(a) = \int f(t)dt$ for if we let the limits be from x to x + Δx, then, $F(x + \Delta x) - F(x) = \int_x^{x+\Delta x} f(t)dt$ and $\lim_{\Delta x \to 0} \frac{F(x + \Delta x) - F(x)}{\Delta x} = \frac{dF}{dx} = \lim_{\Delta x \to 0} \frac{\int_x^{x+\Delta x} f(t)dt}{\Delta x} = f(x)$, as in the proof of Part 1 above.

$$\frac{d(x^3)}{dx} = 3x^2 \qquad\qquad \int 3x^2 dx = x^3 \text{ or } \int x^2 dx = \frac{x^3}{3}$$

$$\frac{dx^{n+1}}{dx} = (n+1)x^n \qquad \int (n+1)x^n dx = x^{n+1} \text{ or } \int x^n dx = \frac{x^{n+1}}{n+1}$$

$$\frac{d(\sin x)}{dx} = \cos x \qquad\qquad \int \cos x\, dx = \sin x$$

$$\frac{d(\cos x)}{dx} = -\sin(x) \qquad -\int \sin x dx = \cos x \text{ or } \int \sin x\, dx = -\cos x$$

$$\frac{de^x}{dx} = e^x \qquad\qquad \int e^x dx = e^x$$

As an example of the use of integrals given above, we determine the area, $_1^2 A_{y=x^3}$ under the curve $y = x^3$ from $x = 1$ to 2.

$$_1^2 A_{y=x^3} = \int_1^2 x^3 dx = \frac{x^4}{4}\Big|_1^2 = \frac{2^4}{4} - \frac{1^4}{4} = \frac{15}{4}$$

The problem of the falling body may now be treated quite elegantly with the calculus. Newton's second law as applied to a body falling only under the force of gravity gives: $F_z = mg = ma_z$ in which z is the coordinate in the direction of the falling body, m the body's mass, and g the acceleration of gravity. Near the earth's surface, Newton's Gravitational Law reduces to $F_z = mg$. We are left with the simple result, $a_z = g$. Thus, $\qquad\qquad\qquad\qquad F_z = mg$ z-axis

$a_z = \dfrac{dv_z}{dt} = g$, and from the Fundamental Theorem,

$v_z(t) - v_z(0) = \int_0^t g dt = gt$. Or, $v_z(t) = v_z(0) + gt$. Here

$v_z(0)$ is the velocity at time 0. If the body falls from rest then $v_z(t) = gt$.

We continue with $v_z(t) = \dfrac{ds_z}{dt} = gt$. Again, using the Fundamental Theorem,

$s_z(t) - s_z(0) = \int_0^t gt\, dt = \dfrac{1}{2}gt^2$. Or, $s_z(t) = s_z(0) + \dfrac{1}{2}gt^2$. If the coordinate system is set up so that the body starts to fall from z = 0, then $s_z(t) = \frac{1}{2}gt^2$. We have derived all of Galileo's results by applying the calculus to Newton's Law of Gravitation and the Second Law of Motion.

Typically, an introductory calculus text devotes considerable space to methods of solving similar but more complex problems of integration; however initially, these do not involve fundamentally new concepts and will not be explored further. Many new concepts do arise in the use of the calculus involving complex variables, vectors, tensors, and other problems with functions with several independent variables; however, this must be pursued at a later stage in your journey.[cxviii] To give you some feel for such extensions and their extraordinary range of influence in descriptions of the universe, I will introduce in the final section of this chapter the concept of partial differential equations (PDEs). These extend the reach of the calculus to functions of several variables. I will illustrate some of their characteristics with an application historically important to the development of PDEs.

Before we move on beyond functions of a single variable, I want to discuss how the concept of integration can be extended beyond continuous functions. We will find that we can extend the range of functions that can be handled by Riemann integration, but ultimately, extremely discontinuous function will lead to a new method of integration that will return us again to the infinities associated with the difference between the rational and the real numbers.

8.5   Looking for trouble; implications of pathological functions

Phenomena in which a sudden rapid change occurs in a system are often modeled as functions with a step changes. The function given below is an example.

$$f(x) = \begin{cases} 3, \text{ for } x<3 \\ 10, \text{ for } x=3 \\ 4, \text{ for } x>3 \end{cases}$$

---

cxviii For applications of the calculus to complex variables see Churchill; vector calculus and partial differential equations are introduced in Aleksandrov, Kolmogorov and, Lavrent'ev. The calculus of vectors and tensors is developed at an advanced level in Lawden and in Wrede.

Clearly the function is discontinuous at the point $x = 3$, and the derivative does not exist at that point. But what about the integral of that function $\int_0^4 f(x)dx$? Recalling the definition of the integral as the limit of a sum may suggest to you that if we break up the sum into two regions, with $x < 3$, and $x > 3$, we may be able to fulfill the requirement that the limit exists as $\Delta x \to 0$. This approach developed by Cauchy[220] is realized in the following form:

$$\int_0^4 f(x)dx = \lim_{a \to 3-} \int_0^a 3dx + \lim_{b \to 3+} \int_b^4 4dx = \lim_{a \to 3-} 3x\Big]_0^a + \lim_{b \to 3+} 4x\Big]_b^4$$

Let $a = 3 - \delta$ and $b = 3 + \delta$ then

$$\int_0^4 f(x)dx = \lim_{\delta \to 0}[3(3-\delta) - 3 \cdot 0] + [4 \cdot 4 - 4(3 + \delta)]$$

$$= \lim_{\delta \to 0} ([9 - 3\delta] + [4 - 4\delta]) = \lim_{\delta \to 0} 13 + 13\delta$$

Therefore, $|\int_0^4 f(x)dx - 13| < \varepsilon$ if $\delta < \varepsilon/13$ and $\int_0^4 f(x)dx = 13$.

In this example $f(x)$ is what is known as a piecewise continuous function. On either side of the discontinuity at a point, the function is continuous. In general, as long as the functions are continuous between a finite number of points of discontinuity, the integral may be calculated. Notice that there is no contribution to the integral at the point of discontinuity $x = 3$, so the integral would still exist even if $f(x)$ is not defined at that point.

Another type of discontinuity occurs when the function is unbounded at a point in the domain of the function or the limits of integration are unbounded. These types of integrals are called improper integrals. For example, the function, $\frac{1}{x^{1/2}}$ integrated from 0 to 2 in the example below is unbounded as x approaches 0. In integrating this function, we will try the same approach as that used with the previous piecewise continuous function.

$$\int_0^2 \frac{dx}{x^{1/2}} = \int_0^2 x^{-1/2}dx \overset{?}{=} \lim_{a \to 0+} \int_a^2 x^{-1/2}dx = \lim_{a \to 0+} \frac{x^{-\frac{1}{2}+1}}{-\frac{1}{2}+1}\Big]_a^2 = \lim_{a \to 0+} 2x^{1/2}\Big]_a^2$$

$$= 2 \cdot 2^{\frac{1}{2}} - 2 \cdot 0^{\frac{1}{2}} = 2\sqrt{2}.$$

More formally, let a $= 0 + \delta$, $\int_0^2 \dfrac{dx}{x^{1/2}} = \lim_{\delta \to 0} 2\sqrt{2} - 2(\delta)^{1/2}$

Therefore, $\left| \int_0^2 \dfrac{dx}{x^{\frac{1}{2}}} - 2\sqrt{2} \right| < \varepsilon$ if $\delta < \dfrac{\varepsilon^2}{4}$ and $\int_0^2 \dfrac{dx}{x^{1/2}} = 2\sqrt{2}$.

The integral is said to converge.

The convergence of improper integrals must be established as indicated in the previous example. In general for a > 0, the integral $\int_0^a x^n dx = \dfrac{x^{n+1}}{n+1}]_0^a$ does not converge if $n < -1$ as x^{n+1} is undefined at $x = 0$. For $n > -1$, the integral converges as $\dfrac{x^{n+1}}{n+1}]_0^a$ can be evaluated in the usual way.

Now in the above example, what about n$= -1$, that is, $\int_0^a \dfrac{dx}{x}$. In this case, the integral does not converge as $\dfrac{x^{n+1}}{n+1}]_0^a$ is undefined for $n = -1$. However, if we change the lower limit to 1, we can see intuitively, by considering the integral as the area under the curve y $= 1/x$, that the integral should exist.

Because of the importance of this integral, I digress a bit to introduce the natural logarithm, ln $(x) = \int_1^x \dfrac{dx}{x}$. From the Fundamental Theorem, $\dfrac{d(\ln x)}{dx} = \dfrac{1}{x}$; thus the slope of the function ln (x) is positive for all $x \geq 1$ and the integral monotonically increases. Also,

ln $(1) = \int_1^1 \dfrac{dx}{x} = 0$. Courant and Robbins show that the function ln (x) has the properties of a logarithm.[221] For example, ln $(ax) =$ ln $(a) +$ ln (x) in the same way that for the common logarithm, base 10, log 1000 $=$ log 10 $+$ log 100 $= 1 + 2 = 3$ since $10^3 = 1000$. Also, ln $(x^n) = n$ ln (x) in the same way as log $(10^3) = 3$ log$(10) = 3$. The base of the natural logarithm was designated as e by Euler in 1736.[222] Hence, $e^{\ln (x)} = x$ as $10^{\log (x)} = x$. However, a proof by Charles Hermite (1822-1901) showing that e was a transcendental number, e $= 2.718281828459 \ldots$, was only published in 1873.[223]

Many common applications are covered satisfactorily by our definition of the integral when extended to piecewise continuous functions and improper integrals, but mathematicians in their search for a precise understanding of the foundations of the calculus would investigate the implications of even more discontinuous functions. A particularly illustrative example is a Dirichlet function,

$f(x) = \begin{cases} 1, & \text{for x irrational} \\ 0, & \text{for x rational} \end{cases}$.[cxix] The function is discontinuous everywhere for no matter how small a region δ we take around any x, f(x) will oscillate between 1 and 0. As a result, the function also has no derivative, but could a meaningful integral of the function be defined that would still be consistent with results for continuous functions?

Let us first look at the simple function g(x) = 1 and take an intuitive approach to evaluating the contributions of the rational and irrational numbers to the integral.

$$\int_0^1 g(x)dx = \int_0^1 dx = x]_0^1 = 1 - 0 = 1.$$

We know from our work on the real numbers that every number in the interval from 0 to 1 is either rational or irrational. Going back to the fundamental definition of the integral, let us try to calculate the contribution of the rational numbers to the integral. Let r(x) = 1 if x is a rational number and 0 otherwise. Because we know that the rational numbers can be put into order with the natural numbers i = 1, 2, 3 . . . (see Chapter 3), each rational number can be covered by an interval Δx_i. Therefore, if c_i is the ith rational number which we cover with the interval Δx_i then,

$$\int_0^1 r(x)dx = \lim_{\substack{\Delta x_i \to 0 \\ 0 \leq c_i \leq 1}} \sum_{i=1}^{\infty} r(c_i)\Delta x_i = \lim_{\Delta x_i \to 0} \sum_{i=1}^{\infty} \Delta x_i.$$

Let $\Delta x_i = \dfrac{\varepsilon}{2^i}$, then $\int_0^1 r(x)dx = \lim_{\varepsilon \to 0} \sum_{i=1}^{\infty} \dfrac{\varepsilon}{2^i} = \lim_{\varepsilon \to 0} \varepsilon \cdot 1 = 0$,

since $\sum_{i=1}^{\infty} \dfrac{1}{2^i}$ forms a geometric series equal to 1.

---

cxix William Dunham, *The Calculus Gallery*, [Math References 10], provides a detailed discussion of pathological functions including the Dirichlet function, pp. 99-101, Riemann's function which has an infinite number of discontinuities yet is Riemann integrable, pp. 108-112, the Weierstrass function which is continuous at every point, but differentiable at none, pp. 140-148; and a general discussion of pathological functions and their relation to the Fundamental Theorem, pp. 171-182. The Calculus Gallery provides a highly readable account of mathematical and historical details in the development of the calculus.

Although the rational numbers are dense, that is, between any two numbers there are an infinite number of rational numbers, the integral over the rational numbers is zero! Mathematically, the rational numbers are said to form a set of measure zero. This is a direct result of the rational numbers being only countably infinite. Recalling that $\int_0^1 dx = 1$, we are therefore left with the conjecture that

if $f(x) = \{ {1, \ \text{for x irrational} \atop 0, \ \text{for x rational}}$, then $\int_0^1 f(x) dx = 1$.

Thus, the entire contribution to the integral seems to come from the irrational numbers. This result should remind you that we have shown that there are more irrational numbers than rational numbers in that the irrational numbers are uncountably infinite.

Now that I have argued that the contribution to the integral of a function of an infinite set of rational numbers is zero, it should be apparent that the contribution due to any finite number of rational numbers will also be zero. A function, which is continuous except at a set of points of measure zero, is said to be continuous almost everywhere. Any countably infinite set of numbers such as the integers is also a set of measure zero.

We have already seen that piecewise continuous functions are Riemann integrable; this situation is concisely covered by Lebesgue's condition for a function to be Riemann integrable by drawing on the concept of measure zero.[224]

Lebesgue's Condition for Riemann Integrability: A necessary and sufficient condition for a bounded function f(x) to be Riemann integrable is that it be continuous almost everywhere (at all but points of a set of measure zero).

The problem with the Dirichlet function is that it is discontinuous everywhere. Our intuitive look at its integral suggests that there should be a way to define integration in a manner that gives a result for the integral of the Dirichlet function and is consistent with the results of Riemann integration when it can be applied. Henri Lebesgue attacked this problem by giving a new definition to the integral which we call the Lebesgue integral.[cxx] Instead of basing the integral on a

---

cxx An introduction to measure theory and the Lebesgue integral is given by S. B. Stečkin in Aleksandrov, Kolmogorov, and Lavrent'ev, Vol. 3, pp. 25-36; see

sum of rectangles with bases on the abscissa (x-axis) and heights defined by y = f(x), his integral divided up the ordinate (y-axis) into intervals Δy_i with an associated value c_i within the interval. The Lebesgue integral is formed from the sum of products of the c_i and the measure of the set I_i of points x_i on the abscissa in which $y_{i-1} \leqq f(x_i) \leqq y_i$. The measure of the set of points is designated as $\mu(I_i)$ hence the contribution to the integral due to c_i is $c_i \cdot \mu(I_i)$. A full description of the concept of measure is beyond us here; however it is closely related to the length of intervals, as illustrated in the summation of intervals that can be made arbitrarily small to show that the measure of the rational numbers is 0. The measure of the simple interval of all points between d and e is simply (d-e). At this point we know enough to give a plausible sketch of the Lebesgue integral of the Dirichlet function f(x).

$$f(x) = \begin{cases} b & \text{for x irrational} \\ a, & \text{for x rational} \end{cases},$$

$$\int_0^1 f(x)dx = \lim_{\substack{\Delta y_i \to 0 \\ 0 \leqq x_i \leqq 1}} \sum_i c_i \mu(I_i) \text{ with } \Delta y_i, c_i, \text{ and } I_i \text{ defined as above.}$$

In calculating this sum, the measure of all points on the x-axis for which y ≠ a or y ≠ b is clearly 0. The measure of all the rational numbers between 0 and 1 is 0 (hence the measure of points with y = a is also 0), and finally the measure of points with y = b in the interval from 0 to 1 is 1. Therefore,

$$\int_0^1 f(x)dx = \lim_{\substack{\Delta y_i \to 0 \\ 0 \leqq x_i \leqq 1}} \sum_i c_i \mu(I_i) = b \cdot 1 = b.$$

The Lebesgue integral was a significant step towards a more abstract theory of the integral compared to the original concept of the area under a continuous curve. In addition to more clearly relating the properties of the real numbers to the integral process, it provided the theoretical basis for mathematical disciplines such as probability in which discrete events in contrast to continuous functions play a key role.[225]

8.6   The calculus brings physics to life

The role of mathematics in the development of physics should be obvious considering the discussion of the relation of the calculus

---

also Dunham, 200-219.

to Newton's Second Law of Motion. Indeed, Newton developed the concepts of the calculus precisely as a means of giving expression to his laws and demonstrating that previous results such as Kepler's Laws of the Planets and Galileo's Law of Falling Objects were consequences of his Laws of Motion and Law of Gravitation. However, the extension and application of the calculus in the nineteenth century to virtually the full realm of physical phenomena then known would result in a wealth of new mathematical techniques. One of the major themes of this period was the extension of the calculus to functions of several variables as required by a universe embedded in space and time. I cannot develop these ideas with any rigor even in the abbreviated form that I have adopted thus far. However, by introducing one of the significant mathematical achievements of this period, I hope to give you a feel for the kinds of advances that would follow from the concepts that I have already introduced.

The problem that I wish to discuss is the problem of the determination of temperature distributions in solids due to heating (or cooling) of the solid's surface. The problem of heat conduction in solids was treated by Jean Baptiste Joseph Fourier (1768 - 1830) in his *Analytic Theory of Heat* published in 1822.[226] Fourier's mathematical development of this problem provides a good illustration of the use of a mathematical model, expression of the model's relation to physical law in space and time, and a method of solution. In solving the problems of heat conduction, Fourier would introduce a new type of infinite series, now known as a Fourier series.[227] The Fourier series like the infinite Taylor series could be used to represent functions, but was made up of sine and cosine functions instead of the polynomials of the Taylor series.

Let us start by solving a heat conduction problem in one dimension. Imagine a wall of thickness Δ. Suppose the outside of the wall in winter is at a temperature T_2. Desiring to stay warm, we would like the inside temperature of the wall to be at temperature T_1. In this age of energy conservation, we might ask, how much heat is necessary to keep the inner temperature at T_1. I assume that you have a reasonable idea what temperature, heat, and energy are. This was certainly not true of anyone in 1822. We now know that heat is just a form of energy. This was first shown and reported in 1843 by James Prescott Joule from experiments transforming mechanical work into heat as measured by the temperature rise of water.[cxxi] At a more fundamental level we know that the source of energy for heat is the random motion of molecules including their translation, rotation, and vibration. Temperature is simply a statistical measure of that molecular motion at our normal level of observation. Heat is therefore the flow of energy due to a temperature difference.

One more concept that we will need is that heat flows from hot to cold. This is a consequence of the Second Law of Thermodynamics. Thinking about heat from a molecular point of view, you should be able to imagine that if there is a temperature difference between two bodies in contact then the higher temperature body with its more vigorous random molecular motions is more likely to transmit some of its energy to the lower temperature body. Thus, heat flowing from hot to cold is a statistical notion, but one whose violation is overwhelmingly improbable.

Fourier would not know any of these ideas with any precision. He did propose a model for heat conduction which I express for heat flow in one direction as: the rate of heat (energy) flowing q_x in a given direction x through a solid is proportional to the derivative (slope) of the temperature $\frac{dT}{dx}$ in that direction. The heat flow per unit time per unit area, called the heat flux will be designated as q''_x.[cxxii] Fourier's model (Law of Heat Conduction) for the rate of heat flow by conduction is:

$$q''_x \propto \frac{dT}{dx}.$$

The constant of proportionality is identified as the thermal conductivity k, a property of the material through which the heat flows. We will designate heat as positive flowing from higher to lower temperature. When the temperature T decreases with distance x, the heat is flowing in the positive x direction, so dT/dx is negative. Therefore following our convention, the heat flowing in the x direction is,

---

cxxi Gamow, G., *The Great Physicists from Galileo to Einstein*, pp. 96-98; see also Einstein, A. and Infeld, Leopold for a discussion of the developments in physics leading to recognition of heat as a form of energy pp. 35 - 51.

cxxii In metric units the flux is given in watts/meter^2 (or possibly more familiar to some in what are known as customary units as BTU/(hour-ft^2)). A watt is a unit of power or energy per unit time. In more fundamental units, a watt is a joule per second. A BTU or British Thermal Unit is energy required to raise a pound of water one degree Fahrenheit. 1 watt/m^2 = 0.3171 BTU/(hr-ft^2).

$$q''_x = -k\frac{dT}{dx}.$$

Now in addition to this model of heat flow, we need a law expressing its relationship to other types of energy. We have already used the Second Law of Thermodynamics to provide the direction of heat flow, the First Law of Thermodynamics or Conservation of Energy says that the heat as energy must be conserved, either remaining constant or changed into other forms of energy. For example, the heat could be used to drive a steam turbine in which case some of the energy of heat would be transformed into the energy to do work. In our simple problem with a wall, no work occurs, but the wall temperature could increase in which case, some of the heat is transformed into increased internal energy U of the wall (the molecules making up the wall now have more energy). Let us start with the simplest case in which conditions at the wall surfaces have remained the same for some time. Therefore, there is no change in the internal energy of the wall with time. The condition in which there are no changes with time is referred to as steady state. Our goal is to determine an equation using the ideas discussed above to determine the relationship of temperature in the wall to the heating of the wall. A schematic of our problem is shown in the next figure as a cross section of the wall.

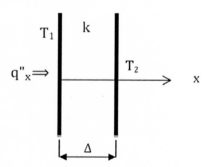

The heat flux at any point x within the wall is designated as $q''_x(x)$. Because the temperature within the wall is not changing with time, the heat flux is constant as any heat energy entering the wall must also be transferred through the wall, that is $q''_x = c$. Therefore, $\frac{dq''_x}{dx} = 0$ Substituting the expression for Fourier heat conduction:

$$\frac{dq_x^{"}}{dx} = \frac{d}{dx}\left(-k\frac{dT}{dx}\right) = 0.$$

This is the ordinary differential equation for the one-dimensional steady state heat conduction in a solid. It is called an ordinary differential equation because temperature is dependent on the single variable x. If the thermal conductivity is constant, then the equation becomes simply,

$$\frac{d}{dx}\left(k\frac{dT}{dx}\right) = k\frac{d}{dx}\left(\frac{dT}{dx}\right) = 0 \text{ or } \frac{d}{dx}\left(\frac{dT}{dx}\right) = \frac{d^2T}{d^2x} = 0$$

Recalling that if c is a constant, then $\frac{d(c)}{dx} = 0$, we have

$\frac{dT}{dx} = C_1$. Here C_1 is some constant, at the moment unknown.

Integrating this result, we have

$\int\frac{dT}{dx}dx = \int C_1 dx$ or $T = C_1 x + C_2$ with another unknown constant C_2 being added.

Notice that taking the derivative of this result twice returns us to the original differential equation. In order to determine the unknown constants we need two additional pieces of information. These are called the boundary conditions of a problem. Because the highest derivative in this problem is a second derivative, we have what is known as a second order ordinary differential equation. In general if the highest derivative is n^{th} order, it will require n boundary conditions.

In our problem, we specify that the temperature on the inner surface of our wall (x = 0) is T_1 and the temperature at the outer surface (x = Δ) is T_2. Therefore,

$T(0) = T_1 = C_1 \cdot 0 + C_2$ or $C_2 = T_1$

$T(\Delta) = T_2 = C_1 \cdot \Delta + C_2 = C_1 \cdot \Delta + T_1$ or $C_1 = (T_2 - T_1)/\Delta$, so the temperature at any x within the wall is given by,

$$T(x) = \frac{(T_2 - T_1)}{\Delta}x + T_1.$$

The heat flux to maintain these temperatures is given by Fourier conduction as,

$$q''_x = -k\frac{dT}{dx} = k\frac{(T_1 - T_2)}{\Delta}.$$

Now let us allow heating to change the temperature of the wall. For this, time t must be added as another variable and $T = T(x, t)$. Because the temperature depends on two independent variables, a new mathematical concept must be introduced, the partial derivative. A partial derivative of a function such as $T(x, t)$ is similar to the derivative; however, it is formed while holding all independent variables constant except the independent variable for which the partial derivative is sought. The partial derivative of T with respect x is indicated as $\frac{\partial T}{\partial x}$ with it being understood that the variable t is being held constant. Therefore, the partial derivatives of $T(x, t)$ with respect to x and with respect to t are:

$$\frac{\partial T}{\partial x} = \lim_{\Delta x \to 0} \frac{T(x + \Delta x,\, t) - T(x,t)}{\Delta x} \text{ and } \frac{\partial T}{\partial t} = \lim_{\Delta t \to 0} \frac{T(x,\, t + \Delta t) - T(x,t)}{\Delta t}.$$

The Fourier conduction in the x-direction is: $q''_x = -k\frac{\partial T}{\partial x}$

Conservation of energy requires that an energy balance reflect that the rate of heat flowing into any section of the wall minus the rate of heat flowing out equals the rate of change in internal energy $\frac{(dU)^{\cdot}}{dt}$ of the wall. Using conservation of energy, we can develop the partial differential equation for temperature from the energy balance of a slice of thickness Δx of the wall during a time change of Δt. First let us determine and expression for the difference between the rate of heat in and the rate of heat out in the slice Δx of a wall of surface area A.

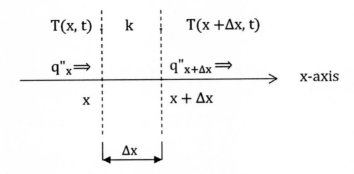

Without formal proof, I will develop an expression for the changes in the heat flux using an approach similar to the Taylor series used in Section 8.2.2. The total rate of heat flowing out a wall of surface area A is:

$$A \cdot q''_{x+\Delta x,t} = A \cdot (q''_{x,t} + \frac{\partial q''_{x,t}}{\partial x}\Delta x + \frac{\frac{\partial^2 q_{x,t}}{\partial x^2}\Delta x^2}{2} + \cdots$$

Therefore, the rate of net heat flowing into the slice Δx of the wall is:

$$A \cdot (q''_{x,t} - q''_{x+\Delta x,t}) = -A \cdot (\frac{\partial q''_{x,t}}{\partial x}\Delta x + \frac{\partial^2}{\partial x^2}(q''_{x,t}) \cdot \Delta x^2/2 + \ldots$$

Substituting Fourier heat conduction:

$$\text{Net Rate of Heat Flow In} = A \cdot (\frac{\partial}{\partial x}(k\frac{\partial T}{\partial x}\big|_{x,t})\Delta x + \frac{\frac{\partial \partial^2}{\partial x^2}(k\frac{\alpha T}{x}\big|_{x,t})\Delta x^2}{2} + \cdots$$

Now we need an expression for the rate of increase in the internal energy of the slice of the wall due to the net heat flux. To quantify the internal energy two additional properties of the wall material must be known, the density of the material, ρ that is its mass per unit volume and the specific heat, c which is the energy absorbed by the material per unit mass and per unit temperature rise ΔT. The increase in internal energy ΔU of a body of mass m and specific heat c is $\Delta U = mc\Delta T$. The mass of the slice of wall is $\rho A\Delta x$ since the volume of the slice is $A\Delta x$. Therefore, in the slice Δx, the average rate of increase in energy $\frac{\Delta U_{\Delta x}}{\Delta t}$ due to a rise in temperature ΔT in time Δt is given by $\rho A\Delta x\Delta T/\Delta t$. At any location x in the wall and time t, the instantaneous rate of change of the temperature T is given as $\Delta t \rightarrow 0$ by its partial derivative with respect to time $\frac{\partial T}{\partial t}\big|_{x,t}$. We will associate this instantaneous temperature change at x with the slice Δx. We could determine the rate of temperature change at the center of the slice x + $\Delta x/2$ through a Taylor-like expansion in Δx, but such terms will vanish when we eventually take the limit as $\Delta x \to 0$. Therefore, we will take the instantaneous rate of the internal energy of the slices as $\rho \Delta x A c \frac{\partial T}{\partial t}$.

Now we are ready to express the energy balance of the slice.

Net Rate of Heat Flow In = Rate of Increase of Internal Energy

$$A \cdot \left(\frac{\partial}{\partial x} \left(k \frac{\partial T}{\partial x} \right) \Delta x + \frac{\frac{\partial \partial^2}{\partial x^2}\left(k \frac{\partial T}{x} \right) \Delta x^2}{2} + \ldots = \rho A \Delta x c \frac{\partial T}{\partial t}.$$

Dividing by the volume $A\Delta x$ of the slice,

$$\frac{\partial}{\partial x} \left(k \frac{\partial T}{\partial x} \right) + \frac{\frac{\partial \partial^2}{\partial x^2}\left(k \frac{\partial T}{x} \right) \Delta x}{2} + \ldots = \rho c \frac{\partial T}{\partial t}.$$ And taking the limit as $\Delta x \to 0$, we have

$$\frac{\partial}{\partial x} \left(k \frac{\partial T}{\partial x} \right) = \rho c \frac{\partial T}{\partial t}.$$

If the thermal conductivity is constant, and identifying $k/(\rho c)$ as the material property known as thermal diffusivity, α we arrive at the time dependent, one-dimensional heat equation.

$$\alpha \frac{\partial}{\partial x} \left(\frac{\partial T}{\partial x} \right) = \frac{\partial T}{\partial t}.$$

Now let's see how we can use this partial differential equation (PDE) to solve a problem. Suppose our wall of thickness Δ and thermal diffusivity α is initially at a constant temperature T_i throughout. Then at some time, which I designate as t =0, the surfaces of the wall (x = 0 and x = Δ) are suddenly brought to the temperature T_s. We would like to know, how the temperature changes within the wall with time.

The method of attacking this problem is a straightforward one with wide applicability to solving problems with PDEs. The method is known as Separation of Variables. We will assume that T(x, t) may be expressed as the product of two functions, each being a function of a single independent variable. Let T(x, t) = $\mathcal{X}(x)\mathcal{T}(t)$. Because $\mathcal{X}$ and $\mathcal{T}$ are each functions of only a a single variable, when taking the partial derivative with respect to x of $\mathcal{X}(x)\mathcal{T}(t)$, $\mathcal{T}(t)$ acts like a constant and the partial derivative of $\mathcal{X}$ is the same as our ordinary derivative, that is $\frac{\partial \mathcal{X}\mathcal{T}}{\partial x} = \mathcal{T}\frac{d\mathcal{X}}{dx}$. Similar results are found when taking the partial derivative with respect to time.

Let us apply our assumption that $T(x, t) = X(x)T(t)$ and see where it leads us.

$$\alpha\frac{\partial}{\partial x}\left(\frac{\partial T}{\partial x}\right) = \frac{\partial T}{\partial t};$$

$$\alpha\frac{\partial}{\partial x}\left(\frac{\partial XT}{\partial x}\right) = \frac{\partial XT}{\partial t};$$

$$\alpha\frac{\partial}{\partial x}T\left(\frac{dX}{dx}\right) = X\frac{dT}{dt};$$

$$\alpha T\frac{d}{dx}\left(\frac{dX}{dx}\right) = X\frac{dT}{dt}.$$

Now this is where the method shows its strength as we can place all functions of x on one side of the equation and those functions of t on the other.

$$\frac{\frac{d}{dx}\left(\frac{dX}{dx}\right)}{X} = \frac{\frac{dT}{dt}}{\alpha T}.$$

Since one side of the equation only varies with x, the other with t, and the variables are independent of each other, the only way for there to be equality is if each side of the equation is equal to the same constant. I choose this constant to be $-\lambda^2$ (A convenient form as we shall see.) The Separation of Variables method has changed our PDE into two ordinary differential equations (ODEs):

$$\frac{dT}{dt} = -\lambda^2\alpha T \text{ and } \frac{d}{dx}\left(\frac{dX}{dx}\right) == -\lambda^2 X.$$

Notice that in both cases after taking the derivative of T or taking two derivatives of X, we must be left with the original functions multiplied by $-\lambda^2$. In the short list of derivatives of functions in Section 8.2.1, we have $\frac{de^x}{dx}=e^x$, $\frac{d}{dx}\frac{d}{dx}(\sin x) = -\sin x$, and $\frac{d}{dx}\frac{d}{dx}(\cos x) = -\cos x$. This suggests that the exponential and sinusoidal functions may be useful to solve the ODEs.

Let us try the functions $T = e^{-\lambda^2\alpha t}$. First however note that if $u = -\lambda^2\alpha t$, then $e^{-\lambda^2\alpha t} = e^u$ and using the chain rule,

$$\frac{de^{-\lambda^2\alpha t}}{dt} = \frac{de^u}{du}\frac{du}{dt} = e^u(-\lambda^2\alpha) = -\lambda^2\alpha e^{-\lambda^2\alpha t}$$

Therefore, $T = e^{-\lambda^2\alpha t}$ is a solution of the ODE, $\frac{dT}{dt} = -\lambda^2\alpha T$.

Now let's look at $\mathcal{X} = \sin(\lambda x)$. Again we will use the chain rule, this time with $u = \lambda x$.

$$\frac{d\sin(\lambda x)}{dx} = \frac{d\sin u}{du}\frac{du}{dx} = \cos u \ (\lambda) = \lambda\cos(\lambda x);$$

$$\frac{d}{dx}\frac{d\sin(\lambda x)}{dx} = \frac{d}{dx}(\lambda\cos(\lambda x)) = \lambda\frac{d\cos u}{du}\frac{du}{dx} = -\lambda^2\sin(\lambda x)$$

Therefore, $\mathcal{X} = \sin(\lambda x)$ is a solution of the ODE, $\frac{d}{dx}(\frac{d\mathcal{X}}{dx}) == -\lambda^2\mathcal{X}$.

Similarly, $\mathcal{X} = \cos(\lambda x)$ is also solution of the ODE, $\frac{d}{dx}(\frac{d\mathcal{X}}{dx}) == -\lambda^2\mathcal{X}$.

Because the derivatives are linear operators, we can add the two solutions for $\mathcal{X}$ multiplied by arbitrary constants A and B. (You can easily verify this by substituting into the ODE for $\mathcal{X}$.)] Therefore, a general solution of the PDE is

$T(x.t) = \mathcal{T}(t)\mathcal{X}(x) = e^{-\lambda^2\alpha t}[A\sin(\lambda x) + B\cos(\lambda x)]$.

Now that we have an expression that satisfies the PDE, we need to be able to satisfy the temperature at the wall surfaces for $t > 0$ and the temperature condition throughout the wall at $t = 0$. The conditions at the wall surface, the boundary conditions, are $T(0) = T(\Delta) = T_s$. Because the derivative of a constant is zero, a new variable, $\theta = T - T_s$ can be used to simplify the boundary condition to $\theta(0) = \theta(\Delta) = 0$. The new PDE is $\alpha\frac{\partial}{\partial x}(\frac{\partial\theta}{\partial x}) = \frac{\partial\theta}{\partial t}$ which is also satisfied by $\theta = e^{-\lambda^2\alpha t}$. $[A\sin(\lambda x) + B\cos(\lambda x)]$.

For $t > 0$, $\theta(0, t) = 0 = e^{-\lambda^2\alpha t}[A\sin(0) + B\cos(0)] = e^{-\lambda^2\alpha t}[0 + B \cdot 1 = Be^{-\lambda^2\alpha t}$.

Therefore to satisfy this boundary condition, $B = 0$ and $\theta = Ae^{-\lambda^2\alpha t}\sin(\lambda x)$.

On the outer surface of the wall, $\theta(\Delta, t) = 0 = Ae^{-\lambda^2\alpha t}\sin(\lambda\Delta)$. This boundary condition is satisfied if $\lambda = n\pi/\Delta$ for $n = 1, 2, 3 \ldots$ Thus the general solution satisfying the PDE and the boundary conditions is:

$$\theta(x, t) = a_1 e^{-(\pi/\Delta)^2\alpha t}\sin\left(\frac{\pi x}{\Delta}\right) + a_2 e^{-(2\pi/\Delta)^2\alpha t}\sin\left(\frac{2\pi x}{\Delta}\right) + \cdots$$

$$= \sum_{n=1}^{\infty} a_n e^{-(n\pi/\Delta)^2\alpha t}\sin\left(\frac{n\pi x}{\Delta}\right)$$

At $t = 0$, for $0 \leqq x \leqq \Delta$, $\theta(x,0) = T_i - T_s$. This is known as the initial condition. Therefore, $T_i - T_s = \sum_{n=1}^{\infty} a_n e^0 \sin\left(\frac{n\pi x}{\Delta}\right) = \sum_{n=1}^{\infty} a_n \sin\left(\frac{n\pi x}{\Delta}\right)$ Thus the initial condition is to be satisfied by an infinite series of sine functions. Such an infinite series is known as a Fourier series. In 1832

Dirichlet determined conditions for which the series converges. In our problem, it may be shown that for the general case with the initial condition $\theta(x,0) = f(x)$ that the coefficients may be calculated as:

$$a_n = \frac{2}{\Delta}\int_0^\Delta f(x)\sin\left(\frac{n\pi}{\Delta}\right)dx \text{ or for a constant temperature } f(x) = \theta_i = T_i - T_s,$$

$$a_n = \frac{2(T_i - T_s)}{\Delta}\int_0^\Delta \sin\left(\frac{n\pi x}{\Delta}\right)dx$$

Integrating,[cxxiii] $a_n = \dfrac{4(T_i - T_s)}{n\pi}$ for n = 1, 3, 5 . . .

$$a_n = 0 \text{ for n } = 2, 4, 6 \ldots$$

and $\theta(x, t) = T - T_s = \dfrac{4(T_i - T_s)}{\pi}\sum_{n=1,3,5\ldots}^{\infty} \dfrac{e^{-\left(\frac{n\pi}{\Delta}\right)^2 \alpha t}}{n}\sin\left(\dfrac{n\pi x}{\Delta}\right).$

Because of the decreasing exponential, the solution is well approximated with just a few terms. Also, because as t→∞,

$e^{-\left(\frac{n\pi}{\Delta}\right)^2 \alpha t} \rightarrow 0$, the steady state solution is $T = T_s$.

The evaluation of the coefficients of the Fourier series is possible because $\int_0^\Delta \sin\left(\dfrac{n\pi x}{\Delta}\right)\sin\left(\dfrac{m\pi x}{\Delta}\right)dx = 0$ for m ≠n. The two sinusoidal functions are said to be orthogonal. Multiplying both sides of $T_i - T_s$ $= \sum_{n=1}^{\infty} a_n \sin\left(\dfrac{n\pi x}{\Delta}\right)$ by $\sin\left(\dfrac{m\pi x}{\Delta}\right)$ and integrating over the limits of 0 to Δ gives the previously stated result for the coefficients a_n of the series. Similar approaches have been developed for other PDEs where Separation of Variables is successful. In these solutions, infinite series using other functions appear which satisfy the ODEs, and are also orthogonal. The theory for such solutions which represent generalized Fourier series was developed by younger colleagues influenced by Fourier, Jean-Jacques-François-Sturm (1805 - 1859) and Joseph Liouville (1809 - 1882).[228]

From the development of the transient heat equation in one dimension, it should be quite apparent that it can be extended to three dimensions. The heat flux in the x-direction q''_x is associated in the PDE with the net rate of heat flow $\dfrac{\partial^2 T}{\partial x^2}$ through the wall slice Δx. Instead of a wall, imagine a volume of dimensions Δx, Δy, and Δz in a Cartesian

---

cxxiii See Appendix J for details of the integration.

coordinate system. The contribution to the PDE from the heat flux in the y-direction q''_y crossing the area $\Delta x \cdot \Delta z$ will be $\frac{\partial^2 T}{\partial y^2}$. Similarly for q''_z, the addition to the PDE is $\frac{\partial^2 T}{\partial z^2}$. Therefore the transient, three-dimensional heat equation with constant properties is:

$$\alpha[\frac{\partial^2 T}{\partial x^2} + \frac{\partial^2 T}{\partial y^2} + \frac{\partial^2 T}{\partial z^2}] = \frac{\partial T}{\partial t}.$$

The heat equation has been extended by noting that the heat flows in three directions. It is natural therefore to express the heat flux as a vector using the Cartesian unit vectors: $\mathbf{q}'' = q_x'' \mathbf{i} + q_y'' \mathbf{j} + q_z'' \mathbf{k} = -[k\frac{\partial T}{\partial x}\mathbf{i} + k\frac{\partial T}{\partial y}\mathbf{j} \ k\frac{\partial T}{\partial z}\mathbf{k}]$. If we associate the Cartesian axes x, y, and z with x_1, x_2, and x_3, then the expression for the heat flux in tensor notation should be apparent: $q''_i = -k\frac{\partial T}{\partial x_i}$. As the heat flux is clearly a vector, $\frac{\partial T}{\partial x_i}$ must also be a vector. The vector $\frac{\partial T}{\partial x_i}$ is known as the gradient of the scalar temperature. Thus the operator $\frac{\partial}{x_i}$ is a vector and in Cartesian vector notation is indicated as $\nabla = (\frac{\partial}{\partial x_1}, \frac{\partial}{\partial x_2}, \frac{\partial}{\partial x_3})$.[cxxiv] We may therefore also express the heat flux vector as $\mathbf{q}'' = -k\nabla T$.

The transient, three dimensional heat equation may also be expressed in tensor notation:

$$\alpha[\frac{\partial^2 T}{\partial x_1^2} + \frac{\partial^2 T}{\partial x_2^2} + \frac{\partial^2 T}{\partial x_3^2}] = \frac{\partial T}{\partial t} \text{ or } \alpha\sum_{i=1}^{3}\frac{\partial}{\partial x_i}\frac{\partial}{\partial x_i}T = \frac{\partial T}{\partial t}.$$

Recalling that a repeated index implies summation in the Einstein convention leads to:

$$\alpha\sum_{i=1}^{3}\frac{\partial}{\partial x_i}\frac{\partial}{\partial x_i}T = \alpha\frac{\partial}{\partial x_i}\frac{\partial}{\partial x_i}T = \frac{\partial T}{\partial t}.$$

---

cxxiv Another approach to the gradient is by introducing the concept of the differential. For a function of one independent variable $y = f(x)$, the differential $dy = f'(x)dx$ (see Labarre, Jr., pp. 122 - 125). Similarly, if T is a function of the Cartesian coordinate $\mathbf{r}=(x, y, z)$, $T = T(x, y, z)$ then, $dT = \frac{\partial T}{\partial x}dx + \frac{\partial T}{\partial y}dy + \frac{\partial T}{\partial z}dz = \nabla T \cdot \mathbf{dr}$.

We have already identified $\dfrac{\partial}{\partial x_i}$ with the vector operator ∇, moreover we have seen that the scalar product of a vector $\mathbf{v}$ and $\mathbf{w}$ may be written $\mathbf{v} \bullet \mathbf{w} = v_i w_i$. This suggests the useful vector form: $\alpha\dfrac{\partial}{\partial x_i}\dfrac{\partial}{\partial x_i}T = \alpha\nabla\bullet(\nabla T) = \dfrac{\partial T}{\partial t}$. Here the operator $\nabla \bullet (\ )$ is known as the divergence operator which must operate on a vector (or tensor) in our case provided by $\nabla T = \dfrac{\partial T}{\partial x_i}$. As should be apparent from the derivation of the heat equation, the divergence of a vector expresses the local net flux of a vector. For example, under steady state conditions the equation becomes $\nabla \bullet (\nabla T) = 0$ and the net heat flux is zero or heat in equals heat out. Another expression for $\nabla \bullet (\nabla T) = 0$ is $\nabla^2 T = 0$ which is known as Laplace's equation. As the operator on a scalar, ∇^2 appears in many situations in mechanics and electromagnetism.

We will now use this convenient vector form to sketch how the heat equation could have been derived without reference to coordinates. For this purpose, we rewrite the equation as:

$$k\nabla\bullet(\nabla T) = \rho c\dfrac{\partial T}{\partial t}$$

Let us look at an arbitrarily shaped body of volume V and surface area S as pictured below (looking somewhat like a potato)

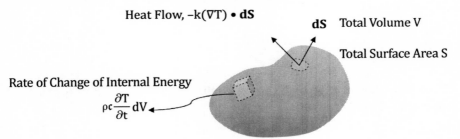

Heat Flow, $-k(\nabla T) \bullet \mathbf{dS}$

$\mathbf{dS}$ Total Volume V

Total Surface Area S

Rate of Change of Internal Energy

$\rho c\dfrac{\partial T}{\partial t}dV$

The material density (mass m per unit volume v is defined by $\rho = \dfrac{dm}{dV}$. Therefore, the differential element of mass $dm = \rho dV$. Integrating over the entire volume of the body, the total mass $M = \iiint_V \dfrac{dm}{dV}dV = \iiint_v \rho dV$. I have used the symbol for a triple integral to emphasize the integration over the entire volume is three-dimensional. Similarly, the total rate of increase of internal energy $\dfrac{dU}{dt} = \iiint_v \rho c\dfrac{\partial T}{\partial t}dV$.

Now we want to express the net rate of heat flow conducted into the body. Heat flows into body across its surface S. The heat flow **dq** across the differential surface area **dS** is the component of heat flux perpendicular to that surface. Recall that the surface area is the outward vector of magnitude dS perpendicular to the surface. Therefore the differential rate of heat flow across **dS** is dq = q" • **dS** = k(∇T) • **dS**. (The negative sign of Fourier's Law of Heat Conduction is dropped because we want the flow opposite to the direction of the surface vector **dS** to be positive.) The total heat into the body across the entire surface area of the body is therefore, q = $\iint_s$ k(∇T) • **dS**. The heat balance for the body may be expressed therefore by the following integral equation:

$$\iint_s k(\nabla T) \cdot dS = \iiint_v \rho c \frac{\partial T}{\partial t} dV.$$

On one side we have a surface integral while the other integral is over the volume. This equation may be greatly simplified using a theorem relating surface to volume integrals. The theorem is variously known as the Divergence Theorem, Gauss's Theorem, or Ostrogradskiǐ's Theorem.

Divergence Theorem: If **A** is a vector defined over the volume V with surface area S, then, $\iint_s \mathbf{A} \cdot d\mathbf{S} = \iiint_v \nabla \cdot \mathbf{A} dV.$[cxxv]

We can easily apply this to our heat balance:

$\iint_s k(\nabla T) \cdot dS = \iiint_v \nabla \cdot k \nabla T dV = \iiint_v \rho c \frac{\partial T}{\partial t} dV$. Now we can rewrite this as:

$$\iiint_v \left[\nabla \cdot k \nabla T - \rho c \frac{\partial T}{\partial t} \right] dV = 0.$$

Since our potato is arbitrary, this can only be true if

$$\nabla \cdot \left(k \nabla T \right) = \rho c \frac{\partial T}{\partial t}.$$

---

cxxv The Divergence Theorem applies over a wide range of conditions; however, constraints on the vector **A** (such as **A** being continuous over V with continuous partial derivatives and a sufficiently "smooth" surface area S) need to be stated for the theorem to be fully rigorous; however, this is beyond what can be introduced here.

Thus we have derived the heat equation without reference to any particularly coordinate system.

WARNING! To solve any particularly problem such as the transient problem of heat through a wall, a coordinate system must be specified. In our case, we used a Cartesian system which was convenient for our geometry. However, in other coordinate systems operators such as $\nabla()$, $\nabla \bullet ()$, or $\nabla^2()$ will look different. This difference is related to the changing orientation of local non-Cartesian coordinate system vectors noted in Section 7.3 and is true for the case of the cylindrical coordinates (r, θ, z) shown in the next figure.

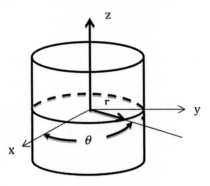

The cylindrical coordinates are related to a Cartesian system with x = r cos θ, y = r sin θ, and z = z. The radial and azimuthal directions associated with r and θ change with location. The Laplacian operator ∇^2 on the scalar temperature T is $\dfrac{\partial^2 T}{r^2} + \dfrac{1}{r}\dfrac{\partial T}{\partial r} + \dfrac{1}{r^2}\dfrac{\partial^2 T}{\partial \theta^2} + \dfrac{\partial^2 T}{\partial z^2}$ instead of its Cartesian version, $\dfrac{\partial^2 T}{\partial x^2} + \dfrac{\partial^2 T}{\partial y^2} + \dfrac{\partial^2 T}{\partial z^2}$ that we derived previously.

One approach to determining the forms in different coordinate systems is through the use of a chain rule for partial derivatives; however, we have gone as far on this part of our journey as possible here. Another is through the use of definitions of operators independent of coordinate systems such as:

$$\nabla \bullet A = \lim_{\Delta V \to 0} \frac{1}{\Delta V} \iint_S A \bullet dS$$ with S being the surface of a body of volume V as described previously.

By applying this definition to an appropriate volume ΔV, the divergence $\nabla \bullet A$ in the coordinate system of interest may be determined. For example instead of the cube $\Delta x \Delta y \Delta z$ with vector (A_x, A_y, A_z) in Cartesian coordinates, a cylindrical volume may be used:

$r\Delta\theta\Delta r\Delta z$ with (A_r, A_θ, A_z). Similar to the development of the heat equation, we can determine the differences in the fluxes of the vector **A** across the surfaces of the cylindrical volume and take the limit as $\Delta V \to 0$. The volume forms six surfaces: $\Delta S_r = r\,\Delta\theta\Delta z$, $\Delta S_\theta = \Delta r\Delta z$, $\Delta S_z = r\,\Delta\theta\Delta r$, and the associated surfaces, $\Delta S_{r+\Delta r}$, $\Delta S_{\theta+\Delta\theta}$, $\Delta S_{z+\Delta z}$.

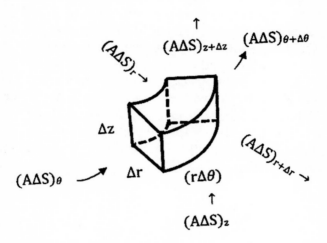

Using the nomenclature shown in the figure above and the Taylor series approach:

$$\iint_S \mathbf{A} \cdot d\mathbf{S} \approx [(A\Delta S)_{r+\Delta r} - (A\Delta S)_r] + [(A\Delta S)_{\theta+\Delta\theta} - (A\Delta S)_\theta] + [(A\Delta S)_{z+\Delta z} - (A\Delta S)_z]$$

$$\approx \frac{\partial\left(A_r r\Delta\theta\Delta z\right)}{\partial r}\Delta r + \frac{\partial(A_\theta \Delta r\Delta z)}{\partial\theta}\Delta\theta + \frac{\partial(A_z r\Delta\theta\Delta r)}{\partial z}\Delta z + \text{higher order terms}$$

$$\frac{1}{\Delta V}\iint_S \mathbf{A}\cdot d\mathbf{S} = \frac{1}{r\Delta\theta\Delta r\Delta z}\iint_S \mathbf{A}\cdot d\mathbf{S} \approx \frac{1}{r}\frac{\left(A_r r\right)}{\partial r} + \frac{1}{r}\frac{\partial A_\theta}{\partial\theta} + \frac{\partial A_z}{\partial z} + \text{higher order terms.}$$

Therefore,

$$\nabla\cdot\mathbf{A} = \lim_{\Delta V\to 0}\frac{1}{\Delta V}\iint_S \mathbf{A}\cdot d\mathbf{S} = \frac{1}{r}\frac{\partial\left(A_r r\right)}{\partial r} + \frac{1}{r}\frac{\partial A_\theta}{\partial\theta} + \frac{\partial A_z}{\partial z}.$$

Now to find $\nabla^2 T = \nabla \cdot \nabla T$ with $\mathbf{A} = \nabla T$, we need a definition of the gradient vector independent of the coordinate system. The gradient of a scalar such as T is the local change of T in a given path direction per unit change in that direction. For example the gradient in the radial and axial path directions, are respectively, $\frac{\partial T}{\partial r}$ and $\frac{\partial T}{\partial z}$.

Since the path length in the θ direction is $r\Delta\theta$, the gradient is $\frac{1}{r}\frac{\partial T}{\partial\theta}$.

Therefore, $\mathbf{A} = (A_r, A_\theta, A_z) = \nabla T = (\dfrac{\partial T}{\partial r}, \dfrac{1}{r}\dfrac{\partial T}{\partial \theta}, \dfrac{\partial T}{\partial z})$ and $\nabla^2 T = \nabla \bullet \nabla T =$

$$\frac{1}{r}\frac{\partial}{\partial r}\left(r\frac{\partial T}{\partial r}\right) + \frac{1}{r}\frac{\partial}{\partial \theta}\left(\frac{1}{r}\frac{\partial T}{\partial \theta}\right) + \frac{\partial}{\partial z}\left(\frac{\partial T}{\partial z}\right) = \frac{\partial^2 T}{r^2} + \frac{1}{r}\frac{\partial T}{\partial r} + \frac{1}{r^2}\frac{\partial^2 T}{\partial \theta^2} + \frac{\partial^2 T}{\partial z^2}.\text{ cxxvi}$$

From the example of the development and solution of the transient heat equation, I hope the rich content of PDEs and their solution is apparent. An introduction to PDEs is given by Sobolev and Ladyzenskaja in Aleksandrov, Kolmogorov, and Lavrent'ev (Chapter VI).

I leave this chapter with an example of a PDE of monumental importance in modern physics, Quantum Mechanic's description of the atom given by Schrodinger's equation. The equation with mathematical forms that you can now recognize is for the wave function ψ of a particle which when multiplied by its complex conjugate gives the probability function for among other thing the location of the particle.

$$-\frac{\left(\dfrac{h}{2\pi}\right)^2}{2m}\nabla^2\psi + V(r)\psi = i\frac{h}{2\pi}\frac{\partial \psi}{\partial t}$$

The equation, developed by Erwin Schrodinger in 1926,[229] expresses the allowed behavior of particles such as the electron (of mass m) in the hydrogen atom in terms of its potential energy V as a function of position $\mathbf{r}$, and is able to give a description of an atomic world which is otherwise completely mysterious from the perspective of classical physics. Planck's constant h in this equation is found in Heisenberg's uncertainty principle and quantifies a fundamental limitation imposed by nature on our ability to know simultaneously the particle position x and momentum p_x to accuracies of Δx and Δp_x. The best we can do is $\Delta x \cdot \Delta p_x \gtrless h/(2\pi)$.[cxxvii] This means that if we know the momentum exactly, $\Delta p_x = 0$, the position is unknown.

---

cxxvi Note using the product rule for derivatives, $\dfrac{1}{r}\dfrac{\partial}{\partial r}\left(r\dfrac{\partial T}{\partial r}\right) = \dfrac{\partial^2 T}{\partial r^2} + \dfrac{1}{r}\dfrac{\partial T}{\partial r}$, and

$\dfrac{1}{r}\dfrac{\partial}{\partial \theta}\left(\dfrac{1}{r}\dfrac{\partial T}{\partial \theta}\right) = \dfrac{1}{r^2}\dfrac{\partial^2 T}{\partial \theta^2}$ since in taking the partial derivative $\dfrac{\partial}{\partial \theta}$, r is constant.

cxxvii A qualitative discussion of the early historical development of Quantum Mechanics is given in Gamow, *The Great Physicists from Galileo to Einstein*, Chapter VII, pp. 209 - 271. Einstein and Infeld (pp. 280 - 294) give a qualitative discussion of probability waves.

Schrodinger's equation illustrates the power of mathematics to express the richness of nature in a concise and elegant form. I ask you to consider the implications of an equation that expresses some of our most fundamental understanding of the reality of the atom, yet is an equation for a wave function which is beyond our direct experience, an abstraction like so many others found in modern physics. We are clearly far beyond the familiar world of Galileo and Newton with their objects in motion accessible to our senses and completely predictable. Thus, our understanding of the physical world at its deepest level appears to be only fully expressible in the abstract language of mathematic.[cxxviii]

---

cxxviii In regard to our understanding of the physical world, Russell in a personal statement defines matter as *"what satisfies the equations of physics,"* Russell, p. 658.

Chapter 9

SET THEORY, THE FOUNDATION

"Later generations will regard set theory as a disease from which one has recovered."—Henri Poincaré [cxxix]

"No one shall drive us from the paradise which Cantor created for us."— David Hilbert [cxxx]

9.1   The basics

As promised by the title of the book, throughout the previous chapters, I have introduced some of the major developments in mathematics building upon their algebraic and geometric foundations, starting with the algebra of the natural numbers and Euclid's geometry. I chose this approach assuming your greater familiarity with introductory ideas of number, algebra, and geometry. However, despite this approach I have frequently found it convenient to make use of, at least superficially, another foundation of mathematics, set theory. While not formally introducing sets, various collections of numbers—natural numbers, integers, and rational numbers—were discussed on our way to determining the properties of the real numbers. In order to characterize the real numbers, it was necessary to look at these various collections of numbers as being capable of consideration as whole entities that is as infinite sets, and despite each being an infinite set to compare them in size. The least upper bound property that differentiates the real numbers from the rational numbers is a property that characterizes the nature of the real numbers as an uncountable infinite set. This and other properties of the real numbers such as denseness, connectivity, and continuity are concisely described using sets.

---

cxxix Poincaré made this comment in 1908 regarding infinite sets; quoted in Kline, p. 203. Poincaré was a leading mathematician of the late nineteenth and early twentieth century with major contributions across all areas of mathematics, see Merzbach and Boyer, pp. 549 - 555.

cxxx Hilbert made this comment in 1926 in regard to Cantor's work on infinite sets; quoted in Kline, p. 204.

The introduction of set theoretic approaches in mathematics is primarily attributable to the work of Georg Cantor with support from his friend Dedekind. Although in Chapter 3, I emphasized the definition of the real numbers in terms of a visualization of Dedekind cuts in the number line, a geometric description; it would be more precise to see this cut as the division of the infinite set of rational numbers. The one-to-one correspondence with the points of the line and the real numbers defined by the cuts is referred to as the Cantor-Dedekind Postulate.[230] Cantor, investigating the characteristics of infinite sets, developed approaches to establish the commonality of the infinities of the natural numbers, integers, and rational numbers and to distinguish them from the infinite set of the real numbers. Encountering much opposition over the concept and implications of infinite sets as well as logical contradictions in Cantor's original conception of sets, a formal axiomatic approach to set theory was needed and was supplied in 1908 by Ernst Zermolo (1871 - 1956) with refinements in 1922 by Abraham Fraenkel (1891-1965).[231] Although this would become a standard part of mathematical theory, it too would lead to even deeper controversies and new insights—the subject of my closing chapter. Despite controversies, the set theoretic approach would provide the language for generalizing and extending properties established for the real numbers in more abstract mathematical formalisms. Among these are topological spaces, now a key element of modern mathematics. In this chapter, I will give an introduction to set theory and topology, emphasizing their relation to the description of the properties of the real numbers.

9.1.1 Definitions and operations in elementary set theory

The elementary concept of a set is simple enough, at least as long as we are considering only finite sets. Sets may be any collection of distinguishable items: the fifty two playing cards in a deck, students taking an exam, pictures at an exhibition, and certainly, any finite collection of natural numbers. The following definition from elementary set theory is due to Cantor:[cxxxi]

---

cxxxi The quotation of Cantor is translated from the German in Breuer, J., p. 4.

Definition of a Set: A set is a bringing together into a whole of definite well-distinguished objects of our perception or thought—which are to be called the elements of the set.

A set can therefore be defined by identifying its elements. The set $\mathcal{A}$ of natural numbers less than six can be represented by a simple listing as $\mathcal{A} = \{1, 2, 3, 4, 5\}$ or by defining a logical property of the set, a style which is often more convenient as $\mathcal{A} = \{$x is a natural number$|$ x $<$ 6$\}$. The latter definition would be read as $\mathcal{A}$ is the set of natural numbers such that x $<$ 6 or set $\mathcal{A}$ is the set for which the proposition is true that the elements are natural numbers less than 6.

Returning to Cantor's definition of a set in terms of its elements, it seems appropriate to define a universal set $\mathcal{U}$ containing all of the elements that are relevant to the particular analysis. This simple idea would ultimately lead to many logical contradictions and require a more sophisticated set theory. However, in elementary set theory (also called naïve set theory), the universal set can provide a helpful approach for finite sets which does not involve such contradictions. Using our example above, the universal set $\mathcal{U}$ is the set $\mathcal{U} = \{1, 2, 3, 4, 5\}$ where the elements of $\mathcal{U}$ are simply listed. The number 2 is an element of $\mathcal{U}$ or symbolically $2 \in \mathcal{U}$. A subset is defined as:

Definition of Subset: For sets $\mathcal{A}$ and $\mathcal{B}$, $\mathcal{A}$ is a subset of $\mathcal{B}$ ($\mathcal{A} \subseteq \mathcal{B}$) if for every ($\forall$) element x of $\mathcal{A}$, x is an element of $\mathcal{B}$ (or symbolically, $\mathcal{A} \subseteq \mathcal{B}$ if $\forall$ x $\in \mathcal{A}$, x $\in \mathcal{B}$).

From the definition of sets, if $\mathcal{A} \subseteq \mathcal{B}$, and $\mathcal{B} \subseteq \mathcal{A}$, then $\mathcal{A} = \mathcal{B}$. If $\mathcal{A} \subseteq \mathcal{B}$, but $\mathcal{B}$ is not a subset of $\mathcal{A}$ ($\mathcal{B} \not\subseteq \mathcal{A}$) then $\mathcal{A}$ is called a proper subset of $\mathcal{B}$ which will be indicated when useful for clarity as $\mathcal{A} \subset \mathcal{B}$.

Examples of subsets formed from $\mathcal{U} = \{1, 2, 3, 4, 5\}$ are the sets of even numbers $\mathcal{E} = \{2, 4\}$, odd numbers $\mathcal{O} = \{1, 3, 5\}$, the smallest number in the set $\mathcal{L} = \{1,\}$ and numbers that are perfect squares $\mathcal{S} = \{1, 4\}$. Sets may be subsets of sets other than of $\mathcal{U}$. For example, the set $\mathcal{L} \subseteq \mathcal{O}$.; however, $\mathcal{S}$ is not a subset of $\mathcal{O}$ since 4 is not an element of $\mathcal{O}$ ($\mathcal{S} \not\subseteq \mathcal{O}$ since 4 $\notin \mathcal{O}$).

The empty set $\emptyset$ is a subset of every set. Suppose $\emptyset$ is not a subset of a set $\mathcal{A}$, then by the definition of subset, there is an element of $\emptyset$ that is not an element of $\mathcal{A}$. However, $\emptyset$ has no elements. Therefore, we have a contradiction, and $\emptyset \subseteq \mathcal{A}$, that is to say, it is a subset of all sets.

The operation of the union of sets is defined below in terms of the elements of sets.

Definition of Union: The union of sets $\mathcal{A}$ and $\mathcal{B}$ ($\mathcal{A} \cup \mathcal{B}$) is the set formed so that for every x an element of $\mathcal{A}$ or x an element of $\mathcal{B}$, x is an elements of $\mathcal{A} \cup \mathcal{B}$;

$A \cup \mathcal{B} = \{x|x \in \mathcal{A} \text{ or } x \in \mathcal{B}\}$.

Using the previous example with $S = \{1, 4\}$ and $O = \{1, 3, 5\}$, $S \cup O = \{1, 3, 4, 5\}$. Note that if $\mathcal{A} \cup \mathcal{B} = \mathcal{A}$, then $\mathcal{B} \subseteq \mathcal{A}$. Some other operations defined in terms of the elements are intersection and complement.

Definition of Intersection: The intersection of sets $\mathcal{A}$ and $\mathcal{B}$ ($\mathcal{A} \cap \mathcal{B}$) is the set formed from elements x for which x is an element of $\mathcal{A}$ and x is an element of $\mathcal{B}$;

$A \cap \mathcal{B} = \{x|x \in \mathcal{A} \text{ and } x \in \mathcal{B}\}$.

Definition of Complement of a Set: The complement of a set $\mathcal{A}$ ($\mathcal{A}^c$) with respect to the universal set $\mathcal{U}$ is the set with elements x members of $\mathcal{U}$ which are not members of $\mathcal{A}$;

$\mathcal{A}^c = \{x| \ x \in \mathcal{U} \text{ and } x \notin \mathcal{A}\}$.

In our example, $S \cap O = \{1\}$. The intersection $O \cap \mathcal{E} = \emptyset$. Such sets are called disjoint sets; that is, the sets have no elements in common.

A helpful way to visualize sets and set operation is through Venn diagrams.[232]

Let the rectangles in the next figures correspond to a universal set $\mathcal{U}$. Sets $\mathcal{A}$ (ellipse), $\mathcal{B}$(circle), C (pentagon), and $\mathcal{D}$ (the rest of the rectangle) are defined within this univese.

$\mathcal{U}$

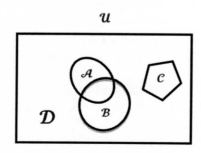

Then we can easily visualize $\mathcal{A} \cup \mathcal{C}$, $\mathcal{A} \cap \mathcal{B}$, and $\mathcal{D}^c$ as the shaded areas in the figures below.

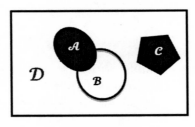

$$\mathcal{A} \cup \mathcal{C}$$

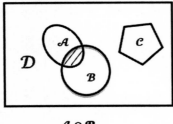

$$\mathcal{A} \cap \mathcal{B}$$

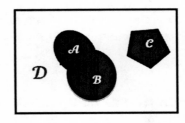

$$\mathcal{D}^c$$

In addition to the operations shown above, the unshaded area of set $\mathcal{A}$ in the Venn diagram of $\mathcal{A} \cap \mathcal{B}$ illustrates the operation of the complement of $\mathcal{B}$ with respect to $\mathcal{A}$, that is x is an element of $\mathcal{A}$ and not an element of $\mathcal{B}$, $(\mathcal{A} - \mathcal{B})$. The elementary definitions of sets, the operations of union, intersection, and complementation of a set, and the existence of a universal set $\mathcal{U}$, and empty set $\emptyset$, are easily shown to be consistent with the set of postulates shown below forming the algebra of sets.[233]

ALGEBRA of SETS (Elementary Set Theory)

For sets $\mathcal{A}$, $\mathcal{B}$, $\mathcal{C}$ ..., members of set $\mathcal{U}$:

S1. Commutative Property of Set Operation: $\mathcal{A} \cup \mathcal{B} = \mathcal{B} \cup \mathcal{A}$ and $\mathcal{A} \cap \mathcal{B} = \mathcal{B} \cap \mathcal{A}$.

S2. Identity Elements for Union and Intersection: $\mathcal{A} \cup \emptyset = \mathcal{A} \cap \mathcal{U} = \mathcal{A}$.

S3. Complement Element: $\mathcal{A} \cup \mathcal{A}^c = \mathcal{U}$ and $\mathcal{A} \cap \mathcal{A}^c = \emptyset$.

S4. Distributive Property: $\mathcal{A} \cup (\mathcal{B} \cap \mathcal{C}) = (\mathcal{A} \cup \mathcal{B}) \cap (\mathcal{A} \cup \mathcal{C})$
$$\mathcal{A} \cap (\mathcal{B} \cup \mathcal{C}) = (\mathcal{A} \cap \mathcal{B}) \cup (\mathcal{A} \cap \mathcal{C})$$

Two useful theorems from the postulates linking complements of unions and intersections of sets are known together as De Morgan's Laws:

De Morgan's Laws: $(\mathcal{A} \cup \mathcal{B})^c = \mathcal{A}^c \cap \mathcal{B}^c$ and $(\mathcal{A} \cap \mathcal{B})^c = \mathcal{A}^c \cup \mathcal{B}^c$

De Morgan's Laws provide examples of another consequence, the principle of duality that states that valid theorems may be obtained by interchanging $\cup$ and $\cap$, and interchanging $\emptyset$ and $\mathcal{U}$. For example, it is easily proved from the basic definitions that $\mathcal{A} \cup \mathcal{U} = \mathcal{U}$ and the principle of duality immediately gives $\mathcal{A} \cap \emptyset = \emptyset$.

The Algebra of Sets given above is known as Boolean algebra after George Boole (1815-1864) who discovered it in establishing a symbolic logic.[234] The correspondences between the algebra of sets and the calculus of propositions of logic (Section 4.2) may be seen by associating sets with propositions ($\mathcal{A}$ becomes the statement a) and the operations of union $\cup$ with the logical conjunction "or" $\vee$, intersection $\cap$ with "and" $\wedge$, and complementation $\mathcal{A}^c$ with negation $\neg a$. The correspondence may be seen in the following examples:

$\mathcal{A} \cup \mathcal{A}^c = \mathcal{U}$ becomes $a \vee \neg a$ which is always a true statement. (Statement a must be true or false.)

$\mathcal{A} \cap \mathcal{A}^c = \emptyset$ becomes $a \wedge \neg a$ which is always a false statement. (Statement a cannot be true and false.)

Using De Morgan's Laws with the appropriate substitutions, logical equivalence ($\leftrightarrow$) is therefore established between the following propositions of logic:

$\neg(a \wedge b) \leftrightarrow \neg a \vee \neg b$ (The negation of statement a and b is true if and only if the negation of statement a or the negation of statement b is true.)

$\neg(a \vee b) \leftrightarrow \neg a \wedge \neg b$. (The negation of statement a or b is true if and only if the negation of statement a and the negation of statement b is true.)

We will not pursue the connections of set theory with logic further (see more details in Eves, pp. 243 - 262) other than noting that logical contradictions can occur in the elementary theory of sets assuming that a set can simply be defined by any property and those members which satisfy that property. One of the famous contradictions is that discovered by Russell who pointed out the contradictory nature of a set X defined as the set of all sets which are *not members of themselves*.[235] For example, a collection of maps that is an atlas is not a map; while in contrast, the list of all lists includes itself. Now any set X must be either a member of itself or not—so we can look at these two possibilities. First, assume that X *is a member of itself*, then by the definition of X, it is not a member of X - a contradiction with our assumption. Alternatively, assume X is not a member of itself. Then it must be in X which is a contradiction with the definition of X. Thus, what seems like a perfectly good definition for a set leads to paradoxical conclusions. Such paradoxes are known in mathematics as antinomies.

As noted in the history outline (Section 1.2.6), Russell also described this contradiction less formally in the paradox of the barber: does a barber shaves himself if he only shaves those who do not shave themselves? Related paradoxes occur with other examples of sets of all sets such as with the set of all ordinal numbers. As we have seen for any transfinite ordinal, there is an even larger ordinal. Thus, an ordinal number exists which is larger than that determined by the set of all ordinal numbers. [236] This was stated by Cesare Burali-Forti (1861 - 1931).[237] From considerations such as these, the need for a formal axiomatic approach to set theory that would avoid paradoxes was recognized.

9.1.2   Axioms of sets

From an axiomatic point of view, we may take the concept of a set and the relation of being a member of a set as undefined terms. We will not delve deeply into this more sophisticated approach. However, we can provide some insight into the formal axiomatic point-of-view of sets by introducing the axioms first stated by Zermolo and now known as the Zermolo—Fraenkel (ZF) axioms.[cxxxii] These are fundamental to the development of the foundations of mathematics. The axioms of set theory have been formulated in a number of different ways starting with Zermolo in 1908. The names of the

---

cxxxii In addition to Zermelo's contributions to the development of the axioms, important contributions were made by a number of mathematicians including Abraham Fraenkel, Thoralf Skolem, and John von Neumann. An historical perspective on the development of the axioms is given by G.H. Moore, *Zermelo's Axiom of Choice, Its Origins Development & Influence*; in particular see pp. 152-154, 269-270 [Math References 26].

axioms are primarily those given by Zermolo. In what follows all of the members of sets are themselves sets.

Zermolo and Fraenkel (ZF) Axioms of Set Theory:[cxxxiii]

ZF1 (Axiom of Extension): Two sets $\mathcal{A}$ and $\mathcal{B}$ are equal if and only if the members of $\mathcal{A}$ and $\mathcal{B}$ are the same.

ZF2 (Axiom of Elementary Sets): There exists a set without members called the empty set (designated as $\emptyset$).

ZF3 (Axiom of Pairing): For any sets $\mathcal{A}$ and $\mathcal{B}$, $\{\mathcal{A}, \mathcal{B}\}$ is a set. (This set is called the unordered pair).

ZF4 (Axiom of Union): For any non-empty set $\mathcal{A}$, there is a set $\mathcal{B}$ consisting of the members of members of set $\mathcal{A}$.

ZF5 (Power Set Axiom): For any set $\mathcal{A}$, there is a set $\mathcal{P}(\mathcal{A})$, called the power set consisting of all subsets of $\mathcal{A}$.

ZF6 (Axiom of Separation): Given a set $\mathcal{X}$ with members x and a function f(x) formed from operations of logic, there exists a set $\mathcal{Y} = \{y \in \mathcal{X} | y = f(x)\}$.

ZF7 (Axiom of Replacement): Given a set $\mathcal{X}$ with members x and a formula $f(x, y)$ formed from operations of logic, there exists a set $\mathcal{Y}$ with members y that satisfy $f(x, y)$.

ZF8 (Axiom of Foundation): Any nonempty set $\mathcal{A}$ contains a set $\mathcal{B}$ with members not members of $\mathcal{A}$.

ZF9 (Axiom of Infinity): Sets with an infinite number of members exist.

Illustrating the struggle over the proper formulation of the axioms, Zermolo did not include ZF9 the Axiom of Infinity in his axioms in 1930. Another axiom of 1908 excluded from his 1930 formulation is the controversial Axiom of Choice. This seemingly simple, independent axiom states:

ZF10 Axiom of Choice: If a set $\mathcal{S}$ is partitioned into sets that are disjoint (sets having no members in common), then there exists a set $\mathcal{T}$ which has exactly one member from each of the disjoint sets.

---

cxxxiii The axioms and their interpretation are adapted from those given by A. G. Hamilton, pp. 115-128 and Stillwell, p. 26.

Now let us give an introductory sense of these axioms. Axiom ZF1 merely confirms the elementary notion that two sets are equal if they have the same members. In ZF2, the first specific set is identified, oddly enough as the set with no members called the empty set or the null set, $\emptyset$. Like the number zero, the empty set plays an important role in the algebra of sets. Axioms ZF3 and ZF4 allow the construction of sets. For example if we have sets $\mathcal{A}$ and $\mathcal{B}$, then $\{\mathcal{A}, \mathcal{B}\}$ is a set. Set $C = \{\mathcal{A}, \mathcal{B}\}$ is called the unordered pair of $\mathcal{A}$ and $\mathcal{B}$. Notice that if $\mathcal{A} = \mathcal{B}$, then $\{\mathcal{A}, \mathcal{B}\} = \{\mathcal{A}\}$, known as a singleton. Axiom ZF4 allows the process to continue through the operation of union. As an example, from the set $\mathcal{D}$ including the members $\mathcal{A}$ and $\mathcal{B}$, the union $\mathcal{A} \cup \mathcal{B}$ can be formed as members of members of $\mathcal{D}$.

From the existence of the single set $\emptyset$, John von Neumann (1903-1957)[238][cxxxiv] constructed the natural numbers. [239]

Let: $\mathbf{0} = \emptyset$, and

$\mathbf{1} = \emptyset \cup \{\emptyset\} = \{\emptyset\}$ that is $\mathbf{1}$ is the set containing the set $\emptyset$. Continuing,

$\mathbf{2} = \mathbf{1} \cup \{\mathbf{1}\} = \{\emptyset, \{\emptyset\}\} = \{\mathbf{0}, \mathbf{1}\}$,

$\mathbf{3} = \mathbf{2} \cup \{\mathbf{2}\} = \{\emptyset, \{\emptyset\}\} \cup \{\{\emptyset, \{\emptyset\}\}\} = \{\emptyset, \{\emptyset\}, \{\emptyset, \{\emptyset\}\}\} = \{\mathbf{0}, \mathbf{1}, \mathbf{2}\}$

.
.
.

$\mathbf{n} + \mathbf{1} = \mathbf{n} \cup \{\mathbf{n}\}$.

Thus the natural numbers, in effect, have been created ex nihilo (out of nothing) from the empty set. Furthermore, the natural numbers as an infinite set may be fulfilled through ZF9, Thus set theory through the natural numbers are, as we have seen, a basis for the real numbers and through analytic geometry, geometry itself.

As we saw in Chapter 3, the concept of the power set established in ZF5 builds ever larger sets with the power set of the natural numbers having the same size or cardinal number as that of the real numbers. Let us first look at the power set of a simple finite set.

---

cxxxiv A fascinating telling of the story of John von Neumann's life and role in the development of the architecture of the modern computer is related in George Dyson's *Turing's Cathedral, the Origins of the Digital Universe* {Other Citation Sources 6]. A brief discussion is included of von Neumann's contribution to the axioms of sets, pp.49-50. An alternative set of axioms due to von Neumann and Paul Bernays is discussed in Hamilton, pp. 145-156.

Let $\mathcal{D} = \{\mathcal{A}, \mathcal{B}, \mathcal{C}\}$. The power set of $\mathcal{D}$ is the set of all its possible subsets $\mathcal{P}(\mathcal{D})$. In this simple case, $\mathcal{P}(\mathcal{D}) = \{\emptyset, \{\mathcal{A}\}, \{\mathcal{B}\}, \{\mathcal{C}\}, \{\mathcal{A}, \mathcal{B}\}, \{\mathcal{A}, \mathcal{C}\}, \{\mathcal{B}, \mathcal{C}\}, \{\mathcal{A}, \mathcal{B}, \mathcal{C}\}\}$. The cardinal number of $\mathcal{D}$ is 3 and that of $\mathcal{P}(\mathcal{D})$ is $8 = 2^3$. If with designate the cardinal number of a set $\mathcal{X}$ as $\#\mathcal{X}$ then, for any finite set, if $\#\mathcal{X} = n$, $\#\mathcal{P}(\mathcal{X}) = 2^n$. This is shown below using the Taylor series expansion about $x = 0$ for $f(x) = (1 + x)^n$. From Chapter 8, we can show that for a natural number n,

$$(1 + x)^n = 1 + f'(0)x + \frac{f''(0)}{2 \cdot 1}x^2 + \cdots + \frac{f^m(0)}{m!}x^m + \cdots + x^n \text{ , where m is the}$$

m^{th} term after the first.

$$= 1 + \frac{n}{1}x + \frac{n(n-1)}{2 \cdot 1}x^2 + \cdots \frac{n(n-1)(n-2)\cdots(n-m+1)}{m!}x^m + \cdots + x^n.$$

For example, $(1+x)^4 = 1 + \frac{4}{1}x + \frac{4 \cdot 3}{2 \cdot 1}x^2 + \frac{4 \cdot 3 \cdot 2}{3 \cdot 2 \cdot 1}x^3 + \frac{4 \cdot 3 \cdot 2 \cdot 1}{4 \cdot 3 \cdot 2 \cdot 1}x^4$

$$= 1 + 4x + 6x^2 + 4x^3 + x^4$$

The coefficient of the mth term can be shown to be the same as the number of combinations without regard to order that can be made of n objects taken m at a time $C\binom{n}{m}$. In the example,

$$(1 + x)^4 = 1 + C\binom{4}{1}x + C\binom{4}{2}x^2 + C\binom{4}{3}x^3 + C\binom{4}{4}x^4.$$

For x=1,

$$(1 + x)^4 = 1 + C\binom{4}{1} + C\binom{4}{2} + C\binom{4}{3} + C\binom{4}{4}. \text{ Therefore,}$$

$2^4 =$ the empty set plus the total number of possible subsets of a set of 4 members taken, 1, 2, 3, and 4 at a time. Therefore, in general,

if $\#\mathcal{D} = n$, $\#\mathcal{P}(\mathcal{D}) = 1 + C\binom{n}{1} + C\binom{n}{2} + \cdots + C\binom{n}{n} = 2^n$.

Axiom ZF6, the Axiom of Separation, is closely relate to ZF7, Axiom of Replacement and is in fact implied by ZF7. [240] Axiom ZF7 may be expressed as the image of a set under the formula of logic f is a set. These axioms do not express specific methods for constructing sets, but rather express the allowed framework for their construction. The Axioms of Separation and of Replacement are more formal ways to express Kline's informal axiom that "any property that can be formalized in the language of the theory [language of logic] can be used to define a set."[241] From an example of an operation we have previously seen, if $\mathcal{D} = \{\mathcal{A}, \mathcal{B}, \mathcal{C}\}$ and $\mathcal{E}=\{\mathcal{B}, \mathcal{C}, \mathcal{F}\}$. The set $\mathcal{G}$ can be formed as the set whose members are members of both $\mathcal{D}$ and $\mathcal{E}$ that is $\mathcal{G} = \{x| \ x \in \mathcal{D}$ and $x \in \mathcal{E}\} = \{\mathcal{B}, \mathcal{C}\}$ or $\mathcal{G}= \mathcal{D} \cap \mathcal{E}$.

Another operation covered under the axioms is that of taking the complement of a set with respect to another set. Again if $\mathcal{D} = \{\mathcal{A}, \mathcal{B}, \mathcal{C}\}$ then the complement of $\mathcal{B}$ with respect to $\mathcal{D}$, $\mathcal{D} - \mathcal{B} = \{x|x \in \mathcal{D}$ and $x \notin \mathcal{B}\} = \{\mathcal{A}, \mathcal{C}\}$.

In elementary set theory, a universal set $\mathcal{U}$, a set of all sets, was introduced including all of the sets in consideration. A universal set is not defined in terms of the ZF axioms since it can, as noted, lead to logical contradictions and is therefore excluded. The axiom ZF8, the Axiom of Foundation restricts $\mathcal{X}$ from being a member of $\mathcal{X}$, thus avoiding contradictions in the axiomatic system such as Russell's paradoxes and others related to the logical consequences of postulating a set of all sets. [242]

When ZF10, the Axiom of Choice is added to ZF1 to ZF9, the axioms are often designated by the abbreviation ZFC. The axiom states that for any set (finite or infinite) partitioned into disjoint sets, a set may be formed by a choice function selecting one member from each of the disjoint sets. Perhaps the most controversial aspect of the Axiom of Choice would be the discovery that it is equivalent to the axiom that all sets may be well-ordered, that is all sets, may be ordered and have a first member.[243] Sets of the real numbers, say $\{x|0 < x < 1\}$, being uncountable and dense, clearly are a challenge to the meaning of this axiom—what is the first element of the set? However, crucial mathematical concepts require the Axiom of Choice such as the equivalence of continuity as defined by sequences to that defined by the $\epsilon - \delta$ approach of Weierstrass/Cauchy. This was not recognized until the twentieth century.[244] The Axiom of Choice is thus an assumption presenting mathematicians with the need to determine circumstances in which the axiom can be consistently and usefully applied.

Issues surrounding the Axioms Choice are the basis for many of the controversies surrounding the use of set theory as a foundation of mathematic and will be discussed in more detail in the final chapter. With this introduction to the axiomatic approach, we will now look at infinite sets.

9.2   Revisiting infinity

9.2.1   Infinite sets and their cardinal number

In Chapter 2, a formal definition of the natural numbers is given with the Postulates of Peano. The idea of infinity is encountered in this definition in the sense that no matter which natural number we choose, there will always be natural numbers that are greater in magnitude. Rather than infinity indicating the potential for ever greater numbers, Cantor envisioned the infinite set of natural numbers including all natural numbers. As the integers, rational numbers, and real numbers all include the natural numbers, it is clear that sets of these numbers are also infinite. If that were the only implication of infinity, then its impact on mathematics would not be great. However, as shown in Chapter 3, Cantor showed that there are different orders of infinity. The natural numbers, integers, and rational numbers share a common infinity while the real numbers are characterized by a higher order of infinity. Cantor developed these concepts by introducing sets which could contain an infinite number of members, such as the set of natural numbers N, and introducing transfinite cardinal numbers to quantify their size, and transfinite ordinal numbers to quantify their size and order. Ultimately, Cantor would find that the logic of his set theory leads to unlimited infinities beyond that of the natural numbers. We will now explore again these infinities using the more precise language provided by sets to describe without proof some of these results.

First let us recall from Chapter 3 the definition of equivalent sets[cxxxv] and cardinal number.

Definition of Equivalent Sets: Two sets A and B are equivalent ($A \sim B$) if a one-to-one correspondence[cxxxvi] may be established between the members of the two sets.

Definition of Cardinal Number: The common property of all equivalent sets (such as A and B) is their cardinal number ($\#A = \#B$).

---

cxxxv Equivalent sets are also known as equinumerous or similar sets.
cxxxvi From Chapters 3 and 5, a one-to-one correspondence for two sets of objects A and B is established if each object in A is paired with a single object in B and conversely. A one-to-one correspondence is also referred to as a bijection.

The equivalence of sets ($\mathcal{A} \sim \mathcal{B}$) may be shown to be an equivalence relation:

$\mathcal{A} \sim \mathcal{A}$; $\mathcal{A} \sim \mathcal{B} \Rightarrow \mathcal{B} \sim \mathcal{A}$; and $\mathcal{A} \sim \mathcal{B}$ and $\mathcal{B} \sim \mathcal{C} \Rightarrow \mathcal{A} \sim \mathcal{C}$.

Using the definition of equivalence and that of a proper subset, Dedekind's definition of finite and infinite sets may be given.

Definition of a Finite Set: A set $\mathcal{A}$ is finite if no proper subset of $\mathcal{A}$ is equivalent to $\mathcal{A}$.

Definition of an Infinite Set: A set $\mathcal{A}$ is infinite if there is a proper subset of $\mathcal{A}$ equivalent to $\mathcal{A}$.

From these definitions it is clear, as shown in Chapter 3, that the sets of positive even and odd natural numbers, integers, and rational numbers are equivalent to the set of natural numbers through the establishment of a one-to-one correspondence. The infinite quality of the natural numbers is also exhibited by the odd numbers being a proper subset of the natural numbers. The cardinal numbers of all these sets are the same. Any set that can be put into a one-to-one correspondence with the natural numbers is said to be countably infinite or denumerable and has a cardinal number $\aleph_0$ as designated by Cantor. Sets that are finite or denumerable are known as countable.

Cantor also showed (Chapter 3) that the real numbers could not be put into a one-to-one correspondence with the natural numbers. The transfinite number representing the real numbers is often designated as C. However, sets such as $\{x|\ 0 < x < 1\}$ can be put into a one-to one correspondence with the whole real number line or other similar sets, for example $\{x\ |\ 5 \leq x \leq 100\}$. Thus, all sets made up of such intervals of the real number line are equivalent and have the cardinal number of C.

Cantor envisioned the transfinite numbers as having order relations like the usual numbers. A key theorem to establishing the ordering of transfinite numbers is the Schröder-Bernstein Theorem.

Theorem S1 (Schröder-Bernstein): For sets $\mathcal{A}$ and $\mathcal{B}$ with $\mathcal{A}_s$ and $\mathcal{B}_s$ being subsets of $\mathcal{A}$ and $\mathcal{B}$, respectively, if for some $\mathcal{A}_s$ and $\mathcal{B}_s$, $\mathcal{A} \sim \mathcal{B}_s$, and $\mathcal{B} \sim \mathcal{A}_s$ then $\#\mathcal{A} = \#\,\mathcal{B}$.[cxxxvii]

---

cxxxvii Breuer, p. 41. Hamilton (p. 63) gives another form of the theorem in terms of injections, that is functions that are one-to-one but not necessarily onto functions (recall a one-to-one and onto function is also called a

The Schröder-Bernstein Theorem gives us another way of evaluating infinite sets formed from the various infinite subsets of rational numbers, integers and natural numbers. As we have seen, the real numbers are not equivalent to any subset of the natural numbers, so as previously shown $C \neq \aleph_0$. In addition, however, the cardinal numbers can be ordered by size. The order theorem stated below may be proved using the Schröder-Bernstein Theorem and the Axiom of Choice.[245]

Theorem S2 (Order of Cardinal Numbers): For sets $\mathcal{A}$ and $\mathcal{B}$ with $\mathcal{A}_s$ and $\mathcal{B}_s$ being subsets of $\mathcal{A}$ and $\mathcal{B}$, respectively, if for some $\mathcal{B}_s$, $\mathcal{A} \backsim \mathcal{B}_s$, but $\mathcal{B} \not\backsim \mathcal{A}_s$ ($\mathcal{B}$ not equivalent to $\mathcal{A}_s$) for any $\mathcal{A}_s$ then $\#\mathcal{A} < \#\mathcal{B}$.[cxxxviii]

As the natural numbers are equivalent to a subset of the real numbers, therefore, $\aleph_0 < C$. (Recall that Cantor showed that the rational numbers are equivalent to the natural numbers both having the cardinal number $\aleph_0$.) While the order of these two cardinal numbers has been established, it does not say whether there is a cardinal number $\aleph_1$ between $\aleph_0$ and C. The assumption that the cardinal number after $\aleph_0$, designated $\aleph_1$, is equal to C is known as the Continuum Hypothesis and remains a lively issue of mathematics. The theorem that for any two transfinite numbers m and n, $m < n$, $m = n$, or $m > n$ is known as the Trichotomy of Cardinal Numbers and has been shown to be equivalent to the Axiom of Choice.[246]

In addition to being ordered, a consistent arithmetic of cardinal numbers may be established for finite and transfinite cardinal numbers. We begin by defining addition of cardinal numbers in terms of the union of sets.[247]

---

one-to-one correspondence; see Appendix G). If f:$\mathcal{A} \dashrightarrow \mathcal{B}$ and g:$\mathcal{B} \dashrightarrow \mathcal{A}$ are injective functions, then there is a bijective (one-to-one and onto) function h:$\mathcal{A} \dashrightarrow \mathcal{B}$. Therefore, $\mathcal{A}$ is equivalent to $\mathcal{B}$. In this form of the theorem, the injective functions f and g take the role, respectively of the statements $\mathcal{A} \backsim \mathcal{B}_s$ and $\mathcal{B} \backsim \mathcal{A}_s$. The theorem says that with the existence of functions f and g, there exists a one-to-one correspondence h from $\mathcal{A}$ to $\mathcal{B}$; therefore, $\mathcal{A} \backsim \mathcal{B}$ and $\#\mathcal{A} = \#\mathcal{B}$.

cxxxviii Breuer, p. 40. Following the approach of Hamilton, this theorem may also be expressed as: $\#\mathcal{A} < \#\mathcal{B}$ if and only if there is an injective function of $\mathcal{A}$ to $\mathcal{B}$, but not one from $\mathcal{B}$ to $\mathcal{A}$; Hamilton, pp. 54, 225.

Definition of Addition of Cardinal Numbers: If $S = \mathcal{A} \cup \mathcal{B}$ and $\mathcal{A} \cap \mathcal{B} = \emptyset$, then $\#S = \#\mathcal{A} + \#\mathcal{B}$.

From the properties of the union of sets, addition of cardinal numbers is commutative and associative, that is, $\#\mathcal{A} + \#\mathcal{B} = \#\mathcal{B} + \#\mathcal{A}$, and $(\#\mathcal{A} + \#\mathcal{B}) + \#\mathcal{C} = \#\mathcal{A} + (\#\mathcal{B} + \#\mathcal{C})$

Looking first at a simple example of finite sets, it is clear that the operation of addition for finite sets takes on its usual meaning. If $\mathcal{A} = \{a, b, c, d\}$ and $\mathcal{B} = \{e, f\}$, $(\mathcal{A} \cup \mathcal{B}) = \{a, b, c, d, e\}$, $\#\mathcal{A} = 4$ and $\#\mathcal{B} = 2$. From the definition of addition, $\#\mathcal{A} + \#\mathcal{B} = 4 + 2 = \#(\mathcal{A} \cup \mathcal{B}) = 6$.

Now let's look at the addition of a finite set $\mathbf{n} = \{1, 2, 3, 4, \ldots, n\}$ and the infinite subset of the natural numbers, $\mathcal{N}_{n+1} = \{n+1, n+2, n+3, \ldots\}$; $\#\mathbf{n} = n$, $\#\mathcal{N}_{n+1} = \aleph_0$. Therefore,

$$n + \aleph_0 = \aleph_0 \text{ since } (\mathbf{n} \cup \mathcal{N}_{n+1}) = \mathcal{N}$$

Similarly, for subsets of $\mathcal{N}$, the even number set $\mathcal{E}$ and odd number set $\mathcal{O}$,

$$\#\mathcal{E} + \#\mathcal{O} = \aleph_0 + \aleph_0 = \#(\mathcal{E} \cup \mathcal{O}) = \#\mathcal{N} = \aleph_0. \text{ In general,}$$
$$\aleph_0 + \aleph_0 + \aleph_0 + \ldots + \aleph_0 = \aleph_0.$$

The same line of reasoning may be used to give results for addition involving the transfinite cardinal number of the continuum C. For example, the union of the natural numbers $\mathcal{N}$ with the set of real numbers between 0 and 1 $\mathcal{R}_{(0,1)}$ includes an infinite set of rational numbers that can be put into a one-to-one correspondence with the natural numbers; however, there are still in the interval an uncountable infinite number of irrational numbers. Therefore,

$$\aleph_0 + C = C.$$

We have also seen that intervals of real numbers such as $(0 \leq x \leq 1)$ and $(1 \leq x \leq 3)$ can easily be shown to have the same cardinal number C by establishing a function from one interval to the other. In this example, the union of the two sets forms the interval $(0 \leq x \leq 3)$ which also has the cardinal number C. This illustrates the general result:

$$C + C = C$$
and
$$C + C + C + \ldots + C = C.$$

Multiplication of finite and transfinite cardinal numbers can be established by introducing the product set $\mathcal{A} \times \mathcal{B}$.[cxxxix]

Definition of Product Set: For $\mathcal{A}$ and $\mathcal{B}$, $\mathcal{A} \times \mathcal{B} = \{(x, y)|\forall x \in \mathcal{A}$ and $\forall y \in \mathcal{B}\}$

If $\mathcal{A} = \{a, b, c\}$ and $\mathcal{B} = \{1, 2\}$, then $\mathcal{A} \times \mathcal{B} = \{(a,1), (a, 2), (b,1),$ $(b, 2), (c, 1), (c, 2)\}$

Note that $\#\mathcal{A} = 3$, $\#\mathcal{B} = 2$, and $\# (\mathcal{A} \times \mathcal{B} = 6$, just as $3 \cdot 2 = 6$. This specific result is generalized for finite and transfinite cardinal numbers:

Definition of Multiplication of Cardinal Numbers: The product $\#\mathcal{A} \cdot \#\mathcal{B} = \#(\mathcal{A} \times \mathcal{B})$.

As in the example above, for finite sets with $\#\mathcal{A} = m$ and $\#\mathcal{B} = n$, $m \cdot n = \# (\mathcal{A} \times \mathcal{B})$.

From the properties of sets, multiplication of cardinal numbers is commutative and associative, that is, $\#\mathcal{A} \cdot \#\mathcal{B} = \#\mathcal{B} \cdot \#\mathcal{A}$, and $(\#\mathcal{A} \cdot \#\mathcal{B}) \cdot \#\mathcal{C} = \#\mathcal{A} \cdot (\#\mathcal{B} \cdot \#\mathcal{C})$.

For $n = \{1, 2, \ldots n\}$, and $\mathcal{N}$, the set of natural numbers, $n\aleph_0 = \#n \cdot \#\mathcal{N} = \#(n \times \mathcal{N})$ and as another example, $\aleph_0\aleph_0 = \#\mathcal{N} \cdot \#\mathcal{N} = \#(\mathcal{N} \times \mathcal{N})$. The two product sets $n \times \mathcal{N}$ and $\mathcal{N} \times \mathcal{N}$ are illustrated below with the product set corresponding to $n \times \mathcal{N}$ having n rows and $\aleph_0$ columns. The product set $\mathcal{N} \times \mathcal{N}$ has $\aleph_0$ rows and $\aleph_0$ columns .

$$
\left.
\begin{array}{llll}
(1,1) & (1,2) & (1,3) & (1, 4)\ldots \\
(2,1) & (2,2) & (2,3) & (2.4)\ldots \\
(3,1) & (3,2) & (3,3) & (3,4)\ldots \\
\vdots & \vdots & \vdots & \vdots \\
(n,1) & (n,2) & (n,3) & (n,4)\ldots
\end{array}
\right\}
\begin{array}{l}
\text{n rows,} \\[1ex]
\aleph_0 \text{ columns}
\end{array}
\left.
\vphantom{\begin{array}{l}1\\2\\3\\4\\5\\6\\7\\8\end{array}}
\right\}
\begin{array}{l}
\aleph_0 \text{ rows} \\[1ex]
\aleph_0 \text{ columns}
\end{array}
$$

or

$$
\begin{array}{llll}
\vdots & \vdots & \vdots & \vdots \ldots
\end{array}
$$

---

cxxxix The product set is also known as the Cartesian product; Breuer, p. 46-49.

The cardinal number of the product $n\aleph_0$ may be seen in this illustration as the cardinal number of the union of n countably infinite sets. This is the same as $\aleph_0 + \aleph_0 + \aleph_0 + \ldots + \aleph_0 = \aleph_0$ with n additions and $n\aleph_0 = \aleph_0$.

The product set array corresponding to the cardinal number of the product $\aleph_0\aleph_0$ should remind you of the method used by Cantor to establish that the rational numbers are countably infinite (Chapter 3). In the array shown above, the array number (m, n) replaces the array of rational numbers m/n shown in Chapter 3. Therefore, just as the array of rational numbers m/ n can be put into a one-to-one correspondence with the natural numbers and has the cardinal number $\aleph_0$, so the cardinal number of the array (m, n) associated with the product set ($\mathcal{N} \times \mathcal{N}$) also has a cardinal number $\aleph_0$. Since the cardinal number of the product set is $\aleph_0$, $\aleph_0\aleph_0 = \aleph_0$. Again this may be generalized as:

$$\aleph_0\aleph_0\aleph_0 \ldots \aleph_0 = \aleph_0$$

In regard to transfinite arithmetic with the cardinal number C, nC = C as it can be regarded as the union of n uncountably infinite sets or n additions of C,

$$nC = C + C + C + \ldots + C = C \text{ (n additions)}$$

The product CC is the cardinal number of the product set of real numbers $\mathcal{R} \times \mathcal{R}$. In the product CC, C may be taken as the cardinal number of the subset of the real numbers on the x-axis of the Cartesian plane $\{x|\ 0 < x < 1\}$ and as the cardinal number of the set on the y-axis, $\{y|\ 0 < y < 1\}$. Therefore $\mathcal{R} \times \mathcal{R}$ is the set $\{(x, y)|\ 0 < x < 1 \text{ and } 0 < y < 1\}$, that is the associated points in the Cartesian plane (x, y). In chapter 3, the cardinal number of this set is shown to be C, therefore, CC=C. This can be generalized as CCC $\ldots$ C = C. This shows that in an n-dimensional space $\mathcal{R}^n$ that $\#\mathcal{R}^n = C$.

Noting that $n < \aleph_0 < C$, and nC = CC = C, it is not surprising then that $\aleph_0 C = C$. More formally, the product set $\mathcal{N} \times \mathcal{R} \sim \mathcal{N} \times \mathcal{R}_{(0,1)}$ with $\mathcal{R}_{(0,1)} = \{x|0 < x < 1)\}$ and $\mathcal{N} \times \mathcal{R}_{(0,1)} \sim \{(1, x)|x \in \mathcal{R}_{(0,1)}\} \cup \{(2, x)|x \in \mathcal{R}_{(0,1)}\} \cup \{(3, x)|x \in \mathcal{R}_{(0,1)}\} \cup \ldots$, which is a countable union of sets of cardinal number C. Since $\#\mathcal{N} = \aleph_0$ and $\#\mathcal{R}_{(0,1)} = C$, therefore $\aleph_0 C = \#(\mathcal{N} \times \mathcal{R}_{(0,1)}) = C + C + C + \ldots = C$.

The results below summarize these concepts.

$$n + \aleph_0 = \aleph_0$$
$$\aleph_0 + \aleph_0 = \aleph_0$$
$$\aleph_0 + \aleph_0 + \aleph_0 + \ldots + \aleph_0 = \aleph_0.$$
$$n + C = C$$
$$\aleph_0 + C = C$$
$$C + C = C$$
$$C + C + C + \ldots + C = C$$

$$n\aleph_0 = \aleph_0$$
$$\aleph_0 \aleph_0 = \aleph_0$$
$$\aleph_0 \aleph_0 \aleph_0 \ldots \aleph_0 = \aleph_0$$
$$nC = C$$
$$\aleph_0 C = C$$
$$CC = C$$
$$CCC \ldots C = C$$

The final arithmetic operation to define is exponentiation. [248] As with the previous operations of addition and multiplication, exponentiation for transfinite numbers needs to be consistent with that of the cardinal numbers of finite sets. First, however, we need a definition for exponentiation of sets.

Definition of Exponents of Sets: For sets $\mathcal{A}$ and $\mathcal{B}$, $\mathcal{B}^{\mathcal{A}}$ denotes the set of all functions mapping $\mathcal{A}$ to $\mathcal{B}$.

The functions mapping $\mathcal{A}$ to $\mathcal{B}$ need only satisfy the requirement that every member of $\mathcal{A}$ is mapped into a single member of $\mathcal{B}$, that is only has one image. To give insight into this definition, let's look at its meaning when $\mathcal{A}$ and $\mathcal{B}$ are finite sets. Let $\mathcal{A} = \{a, b, c\}$ and $\mathcal{B} = \{1, 2\}$. The following 8 functions f_i ($i = 1$ to 8) are possible in which for example (a, 1) is a mapping from a to 1:

$f_1 = (a, 1), (b, 1), (c,1), f_2 = (a, 2), (b, 2), (c,2), f_3 = (a, 1), (b, 1), (c,2), f_4 = (a, 1), (b, 2), (c,1), f_5 = (a, 2), (b, 1), (c,1), f_6 = (a, 2), (b, 2), (c,1), f_7 = (a, 2), (b, 1), (c,2), f_8 = (a, 1), (b, 2), (c,2)$.

Notice that $\#\mathcal{A} = 3$ and $\#\mathcal{B} = 2$, $\#\mathcal{B}^{\#\mathcal{A}} = 2^3 =$ the number of functions f_i mapping $\mathcal{A}$ to $\mathcal{B}$. This result is generalized through the following definition.

Definition of Exponents of Cardinal Numbers: For sets $\mathcal{A}$ and $\mathcal{B}$, $\#(\mathcal{B}^{\mathcal{A}}) = \#\mathcal{B}^{\#\mathcal{A}}$.

An important example of this definition with a transfinite cardinal exponent is $2^{\aleph_0}$. Let $\mathcal{A} = \mathcal{N}$ and $\mathcal{B} = \{0, 1\}$. Then, $\#\mathcal{A} = \aleph_0$ and $\#\mathcal{B} = 2$ functions f_i from $\mathcal{A}$ to $\mathcal{B}$ can be represented as a mapping from $(1, 2, 3, 4, 5, 6, 7, \ldots)$ to images such as $(0, 1, 1, 0, 1, 0, 0 \ldots)$. In turn, a one-to-one correspondence with these images can be made with binary nonterminating fractions as 0.0110100 . . . . As explained in Chapter 3, the infinite set of these numbers is equivalent to the real number between 0 and 1; hence, $2^{\aleph_0} = C$. A similar mapping from $\mathcal{N}$ to the set of decimal numbers 0 to 9 allows us to conclude that $10^{\aleph_0} = C$ or in general $n^{\aleph_0} = C$.

From these, the results below follow:

$C^n = (2^{\aleph_0})^n = 2^{\aleph_0 n} = 2^{\aleph_0} = C$
$C^{\aleph_0} = (2^{\aleph_0})^{\aleph_0} = 2^{\aleph_0 \aleph_0} = 2^{\aleph_0} = C$
Furthermore noting that $2 < \aleph_0 < C$,
$\aleph_0^{\aleph_0} = C$ is consistent with $2^{\aleph_0} = C$ and $C^{\aleph_0} = C$.[cxl]

For finite sets, we saw previously that for $\mathcal{A}$, the power set $\mathcal{P}(\mathcal{A})$ has a cardinal number $\#\mathcal{P}(\mathcal{A}) = 2^n$ where n = $\#\mathcal{A}$. From $2^{\aleph_0} = C$, one can infer that the cardinal number $\#\mathcal{P}(\mathcal{N}) = \#\mathcal{R}$, the cardinal number of the power set of the natural numbers is the cardinal number of the real numbers.[cxli]

Now one might ask if C is the largest infinity. An answer to this question lies in the result proved by Cantor that $\#\mathcal{P}(\mathcal{A}) > \#\mathcal{A}$, or $2^{\#\mathcal{A}} > \#\mathcal{A}$.[249] From this relation, ever greater transfinite cardinal numbers can be created as $\mathcal{P}(\mathcal{P}(\dots \mathcal{P}(\aleph_0) \dots))$ to form the sequence:

$$\aleph_0, \; 2^{\aleph_0}, \; 2^{2^{\aleph_0}}, \; 2^{2^{2^{\aleph_0}}}, \dots$$

When Russell became aware of this possibility he felt that there must be a mistake in Cantor's logic as he believed that there must be a greatest transfinite set, but he eventually came to agree with Cantor.[250] Thus, there is no greatest transfinite cardinal number; there are ever higher levels of infinity; and there cannot be a set of all sets.

9.2.2   The procession of successors to and from infinity; ordinal numbers

From Chapter 3 and the previous section, it should be clear that only the size of sets, whether finite or infinite, is ranked by their cardinal number. However, another important characteristic

---

cxl Hamilton provides additional insight, p. 79.
cxli Formal proof is given by Hamilton, pp. 67, 78.

introduced in Chapter 3 is the order of the members of sets. For example, the infinite set of natural numbers $\mathcal{N} = \{1, 2, 3, 4, \ldots\}$ is intuitively different from the infinite set of odd natural numbers followed by even natural numbers $\mathcal{N}_{O\&E} = \{1, 3, 5, 7, \ldots 2, 4, 6, 8, \ldots\}$ because of order. In both sets there is a first member, 1. Also in both cases there is a rule for ordering the members a_n of the set. For $\mathcal{N}$, a_m is before a_n if $a_m < a_n$. In the case of $\mathcal{N}_{O\&E}$, if a_m and a_n are both odd or both even then a_m is before a_n if $a_m < a_n$; if a_m is odd and a_n is even then a_m is before a_n. Another difference is that $\mathcal{N}$ has only one member which does not have a predecessor, 1 while $\mathcal{N}_{O\&E}$ has two, 1 and 2; however, in both cases every member has a successor. Despite the differences in ordering, both sets have a cardinal number of $\aleph_0$.

There are many other ways of arranging sets of numbers other than simply ordering by magnitude. For example in Chapter 3, the integers were put into a one-to-one correspondence with the natural numbers through the set $\{0, 1, -1, 2, -2, \ldots\}$. The integers could also be described by a set with no first or last number, $\{\ldots -3, -2, -1, 0, 1, 2, 3, \ldots\}$. The infinite set of rational numbers $\mathbb{R} = \{r \mid r > 0\}$ appears to be one that has no first number, and it is not immediately obvious how to define successive members in the set. But as discovered by Cantor, $\mathbb{R}$ can be ordered as a one-to-one correspondence with the natural numbers (see Chapter 3.) so as to contain all of the rational numbers greater than 0; $\mathbb{R} = \{1, 1/2, 2, 3, 1/3, \ldots\}$.

To characterize the types of differences of order in infinite sets, Cantor introduced the transfinite ordinal numbers. The transfinite ordinal numbers and order principles of sets would prove to be fundamental to the understanding of the foundations of mathematics. Two questions closely related to the transfinite ordinal numbers are the question of whether sets of real numbers can be ordered and whether there is a transfinite cardinal number between $\aleph_0$ and C. I can only just begin to describe the many profound issues raised by these questions, but I wish to take a first step towards an understanding of the meaning of these questions.

As a start, we need to have a mathematical definition of what is meant by order. The definition is supplied by what is known as an order relation. Recall in Chapter 2, an equivalence relation is defined in terms of reflexive, symmetric, and transitive properties. An order relation, between members x and y of a set $\mathcal{X}$, will be denoted as $x \preceq y$. It is said to exist if for every x, y, and z of $\mathcal{X}$ the following properties are satisfied: reflexivity $x \preceq x$; anti-symmetry $x \preceq y$ and $y \preceq x \Rightarrow x = y$; and transitivity $x \preceq y$ and $y \preceq z \Rightarrow x \preceq z$. [251] The symbol $\preceq$ is chosen to indicate such a relation as it reminds us of the traditional symbol for less than or equal $\leqq$ which may be used to order the set of natural numbers $\mathcal{N}$ ={1, 2, 3, . . .} However, as with equivalence relations, there are other examples of order relations. For example, if **x, y**, and **z** are sets in $\mathcal{X}$, then the order relation is satisfied by $\subseteq$ (is a subset of). The symbol $\preceq$ will be used to represent any order relation to emphasize that it is not necessarily one based on comparisons of magnitude.[cxlii]

To further clarify the concept of ordered sets, note that two sets $\mathcal{X}$and $\mathcal{Y}$ are similarly ordered $\mathcal{X} \simeq \mathcal{Y}$ (called an isomorphic order) if a function f(x) provides a one-to-one correspondence between $\mathcal{X}$ and $\mathcal{Y}$ preserving the order of the set members.[252] This means that for any members a and b of $\mathcal{X}$ ordered by some relation R_1 so a $\preceq$ b with f(a) = c, f(b) = d , and c and d members of $\mathcal{Y}$ ordered by R_2, then c $\preceq$ d. For example, the set of positive integers $\mathcal{I}_p$ = {1, 2, . . .} with $\leqq$ as R_1 and the set of negative integers $\mathcal{I}_n$ = {−1, −2, . . .} with $\geqq$ as R_2 are similar as the one-to-one correspondence f(x) = −x preserves order.

Sets such as $\mathcal{S}_1$ = {. . . , 3, 2, 1} and $\mathcal{S}_2$ ={1, 3, 5, . . . , 2, 4, 6, . . .} are not similarly ordered with $\mathcal{I}_p$ since a one-to-one correspondence is impossible with $\mathcal{S}_1$ having no first member and $\mathcal{S}_2$ having two members without a predecessor. A number without a predecessor is known as a limit ordinal.

Of particular significance to our questions concerning the ordering of the real numbers are well-ordered sets. A set $\mathcal{A}$ is well-ordered if every non-empty subset of $\mathcal{A}$ has a first member. An example of particular interest is the well-ordered set of the natural numbers $\mathcal{N}$ including 0. Previously we stated that the natural numbers could be generated as sets under the ZF axioms with:

$$0 = \emptyset, 1 = 0 \cup \{0\} = \{\emptyset\}, 2 = 1 \cup \{1\} = \{\emptyset, \{\emptyset\}\}, 3 = 2 \cup \{2\} = \left\{\emptyset, \{\emptyset\}, \{\emptyset, \{\emptyset\}\}\right\} \cdots$$
$$n + 1 = n \cup \{n\} \cdots$$

For any finite set, we define as a set the ordinal number **n+1** ={**0, 1, 2, 3, . . . , n**} the set of all predecessors of **n+1** with each member

---

cxlii Another definition providing a consistent approach to order relations is that known as a linear order. It is defined as non-reflexive, anti-symmetric, and transitive: x does not precede x, x precedes y $\Rightarrow$ y succeeds x, and x precedes y and y precedes z $\Rightarrow$ x precedes z. As an example, the order relation for the natural numbers can be defined as x<y. More generally the relation is denoted as x $\prec$ y; see Breuer, p. 56-57, Meserve, p. 14, and Stillwell p. 33.

equal to the set of its predecessors.[253] The axiom of infinity ZF9 allows us to define the ordinal number of the well-ordered set of all finite numbers as: $\omega = \{0, 1, 2, 3, \ldots\}$. The ordinal number ω is therefore countable although it is the first transfinite ordinal and the least upper bound of the set $\{0, 1, 2, 3, \ldots\}$.

Now where can we go from here? By analogy with the finite ordinals,

$\omega + 1 = \omega \cup \{\omega\} = \{0, 1, 2, 3, \ldots \omega\}$; $\omega + 2 = \omega + 1 \cup \{\omega + 1\} = \{0, 1, 2, 3, \ldots \omega, \omega + 1\} \ldots$

And $\omega + \omega = \omega \cdot 2 = \{0, 1, 2, 3, \ldots \omega, \omega + 1, \omega + 2, \ldots\}$.

An example of the ordered set $\omega + 1$ is $\{1, 2, 3, \ldots, 0\}$; while a representative set for $\omega \cdot 2$ is $\{1, 3, 5, \ldots, 2, 4, 6, \ldots\}$. The ordinal number ω like 2 in the example of $\omega \cdot 2$ is a limit ordinal. This is a good time to remind you that as discussed in Chapter 3 in regard to the Hilbert Hotel, $1 + \omega = \omega$, but $1 + \omega \neq \omega + 1$.

Successive ordinal numbers continue as shown in Chapter 3 to $\omega^2 \ldots \omega^3 \ldots \omega^\omega \ldots \omega^{\omega^{\omega^\omega}}$ and beyond. All of these ordinal numbers, however, are countable as in the Hilbert Hotel, and the cardinal number for these sets is therefore $\aleph_0$. We know from the example of the real numbers that there must be uncountable sets. Let ω_1 be the least upper bound of the set of all countable ordinals. The set ω_1 must then be *uncountable* otherwise there would be a countable successor greater than ω_1.[254]

If $\aleph_0$ is the cardinal number of the countable sets, what is the cardinal number of ω_1. Cantor called this cardinal number $\aleph_1$. He proposed that the cardinal number of the set of all countable ordinals is equal to the cardinal number of the real numbers which is the power set of the natural numbers $\mathcal{P}(\mathcal{N})$. Therefore, $\aleph_1 = 2^{\aleph_0} = C$. This is known as the Continuum Hypothesis and implies that there is no cardinal number between $\aleph_0$ and C.[255] The identification of $\aleph_1$ with $2^{\aleph_0} = C$ seems very appealing, as it was for Cantor; however, these two quantities are defined in very different and not clearly connected ways. Since $\aleph_1$ is the cardinal number of the set of all countable, well-ordered sets, it implies that the set of real numbers is also well-ordered. If sets of the real numbers are well-ordered, then theorems of the real numbers could be proved through mathematical induction similar to our proofs with the natural numbers. In 1883, Cantor had proposed as a "law of thought" that every set could be well-ordered. The first proof was stated in 1904 by Zermelo using the Axiom of Choice. The proof was controversial and no specific ordering of the real numbers was given.[cxliii] Eventually it would be proved that the Axiom of Choice was equivalent to Well-Ordering for the ZF axioms of set theory.[256] Along the way there would be considerable clarification into the foundations and limitations of mathematics, as related to the Axiom of Choice, Well-Ordering, and the Continuum Hypothesis, as discussed in my final chapter. Nevertheless the use of set theoretic approaches would bring precision to the expression of properties of the real numbers and create new abstract spaces, by merging and extending geometric and algebraic approaches.

9.3   Sets and the space of real numbers

9.3.1   Open and closed sets; neighborhoods, interior, and accumulation points

Let us start the discussion of sets of the real numbers with the simple notion of intervals of the real number line, a concept that was useful in defining limits, continuous functions, and the derivative. Recall the definition of limit in Chapter 5, $\lim_{x \to c} f(x) = L$, if for every ε we can find a region δ such that for all x with $|x-c| < \delta$, $|f(x) - L| < \varepsilon$. From the meaning of absolute value, the expression $|x-c| < \delta$ can be written as $c - \delta < x < c + \delta$. This is an example of an open interval in which x can vary between $c - \delta$ and $c + \delta$. This is usually expressed symbolically as $(c - \delta, c + \delta)$. The parentheses here denote an open interval (not to be confused in the current context with coordinates.) In general then (a, b) refers to the open interval $a < x < b$. If we defined δ as $|x - c| \leq \delta$, then the interval is $c - \delta \leq x \leq c + \delta$ which is known as a closed interval denoted as $[c - \delta, c + \delta]$. The difference between the intervals is that the closed interval contains the endpoints a and b. In general, [a, b] denotes $a \leq x \leq b$. Intervals that are neither open nor closed would be (a, b] or [a, b) representing respectively, $a < x \leq b$ and $a \leq x < b$. These are sometimes called half-open intervals.

From our understanding that the rational and real numbers are dense, we know that for every c in the open interval (a, b) and any selected $\delta > 0$, no matter how small, there exists a real number x not equal to c in the open interval $(c - \delta, c + \delta)$. The open interval is called

cxliii A detailed historical account of the axiom of choice and surrounding issues such as well-ordering is given by Moore. Chapter 1, pp. 5 - 84, pp. 88 - 92, focuses on the early history.

a neighborhood of c. More generally for sets, if every neighborhood of a point c contains points of the set different from c, then c is known as an accumulation point of the set. In regard to the real numbers, every neighborhood of a point c contains not only a point different from c, but an infinite number of points. In the closed interval [a, b], every point is an accumulation point; however, a and b are also accumulation points of the open interval (a, b) although a and b are not part of the open interval. This is because any neighborhood of a or b will include points of the open interval (a, b).[cxliv]

Another way to characterize points is as an interior point. An interior point of an interval, or a set, is a point for which there exists at least one neighborhood of the point entirely within the interval or set. For example, all of the points of the interval of real numbers (a, b) are interior points, whereas points a and b of the closed interval [a, b] are not, as any neighborhood of a or b will enclose points not in the interval.

With these definitions, the following definitions are given for the more general case of sets of real numbers.[257]

Definition of an Open Set: A set is open if all of the points of the set are interior points.

Definition of a Closed Set: A set is closed if it contains all of its accumulation points.

In the following examples, all of the sets are subsets of the real number line.

Example 1: {(a, b)} is open and {[a, b]} is closed.

Example 2: Any finite set of numbers, such as {1, 2, 3, 4, 5} has no accumulation points and no interior points. The set is therefore closed. The set of all natural numbers $\mathcal{N}$ = {1, 2, . . .} although containing an infinite number of points like intervals of the real or rational numbers also has no accumulation points and is closed.

Example 3: In the set of rational numbers in the closed interval [a, b], all of the rational numbers are accumulation points as are the

---

cxliv Breuer, pp. 70 - 71; as noted by Labarre, pp. 78 - 81, accumulation points are also known as limit points.

irrational numbers. The set has no interior points. (Between any two rational numbers, there are an infinite number of irrational numbers.).

Example 4: The set {0, 1, 1/2, 1/3, 1/4 . . .} includes its only accumulation point 0 and is therefore closed.

Example 5: A set may be neither open nor closed as with the set {1, 1/2, 1/3, 1/4 . . .} which does not include its accumulation point, 0 and not every point is an interior point.

Example 6: The singleton set {5} is closed as it has no accumulation points.

Example 7: The empty set ∅, having no points, has no accumulation points, so it could be said to be closed. Similarly with respect to interior points, it may also be considered to be open. Thus, in regard to sets, open does not mean not closed, and closed does not mean not open. This will be clarified in the section in which topological spaces are introduced.

Example 8: The union of any number of open sets is open as with
{(0, 1)} ∪ {(3, 4)} = {(0,1), (3,4)} is open as all points in the set are interior points. Note, however, that this set is not an interval.

Example 9: The intersection of a finite number of open sets is open as with {(−1/2, 1/2)} ∩ {(−1/3, 1/3)} ={(−1/3, 1/3)}; however, note that

$$\bigcap_{1}^{\infty} \{(-\frac{1}{n}, \frac{1}{n})\} = \{(-1,1)\} \cap \left[\left(-\frac{1}{2}, \frac{1}{2}\right)\right] \cap \left[\left(-\frac{1}{3}, \frac{1}{3}\right)\right] \ldots = \{0\}$$ which is a closed set.

9.3.2 The Bolzano-Weierstrass Theorem

I would like to use the framework of sets to provide another approach to distinguish the real numbers from the rational numbers. However, it is useful to recall how these two number systems are the same. We showed in Chapter 2, that both systems satisfy the requirements of an ordered field. Moreover, they both are dense sets in the number line. Recall that a dense set is defined as one in which between any two points of the set, there is at least one point. The open and closed intervals of rational numbers are dense while intervals of the real number line are dense in both the rational and irrational numbers. [258] So it is not denseness that makes the difference.

In Chapter 3, the difference was described by the Least Upper Bound Property; however, the differences may also be characterized in a key alternative theorem using the concepts of sets described in the previous section.

Bolzano-Weierstrass Theorem: Every bounded infinite set of real numbers has at least one accumulation point.[cxlv]

The Bolzano-Weierstrass Theorem may be shown to be a consequence of the Least Upper Bound Property (also referred to in Chapter 3 as the Postulate of Continuity). However, rather than deriving the Bolzano-Weierstrass Theorem from the properties of the real numbers with the Least Upper Bound Property, Bolzano-Weierstrass can be taken as a fundamental axiom allowing the rational numbers to be expanded to the real numbers. Without providing the proof that it leads to the properties of the real numbers, I will at least motivate its plausibility by looking at a bounded infinite set of rational numbers that does not have an accumulation point.

In Chapter 3 in making estimates x_n of $\sqrt{2}$, we developed a sequence of rational numbers in decimal notation that is ever increasing, but always satisfying the condition, $x_n^2 < 2$. The sequence of these estimates is 1, 1.4, 1.41, 1.414 . . . . The sequence forms an infinite set of rational numbers bounded by the condition that for every n, $x_n^2 < 2$. Thus, the set satisfies the Bolzano-Weierstrass conditions. However, there are no neighborhoods of any point in the set of rational numbers with an infinite number of points, hence there are no accumulation points. The only accumulation point is $\sqrt{2}$ which requires us to expand our definition of the set to the real numbers. The example given above suggests that the Bolzano-Weierstrass Theorem may also be expressed alternatively in terms of sequences.

---

cxlv Bernhard Bolzano (1781 - 1848), a Czechoslovakian priest who before Weierstrass discovered both the theorem on bounded infinite sets and accumulation points as well as a function that was continuous but nowhere differentiable. Also, he anticipated the differences between the infinity of the real numbers and integers, but his results seem to have been overlooked and were only rediscovered later; Merzbach and Boyer, pp. 457 - 458, 534.

Bolzano-Weierstrass Theorem for Sequences: Every bounded infinite sequence of real numbers has at least one sequential accumulation point.[cxlvi]

Just as we saw in Euclidean geometry that there are many postulates that are equivalent to the Parallel Postulate, so there are a number of postulates that can be equivalently used to expand the rational numbers to the real numbers. The Least Upper Bound Property discussed in Chapter 3 is sufficient to produce the real numbers from the rational numbers; however, other approaches are that of the Nested Intervals (Chapter 3), Cauchy Sequences (Chapter 6), and the Bolzano-Weierstrass Theorem discussed above.[cxlvii] All of the approaches other than that of the Least Upper Bound Property require in addition an explicit statement of the Archimedean Property (for any rational number r, there is a natural number n > r). However, with this caveat all of the approaches can be shown to be equivalent to the real numbers developed through the Dedekind Cuts (Chapter 3). For convenience, I restate here the various postulates used to expand the rational numbers below:

Least Upper Bound Property: Every nonempty subset of the real numbers $\mathcal{R}$ with an upper bound has a least upper bound.

Nested Interval Property: For sets of nested intervals of real numbers $I_n = \{[a_n, b_n]\}$ with $I_{n+1} \subseteq I_n$, only one real number x belongs to each of the intervals ($\bigcap_{n=1}^{\infty} I_n = x$).

Cauchy Property: Every convergent Cauchy sequence converges to a real number.

Bolzano-Weierstrass Property: Every bounded infinite set of real numbers has at least one accumulation point.

---

cxlvi Schramm, M. J., *Introduction to Real Analysis,* p. 168 - 169, [Math References 30]. Schramm use the term cluster point for accumulation point and sequential cluster point for an accumulation point in the sequence.

cxlvii The various postulates used to define the real numbers and the interrelationships between the postulates are the principal subject of M. J. Schramm's *Introduction to Real Analysis.* In addition, there is an introduction to logic and sets. Schramm also discusses the Heine-Borel Theorem involving the concept of compact sets which is beyond that which can be covered here. The various approaches to the real numbers are also summarized by Stečkin in Aleksandrov, Kolmogorov, and Lavrent'ev, Vol. 3, Part 5, p. 14 - 17.

A common theme of these properties can be seen in the problem of finding a number that satisfies $x^2 = 2$. In the case of each property, notice that in constructing an appropriate set or sequence of values to approach the solution, the property cannot be satisfied within the rational numbers and can only be satisfied through acceptance of the property as defining the expansion of the rational numbers to the real numbers. In the rational numbers: the set of numbers $\{x_n \mid x_{n+1} > x_n$ and $x_n^2 < 2\}$ has no least upper bound; the intersection of nested intervals about $\sqrt{2}$ is the empty set; the Cauchy sequence does not converge to a rational number; and as we have seen a bounded infinite set has no accumulation point. In each case, the real number, $\sqrt{2}$ defined through these properties does the job.

One other way to build the real numbers is through the concept of connected sets. The real numbers can be described as ordered connected field. We will investigate this along with its relation to continuous functions.

9.3.3   Connectivity and functions

We have seen repeatedly that there are more irrational numbers amongst the real numbers than rational numbers. From the point of view of sets, one consequence of the difference between the set of rational numbers and real numbers is that unlike the set of real numbers, the set of rational numbers is disconnected. A general definition to describe such sets of numbers is given below:[259]

Definition of Disconnectedness: A set $S \subseteq \mathcal{R}$ is disconnected if and only if there exist open disjoint sets $\mathcal{A}$ and $\mathcal{B}$ ($\mathcal{A} \cap \mathcal{B} = \emptyset$) such that: $\mathcal{A} \cap S \neq \emptyset$ and $\mathcal{B} \cap S \neq \emptyset$; and $S \subseteq \mathcal{A} \cup \mathcal{B}$.

A set that is not disconnected is connected. As a classic example of a disconnected set, S is the set of all rational numbers. Let $\mathcal{A} = \{x_n$ is rational $\mid x_n^2 \leqq 2\}$ and $\mathcal{B} = \{x_n$ is rational $\mid x_n^2 > 2\}$. The set S is disconnected as: $\mathcal{A}$ and $\mathcal{B}$ are disjoint sets ($\mathcal{A} \cap \mathcal{B} = \emptyset$); $\mathcal{A} \cap S \neq \emptyset$ and $\mathcal{B} \cap S \neq \emptyset$; and $S = \mathcal{A} \cup \mathcal{B}$. The sets $\mathcal{A}$ and $\mathcal{B}$ form the cut in the rational numbers, discovered by Dedekind, that defines the real number $x = \sqrt{2}$. Because between any two rational numbers there is an infinite set of irrational numbers, the only sets of rational numbers that can be said to be connected are singletons $\{r\}$ in which r is any rational number.

Using any of the various possible postulates that we have discussed to extend the rational to the real numbers, it can be shown that the entire real number line $(-\infty, \infty)$ and any of its intervals form a connected set. These intervals include the bounded open, closed, and half-open intervals (a, b), [a, b], (a, b], and [a, b} as well as those intervals with no upper bound, (a, ∞), $[a. \infty)$ or lower bound $(-\infty, b)$ and $(-\infty, b]$.[260] Alternatively, starting with the real numbers as a connected ordered field, the following theorem may be proved:

Theorem for Connected Ordered Fields: Any connected ordered field has the Least Upper Bound Property

Therefore, a final approach to the real numbers is to define them as a connected ordered field (while recalling that the rational numbers only form an ordered field).[261]

Now we want to see how the concept of a connected set relates to functions, but first let's look at functions in the context of sets. In Chapter 5, functions of a real variable such as $f(x) = x^3$ were introduced and interpreted as curves in the Cartesian plane. Functions may also be thought of as subsets of the product set of real numbers $\mathcal{R} \times \mathcal{R}$ which is sometimes expressed as f: $\mathcal{R} \to \mathcal{R}$. The function $f(x) = x^3$ is an example. A member of this product set would be the ordered pair (2, 8). The domain of the function is the set of real numbers constituting the independent variable. The codomain corresponds to the dependent variable which in the example $f(x) = x^3$ is also the entire real number line. In general, we can define functions of real numbers as f: $\mathcal{A} \to \mathcal{B}$. In this description $\mathcal{A}$ is the domain and $\mathcal{B}$ is the codomain. If $\mathcal{B}$ is a subset of a larger set, it is often referred to as the range. The set $\mathcal{B}$ is the image of the set $\mathcal{A}$ under the function f. (Alternatively, this may be expressed as $f(\mathcal{A}) = \mathcal{B}$) This relationship can be quite general; however, certain types of functions are particularly useful and given specific names (see also Appendix G). These types of functions are again described here emphasizing the language of sets.[cxlviii]

cxlviii Various authors use different names for these functions. The names used here are consistent with Labarre, Jr., pp. 11-16; Hamilton, pp., 54, 56, 114; Schramm, p. 32; see also B. Mendelson, *Introduction to Topology*, p. 11 - 14.[Math References 23].

Definition of a (Single Valued) Function: The function f: $\mathcal{A} \to \mathcal{B}$ is a function mapping $\mathcal{A}$ to $\mathcal{B}$ if for every member x of $\mathcal{A}$, only one member y of $\mathcal{B}$ exists such that $y=f(x)$.

Definition of One-to-One (Injective) Function: The function f: $\mathcal{A} \to \mathcal{B}$ is a one-to-one function if for every member x of $\mathcal{A}$ there exists only one member y of $\mathcal{B}$ such that $y=f(x)$ and if $f(x_1) = f(x_2)$, then $x_1 = x_2$.

Definition of an Onto (Surjective) Function: The function f: $\mathcal{A} \to \mathcal{B}$ is a function of $\mathcal{A}$ onto $\mathcal{B}$ if for every member y of $\mathcal{B}$, there exists a member x of $\mathcal{A}$ such that $y=f(x)$.

Definition of a Function as a One-to-One Correspondence (Bijective): A function is a one-to-one correspondence if it is a one-to-one and onto function.

Examples of functions: f: $\mathcal{A} \to \mathcal{B}$

$\mathcal{A} = \{1, 2, 3, 4\}$ $\quad\quad\quad\quad$ $\mathcal{A} = \{1, 2, 3, 4\}$

$\mathcal{B} = \{100, 200, 300, 400\}$ $\quad$ $\mathcal{B} = \{100, 200, 300\}$

Mapping $\mathcal{A}$ to $\mathcal{B}$ $\quad\quad\quad$ $\mathcal{A}$ onto $\mathcal{B}$

$\quad\quad 1 \to 100$ $\quad\quad\quad\quad\quad\quad\quad 1 \to 100$

$\quad\quad 2 \to 200$ $\quad\quad\quad\quad\quad\quad\quad 2 \to 200$

$\quad\quad 3 \to 300$ $\quad\quad\quad\quad\quad\quad\quad 3 \to 300$

$\quad\quad 4 \nearrow 400$ $\quad\quad\quad\quad\quad\quad\quad 4 \nearrow$

$\mathcal{A} = \{1, 2, 3, 4\}$ $\quad\quad\quad\quad$ $\mathcal{A} = \{1, 2, 3, 4\}$

$\mathcal{B} = \{100, 200, 300, 400, 500\}$ $\quad$ $\mathcal{B} = \{100, 200, 300, 400\}$

One-to one $\quad\quad\quad\quad\quad\quad$ One-to-one and onto

$\quad\quad 1 \to 100$ $\quad\quad\quad\quad\quad\quad\quad 1 \to 100$

$\quad\quad 2 \to 200$ $\quad\quad\quad\quad\quad\quad\quad 2 \to 200$

$\quad\quad 3 \to 300$ $\quad\quad\quad\quad\quad\quad\quad 3 \to 300$

$\quad\quad 4 \to 400$ $\quad\quad\quad\quad\quad\quad\quad 4 \to 400$

$\quad\quad\quad 500$

If the function f is a one-to-one correspondence (one-to-one and onto) then an inverse function f^{-1} exists. In this case, $f(\mathcal{A})$ maps $\mathcal{A}$ onto $\mathcal{B}$ and $f^{-1}(\mathcal{B})$ maps $\mathcal{B}$ onto $\mathcal{A}$; thus $f^{-1}(\mathcal{B}) = f^{-1}(f(\mathcal{A})) = \mathcal{A}$. In terms of the product set $\mathcal{A} \times \mathcal{B}$ with ordered pairs (x, y), this corresponds to the following definition:

Definition of Inverse Function: If f is a one-to-one function from $\mathcal{A}$ onto $\mathcal{B}$ with $f(\mathcal{A}) = \{(x, y) | \forall\ x \in \mathcal{A}$, there exist a $y = f(x)$, $\forall\ y \in \mathcal{B}\}$ then f^{-1} is the inverse function (one-to-one) from $\mathcal{B}$ onto $\mathcal{A}$ with $f^{-1}(\mathcal{B}) = \{(y,x)\} | \forall\ y \in \mathcal{B}$, there exists an $x = f^{-1}(y) \in \mathcal{A}\}$.

If the function f: $\mathcal{R} \rightarrow \mathcal{R}$ is not a one-to-one and onto function (one-to-one correspondence), an inverse image from $\mathcal{B} \subseteq \mathcal{R}$ may still be formed into $\mathcal{R}$ under the function f as $g(\mathcal{B}) = \{x \in \mathcal{R}\ |\ f(x) \in \mathcal{B}\}$. The function $g(\mathcal{B})$ is described as the inverse image of $\mathcal{B}$ under the function f and may, with this understanding, indicate $f^{-1}(\mathcal{B}) = g(\mathcal{B})$. This does not depend on the existence of an inverse as defined in the definition above. However, in these cases, if $f(\mathcal{A}) = \mathcal{B}$, $g(f(\mathcal{A}))$ may not be equal to $\mathcal{A}$. As an example, take as f: $\mathcal{R} \rightarrow \mathcal{R}$ with $f(x) = x^2$. Then, $f(\{2\}) = \{4\}$; however, $g(\{4\} = \{-2, 2\}$.[cxlix]

Now we want to use the concept of functions of sets to describe whether a function is continuous. Previously in Chapter 5, continuous functions were identified by introducing the concept of limit in which $\lim_{x \to a} f(x) = f(a)$ if for any ε, there exists a region $|x - a| < \delta$ in which $|f(x) - f(a)| < \varepsilon$. As the selected ε and δ may be considered to be neighborhoods along the y-axis and x-axes,[cl] the following definition of a continuous function may be shown to be equivalent:[262]

Definition of Continuous Function: A function f: $\mathcal{R} \rightarrow \mathcal{R}$ is continuous if for any open set $\mathcal{S}$, $f^{-1}(\mathcal{S})$ is open.

With this definition of a continuous function in terms of sets, it is then natural to ask about functions of connected sets. A consequence of the definition of a continuous function and of connectedness is the following theorem:[263]

Theorem on Continuous Mappings of Connected Sets: If $\mathcal{S}$ is a connected set and the continuous function f: $\mathcal{S} \rightarrow \mathcal{R}$, then $f(\mathcal{S})$ is connected.

---

cxlix For further discussion see Schramm, pp. 129-130.

cl If instead of using sets to define neighborhoods, we can define them in terms of distances between points such as $|x - a|$, we have what is known as a metric space. Metric spaces are a subset of the more general concept of a topological space discussed in the next section. I will not pursue the details of this approach here; however, a discussion of its relation to topological spaces is given V. I. Krlov in in Aleksandrov, Kolmogorov, and Lavrent'ev, Vol. 3, Chapter XVIII, pp. 159 - 162, 221 - 224, and Mendelso, pp. 29 - 68, 70 - 73.

Thus, connectedness is preserved under transformations of sets by continuous function. Also it may be shown that closed intervals will be transformed into closed intervals in $\mathcal{R}$. One property of the real numbers that perhaps seems to follow more intuitively from connectedness than from the other properties that take the rational numbers to the real numbers is the Intermediate Value Theorem. The theorem is a direct result of the mapping of closed into closed intervals by a continuous function.[cli]

Intermediate Value Theorem: Let $S = \{[a, b]\}$ and f: $S \to \mathcal{R}$ be a continuous function, for any X with f(a) < X < f(b), there exists an x$\in$ $\{[a, b]\}$ with f(x) = X.

The Intermediate Value Theorem is just one example of the theorems used in the calculus that can be proved using the properties of sets forming what is known as a topological space. Topology provides an elegant foundation for those topics forming the subject of analysis which had its beginnings in the calculus. However, at this stage of your math background only a brief peek can be given. I will introduce the subject of topology by first defining the topological space of the real numbers using the background we have acquired in sets.

9.4   The topology of the real number line and beyond

The development of non-Euclidean geometries in the nineteenth century was just the beginning of the broadening of mathematicians' understanding of geometry. We have previously mentioned the generalization to Riemann geometries and in the history outline mentioned Klein's classification of geometries in terms of invariants of geometry under various transformations. With our discussion in the last section of the role of continuous functions of sets in preserving properties such as connectedness, it should not seem surprising, that the concept of geometric space and its transformation under various functions should be generalized to sets of points, neighborhoods, and transformations without relation to traditional geometry. This generalization would eventually become topology.[clii]

---

cli A discussion of the Intermediate Value Theorem and connectedness is given in Schramm, pp. 196 - 205.
clii The development of topology is discussed in Merzbach and Boyer, pp. 568 - 570 and V. I. Krlov in Aleksandrov, Kolmogorov, and Lavrent'ev, Vol. 3,

Major contributors in the beginning of the twentieth century were
David Hilbert, Henri Poincaré, and Maurice Fréchet (1878 - 1973).
An early realization of the use of sets to a generalized space in
which only the relationships among the set elements are important
was that developed in 1914 by Felix Hausdorff (1868 - 1942). As
topology became a central part of mathematics, there would be many
significant contributors in the first half of the twentieth century
including: L. E. J. Brouwer (1882 - 1966)[264], Hermann Weyl (1885 -
1955), P. S. Aleksandrov (1898 - 1982), and A. N. Kolmogorov (1903
- 1987). Many of the ideas of topology may be illustrated by properties
of sets of the real numbers.

Let us consider the set $\mathcal{J}$ of all open intervals of the real number
line. The set $\mathcal{J}$ may be defined as $\mathcal{J}$ = {the open interval (a, b) | $\forall$ a and
b $\in \mathcal{R}$ and a < b}. From previous discussion, we know that the intervals
are connected and form open sets in $\mathcal{R}$. The union of an arbitrary
number of these intervals of $\mathcal{J}$ is also an open set. For example, (0, 1)
$\cup$ (1, 2) is an open set as well as (0, $\sqrt{5}$) $\cup$ (2, 5) = (0, 5). In the
first case, (0, 1) $\cup$ (1, 2), the set is open, as all the points are interior
points, but it is no longer an interval. In the second case, the result
of the union is still an open interval, hence also an open set. Even
an unlimited number of unions of open sets is still open, as in the
example, $\mathcal{A}_n = \left\{\left(-1+\dfrac{1}{n}, 1+\dfrac{1}{n}\right)\right\}$, and $\bigcup_{n=1}^{\infty} \mathcal{A}_n$ = {(-1,2)}. In contrast, an
arbitrary number of intersections of open intervals is not necessarily
open. As an example, again let $\mathcal{A}_n$ = {(−1 + 1/n, 1 + 1/n)}. Then,
$\bigcap_{n=1}^{\infty} \mathcal{A}_n$ = [-1,1], a closed interval. However, any finite number of
intersections of open intervals or of open sets is open. It can be shown
that any open set in $\mathcal{R}$ can be formed as the union of a countable
number of open intervals.[265]

With these examples, we consider the set $\mathcal{O}$ = {all open sets in $\mathcal{R}$}.
Then if $\mathcal{O}_\alpha$ is an open set in $\mathcal{R}$ with α an index selecting the specific open
set, then the union over all sets $\bigcup_\alpha \mathcal{O}_\alpha \subseteq \mathcal{R}$ and the finite intersections
such as $\mathcal{O}_{\alpha1} \cap \mathcal{O}_{\alpha2} \subseteq \mathcal{R}$ are members of $\mathcal{O}$. With the addition of the
empty set $\emptyset \subset \mathcal{O}$, then the set $\mathcal{O}$ forms what is known as the usual
topology on $\mathcal{R}$. In this topology on $\mathcal{R}$, because of the properties of the

---

Chapter XVIII, pp. 193 - 212, 218 - 224. Eves discusses the development and
basics of Hausdorff, metric, and topological spaces, pp. 229 - 234. A formal
introductory development of topology including metric spaces is given by B.
Mendelson.

real number, every point x is contained within an open set $\mathcal{N}(x) =$ $\{x \mid x - \varepsilon < x < x + \varepsilon\}$ of $\mathcal{R}$ called a neighborhood of x, and every point x is an accumulation point. The definition of a general topology follows the pattern established above:

Definition of Topology $\mathcal{T}$ on a set $\mathcal{X}$: Let $\mathcal{T}$ be a collection of subsets $\mathcal{O}_\alpha$ of $\mathcal{X}$, then $\mathcal{T}$ is a topology on $\mathcal{X}$ if: $\emptyset \in \mathcal{T}$ and $\mathcal{X} \in \mathcal{T}$, $\cup_\alpha \mathcal{O}_\alpha$ $\in \mathcal{T}$, and all finite intersections of the $\mathcal{O}_\alpha \in \mathcal{T}$. The pair $(\mathcal{X}, \mathcal{T})$ is known as a topological space. The subsets $\mathcal{O}_\alpha$ are considered open sets.

Example 1: For any set $\mathcal{X}$, a topology is formed from the power set $\mathcal{T} = \mathcal{P}(\mathcal{X})$ which includes all the subsets of $\mathcal{X}$. Thus, the union of any number of sets is in $\mathcal{T}$ as well as the intersection of sets. This topological space is known as a discrete topological space.

Example 2: A simple topology is formed on $\mathcal{X}$ if $\mathcal{T} = \{\mathcal{X}, \emptyset\}$. This is known as an indiscrete topological space.

Example 3: A finite topology may be formed from $\mathcal{X} = \{a, b, c, d\}$ in which members a, b, c, and d are undefined. Then the definition of a topology on $\mathcal{X}$ is satisfied by $\mathcal{T}_1 = \{\mathcal{X}, \emptyset, \{a\}, \{b\}, \{a, b\}, \{b, c, d\}\}$. As noted in the definition of a topological space, the subsets of $\mathcal{X}$ in $\mathcal{T}_1$ are considered to be open sets. Let $\mathcal{S} = \{\mathcal{X}, \emptyset, \{a\}, \{a, b\}, \{b, c, d\}\}$. The set $\mathcal{S}$ is not a topology on $\mathcal{X}$.[cliii]

Example 4: A topology on the real numbers $\mathcal{R}$ is formed from the set $\mathcal{T}$ of all open intervals of the form (x, ∞), that is $\mathcal{T} = \{\mathcal{R}, \emptyset, \{(x, \infty)\} \mid \forall x \in \mathcal{R}\}$.

An important concept in topology is the preservation of properties of spaces under transformations by continuous functions. We have already seen conditions for which sets maintain the property of connectedness under continuous transformation. More generally a continuous transformation between topologies maintaining such properties is a homeomorphism and the topologies are said to be homeomorphic.

Definition of Homeomorphic Topologies: Two topologies $(\mathcal{X}, \mathcal{T}_1)$ and $(\mathcal{Y}, \mathcal{T}_2)$ are homeomorphic if and only if there exists continuous functions f: $\mathcal{X} \to \mathcal{Y}$ and g: $\mathcal{Y} \to \mathcal{X}$. The functions g and f define a homeomorphism between $(\mathcal{X}, \mathcal{T}_1)$ and $(\mathcal{Y}, \mathcal{T}_2)$.

Not surprisingly in the usual topology on $\mathcal{R}$, the open interval $(0, 1)$ is homeomorphic with any other interval (a, b) with $y = f(x)$ $= (b - a)x + a$ and $x = f^{-1}(y) = \frac{y - a}{b - a}$. Similarly, the interval $(0, 1)$ is

---

cliii Further examples of topologies are given by Mendelson, pp. 70 – 72.

homeomorphic to the whole real number line $\mathcal{R}$ with $y = f(x) =$ $\tan\left(\frac{\pi}{2}(2x - 1)\right)$ and $x = f^{-1}(y) = \frac{1}{\pi}\arctan(y) + \frac{1}{2}$. (The arctan(y) is the inverse of the tangent function in that if $y = \tan(x)$, then arctan(y) =x.) Of course in all cases, the space is connected.

While we have focused on the real number line, the topological spaces may be formed on the Cartesian plane $\mathcal{R}^2$ which can be considered as the product space $\mathcal{R} \times \mathcal{R}$. Similarly topologies may be formed in the three dimensional space $\mathcal{R}^3$ associated with the product space $\mathcal{R} \times \mathcal{R} \times \mathcal{R}$ or the abstract n-tuple space $\mathcal{R}^n$. In $\mathcal{R}^2$, an equivalent of an open interval on the real number line is the set formed within a circle centered at the point (a, b): $\mathcal{D}(a, b, r) = \{(x, y) \mid (x - a)^2 + (y - b)^2 < r^2)\}$. Similarly, an open interval in $\mathcal{R}^3$ corresponds to the inside of a sphere. Homeomorphisms in $\mathcal{R}^2$ can be described as f: $\mathcal{R}^2 \rightarrow \mathcal{R}^2$. As an intuitive example, a circle is homeomorphic to an ellipse or a sphere to a ellipsoid as transformed through a continuous function in either direction as illustrated in the next figure. However, in $\mathcal{R}^2$ an annulus (ring formed by concentric circles cannot be similarly transformed into a circle nor a torus (donut) into a sphere in $\mathcal{R}^3$. In the sense of this example, topology may be thought of as the study of transformations of spaces and their impact on adjacent points or sepaate points.

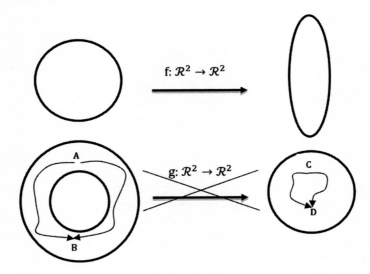

We can also form closed paths in spaces by beginning and ending at the same point. In the circle if we travel clockwise from C to D and then continue clockwise in the reverse direction of the second path, then a close path is formed. Within the circle, any closed path can be contracted indefinitely through transformations. When this is possible, the space is simply connected. The property of being simply connected is another topological; property. Clearly the annulus is not simply connected. Another property of a simply connected space is that a closed path viewed as a cut in the space splits it in two. In the case of the torus a cut is possible that leaves it simply connected. The consideration of the impact of such cuts provides a means of classifying spaces that are homeomorphic. In explaining topology, the observation is often made that to a topologist a donut and a coffee cup are the same as one can be transformed into the other by continuous transformations. Beyond this amusing observation, topology provides the means to determine fundamental relationships between complex geometric and abstract spaces.

The discussion above is just the tiniest step towards modern approaches in mathematics. The discipline of topology provides a powerful tool for the description of geometries, patterns, and general relationships interpreted as abstract spaces. Some classic topics of topology include characterizations of abstract relationships interpreted as surfaces, graphs, knots, and links and the determination of relationships of various homeomorphisms to other non-homeomorphic spaces. Some specific well-known introductory examples used to give a sense of the subject matter of topology are the characteristics of the Möbius band, a single-sided closed surface that can be formed by connecting the ends of a strip of paper after a single twist; the general relationship between vertices, edges and surfaces of polyhedrons (a relationship discovered by Euler in 1758); and optimizations of paths (with, as an example, Euler's proof in 1736 that that it was impossible to walk across a set of bridges in Königsberg, Prussia, each only once, and return to the starting point of the walk).[266] A qualitative introduction to these ideas is given by Stahl[267] and Courant and Robbins[268] with a more formal development of topological concepts of connectedness and path connectedness by Mendelson.[269] From the point-of-view of this brief introduction, perhaps it suffices to say that the concepts developed in topology bring together thousands of years of development of number, geometry, and the processes of the rational representation of relationships in mathematical form.

Chapter 10

THE SCIENCE OF RELATIONSHIP, EXPERIENCE, AND IMAGINATION

"But why do we not postulate that through any three points it shall be possible to draw a straight line? . . . Because this postulate contains a contradiction. Very well, then, what we have to do first is to prove that these other postulates of ours do not contain any contradiction. Until we have done that, all rigor, strive for it as we will, is so much moonshine."—Gottlob Frege[cliv]

". . . for every formal system of mathematics there are statements which are expressible within the system but which may not be decided from the axioms of that system, and that those statements are even of a relatively simple kind, namely, belonging to the theory of positive whole numbers."—Kurt Gödel[clv]

In the previous nine chapters, I have presented a sampling of achievements in mathematics developed over thousands of years that I hope you will agree is astonishing. Now that many of the ideas discussed in the history outline have been illustrated, it is an opportune moment to take a quick look back to review with new understanding the sweep of mathematics from the beginning consciousness of numbers to the beginning of the twentieth century. All of the developments of mathematics to that point had set the stage, and would seem to have made inevitable, the ensuing struggle over the foundations of mathematics that occurred in the first half of

---

cliv The quote is cited in Kline (p. 192) from Frege's *Foundations in Arithmetic* (1884). Frege in 1903 would just complete Volume II of his *Fundamental Laws of Mathematics* in which he derived basic concepts of number systems from logic when Russell sent him a letter indicating that his use of the set of all sets led to contradictions. Frege responded that, "A scientist can hardly meet with anything more undesirable than to have the foundation give way just as the work is finished," (Kline, pp. 217- 218).

clv The quote is cited in Stillwell (p. 75) from a letter to Zermelo in 1931 regarding Gödel's First Completeness Theorem.

the twentieth century. The struggle, which I shall discuss following our quick look back, would lead to new directions, controversies, and questions while providing mathematicians with a focus for a meditation upon the very meaning of mathematics. The intellectual struggle would end one view of mathematics as a source of certain truth; however, it would leave mathematics with new potentials and its familiar place as the source for new imaginative descriptions of relationships and patterns (whether of fully understood significance or not). As the final story told here in the ongoing story of mathematics, the struggle over foundations is a fitting summary of the efforts that have created and continue to create modern mathematics.I must at the end, however, necessarily leave the certainty of our tale of the past with only the certainty that it is a discipline that can provide a lifetime of intellectual pleasure for those who will study its language and, thanks to the efforts of the mathematicians, a continuing source of new ways of describing the patterns of the universe.

10.1 A quick look back

We began our story of numbers in the history outline with the image of notches found on wolf bones clearly indicative of a notion of counting. The sense of number combined with the consciousness of form attested to by the famous cave paintings of the same period would amazingly develop over the millennia to a symbolic language that would eventually reveal secrets of the atom. Along the way, the concepts of number, algebra, and geometry would be developed not only in the service of meeting humanity's practical needs, but in response to a curiosity in the power of mathematics to describe and to form coherent patterns. Perhaps, the earliest examples of this tendency are to be found in the Pythagoreans' belief in number as the essence of the universe and the Platonic notion of geometric figures as ideals that could be only reached through the mind. In parallel with this notion would be the Greeks' discovery of the deductive or axiomatic method, resting on foundations presumed to be absolute truths. The Greeks discovered that the deductive method, working only with these truths, would allow the relationships of the ideals to be known far beyond the powers of experimental evidence. The axiomatic method as an approach for other parts of mathematics would lie dormant for two thousand years, but as the accepted model of the time for absolute truth in mathematics, it would provide the seeds for new forms of mathematics. Ultimately the axiomatic method would be a time-bomb leading to questions going to the very core of the meaning of mathematics.

While geometry led to a structured deductive approach, in contrast, the development of a pragmatic understanding of numbers would lead likewise to a pragmatic approach to algebra. The ability of the Babylonians to devise verbally specified methods for solving quadratic equations in the absence of general methods or an understanding of symbolic representation is remarkable. Their development of the sexagesimal system and associated arithmetic operations, as well as approximations for numbers that would eventually be understood as irrational numbers attests to the practical needs for calculation and to the hold of numbers on the imagination of the ancients. Concepts of numbers and their operation would continue to be developed for thousands of years, particularly in Indian and Islamic communities with the decimal representation of numbers, the related expansion of the natural numbers to negative and rational numbers, and discoveries of algebraic techniques. These developments brought mathematics to a critical point that would create the conditions to inspire the creation of symbolic techniques to represent the patterns and operations of numbers pragmatically discovered over the centuries. The confluence of symbolic representation and the insights of Descartes, which would become known as analytic geometry, then began the synergistic explorations of geometry and algebra. The exploration of algebraic representation of geometry as curves and properties such as tangents, and their implications for solutions of equations would go beyond practical necessity to become a fascination with the relationships implied by the symbolic representations.

With these developments in place, the stage was set for Newton's and Leibniz's discovery of the calculus which would provide the model for mathematics and science for the next two centuries. While Newton in a bow to geometry would clothe the proofs of his Gravitational Law and Laws of Motion in geometrical garb, Leibniz's more nimble and accessible symbolic representation would win the day and inspire an explosion in new mathematical discoveries and applications to science. The relationship between the needs of science and discoveries in mathematics had always been close, but the discovery of the calculus, pushed mathematics to new levels of creativity in the search for solutions to scientific problems following the model of the mechanics of Newton. We have seen some of these new creations in the extension of mathematics to complex numbers, vectors, tensors, matrices and partial differential equations. These new creations occurred even while the foundations of mathematics that supported the calculus had yet to be put in place, in particular, the notion of limit and the real numbers. Despite the lack of a firm foundation, many new discoveries in mathematics occurred, driven as much by the fascinating patterns and intricacies of the subject as by the needs of science. Euler's discoveries with infinite series, his famous relationship between $e^{i\theta}$ and the trigonometric functions, representations of π, operations with complex numbers, solutions to many types of ordinary differential equations, and contributions to the understanding of the distribution of prime numbers are illustrations from just this one great mathematician of the growth of mathematics as its own subject independent of its service to science.

The need to put the calculus and other associated concepts on a firm foundation occurred in the period in which the meaning of the axiomatic approach was clarified by the discovery of Lobachevsky and Bolyai that a new consistent geometry could be established by simply changing one axiom in Euclid's system. This insight was further extended by the new abstract geometries described by Riemann. If axioms were not self-evident truths, but founding assumptions selected to form a consistent perhaps useful system, it began to seem apparent that a proof of the consistency of the axiomatic basis of mathematics should be established. The need for this basis was made more urgent in the latter nineteenth century as the concepts of infinite sets and transcendental numbers proposed by Cantor took mathematics farther and farther from the familiar illustrations of experience and science that had done so much to inspire developments in mathematics. Despite the challenge of creating a foundation for all of mathematics, the unprecedented successes of mathematics in the nineteenth century led Hilbert to believe that an axiomatic approach could establish the foundations of mathematics on bedrock of unquestionable truth.

10.2 Competing visions of the foundations of mathematics

In 1900, Hilbert addressed his fellow mathematicians at the Second International Congress held in Paris. In his paper entitled Mathematical Problems, he presented twenty-three problems particularly selected to advance the discipline of mathematics. Of the twenty-three, he only spoke of ten in his address, presumably considered the most important.[270] The second problem was to prove that the axioms of arithmetic were consistent. The resolution of this problem was meant to be the basis for the foundations of mathematics and was to be a major focus of Hilbert and many of his students from that time. In many ways, the mathematical context in which Hilbert sought to solve this problem was given by his first problem—the resolution of the continuum hypothesis and the related question of whether all sets of real numbers can be well-ordered.[271]

The concepts of infinite sets, transfinite numbers, and the real numbers as well-ordered sets discovered by Cantor were surrounded by controversies as many mathematicians adamantly refused to accept the idea of an infinite set. Those who rejected Cantor's work saw in it concepts that were foreign to the intuitions of the mind and farther and farther from the familiar illustrations of experience and science that had done so much to inspire developments in mathematics. Moreover, they rejected Cantor's proofs such as the existence of transcendental numbers because they did not provide methods for constructing the numbers. The controversies would ultimately result in a philosophy of mathematics called intuitionism that rejected the infinite as conceived by Cantor. Others accepting infinite sets would vigorously compete for the prize of establishing the meaning of mathematics. Thus, these controversies along with paradoxes surrounding set theory, that we previously discussed, fairly begged to be resolved through creation of an unassailable foundation of mathematics. Four main approaches were taken depending on the foundation materials deemed to be essential to the construction of mathematics. These approaches are known as: logicism (logic based), formalism (the axiomatic approach of Hilbert), set-theoretic, and intuitionism.[clvi] As we shall see, none could be wholly successful, but each provides important insight into mathematics, particularly when contrasted with each other.

---

clvi Breuer, pp. 86 - 92, Eves, pp. 266 - 271. A detailed discussion of the philosophic arguments between the various contending groups is given by Kline. Chapter X, "Logicism versus Intuitionism" pp. 216 - 244, and Chapter XI, "The Formalist and Set-Theoretic Foundations," pp. 245 - 257.

10.2.1 The logistic approach

Logicism had roots going back to Leibniz's belief that mathematics could be built entirely on the basis of logic. Attempts had been made by a number of mathematicians, but the most comprehensive was that of Whitehead and Russell in their *Principia Mathematica* [Reference 32] published from 1910 to 1913.[272] The approach is axiomatic starting with undefined terms and postulates of logic. For example, it is postulated that for propositions p and q, asserting that the propositions p and $p \Rightarrow q$ are true allows the assertion that q is true to be made. From the axioms, the laws of logic are constructed along with the introduction of classes (sets) with members defined by propositions and the concept of relationship between members of the classes. This leads to the definition of natural numbers through the one-to-one correspondence of classes. In other words if two classes are in a one-to-one correspondence, they have the common property of number. However, such classes may have other properties in common than what we want to define by number. Therefore, Whitehead and Russell defined number with the unique class of all classes which are equivalent to the given class. As a possible extension of this concept, the class of real numbers would include all rational numbers, integers, and natural numbers.

The definition of such classes should recall the paradoxes noted by Russell generated by the concept of a set of all sets. Whitehead and Russell solved this problem by defining a hierarchy of classes called types in which "whatever involves all members of a collection must not itself be a member of the collection."[273] Using this approach they avoided paradoxes, however, the result was a complex system in which the real numbers consisted of different types since the irrational numbers were generated from the rational numbers, the rationals from the integers, and the integers from the natural numbers. In order to deal with this hierarchy, Whitehead and Russell introduced a new axiom called the Axiom of Reducibility. I will not go into its meaning and use other than to make the point that this new axiom was not perceived as fundamental to the foundations of logic. As noted by Whitehead and Russell in their 2nd edition of the *Principia Mathematica*, "This axiom has a purely pragmatic justification; it leads to the desired results and no others. But clearly it is not the kind of axiom with which we can rest content."[274] The Axiom of Reducibility was not the only axiom that Whitehead and Russell needed to complete their system that was not perceived as an accepted truth, fundamental to logic. They also had need for an Axiom of Infinity to allow infinite sets and the Axiom of Choice. The use of these axioms raised the questions: are these axioms of logic and in what sense are they true. This would lead to the greater question, could mathematics be derived purely from logic. Certainly one could point to the many innovations in mathematics inspired by experimental inputs from physics suggesting it could not. Furthermore, from the point-of-view of Hilbert's problem, if the axioms of a logistic system could not be considered as absolutely true, then the system did not meet Hilbert's needs in that it still must be proved to be consistent.

10.2.2 Formalism and the axiomatic approach

Hilbert was the champion of the axiomatic approach. As he said in his paper of 1925, "the goal of my theory is to establish once and for all the certitude of mathematical methods."[275] Hilbert had already in 1899 put Euclid's geometry into a purely axiomatic form addressing the inconsistencies and supplying required postulates to complete Euclid's system. In doing so, he underscored the understanding of the system as a purely logical structure depending on the acceptance of the postulates as true.[276] Although for millennia, the truth of Euclidean geometry had been accepted through its identification with physical space, Hilbert's axiomatic approach made it clear that Euclidean geometry could be *interpreted* as physical space, but that any other model that fit the requirements of the undefined terms and postulates is another acceptable model. Once the postulates were no longer considered to be absolute truths, it was no longer true that they must necessarily lead through the laws of logic to true theorems. It became necessary to demonstrate that the use of the postulates would not lead to contradictions—thus, Hilbert's plea for the demonstrations of consistency in mathematics.

Using the medium of analytic geometry, Hilbert proved that Euclidean geometry was consistent if the system of the real numbers could be proved to be consistent. This was the source of his second problem, to prove the consistency of arithmetic, at the Second International Congress of 1900. Hilbert's approach to this problem was to distill mathematics into a completely abstract symbolic form in which the postulates defined the allowed manipulations of the symbols from which further theorems could be generated. The classical system of logic could be conveniently applied to this approach with the existing forms of symbolic logic. Thus, the system was completely formal in the sense that there need not be any reference to the meaning of the symbols. However, this method of building mathematical systems still did not answer the question of whether the resulting system was consistent. To answer this question, Hilbert and his students proposed a "proof theory" formed with axioms of logic considered to be free of all objections. In this approach, proofs of existence by contradiction, the Axiom of Choice, and infinite sets were unacceptable, although the older potential infinities were allowed. With his formal construction of mathematics and proof theory, by 1928 Hilbert was confident that the consistency of arithmetic could be proved. [277]

In addition to seeking a proof of consistency for a mathematical system, Hilbert also believed it was necessary that a mathematical system be complete. By this he meant that any statement expressible in the system could be shown to be true or false.[278] This sentiment harkens back to Aristotle's logic law of the excluded middle which required any statement to be either true or false. By 1930, some progress had been made using Hilbert's formalistic approach. In 1930, Gödel had shown that first order logic was complete. However, this victory would be short lived as in the next year, Gödel proved that it was impossible meet Hilbert's goal of proving the consistency of the real number system. In addition to making the fulfillment of Hilbert's approach impossible, it would have far reaching implications for mathematics in general. However, for the intuitionists who believed that mathematics was founded on intuitive ideas such as the whole numbers and their operations which needed no justification, Gödel's proof was, in their view, somewhat beside the point as the intuitionists were not focused on consistency. In any case, the formalistic approach, having no reference to the meaning of its symbols, did not have an appeal to intuitionists. Before discussing the work of Gödel, the approach of the intuitionists will be explored including their criticism of logicism, formalism, and the previously introduced set theoretic approach initiated by Zermelo.

10.2.3 Intuitionism

The understanding of mathematics by those who would eventually come to be known as intuitionists began in reaction to the revolutionary insights of Cantor regarding infinite sets. The infinite had since the time of the Greeks been conceived of as the unlimited potential of numbers, but not an actual number.[279] Cantor challenged this concept by imagining infinite sets as existing entities and quantifying them with transfinite cardinal and ordinal numbers with an associated arithmetic. Objections would be vigorously raised that such concepts had no place in mathematics because the logic used by Cantor only properly applied to finite sets and finite operations. As such the infinite sets were beyond the experience and intuition that the critics saw as the fundamental basis of mathematics.

An early and perhaps the most impassioned opponent of Cantor was Kronecker. Kronecker was a member of the German Academy of Sciences and professor at the prestigious University of Berlin where he was one of Cantor's instructors. Kronecker rejected the existence of Cantor's infinite sets as beyond intuition. He believed that the foundation of mathematics rested on the intuitive concept of the integers from which the rest of mathematics flowed without the need for more complex constructs such as those that would be proposed in schools of logicism or formalism. Moreover, he believed that the existence of mathematical entities should be proved by constructive methods of a finite number of steps. Cantor's existence proof of transcendental numbers which did not provide a means for constructing the numbers was therefore unacceptable to Kronecker. When Lindemann was able to prove that π was transcendental, Kronecker asked Lindemann "Of what use is your beautiful investigation regarding π? Why study such problems since irrationals do not exist?" Here his objection was to proofs that did not provide a method of calculating the irrational number. The vehement objections of Kronecker led him to call Cantor a charlatan, block publication of Cantor's papers, and block a position for Cantor at the University of Berlin. It was during this period that Cantor began to have the mental difficulties that would end his productive career. However, on and off for the rest of his life, Cantor would work on a key problem of his transfinite numbers, the Continuum Hypothesis. This problem would eventually be shown to be unsolvable like the proof of Euclid's Parallel Postulate.[clvii]

---

clvii Brief discussions of the conflicting issues between Cantor and Kronecker are given in Kline, pp. 203, 214, 232 and Merzbach and Boyer, pp.542 - 543. A detailed account is given by Amir D. Aczel, p. 131 - 137. Aczel's book gives a narrative of the development of the concept of infinity from the time of the ancient Greeks, including aspects of the lives of contributors such as Galileo, Bolzano, Weierstrass, Dedekind, Cantor, and Gödel. Aczel also discusses many non-mathematical esoteric concepts inspired by the contemplation of infinity.

Objections like those of Kronecker to Cantor's work set the stage for the development of the formal stance towards the foundations of mathematics called intuitionism. Many distinguished mathematicians would be proponents of this approach, among them Lebesgue and Poincaré who we have met previously. The most definitive statement of this point-of-view was given by Luitzen E. J. Brouwer (1881 - 1966).[280] Brouwer characterized mathematics as a self-evident, intuitively clear, product of the mind, independent of external reality in contrast to the undefined terms and postulates of the axiomatic approach. Similarly, Brouwer viewed logic as formed from the intuitive concepts of mathematics, not the other way around. Thus, intuitionism rejected both the goals of logicism and the axiomatic approach of formalism.

Brouwer, like Kronecker, rejected infinite sets, and existence proofs which were not constructive—both found in logistic and set-theoretic approaches. In rejecting processes involving the infinite, Brouwer would also therefore reject for such processes a basic law of logic accepted since the time of Aristotle, the Law of Excluded Middle. This meant that in addition to a proposition being either true or false, it could also be undecidable. This was, of course, anathema to Hilbert's goal of proving that mathematical system of the real numbers was complete. As an example, the unresolved Goldbach conjecture that every even number greater than 2 is the sum of two prime numbers is considered by traditional logic to be either true or false, but in the absence of a proof may be considered undecidable by the intuitionists. Fermat's Last Theorem is, however, an example of a conjecture that remained a conjecture for centuries until it was finally proved to be true in 1995.

With the rejection of non-constructive proofs, the intuitionists of course rejected the Axiom of Choice in which there was no specified method of selecting the choices and which included the possibility of an infinite number of choices. The Well-Ordering Theorem that was proved by Zermelo using the Axiom of Choice was therefore rejected along with its conclusion that sets of the real numbers must be capable of being well-ordered. The lack of a specific method to produce a well-ordered set of the real numbers was, of course, consistent with the intuitionists' position. Thus the intuitionists found the set-theoretic approaches to be as suspect as logicism and the formalist approach of Hilbert—not surprising given the origins of set theory in Cantor's work.

The approach taken in intuitionism is not without cost. Gone along with the Axiom of Choice and infinite sets are the Bolzano-Weierstrass Theorem, the Dedekind cuts, and equivalence of the definitions of continuity by the sequential and the $\varepsilon - \delta$ methods.[281] Considering also the complications introduced by Whitehead and Russell in their approach to defining a least upper bound which is the least upper bound in a hierarchy of classes called types, and it would be fair to see the theoretical understanding of real numbers in chaos. However, despite the many disagreements among mathematicians concerning the foundations of mathematics, no fatal contradictions have occurred with the use of the real number system, to some extent supporting the intuitionists. In hindsight, this suggests that what was needed was an understanding of the limitations on what could be proved about the consistency of a mathematical system. An unexpected result was given by Gödel.

10.3 Gödel's first and second theorem—the closing of one door

A key element in the implementation of Hilbert's formalistic approach was the use of symbols for all mathematical concepts and operations. Postulates and propositions were represented as strings of symbols, and a proposition is proved by using the allowed manipulations of the strings of symbols until the desired statement is obtained. Recalling that the axiomatic method begins with undefined terms, the replacement of concepts and operations with symbols underscores the point that in the formalistic approach, the symbols are abstractions that have no intrinsic meaning although meaning can be assigned through an interpretive model.

Gödel's goal was to use the formalistic approach to answer the question of whether a mathematical system that encompassed the arithmetic of the natural numbers such as established by Whitehead and Russell in their *Principia Mathematica (PM)* could be shown to be consistent and complete. Gödel would use *PM* as his example of a formal axiomatic system encompassing the arithmetic of natural numbers, but his results would apply to any such system including that of the set-theoretic ZF axioms. He would take a further step in abstraction beyond Hilbert's symbolic approach by replacing all symbols and strings of symbols with numbers. Thus, any proposition or set of propositions forming a proof that could be expressed by the system of *PM* was represented by a single number (called a

Gödel number). Symbolic developments in logic and the structure of *PM* were already in place for the use of Gödel in his approach to the consistency problem. Gödel, using his ingenious method of representing propositions as numbers proved the following two theorems in his paper published in 1931:[282]

Gödel's Incompleteness Theorem: Any consistent formal system sufficient to encompass the arithmetic of the natural numbers is incomplete.

Gödel's Consistency Theorem: Any formal system sufficient to encompass the arithmetic of the natural numbers cannot be proved to be consistent within the rules of the system.

The first theorem says that there are propositions within the system which cannot be proved to be true or false using the rules of the system. In other words, there are undecidable propositions. The second theorem says that systems such as *PM* cannot be proved to be consistent. Thus, Gödel's theorems were a one-two punch delivering a knockout blow to Hilbert's desire to use the axiomatic approach whether formalistic, logistic or set-theoretic to create a foundation of mathematics that was proved to be consistent and complete.

Gödel's proofs of these theorems are quite dense and complex, but I will provide some of its highlights by introducing a simplified view of Gödel's numbers following the approach of Nagel and Newman.[clviii] The formal system investigated is that "obtained by superimposing on the Peano axioms [with 0 as the first number] the logic of *PM*."[283] Gödel's basic building blocks for this system include: zero, 0; the succession operation, for example, 0^+ or in Gödel's notation $f0$; negation, $\neg$; the conjunction "or", $\lor$; the quantifying statement "for all," $\forall$; left and right parentheses, ( ); and numerical variables, x, y, as

---

clviii An expanded sketch of Gödel's theorems beyond that provided here may be found in Ernest Nagel and James R. Newman's, *Gödel's Proof*, pp. 68 - 108, [Math References 27]. Nagel and Newman also discuss Gödel's theorem in the broader historical context of logic and the axiomatic method. Gödel's paper, "On Formally Undecidable Propositions of Principia Mathematica and Related Systems," is reprinted in Stephen Hawking's, *God Created the Integers, the Mathematical Breakthroughs that Changed History*, pp. 1263 - 1284, [Math References 14]. Along with this paper and commentary by Hawking (pp. 1253 - 1262), other great works of many of the mathematician encountered here are similarly reprinted with illuminating comments and historical background.

well as variables representing logical statements. In order to construct a correspondence between numbers and the axioms and propositions of *PM*, Gödel assigned a number to the elementary symbols of *PM*. The table below is indicative of Gödel's approach.

Some Symbols of *PM* with Gödel Assigned Numbers[284]

0	f	¬	∨	∀	(	)	x	y
1	3	5	7	9	11	13	15	17

From the assignment of numbers to the elementary symbols, a single number could be calculated corresponding to a formula represented by the symbols. This was accomplished through the identification of the Gödel number of the symbol with the power of a prime number and with the order of the symbols corresponding to the order of increasing primes. As an illustration, the Gödel number of the formula fragment $(\neg x)\vee y$ is: $2^{11} \cdot 3^5 \cdot 5^{15} \cdot 7^{13} \cdot 11^7 \cdot 13^{17}$. This should be clear as the Gödel numbers for the symbols that make up $(\neg x)\vee y$ are in order: 11, 5, 15, 13, 7, and 17. This is an enormous number for such a small formula, but whatever it is, the Fundamental Theorem of Arithmetic (Section 2.3.3) says that it represents a unique formula because any number is uniquely factored into its primes. Note that not all numbers can be Gödel numbers. For example 70 is not because the second prime number 3 is not a factor, although 2, 5, and 7 are.

With Peano's axioms and the definitions and axioms of logic from *PM* as a base, Gödel then proved that any formula within *PM* can be represented by a Gödel number. On the way to building the propositions of *PM*, there are therefore representations that involve such things as existence as in "there exists" (∃) logical implication (⇒); equality, (=), the operation of addition (+), and multiplication (·). Any natural number can be expressed through the successor operation, for example 5 is expressed as *fffff* 0. In considering the ways in which complex statements can be constructed, it is useful to recall the example that the implication p ⇒ q can be expressed as $(\neg p)\vee q$.

The same approach that is used for individual formulas can be used to represent a sequence of formulas forming a proof. For example suppose a proof consists of a sequence of three formulas with Gödel numbers of k, l, and m leading to a conclusion with Gödel number n. Then the number for the proof, call it g, is $g = 2^k \cdot 3^l \cdot 5^m \cdot 7^n$. An interesting relationship is formed between the number g and

n. The number g represents the proof of the proposition whose Gödel number is n. This is a central insight into Gödel's theorems.

Gödel defined a formula xBy consistent with the symbols of *PM* with the meaning that the sequence of formulas with Gödel number x is a proof of the formula with Gödel number y. As it is consistent with *PM*, a Gödel number can be calculated for this expression (recall the variable y is assigned a number as an elementary symbol). We can use this formulation to express the provocative statement; there is a valid formula of *PM* that is not provable in *PM*. Such a statement about the system itself instead of conclusions derived from the system is known as a meta-mathematical statement. Symbolically, the statement may be expressed as: ¬(∃x)xBy where the symbol ∃ stands for there exists, so the symbols mean that there does not exist a Gödel number x that is the proof of the statement with Gödel number y. Now, since y is a variable, the statement cannot be said to be true or false until we know what y stands for. Gödel made an ingenious choice within *PM* for y (see footnote clix below), allowing a statement G, to be expressed as ¬(∃x)xBg with g being the Gödel number of G.[clix] In other words the formula G with Gödel number g states that it is not provable in *PM*. This background allows us to see Gödel's theorems.

Let us start by supposing that the statement G is provable within *PM*. Now G is the statement of *PM* that G is not provable within *PM*. Therefore as shown in detail by Gödel, ¬G is also provable within *PM*.[clx] Thus, *PM* is inconsistent as we have obtained a contradiction. For *PM* to be consistent, then G must be unprovable, that is undecidable within PM. Note that either G or ¬G must be

_____

clix Nagel and Newman (pp. 89 - 98) motivate the selection of y by noting that a symbolic formula of *PM*, abbreviated as Sub(y, 17, y), can be formed which stands for the substitution of the Gödel number of some statement y wherever the numeral 17 (corresponding to the Gödel number of the variable y) appears in the statement y. Although, y is still a variable, the Gödel number of the statement, ¬(∃x)xB Sub(y, 17, y) can be calculated as a specific number which is designated as n. In other words, ¬(∃x)xB Sub(y, 17, y) is the statement that has a Gödel number n. The statement G is now defined as ¬(∃x)xB Sub(n, 17, n). The Gödel number of Sub(n, 17, n) is the number formed by substituting the symbols for the number n for the number 17 into the formula that has n as a Gödel number itself. This is the very definition of G; therefore, g = Sub(n, 17, n) is the Gödel number of G. Therefore, the statement G, which is ¬(∃x)xB g, is now fully defined in *PM*.

clx A summary of Gödel's reasoning is given by Nagel and Newman, pp.98 - 108 (see in particular fn. 35, pp. 100 - 101).

true, therefore either way, *PM* is incomplete because there is a true statement of *PM* which cannot be proved in *PM*. However, if G is not provable in *PM*, then indeed G is true. A closely related concept discussed by Nagel and Newman is that if at least one statement using the rules of a formal system such as *PM* can be shown to be true, but not provable by the formal system, then the system is consistent.[clxi]

So we finish by noting that if *PM* is consistent then it must be incomplete and that the consistency of *PM* cannot be proved within *PM*. Gödel used *PM* as his example, but his proofs applied to any formal system capable of encompassing the arithmetic of the natural numbers. With this proof, the mansion that Hilbert wished to build collapsed in ruins.

10.4 Imagination and the limitless possibilities of mathematics

Gödel's discoveries about consistency and completeness of formal systems would spark deeper investigations into their implications for the foundations of mathematics just as the discovery of non-Euclidean geometry had led to new paths for mathematics in the nineteenth century. With Hilbert's expected solution to fundamental questions of mathematics no longer a possibility, just what were the implications of Gödel's theorems for the maelstrom of questions concerning the Continuum Hypothesis, infinite sets, the Axiom of Choice with its implications for the Well-Ordering Theorem, and the meaning of mathematics itself.

Gödel had proved that in any formal, sufficiently complex and consistent system, there would be undecidable statements thus denying Hilbert's belief [285] that all statements were decidable. But, could one determine in advance that such statements were undecidable. Recall that for two thousand years, mathematicians mistakenly believed that Euclid's Parallel Postulate was provable. Hilbert believed that a procedure could be established to determine if a statement was provable or disprovable—the Entscheidungsproblem (decision problem).[286] In 1936, Alonzo Church (1903 - 1995) put this problem to rest by proving that for any consistent formal system, sufficient to encompass the arithmetic of the natural numbers, there

---

clxi This is the flipside of the statement that in an inconsistent system, any statement can be proved by the rules of the system; Nagel and Newman, pp. 50-51.

is no general procedure to decide which propositions are decidable within the system.[287] [clxii]

Gödel continued to try and understand the implications of his findings that consistent systems are incomplete. In 1940, he proved that if the ZF axioms of sets were consistent, then the systems formed by the addition of the Axiom of Choice (AC) and the Continuum Hypothesis (CH) are also consistent. Again assuming ZF is consistent, Paul Cohen (1934 - 2007)[288] proved, in 1963, that AC and CH are independent of the ZF axioms. Thus they are undecidable axioms in ZF. As independent axioms, Cohen proved that ZF can form a consistent system by either adding AC as an axiom or by assuming as an axiom that AC is false, (¬AC). Furthermore, Cohen proved that if AC is added to ZF, then CH still cannot be proved; thus ZF + AC + ¬CH is also consistent. However, the addition of a generalized form of CH to ZF allows AC to be proved.[289]

As all of this should make clear, mathematics cannot be absolute and depends upon the axioms that are selected with the resulting open question—which axioms should be selected. The Axiom of Choice is crucial to many of the theorems of math; however, one example shows that the choice of axioms must be complemented by intuition with an understanding of the type of results that are sought. This is illustrated by the Banach—Tarski paradox.[clxiii] Using the Axiom of Choice, Banach and Tarski proved that in n-tuple spaces of the

---

clxii Also in 1936, Alan Turing (1912 - 1954) received the proofs of his paper "On Computable Numbers with an Application to the Entscheidungsproblem" only days after reaching Princeton University. There he would be supervised in his doctoral studies by Church. Unbeknownst to Turing, his paper covered issues closely related to those covered in Church's work through a description of deterministic computing that described the mathematical processes that became known as the a Turing Universal Computing Machine. In his paper, Turing showed, in essence, that there were no procedures to determine if a computer program would complete its computation. The approach of Turing would provide a new context to the issue of decidability that would become particular relevant as computers became a reality under the leadership of von Neumann. After receiving a PhD, Turing would return to the UK in 1938 where he was a major contributor during World War II to the breaking of the German ENIGMA code. For his efforts, he received the Order of the British Empire. Turing committed suicide in 1954. Aspects of Turing's brilliant career, particular his collaboration with von Neumann may be found in G, Dyson, pp. 243 - 265, pp. 334 - 335.

clxiii Stefan Banach (1892 - 1945) and Alfred Tarski (1901 - 1983) developed the paradox independently; Aczel, p. 183 - 184; Moore, pp. 284-285.

real numbers $\mathcal{R}^n$, that for n $\geqq$ 3, any bounded set containing interior points, that is objects such as spheres in 3-dimensional space and analogous objects in higher spaces, could be decomposed and shown to be equivalent. In other words, by invoking the Axiom of Choice, one could prove as in Eves' vivid description that a pea is equivalent to the sun or in Kline's that the earth is equivalent to a basketball. [290] As discussed by Hamilton, the use of the Axiom of Choice also implies the existence of non-measurable sets of real numbers bringing into question, for such axiomatic systems, concepts using measure (which we discussed in regard to Lebesgue integration).[291]

While a variety of variations of ZF with added axioms have been shown to be consistent, mathematicians are now left with the decision of which to choose. The choice is therefore dictated by experience with the results, and the utility or fascination of the results for their discoverer. As a further complication, axiomatic systems could be shown to be consistent when embedded in larger systems with added axioms. However, Gödel's Incompleteness Theorem applies to these also, so the larger systems are similarly incomplete, and the logical implications of these systems must also be explored through experience.

One response to this perplexing situation was given under the penname of Nicolas Bourbaki:

> "Historically speaking, it is of course quite untrue that mathematics is free from contradiction; non-contradiction appears as a goal to be achieved, not as a God-given quality that has been granted to us once for all. . . . There are now twenty-five centuries during which the mathematicians have had the practice of correcting their errors and thereby seeing their science enriched, not impoverished, this gives them the right to view the future with serenity."

Nicolas Bourbaki is the pseudonym of a French group of mathematicians of the twentieth century producing texts on fundamental structures of mathematics emphasizing the axiomatic approach.[clxiv] To my mind, it is a pragmatic and honest statement,

---

clxiv Merzbach and Boyer, pp., 578-580. The quote is cited in Kline (p. 320) from the *Elements of Mathematics* published by the Bourbaki group of mathematicians.

and certainly reflects the truth that mathematics has continued to expand its techniques and influence as I will discuss below; but first let me briefly comment on another issue that has accompanied the investigations into foundations of mathematics.

In addition to the uncertainty in mathematics caused by the revelations of Gödel, another reality for the discipline of mathematics is its increasingly abstract and specialized nature which followed the investigations into the logic of its foundations. Until the mid-nineteenth century, much of mathematics had been inspired by its success in representing the physical world and could be followed by much of the mathematics community. The consistency of successful mathematics was, in essence assured by its mirroring of the real world. However, with the extension of mathematics to concepts such as topology and sets including infinite sets and transfinite numbers, and with the focus of mathematicians shifting towards abstract objects rather than the examples of nature, mathematicians became distanced from such comforting sources of inspiration. Mathematicians increasingly chose to work in more exotic worlds dictated by their own logic and the imagination. Moreover, the abstract character of mathematics as well as its enormous expansion meant, like in many other disciplines, that no one person could be expected to be an expert in all phases of mathematics. Kline indeed writes of the possible isolation of mathematics, and its turning inwards, potentially resulting in the end of its record of unexcelled successes. [292]

While I am only a mere observer, enjoying the pleasures of exploring the many intricately interconnected rooms of the mathematical mansion, I will presume to comment. It seems to me that the ambiguities and abstractions that the twentieth century has introduced into mathematics should be liberating in that they provide a more sympathetic correspondence with the overwhelming diversity of reality while increasing the richness of the mathematical experience. It is in fact a glimpse of the richness of this experience that I hope to have passed on to you. Moreover, despite the struggles of the past to understand the foundations of mathematics, the discipline has continued to have an extraordinary vitality. One excellent sourcebook to view this vitality from a mid-twentieth century perspective is Newman's compendium in four volumes, *The World of Mathematics* [Math References 28]. Newman surveys the richness of mathematics from a historical perspective and delves into its development with essays by great contributors accompanied by commentaries, including essays by many mathematicians covered briefly here: Newton, Euler, Dedekind, Russell, Tarski, Turing, von Neumann, and many others not covered here. However, the essays on the relationship of mathematics to other disciplines is particularly revealing of the vitality of mathematics. Among the essays of Newman's collection are those giving a mathematician's perspective on aesthetics, art, artificial intelligence, economics, ethics, physics, psychology, and sociology. A more recent look into the vitality of mathematics is acquired through an internet search of mathematics research conferences.[clxv] Such conferences will be found to abound throughout the world with numerous conference sessions on algebra, differential equations, geometry, logic, number theory, and topology—just to mention categories discussed in this book. The enduring relevance of mathematics is attested to by conferences jointly focusing on theory and applications such as artificial intelligence, complex networks, cryptology, dynamic systems, economics, and pattern recognition not to mention its continuing vital role in the sciences.

To what can we attribute the extraordinary success of mathematics in describing patterns of the universe? Perhaps a clue is given by those occasions when mathematical developments have preceded their application. An example previously mentioned is the development of Riemann geometries and the specification of their tensor properties. Although Riemann was undoubtedly motivated by the desire to understand physical space, his generalization went well beyond that in abstraction. When fifty years later Einstein discovered his Theory of General Relativity, the mathematical apparatus to express his ideas were already in place and could not be expressed without them. An amusing example is Werner Heisenberg's early development of the physics that would become known as Quantum Mechanics. In 1924, after Heisenberg related to a colleague his formulation of allowed states of energy transformation of electrons in the atom through manipulation of tables of numbers, he was informed that the tables were matrices.[293] In both these examples, mathematicians seemed to have discovered abstractions independently from their capabilities to reflect specific physical realities. Of course, there are many examples to illustrate a direct link between mathematical and scientific discoveries. Newton's discovery of the calculus motivated directly by his development of his Laws

clxv See for example, http://www.conference-service.com/conferences/mathematics.html

of Motion and Universal Gravitation is certainly one of the classic examples. In any case, the relationship of the images discovered in the mind to reality seems to be a key to an understanding of mathematics' success.

Mathematics, like our images of the everyday world, occurs in the mind. Science tells us, however, that the images of the natural world are initiated by profoundly complex realities far beyond familiar images. As a species, the human mind evolved in reaction to the external world, and children's minds develop as they encounter the world, fashioning for themselves the sense of space and time, and cause and effect that brings comprehension to the familiar world. Yet within the mind are the capabilities of discovering and expressing complex patterns of the universe that are completely foreign to our everyday experiences of the external world. Of this miraculous ability, I can only say that it seems to express an inherent connection between the mind and the structure of the universe. Of the modes of expression of the mind, mathematics has been unsurpassed in its ability to reveal the universe beyond the surfaces of familiar perception.

Speaking of the relationship between the mind and nature, the physicist Arthur Eddington (1882 - 1944) whose expedition provided the earliest support for General Relativity, had this to say:

> "We have found that where science has progressed the farthest, the mind has regained from nature that which the mind has put into nature. We have found a strange footprint on the shores of the unknown. We have devised profound theories, one after another to account for its origins. At last we have succeeded in reconstructing the creature that made the footprint. And Lo! It is our own."[294]

In a similar vein, Einstein said this of the mind, mathematics, and nature:

> "Our experience hitherto justifies us in believing that nature is the realization of the simplest conceivable mathematical ideas. I am convinced that we can discover by purely mathematical construction the concepts and the laws connecting them with each other, which furnish the key to the understanding of natural phenomena. Experience may suggest the appropriate mathematical concepts, but they most certainly cannot be deduced from it. Experience remains, of course, the sole criterion of the utility of a mathematical construction. But the creative principle resides in

mathematics. In a certain sense, therefore, I hold it true that
pure thought can grasp reality as the ancients dreamed."[295]

In the past, creativity in mathematics has been energized by its close association with physics. In our time, while we get closer to understanding the origins of the universe in the Big Bang, the process of discovery has continued to identify new mysteries. Physicists talk of dark matter and energy, multiverses, and explanations of the universe that require many dimensions beyond those of space and time.[296] It is in just such an environment, not to mention the pervasive expansion of mathematical methods in biological sciences, information and communication theory, economics, and social sciences that we can continue to look optimistically for new discoveries in mathematics.

The theoretical physicist Freeman Dyson[clxvi] in his Gifford Lectures given in Aberdeen, Scotland in 1985 provided a wonderful epilogue for the story that I have told here. Of his continuing optimism for mathematics, Dyson left no doubt:

> "*After the initial shock was over, the mathematicians realized that Gödel's theorem, in denying them the possibility of a universal algorithm to settle all questions, gave them instead a guarantee that mathematics can never die. No matter how far mathematics progresses and no matter how many problems are solved, there will always be, thanks to Gödel, fresh questions to ask and fresh ideas to discover.*"[297]

To those who continue to follow the road of mathematics seeking to enjoy the riches that await us in the discoveries of the mathematicians, I see a lifetime of pleasure, fascination, and new understanding of patterns and relationships. To my readers who choose to join the mathematicians in their journey, I humbly bow.

---

clxvi Freeman Dyson (1923 -) came to Princeton in 1948 working in the illustrious environment of the Institute for Advanced Study at the time von Neumann was leading activities on computers. A major contributor to modern physics, particularly quantum electrodynamics, he has also been active at the interface between science and the public, being known for his skepticism on global warming. He is the father of George Dyson, author of *Turing's Cathedral*.
http://www.sns.ias.edu/sites/default/files/files/Dyson_Biography_detailed (1).pdf
(http://www.nytimes.com/2009/03/29/magazine/29Dyson-t.html?page wanted=all&_r=0).

Appendix A: Lemmas in support of Theorem ℕ8 (Order)

Lemma ℕ4 (1): If $m \neq n$, then $m^+ \neq n^+$

Let us proceed by an indirect proof:

Assume $m^+ = n^+$
Then by Postulate ℕ4, $m = n$ which is a contradiction.
Therefore, $m^+ \neq n^+$
Q.E.D

Lemma ℕ4(2): $n \neq m + n$

For $n = 1$: $1 \neq m + 1 = m^+$	Postulate ℕ3
$\Rightarrow$ true for $n = 1$	
Hypothesis for n: $n \neq m + n$	
Must show: $n^+ \neq m + n^+$	
$\qquad n \neq m + n$	By hypothesis
$\qquad n^+ \neq (m + n)^+$	Lemma ℕ4(1)
$\qquad n^+ \neq m + n^+$	Definition ℕ2

True for $n = 1$ and for n^+ if true for $n \Rightarrow$ Lemma ℕ4(2) is true for all n.
Q.E.D

Appendix B: Proof of the distributive property for the integers

Theorem $\mathbb{I}3$ (Distributive Property): $[m, n] \, ([h, i] + [k, j]) = [m, n] \cdot [h, i] + [m, n] \cdot [k, j]$

$$[m, n]([h, i] + [k, j]) = [m, n] \cdot [h + k, i + j] \qquad \text{Definition } \mathbb{I}3$$
$$= [m(h + k) + n(i + j), m(i + j) + n(h + k)] \qquad \text{Definition } \mathbb{I}4$$
$$= [m \cdot h + m \cdot k + n \cdot i + n \cdot j, m \cdot i + m \cdot j + n \cdot h + n \cdot k]$$
$$\text{Distributive Postulate } \mathbb{N}_c 7$$
$$= [(m \cdot h + n \cdot i) + (m \cdot k + n \cdot j), (m \cdot i + n \cdot h) + (m \cdot j + n \cdot k)]$$
$$\text{Associative and Commutative Postulates } \mathbb{N}_c 3, \mathbb{N}_c 5$$
$$= [(m \cdot h + n \cdot i), (m \cdot i + n \cdot h)] + [(m \cdot k + n \cdot j), (m \cdot j + n \cdot k)]$$
$$\text{Definition } \mathbb{I}3$$
$$= [m, n] \cdot [h, i] + [m, n] \cdot [k, j] \qquad \text{Definition } \mathbb{I}4$$

Q.E.D.

Appendix C: Proof of the cancellation theorem for integer multiplication

We will prove the cancellation theorem by an indirect proof based upon the Order Postulate ($\mathbb{I}_c$11, I) for Integers:

$\mathbb{I}_c$**11 Order Postulate:** For integers K, L, M and N,

I.   Only one of the following is true: M = N, N = M + K, or M = N + J, (M = N, M < N, M > N).

Theorem $\mathbb{I}$11 (Cancellation Property for Multiplication): If K · M = K · N, then N = M

Assume that N > M, then

N = M + L	Order Postulate ($\mathbb{I}$11$_c$, I)
K · N = K (M + L)	By hypothesis
K · N = K · M + K · L	Distributive Postulate $\mathbb{I}_c$7

Contradicts, K · M = K · N, therefore N $\not>$ M

A similar argument assuming M < N leads to a contradiction and M $\not<$ N. Therefore, by the Order Postulate M = N.

Q.E.D.

Appendix D: Propositions E1 to E28 of Euclid (Book I)clxvii

IE1 On a given finite straight line to construct an equilateral triangle.

IE2 To place at a given point (as an extremity) a straight line equal to a given straight line.

IE3 Given two unequal straight lines, to cut off from the greater a straight line equal to the less.

IE4 If two triangles have the two sides equal to the two sides respectively, and have angles contained by the equal straight lines equal, they will also have the base equal to the base, the triangle will be equal to the triangle, and the remaining angles will be equal to the remaining angles respectively, namely those which equal sides subtend.

IE5 In isosceles triangles the angles at the base are equal to one another, and if the equal straight lines be produced further, the angles under the base will be equal to one another.

IE6 If in a triangle two angles be equal to one another, the sides which subtend the equal angles will also be equal to one another.

IE7 Given two straight lines constructed on a straight line (from its extremities) and meeting in a point, there cannot be constructed on the same straight line (from its extremities) and on the same side of it, two other straight lines meeting in another point and equal to the former two respectively, namely each to that which has the same extremity with it.

IE8 If two triangles have the two sides equal to the two sides respectively, and have also the base equal to the base, they will also have the angles equal which are contained by the equal straight lines.

IE9 To bisect a given rectilineal angle.

IE10 To bisect a given straight line.

IE11 To draw a straight line at right angles to a given straight line from a given point on it.

IE12 To a given infinite straight line, from a given point which is not on it, to draw a perpendicular straight line.

---

clxvii Quoted from Heath, Vol. 1 (Book I); see also Bunt, Jones, and Bedient, pp. 147-169. The first twenty eight propositions of Euclid do not make use of his fifth postulate, the Parallel Postulate.

IE13 If a straight line set up on a straight line make angles, it will make either two right angles or angles equal to two right angles.

IE14 If with any straight line, and at a point on it, two straight lines not lying on the same side make the adjacent angles equal to two right angles, the two straight lines will be in a straight line with one another.

IE15 If two straight lines cut one another, they make the vertical angles equal to one another.

IE16 In any triangle, if one of the sides be produced, the exterior angle is greater than either of the interior and opposite angles.

IE17 In any triangle two angles taken together in any manner are less than two right angles.

IE18 In any triangle the greater side subtends the greater angle.

IE19 In any triangle the greater angle is subtended by the greater side.

IE20 In any triangle two sides taken together in any manner are greater than the remaining one.

IE21 If on one of the sides of a triangle, from its extremities there be constructed two straight lines meeting within the triangle, the straight lines so constructed will be less than the remaining two sides of the triangle, but will contain a greater angle.

IE22 Out of three straight lines, which are equal to three given straight lines, to construct a triangle; thus it is necessary that two of the straight lines taken together in any manner should be greater than the remaining one.

IE23 On a given straight line and at a point on it to construct a rectilineal angle equal to a given rectilineal angle.

IE24 If two triangles have the two sides equal to the two sides respectively, but have the one of the angles contained by the equal straight lines greater than the other, they will also have the base greater than the base.

IE25 If two triangles have the two sides equal to the two sides respectively, but have the base greater than the base, they will also have the one of the angles contained by the equal straight lines greater than the other.

IE26 If two triangles have the two angles equal to the two angles respectively, and one side equal to one side, namely, either the side adjoining the equal angles, or that subtending one of the equal angles, they will also have the remaining sides equal to the remaining sides and the remaining angle to the remaining angle.

400 Robert G. Bill

IE27 If a straight line falling on two straight lines make the alternate angles equal to one another, the straight lines will be parallel to one another.

IE28 If a straight line falling on two straight lines make the exterior angle equal to the interior and opposite angle on the same side, or the interior angles on the same side equal to two right angles, the straight lines will be parallel to one another.

Appendix E: Variation of the angle of parallelism with distance

A proof that $\Pi(d_{PQ})$ decreases with increasing distance d_{PQ} is given by A. D. Aleksandrov.[clxviii] Prior to this, he proves without using the Parallel Postulate that if a line cutting two other straight lines forms equal alternate interior angles, a common perpendicular may be formed between the two straight lines. The proof that the angle of parallelism $\Pi(d_{PQ})$ decreases as d_{PQ} increases is outlined below.

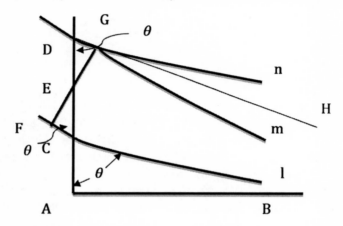

In the figure, line AD is perpendicular to line AB. Line l is constructed as a limiting parallel to AB and intersects AD at point C at the angle of parallelism θ or $\Pi(d_{AC}) = \theta$. Line n intersects point D also at an angle θ. From the prior proof of Aleksandrov, a common perpendicular, FG, can be constructed between line l and n with $\angle GDE = \angle FCE = \theta$ because θ is the same for line l and n. At G, a line m can also be produced parallel to l at some angle less than 90° to FG since n is perpendicular to FG. Therefore, a point H can be placed between the angle formed by lines n and m. The line DH must therefore also be parallel to l and AB, but $\angle ADH < \theta$. Therefore, the angle of parallelism at D is less than θ, or $\Pi(d_{AD}) < \Pi(d_{AC})$.

---

clxviii Aleksandrov, A. D. in Aleksandrov, A.D., Kolmogorov, A.N., Lavrent'ev, M.A. (eds.), *Mathematics, Its Content and Meaning*, [Math References 2], Vol. 3, Chapter XVII, pp. 108- 110.

Appendix F: Derivation of fundamental relations of sides and angles of triangles in spherical geometry

Let us look at an arbitrary triangle △ABC, on the surface of a sphere of radius r.[clxix]

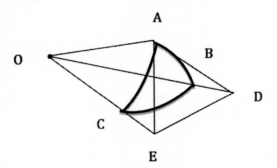

From the center of the sphere, O, radii of length r are drawn to points A, B, and C of the triangle. The straight line AE is produced perpendicular to OA in the plane OAC and intersects the extension of the straight line OC. Similarly, the straight line AD is formed intersecting the extension of OB to OD. By their construction, ∠OAE and OAD are right angles. As planes through OAD and OAE form lines AB and AC, ∠EAD = ∠CAB. Note also that by construction arcs BC = r · ∠BOC = r · ∠DOE, AC = r · ∠AOC = r · ∠AOE, and AB = r ·∠AOB = r · ∠AOD

From the Law of Cosines (Section 4.3.4) for △ODE and △ADE:

$$DE^2 = OD^2 + OE^2 - 2 \cdot OD \cdot OE \cos (\angle DOE)$$
$$= OD^2 + OE^2 - 2 \cdot OD \cdot OE \cos (BC/r); \text{ also,}$$
$$DE^2 = AD^2 + AE^2 - 2 \cdot AD \cdot AE \cos (\angle EAD)$$

Because ∠OAD and ∠OAE are right angles: $OD^2 = OA^2 + AD^2$ and $OE^2 = OA^2 + AE^2$. Substituting for OD^2 and OE^2 in the first equation for DE^2 and subtracting the second equation for DE^2, we obtain:

$$0 = 2 \cdot OA^2 + 2 \cdot AD \cdot AE \cos (EAD) - 2 \cdot OD \cdot OE \cos (BC/r); \text{ or}$$
$$\cos(BC/r) = (OA/OE) \cdot (OA/OD) + (AE/OE) \cdot (AD/OD) \cos(EAD)$$

---

clxix Todhunter shows that the derivation is valid even in such cases as triangles with angles greater than a right angle, pp.18-20.

From the definitions of sine and cosine:

$OA/OE = \cos(AC/r)$, $OA/OD = \cos(AB/r)$, $AE/OE = \sin(AC/r)$, $AD/OD = \sin(AB/r)$; therefore, after substitution,
$\cos(BC/r) = \cos(AC/r) \cdot \cos(AB/r) + \sin(AC/r) \cdot \sin(AB/r) \cdot \cos(\angle EAD)$

As in the earlier proof of the Law of Cosines we will simplify our equation using Euler's notation: $a = BC$ (opposite vertex A), $b = AC$ (opposite vertex B), $c = AB$ (opposite vertex C) and $\angle A = \angle CAB = \angle EAD$. This leads to the more easily recalled formula for $\cos(a/r)$. A similar derivation can be developed for $\cos(b/r)$ and $\cos(c/r)$ noting that $\angle B = \angle ABC$, and $\angle C = \angle ACB$. With these substitutions, we have the fundamental formulas for the sides and angles of triangles in spherical geometry:

$\cos(a/r) = \cos(b/r) \cdot \cos(c/r) + \sin(b/r) \cdot \sin(c/r) \cdot \cos(A)$,
$\cos(b/r) = \cos(c/r) \cdot \cos(a/r) + \sin(c/r) \cdot \sin(a/r) \cdot \cos(B)$,
$\cos(c/r) = \cos(a/r) \cdot \cos(b/r) + \sin(a/r) \cdot \sin(b/r) \cdot \cos(C)$.

Appendix G: Classification of functions

The function $y = f(x) = mx + b$ is an example of a function with a one-to-one correspondence between the independent variable x and the dependent variable y. The entire real number line is the domain of the independent variable. The codomain and the range of the dependent variable are also the entire real number line. The function is single valued, also satisfying the requirement that if $f(x_1) = f(x_2)$, then $x_1 = x_2$. When there is a one-to-one correspondence an inverse function f^{-1} can be defined such that $f^{-1}(f(x)) = x$. Other types of functions do not satisfy the full requirements of a one-to-one correspondence. Definitions of such functions and comparison with the requirements of a one-to-one correspondence are given below with examples in which the domain and codomain are taken as the entire real number line.

Function: For all x in the domain, there exists a single value $f(x)$ in the codomain. (This is a requirement for a function sometimes indicated as a single valued function)
Example: $y = f(x) = x^2$. Each value of x of the domain is mapped to a single value in the range. Note, however, that $f(x) = f(-x) = x^2$ for example $f(2) = f(-2) = 4$. Also, although the domain is the entire real number line, the range is only the real numbers greater or equal to zero.

One-to-one (Injective) Function: For all x in the domain, there exists only a single value $f(x)$ in the range such that if $f(x_1) = f(x_2)$, then $x_1 = x_2$.
Example: $y = f(x) = 10^x$. Each value of x in the domain is mapped to a single number in the codomain; however, the function only takes on the values of the positive real numbers.

Onto (Surjective) Function: For every y of the codomain, there exists an x such that $y = f(x)$.
Example: $y = f(x) = \log(x)$. For every y in the codomain (the entire real number line), there is an $x = 10^y$. However, the function $f(x)$ is only defined for $x > 0$, and therefore not an an injective function from

clxx Various authors use different names for these functions. The names used here are consistent with the definitions in: Labarre, Jr., pp. 11-16, [Math References 19]; Schramm, p. 32, [Math References 30]; B. Mendelson, p. 11 - 14,[Math References 23]. The definitions are also consistent with their use in Hamilton, pp., 54, 56, 114, Math References 13].

all of the real numbers. With the restriction to $x > 0$, $f^{-1}(f(x)) = f^{-1}(\log x) = 10^{\log x} = x$.

One-to-One Correspondence (Bijective or One-to-One and Onto):
For every x of the domain and every y of the codomain, $y = f(x)$ exists and $f(x_1) = f(x_2)$ if and only if $x_1 = x_2$.
Example: $y = f(x) = x^3$. The function is one-to-one and onto being defined for all x of the domain and all y of the codomain, the real number line.

Appendix H: Proof of trigonometric identities for sums of angles

The Euler identity is $e^{i\theta} = \cos\theta + i\sin\theta$, therefore

$e^{i(\alpha+\beta)} = \cos(\alpha+\beta) + i\sin(\alpha+\beta)$; however,

$e^{i(\alpha+\beta)} = e^{i\alpha} \cdot e^{i\beta} = (\cos\alpha + i\sin\alpha) \cdot (\cos\beta + i\sin\beta)$

$\qquad = (\cos\alpha \cdot \cos\beta - \sin\alpha\sin\beta) + i(\sin\alpha \cdot \cos\beta + \cos\alpha \cdot \sin\beta)$

The real part of $e^{i(\alpha+\beta)} = \cos(\alpha+\beta)$ and the imaginary part of $e^{i(\alpha+\beta)} = \sin(\alpha+\beta)$.

Therefore, equating real parts, $\cos(\alpha+\beta) = \cos\alpha \cdot \cos\beta - \sin\alpha\sin\beta$;

and

equating imaginary parts, $\sin(\alpha+\beta) = \sin\alpha \cdot \cos\beta + \cos\alpha \cdot \sin\beta$

Similarly, $\cos(\alpha-\beta) = \cos\alpha \cdot \cos\beta + \sin\alpha\sin\beta$

and $\sin(\alpha-\beta) = \sin\alpha \cdot \cos\beta - \cos\alpha \cdot \sin\beta$

Appendix I: Transformation of a second degree equation by rotation

Let's look at $5x^2 + 3xy + y^2 - 5 = 0$ to further illustrate the rotation transformation of the general second degree equation

$$Ax^2 + 2Bxy + Cy^2 + 2Dx + 2Ey + F = 0.$$

Using the transformation for rotation of coordinates through an angle θ, the term in xy may be eliminated if,

$1/\tan 2\theta = \cot 2\theta = (A - C)/2B$ with $\cot \theta$ being the cotangent function.

In the example, $A = 5$, $B = 3/2$, $C = 1$, $D = E = 0$, and $F = -5$. The invariant $\Gamma = AC - B^2$ determines which conic is represented by the equation.[clxxi] In this example, $\Gamma = 5 \cdot 1 - (3/2)^2 = 2.75 > 0$; therefore we expect the curve to be an ellipse. $\cot 2\theta = (5 - 1)/(2 \cdot 3/2) = 4/3$ or $\tan 2\theta = 3/4$. (Using a calculator, you will find the angle, $2\theta \approx 36.87°$ and therefore, the angle of rotation, $\theta \approx 18.43°$.) Since $\tan 2\theta = \sin 2\theta / \cos 2\theta$, the tangent of an angle of a right triangle is ratio of the side opposite the angle divided by the adjacent side. For $1/\cot 2\theta = \tan 2\theta = 3/4$, a right triangle with one angle equal to 2θ, must have sides proportioned as shown in the accompanying figure; $\sin 2\theta = 3/5$ and $\cos 2\theta = 4/5$.

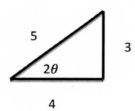

We can use trigonometric identities to show that $\cos^2 \theta = \frac{1}{2}(1 + \cos 2\theta)$ and $\sin^2 2\theta = \frac{1}{2}(1 - \cos 2\theta)$.[clxxii] Therefore, in our example $\cos^2 \theta = 9/10$ and $\sin^2 \theta = 1/10$. We shall also have need of $\cos \theta \cdot \sin \theta =$

$$\sqrt{\cos^2 \theta \cdot \sin^2 \theta} = \sqrt{\frac{9}{10} \cdot \frac{1}{10}} = 3/10.$$

---

clxxi If $\Gamma > 0$, the curve is an ellipse; $\Gamma = 0$, a parabola; and $\Gamma < 0$, a hyperbola.
clxxii We have the identities $\cos^2 \theta + \sin^2 \theta = 1$, and $\cos^2 \theta - \sin^2 \theta = \cos 2\theta$, Adding these two equations or subtracting the two equations gives the results shown after division by 2.

Using the rotation transformation,

$x = x' \cos \theta - y' \sin \theta$

$y = x' \sin \theta + y' \cos \theta$

we have after substitution into $5x^2 + 3xy + y^2 - 5 = 0$:

$5(x'\cos \theta - y'\sin \theta)^2 + 3(x'\cos \theta - y'\sin \theta) \cdot (x'\sin \theta + y'\cos \theta) + (x' \sin \theta + y'\cos \theta)^2 - 5 = 0$

After substitution for $\cos^2 \theta$, $\sin^2 \theta$, and $\cos \theta \cdot \sin \theta$ from the trigonometric identities, and simplification we get,

$5.5x'^2 + 0.5y'^2 = 5$ or in standard form, $x'^2 /(10/11) + y'^2 /10 = 1$

Note that in the equation after transformation Γ is still equal to $2.75 = 5.5 \cdot 0.5$.

Appendix J: Integration of $\dfrac{2(T_i - T_s)}{\Delta} \int_0^\Delta \sin\left(\dfrac{n\pi x}{\Delta}\right) dx$

$$a_n = \frac{2(T_i\text{-}T_s)}{\Delta} \int_0^\Delta \sin\left(\frac{n\pi x}{\Delta}\right) dx$$

Let $u = \dfrac{n\pi x}{\Delta}$, then

$$\frac{d\left(\cos\left(\dfrac{n\pi x}{\Delta}\right)\right)}{dx} = \frac{d(\cos u)}{du}\frac{du}{dx} = -\sin(u)\left(\frac{n\pi}{\Delta}\right) = -\sin\left(\frac{n\pi x}{\Delta}\right)(n\pi/\Delta).$$

$$a_n = \frac{2(T_i - T_s)}{\Delta} \int_0^\Delta \sin\left(\frac{n\pi x}{\Delta}\right) dx = \frac{2(T_i - T_s)}{\Delta} \cdot \left(-\frac{\Delta}{n\pi}\right) \int_0^\Delta \sin\left(\frac{n\pi x}{\Delta}\right) \cdot \left(-\frac{n\pi}{\Delta}\right) dx$$

$$= \frac{2(T_i - T_s)}{\Delta} \cdot \left(-\frac{\Delta}{n\pi}\right) \int_0^\Delta \frac{d\left(\cos\left(\dfrac{n\pi x}{\Delta}\right)\right)}{dx} dx = -\frac{2(T_i - T_s)}{n\pi} \cdot \cos\left(\frac{n\pi x}{\Delta}\right)\Big|_0^\Delta$$

$$= -\frac{2(T_i - T_s)}{n\pi}\left[\cos(n\pi) - \cos(0)\right]$$

$$= -\frac{2(T_i - T_s)}{n\pi}\left[-1 - 1\right] \text{ for n odd}$$

$$= -\frac{2(T_i - T_s)}{n\pi}\left[1 - 1\right] \text{ for n even}$$

$$a_n = \frac{4(T_i - T_s)}{n\pi} \text{ for } n = 1, 3, 5 \ldots$$
$a_n = 0$ for n = 2, 4, 6 ...

THE MATHEMATICAL REFERENCES

The references listed below, in addition to supporting and expanding upon the various technical and historical points made in the text, are in my opinion good examples of choices for continuing your journey in mathematics. With the introductions given here, I believe that you will now have the background to take advantage of their greater depth and more advanced approaches. I particularly recommend Eves' *Foundations and Fundamental Concepts of Mathematics* and Stahl's *Geometry from Euclid to Knots*. Even in the more advanced references, you will find much that is interesting, lucid and illuminating. However, those references that are particularly more advanced and perhaps should be entertained at a point further down the road are marked with an asterisk. Of those, I note however that *Mathematics, Its Contents and Meaning* edited by Aleksandrov, A. D., Kolmogorov, A. N., Lavrent'ev, M. A, is somewhat in a class by itself in its comprehensive nature and attention to clarity in bridging the gap between introductory and advanced concepts. Of the historical works, Kline's *Mathematics, The Loss of Certainty*, is particularly recommended for its compelling narrative in contrast to more encyclopedic approaches and, I believe it will be greatly enhanced through the subjects covered in my survey of mathematics.

1. Aczel, A. D., *The Mystery of the Aleph; Mathematics, the Kabbalah, and the Search for Infinity,* Washington Square Press, Pocket Books, New York, 2000.
2. *Aleksandrov, A. D., Kolmogorov, A. N., Lavrent'ev, M. A., (eds.) *Mathematics, Its Contents and Meaning*, (translated and edited by S. H. Gould), Dover Publications, Inc., New York, (three volumes bound as one), Vol. 1, Vol. 2, Vol. 3, 1999.
3. Ball, W. W. Rouse, *A Short Account of the History of Mathematics*, Dover Publications, Inc., New York, 1960.
4. Breuer, J., *Introduction to the Theory of Sets*, Dover Publications, New York, 2006.
5. *Bonola, R., *Non-Euclidean Geometry (with a Supplement Containing, The Theory of Parallels* by Nicholas Lobachevski and *The Science of Absolute Space* by John Bolyai, translated by George Bruce Halstead), Dover Publications, New York, 1955.

6. Bunt, L. N. H., Jones, Phillip S., and Bedient, Jack D., *The Historical Roots of Elementary Mathematics*, Dover Publications, New York, 1988.
7. *Churchill, R. V., *Complex Variables and Applications*, McGraw Hill, New York, 1960.
8. Courant, R. and Robbins, H., *What is Mathematics?*, 2nd edition, revised by Ian Stewart, Oxford Press, Oxford, 1995.
9. Davis, P. J., *The Mathematics of Matrices*, Blaisdell Publishing Co., Waltham, MA, 1965.
10. Dunham, W., *The Calculus Gallery*, Princeton University Press, Princeton and Oxford, 2005.
11. Eves, H., *Foundations and Fundamental Concepts of Mathematics*, Dover Publications, Inc., New York, 1990.
12. Halsted, G. B. (editor and translator), *Girolamo Saccheri's Euclides Vindicatus*, Chelsea Publishing Co., New York, 1986.
13. Hamilton, A. G., Numbers, sets and axioms, Cambridge University Press, Cambridge, 1982.
14. *Hawking, S., *God Created the Integers, the Mathematical Breakthroughs that Changed History*, ed. with commentary by S. Hawking, Running Press, Philadelphia, 2007.
15. Heath, T. L., *Euclid, The Thirteen Books of the Elements*, translated with introduction and commentary by Sir Thomas L. Heath, Vol. I, (Books I and II), Dover Publications, Inc., New York, 1956.
16. Heath, T. L., *Euclid, The Thirteen Books of the Elements*, translated with introduction and commentary by Sir Thomas L. Heath, Vol. 2, (Books III-IX), Dover Publications, Inc., New York, 1956
17. Heath, T. L., *Euclid, The Thirteen Books of the Elements*, translated with introduction and commentary by Sir Thomas L. Heath Vol. 3, (Books X-XIII), Dover Publications, Inc., New York, 1956.
18. Kline, M., *Mathematics, The Loss of Certainty*, Oxford University Press, Oxford, 1980.
19. Labarre, A. E., Jr., *Intermediate Mathematical Analysis*, Dover Publications, Inc., New York, 2008.
20. *Landau, E., *Foundations of Analysis*, Chelsea Publishing Co., New York, 1951.
21. *Lawden, D., F., *Introduction to Tensor Calculus, Relativity, and Cosmology*, Dover Publications, Inc., New York, 2002.

22. *McCleary, J., Geometry from a Differentiable Viewpoint, Cambridge University Press, Cambridge, UK, 1997.
23. *Mendelson, B., Introduction to Topology, Dover Publication, Inc., New York, 1990.
24. Merzbach, U. C. and Boyer, C. B., A History of Mathematics, John Wiley & Sons, Inc., Hoboken, NJ, 2011.
25. Meserve, B. E., Fundamental Concepts of Algebra, Dover Publications, Inc., New York, 1990.
26. *Moore, G. H., Zermelo's Axiom of Choice, Dover Publications, New York, 2013.
27. Nagel, E. and Newman, J. R., Gödel's Proof, ed. with a new forward by D. R. Hofstadter, New York University Press, New York, 2001.
28. Newman, J. R., The World of Mathematics, A small library of the literature of mathematics from A'h-mosé the Scribe to Albert Einstein presented with commentaries and notes, 4 Vols., Simon and Schuster, New York, 1956.
29. Ross, D. A., Master Math: Trigonometry, Course Technology, Cengage, Boston, 2010.
30. Schramm, M. J., Introduction to Real Analysis, Dover Publications, Inc., New York, 1996.
31. Singh, S., Fermat's Enigma: The Epic Quest to Solve the World's Greatest Mathematical Problem, Anchor Book, New York, 1997.
32. Stahl, S., Geometry from Euclid to Knots, Dover Publications, Inc., New York, 1982.
33. *Stillwell, J., Roads to Infinity, A. K. Peters, Ltd., Natick, MA, 2010.
34. *Thurston, H. A., The Number System, Dover Publications, Inc., New York, 1967.
35. Todhunter, I., Spherical Trigonometry for the Use of Colleges and Schools, with Numerous Examples, fifth edition, Macmillan and Co., London, 1886; an excellent source on spherical geometry may be found at www.gutenberg.org/ebooks/19770Cached Nov 12, 2006.
36. *Whitehead, A. N. and Russell, B., Principia Mathematica, 3 Vols., Cambridge University Press, 1st ed. 1910 - 1913, 2nd ed. 1925 - 1927.
37. *Wrede, R. C., Introduction to Vector and Tensor Analysis, Dover Publications, Inc., New York, 1972.

OTHER CITATION SOURCES

1. Barrow, J. D., *The Book of Universes,* W. W. Norton and Company, New York, 2011.
2. Carrol, L., (Charles Dodgson), *The Complete works of Lewis Carrol*, The Modern Library, Random House, New York.
3. Cohen, I. B. and Whitman, A., *Isaac Newton, The Principia, A New Translation*, preceded by *A Guide to Newton's Principia* (I.B. Cohen), University of California Press, Berkeley and Los Angeles, 1999.
4. Drake, Stillman, *Discoveries and Opinions of Galileo*, translated by Stillman Drake, Anchor Books, Random House, New York, 1957.
5. Dyson, F. J., *Infinite in All Directions, Gifford Lectures Given at Aberdeen, Scotland (April - November 1985),* Harper and Row, Publishers, New York, 1988.
6. Dyson, G., *Turing's Cathedral, the Origins of the Digital Universe*, Pantheon Books, 2012.
7. Einstein, A., Relativity, *The Special and General Theory*, Routledge Classics, London and New York, 2001
8. Einstein, A. and Infeld, L., *The Evolution of Physics from Early Concepts to Relativity and Quanta,* Simon and Schuster, New York, 1966.
9. Galileo, G., *Two New Sciences*, translated with new introduction, notes, and, *History of Free Fall: Aristotle to Galileo* by S. Drake, Wall and Emerson, Inc., Toronto, 1989
10. Gamow, G., *One, Two, Three, Infinity*, Dover Publications, New York, 1988.
11. Gamow, G., *The Great Physicists from Galileo to Einstein,* Dover Publications, Inc., New York, 1988.
12. Kriwaczek, P., *Babylon, Mesopotamia and the Birth of Civilization*, Thomas Dunne Books, St. Martin Press, New York, 2012.
13. Omnès, R., *Quantum Philosophy, Understanding and Interpreting Contemporary Science*, translated by Arturo Sangalli, Princeton University Press, Princeton, NJ, 1999.
14. Plato, *The Republic,* translated by R. W. Sterling and W. C. Scott, W. W. Norton and Company, New York, 1985.
15. Russell, B., A History of Western Philosophy, Simon and Schuster, New York, 1945.

16. Thoreau, H. D., Walden or Life in the Woods, Dover Publications, Inc., New York, 1995.
17. White, M., *Isaac Newton, the Last Sorcerer,* Helix Books, Addison Wesley, Reading, MA, 1997.
18. Whitehead, A. N., *Science and the Modern World*, The Free Press, Simon and Schuster, New York, 1967.

END NOTES

Chapter 1: IN THE BEGINNING

1   Bunt, Jones, and Bedient, *The Historical Roots of Elementary Mathematics*, pp. 2-3 (Math References 6).

2   Ibid., p. 6-7.

3   Ibid., pp. 8-28.

4   Merzbach and Boyer, *A History of Mathematics*, pp. 23-25, [Math References 24].

5   Ibid., pp. 29-31.

6   Ball, *A Short Account of the History of Mathematics*, pp. 6-7, [Math References 3].

7   Bunt, Jones, Bedient, pp. 58-62.

8   Ball, pp. 14-17.

9   Ibid., pp. 19-28.

10   Heath, *Euclid, The Thirteen Books of the Elements*, Vols. 1, 2, 3[Math References 15-17].

11   Kline, *Mathematics, The Loss of Certainty*, pp. 20-21 [Math References 18]; Merzbach and Boyer, pp. 88-89.

12   Kline, pp. 81-85.

13   Ibid., pp. 11-15.

14   Ball., pp 254-257.

15   Ball, p. 60.

16   Merzbach and Boyer, pp. 160-164; see also Ball, pp. 103-110.

17   Kline, 113-126.

18   Merzbach and Boyer, pp. 186-202.

19   Ibid., pp. 206-212; see also Ball, pp. 155-158.

20   Ball, p. 164.

21   Ibid., pp. 217-221.

22   Ibid., pp. 221-225.

23   Kline, p. 116.

24   Ball, pp. 229-234.

25   Ibid., pp.239-243.

26   Ibid., pp. 268-278.

27   Kline, p. 114-115, 123.

28   Merzbach and Boyer, pp. 320-322.

29   Ibid., pp 322-324, pp. 356-358.

30   Ibid., pp. 116-118, pp. 303-306, pp. 324-325.

31   Ball, pp. 319-352.

32   Ibid., pp. 353-366.

33   Kline, pp. 35-41.

34   Kline, pp. 52-54.

35   Ball, pp. 248-249.

36 Merzbach and Boyer, pp. 363-364.
37 Kline, 128-130.
38 Ball., pp. 374-377.
39 Ibid. pp. 393-400.
40 Ibid., pp. 401-412.
41 Ibid. pp. 412-421.
42 Ibid., p. 327.
43 Mertzbach and Boyer, pp. 409-411.
44 Kline, p. 146.
45 Kline, p. 135.
46 Ball. pp. 469-471.
47 Merzbach and Boyer, p. 455.
48 Ibid., p. 534.
49 Ibid., p. 452.
50 Ibid., p. 564-568.
51 Ibid., pp. 536-538.
52 Eves, *Foundations and Fundamental Concepts of Mathematics*, pp. 179-183, [Math References 11].
53 Merzbach and Boyer, p. 538-543.
54 Eves., pp. 224-229.
55 Stahl, *Geometry from Euclid to Knots*, p. 81 [Math References 32].
56 Kline, pp. 79-80.
57 Heath, Vol. 1, Proposition 32, p 316-317.
58 Heath, Vol. 1, Proposition 47, p 349-350
59 Kline, pp.83-84.
60 Ibid., pp. 85-86; Merzbach and Boyer, pp. 496-498.
61 Merzbach and Boyer, pp. 465-475.
62 Kline, pp. 81-85.
63 Merzbach and Boyer, pp. 496-497.
64 Kline, pp. 89-92; see also Merzbach and Boyer, pp. 510-514.
65 Merzbach and Boyer, pp. 515-519.
66 Ibid., p. 479.
67 Eves, p. 124.
68 Merzbach and Boyer, pp. 520-521.
69 Eves, p. 181.
70 Eves 191; see also Merzbach and Boyer, pp. 524-525.
71 Kline, p. 89.
72 Eves, pp. 82-86.
73 Kline, p. 191.
74 Ibid., pp. 258-260.
75 Merzbach and Boyer, pp. 537, 560; Kline 218-223.
76 Kline, pp. 254-256.
77 Eves, pp. 263-264.
78 Kline. pp. 260-263.
79 Ibid., 260.

80 Merzbach and Boyer, pp. 490-491.
81 Ibid., p. 484, pp. 499-501.
82 Ibid., p. 568.

Chapter 2: A UNIVERSE OF NUMBERS

83 Ball, p. 276.
84 Eves, p. 255.
85 Ibid., p. 255.
86 Heath, Vol 1. (Book I), p.252.
87 Eves, pp. 190-191.
88 Eves, pp. 183-185.
89 Kline, pp. 118-119, 153-156.
90 Eves, p. 180.
91 Heath, Vol 2. (book VII), pp. 277-278.
92 Ball, p. 83-84.
93 Heath, Vol. 2, (Book IX, Prop. 20), pp. 412-413; see also Meserve, p. 65.
94 Heath, Vol. 2 (Book VII, Prop. 31, 32)., pp. 331-332.
95 Heath, Vol. 2. (Book IX, Prop. 14) pp. 402-403.
96 Merzbach and Boyer, pp. 75, 103.
97 Heath, Vol. 2, pp. 296-300.
98 Singh, Simon, *Fermat's Enigma: The Epic Quest to Solve the World's Greatest Mathematical Problem*, p.279 [Math References 31].
99 Heath, Vol. 3 (Book 10, Lemma 1 prior to Prop. 29), pp. 63-64; see also Bunt, Jones, and Bedient, p.79.
100 Merzbach and Boyer, p. 418.
101 Meserve, p. 17.
102 Bunt, Jones, and Bedient, p. 222.
103 Ibid., pp. 49-50.

Chapter3: COUNTING TO INFINITY

104 Eves, 222.
105 Merzbach and Boyer, p. 89.
106 Eves, pp. 196-199.
107 Ibid., pp. 180-183.
108 Ibid. p. 86.
109 Ibid. 227-228.
110 Courant and Robbins, *What is Mathematics?*, revised by I. Stewart, pp. 103-104, [Math References 8]; see also Eves, p. 227.
111 Ball, p. 67; see pp. 64-77 for other achievements and biographical summary.
112 Kline, p. 232; see also Merzbach and Boyer, p. 546.
113 Courant and Robbins, p.107.
114 Ibid., pp. 103-107.

115 Merzbach and Boyer, pp. 559-560.
116 Meserve, p. 260.
117 Kline, p. 117.
118 Ball, p. 224.
119 Kline, p. 178.

Chapter 4: GEOMETRY SHOWS THE WAY

120 Heath, Vol. 1, p. 1.
121 Ibid., p.121.
122 Kline, p. 82.
123 Omnès, *Quantum Philosophy*, pp. 250-252, [Other Citation Sources 13].
124 Kline., pp. 62 -63.
125 http://www.whitehouse.gov/omb/budget/historicals;
126 U.S National Academy of Sciences, "STRONG EVIDENCE ON CLIMATE CHANGE UNDERSCORES NEED FOR ACTIONS TO REDUCE EMISSIONS AND BEGIN ADAPTING TO IMPACTS," http://www8.nationalacademies.org/onpinews/newsitem.aspx?RecordID=05192010, November 22, 2012.
127 White, M., *Isaac Newton, the Last Sorcerer,* p. 343 and p. 384, fn.1, [Other Citation Sources 17].
128 Kline, p. 155, pp. 183-189.
129 Eves, p.253
130 Ibid., p. 255.
131 Ibid, p. 246, fn. 4.
132 Heath, Vol. 1 (Book I), pp. 153-155.
133 Eves, p. 40.
134 Bunt, Jones, and Bedient, p. 154.
135 Heath, Vol. 1 (Book I), pp. 241-243.
136 Ibid., pp. 238-240.
137 Ibid., pp. 279-280.
138 Ibid., pp. 280-281.
139 Ibid., p. 224.
140 Eves, p. 52.
141 Heath, Vol. 1, p. 220.
142 Eves, pp. 52-53.
143 Heath, Vol.2 (Book VI), p. 188.
144 Heath, Vol. 1, (Book II), pp. 403-409.
145 Merzbach and Boyer, pp. 146-147.
146 Ibid., p. 409.
147 Heath, Vol. I, pp. 204-220.
148 Eves, pp. 61 -62.
149 Ibid., pp. 63-64 (see also Merzbach and Boyer, 496-498.).
150 Halsted, *Girolamo Saccheri's Euclides Vindicatus*, pp. 29-37 [Math References 12]; Bonola, *Non-Euclidean Geometry*, p. 57, [Math References 5].
151 Merzbach and Boyer, pp. 420-421.

152 Eves., p.62.
153 Ibid., p. 58.
154 Bonola, pp. 84-86.
155 Aleksandrov, *Mathematics, Its Content and Meaning*, Vol. 3, pp. 114-115, fn. * pp. 115 (References 2); also Eves, 63-64.
156 Halsted, pp. 59-61.
157 Bonola. pp. 44-46.
158 Ibid., pp. 55-56.
159 Heath, Vol. 1, pp. 216-217.
160 Eves, pp. 63-65.
161 Aleksandrov, Vol. 2, Chapter VII, pp. 68, 80-82, 89-91, 97.
162 Ibid., pp. 93-97.
163 Bonola, pp. 132-133; Aleksandrov, Vol. 3, pp. 114-115.
164 Eves, p. 66-67.
165 Aleksandrov, Vol3, p. 111 -112.
166 Ibid., p. 188.
167 Ibid., pp. 115-121.
168 Merzbach and Boyer, p. 500.

Chapter 5: THE BRIDGE BETWEEN ALGEBRA AND GEOMETRY

169 Merzbach and Boyer, p. 317.
170 Eves, pp. 94-98.
171 Ball, pp. 46-47.
172 Ibid., pp. 77-83.
173 Merzbach and Boyer, pp. 130-141.
174 Ibid., pp. 26-28.
175 Ibid., pp. 149-151.
176 Ibid., p. 320,
177 Ibid. 409.
178 Ibid. p. 452.
179 Labarre, Jr., *Intermediate Mathematical Analysis,* pp. 14-15, (Math References 19).
180 Ibid., p. 49.
181 Meserve, p. 126.
182 Ball, p. 157.
183 Merzbach and Boyer, p. 475.
184 Delone in Aleksandrov, Kolmogorov, and Lavrent'ev, Vol. 1, Part 1, Chapter IV, pp. 266-268.
185 Merzbach and Boyer, pp. 255, 257, 259-260; see also B. N. Delone in Aleksandrov, Kolmogorov, and Lavrent'ev, Vol. 1, Part 1, Chapter IV, pp. 268-270.
186 Meserve, p. 153.
187 Merzbach and Boyer, pp. 275-276.
188 Meserve, pp. 142-143.

Chapter 6: ONE DARN THING AFTER ANOTHER; INFINITE SEQUENCES AND THE REAL NUMBERS

[189] Bunt, Jones, and Bedient, pp. 50-51.
[190] Ibid., pp. 5-6, pp. 39-40.
[191] Heath, Vol. 2, Book IX, pp. 420-421.
[192] Kline, pp. 140-144.
[193] Merzbach and Boyer, p. 404.
[194] Kline, pp. 142-143.
[195] Merzbach and Boyer, p. 409.
[196] Ibid., pp. 238-242.
[197] Labarre, Jr., pp. 137-141.
[198] Stečkin in Aleksandrov, Kolmogorov, and Lavrent'ev, Vol. 3, Part 5, p. 14-17.
[199] Labarre, Jr. pp. 65-67.
[200] Labarre, Jr., p. 60.
[201] Ball, pp. 232-233.
[202] Delone, B. N. in Aleksandrov, Kolmogorov, and Lavrent'ev, Vol. 1., pp. 266-268.

CHAPTER 7: THE NUMBERS MOVE IN SPACE; ROTATIONS, CONICS, VECTORS, TENSORS, AND MATRICES

[203] Ball, pp. 48-49, 245-247; Wrede, R. C., *Introduction to Vector and Tensor Analysis*,] p. 1, [Math References 37].
[204] Merzbach and Boyer, pp. 300-301.
[205] Aleksandrov in Aleksandrov, Kolmogorov, and Lavrent'ev, Vol. 3, pp. 164-168.
[206] Lawden, *Introduction to Tensor Calculus, Relativity, and Cosmology* pp. 130 -131, (Math References 21).
[207] Einstein, *The Special and General Theory*, pp. 127-129, [Other Citation Sources 7]; Einstein and Infeld, *The Evolution of Physics, from Early Concepts to Relativity and Quanta* pp. 238-239, [Other Citation Sources 8]; Lawden, p.150.
[208] Faddeev in Aleksandrov, Kolmogorov, and Lavrent'ev, Vol. 3, pp. 61-74.
[209] Davis, P. J., *The Mathematics of Matrices*, pp. 294-295, [Math References 9].
[210] Eves, p. 122-124.
[211] Faddeev in Aleksandrov, Kolmogorov, and Lavrent'ev, Vol. 3, pp. 43-44; see also Davis, pp. 112-113.

CHAPTER 8: MAKING A LOT OUT OF THE INFINITESIMAL

[212] Galileo, p. 154.
[213] Courant and Robbins, pp. 475-476.

214 Lavrent'ev and Niloĺskiĭ in Aleksandrov, Kolmogorov, and Lavrent'ev, Vol. 1, p. 85, pp. 97-101; Courant and Robbins, pp. 307-308.
215 Courant and Robbins, p. 430-431.
216 Lawden. pp. 39-46.
217 Ibid., p. 40-41.
218 Merzbach and Boyer, pp. 115-116.
219 Courant and Robbins, pp. 436-439.
220 Dunham, *The Calculus Gallery*, pp. 99-100, [Math References 10].
221 Ibid, pp. 443-446.
222 Merzbach and Boyer, p. 408.
223 Ibid., p. 546.
224 Labarre, Jr, p. 167-168 with supporting material pp. 160-167.
225 Merzbach and Boyer., 573-575.
226 Ball., pp. 432-433.
227 Merzbach and Boyer, pp. 450-452.
228 Ibid., p. 450, p. 544.
229 Gamow, *The Great Physicists from Galileo to Einstein,* pp. 252-253 [Other Citation Sources 11].

CHAPTER 9: SET THEORY, THE FOUNDATION

230 Merzbach and Boyer, pp. 536-538.
231 Kline pp. 253-255.
232 Eves, pp. 214-215.
233 Ibid., pp. 216-217.
234 Ibid., p. 221; Hamilton, p. 106.
235 Eves, p. 264.
236 Hamilton, pp. 201-202, *Numbers, sets, and axioms, the apparatus of mathematics,* [Math References 13]
237 Breuer, p. 95, *Introduction to the Theory of Sets,*[Math References 4]
238 Merzbach and Boyer, p. 583.
239 Stillwell, p. 27, Hamilton, p. 134.
240 Hamilton, pp. 121 -126.
241 Kline, p. 255.
242 Hamilton, p. 127.
243 Eves, pp. 296-299; Stillwell, *Roads to Infinity,* pp. 39-40, 59-61, [Math References 33].
244 Moore, *Zermelo's Axiom of Choice,* p. 14, [Math References 26], Hamilton, p. 187.
245 Ibid., p. 170.
246 Moore, p. 167-171.
247 Hamilton., p. 75; Breuer, p. 44-46.
248 Hamilton, pp. 77-79; Breuer, pp. 49-52.
249 Stillwell, pp. 24-25; Hamilton, p. 61.
250 Kline, p. 202.

251 Hamilton, p. 83.
252 Breuer, pp. 57-60.
253 Stillwell, pp. 33-35; Hamilton, 134-136.
254 Stillwell, pp. 29, 35; Hamilton, p. 203.
255 Stillwell, p. 37.
256 Moore, p. 296.
257 Labarre, Jr., pp. 84-88.
258 Breuer, p. 73; Hamilton, p. 24-25; Labarre, Jr., p. 51-53.
259 Schramm, *Introduction to Real Analysis,* pp. 199-200, [Math References 30].
260 Ibid., pp. 197-198.
261 Ibid., pp. 76-79, 202.
262 Ibid., pp. 133-136.
263 Ibid., pp. 202-204.
264 Merzbach and Boyer, pp. 561-562.
265 Labarre, Jr., pp. 84-86.
266 Stahl, pp. 276, 296.
267 Ibid., Chapter 10, "Informal Topology", Chapter 11, "Surfaces," and Chapter 12, "Knots."
268 Courant and Robbins, pp. 235-269.
269 Mendelson, *Introduction to Topology,* pp. 112-128, 135-155, [Math References 23].

CHAPTER 10: THE SCIENCE OF RELATIONSHIP, EXPERIENCE, AND IMAGINATION

270 Merzbach and Boyer, pp. 559-563.
271 Kline, pp. 195-196; Merzbach and Boyer, pp. 559-560,
272 Kline, pp. 216-223; see also Eves, pp. 267-268; Merzbach and Boyer, pp. 389, 560.
273 Kline, p. 221.
274 Ibid., p. 223-224.
275 Ibid., p. 246.
276 Eves, pp. 82-86.
277 Kline, p. 246-251.
278 Ibid., pp. 258-260.
279 Ibid., p. 199.
280 Ibid., p. 234-238; see also Eves, pp. 268-269.
281 Breuer, p. 91; see also Kline, p. 238.
282 Eves, pp. 299-303; Kline, p. 261.
283 Gödel, K., "On Formally Undecidable Propositions if Principia Mathematica and Related Systems", in Hawking, *God Created the Integers, the Mathematical Breakthroughs that Changed History* p. 1265, [Math References 14].
284 Ibid., pp. 1265-1268.

285 Kline, p. 259.
286 G. Dyson, *Turing's Cathedral* p.94, [Other Citation Sources 6]
287 Kline, pp. 266-267; Eves, p. 300.
288 Merzbach and Boyer, p. 560.
289 Kline, p. 268-269; Eves, 228-229; Hamilton, pp. 159-160, 228; Stillwell, p. 169.
290 Eves, pp. 298-299, Kline, pp. 269-270.
291 Hamilton, pp. 184-186.
292 Kline, Chapter XIII," The Isolation of Mathematics," pp. 278-306.
293 Omnès, p. 142.
294 Kline, p. 341.
295 Ibid., pp. 346-347.
296 Barrow, J. D., *The Book of the Universes,* [Other Citation Sources 1].
297 F. Dyson, *Infinite in All Directions,* [Other Citation Sources 5

INDEX

Abel, Niels Henrik, 225, 233 fn. lxxxv
Abelian group, 38
Analytic geometry 27-28, 39, 346, 376, 380; Cartesian coordinates and the straight line, 205-207; interpretation of Euclidean geometry, 207-211; ellipse, 212-213; parabola, 213-214; hyperbola, 214-215; see Conics (three-dimensions)
Ancient mathematics, China, India, Mayan, 22 fn. vi, 8 fn. xi
Apollonius, 212
Archimedes, 121, 220, 308
Archimedean property, 108 fn. xxxviii, 192 fn. lxx, 364
Argand, Robert, 39, 131
Aristotle, 23, 40, 53, 103, 107, 138, 145, 146, 258, 261, 381, 383
Associative property of numbers, 46-47; group properties 38; natural numbers: 60, proofs, 55, 58; integers, 65, 71; rational numbers, 84, 86, 91; real numbers, 114, 115; complex numbers, 133
Axiomatic method, 23, 36, 38-41; comparison with scientific method, 143-144, 145; classical Greece, 152; influence of matric algebra, 289; nineteenth century understanding of, 377; Hilbert's understanding, 156-157, 156 fn. lv, 380-381; limitations proved by Gödel, 384-385; see Euclid (axiomatic methods); ZF axiomatic set theory
Axiom of Choice (AC), 344 fn. cxxxii, 345, 348, 351, 259-260, 260 fn. cxliii; Banach—Tarski paradox, 389-390; consistency and AC, 389; in logicism, 380; in

formalism, 381; in intuitionism, 383; impact of rejection, 384
Babylonian mathematics, 20-22, 215, 225, 233, 376; approximation of irrational numbers, 233, 243; sexagesimal system, 94-95, 174; solution to quadratic equation, 21,21 fn. v
Banach—Tarski paradox, 389-290, 389 fn. clxiii
Barrow, Isaac, 28
Beltrami, Eugenio, 190, 202, 203
Berkeley, Bishop George, 32
Bernoulli, Jacques, 31 fn. xv
Bolyai, Johann, 36, 177, 183, 185 fn. lxvi, 190, 193, 204, 377
Bolzano, Bernhard, 363 fn. cxliv, 382 fn. clvii
Bolzano—Weierstrass Theorem, 363-365, 384
Boole, George, 145, 146 fn. li, 343
Bourbaki group, 390, 390 fn. clxiv
Bourbaki, Nicolas 390
Brahe, Tycho, 24 fn. viii
Brouwer, L. E. J., 370, 383
Calculus, complex variables, 315 fn. cxviii; derivative: chain rule, 299-300, definition and examples, 294-298; of sums and products, 298-299, Fundamental Theorem, 310-314, 318 fn cxix; integral: as area under curve, 305-308, definition of Riemann integral, 308-309, general properties, 309-310; maxima, 295; overview, 291-294; see Lebesgue, Leibniz, Newton, Riemann, Vector
Cantor, Georg, 35; cardinal number, 106-111, 118-121, 123-127, 349–356; continuum hypothesis, 359, 382; letter

with vector (stress tensor),
271-274; examples (alternating
and Kronecker delta tensor)
279-280; General Relativity,
276-279; heat equation, 331;
metric tensor, 274-276, 276
fn. ciii; notation, 273-274;
transformation by rotation of
Cartesian axes, 273-274
Thales of Miletus, 22
Topology, 42, 369-370 fn.
clii, 373; definition and
examples, 370-371, 371 fn.
cliii; early contributors, 370;
homeomorphic, 371-372;
homotopic paths, 373; simply
connected paths, 373
Transformation, 42, 369; Cartesian
tensor, 274; Cartesian vector,
267-268; homeomorphic
topology, 371-372;
Lorentz, 268-270, 302-305;
non-Euclidean space, 275-276,
276 fn. civ; of sets by continuous
functions, 368-369; rotation in
the plane, 267-268, Appendix I,
Viète, 248-249,
Transcendental numbers, 105;
121-122; e, 31 fn. xv, 245,
317; Hilbert number, Liouville
number, π, 121-122; views of
intuitionists, 378, 382
Trigonometric functions, 25-26, 27,
31, 173-176, 176 fn. lxi; 215,
216; derivatives of, 297-298;
Euler identity and Euler
equation, 246; law of cosines
and law of sines, 175-176; proof
of trigonometric Identities for
sums of angles, Appendix H, 406;
use in rotational transformation
of a second degree equation,
253-256, 256 fn. xcii, Appendix I,
407-408
Turing, Alan, 389 fn. clxii

Vector, 37, 258-268, 258 fn.
xcvi; calculus, 315 fn. cxviii,
330-336; complex numbers
259; geometric interpretation:
addition, 260-261, law of
cosines, 263-264, lines
and planes, 264, scalar
product, 262-263, triple
product as volume, 266-267,,
transformation by rotation of
Cartesian axes, 267-268,, unit
vectors, 265,vector product,
264-266; gradient, 263, 263 fn.
cxxiii; relativistic four-vector,
302-305; Euclidean vector space,
259-260, 259 fn. xcvii;
Viète, François, 27, 227, 248
Weierstrass, Karl, 33, 39;
Bolzano-Weierstrass Theorem,
362-365, 384, 363 fn. cxlv;
definition of limit of a function,
221; definition of limit of
a sequence, 235; limit and
continuous functions, 348;
Weierstrass function, 318 fn. cxix
Well-defined operations, 65 fn. xxvii
Well-Ordering Theorem, 128,
359-360, 360 fn. cxlii, 383; see
also Sets (well ordered)
Wessel, Caspar, 39, 131
Whitehead, Alfred North, logic
and mathematics (*Principia
Mathematica*: Whitehead, A. N.
and Russell), B., 17 fn. I, 40, 41,
379, 384; perception and reality,
139 fn. xlviii
Zermelo, Ernst, 40; letter from Gödel,
374, 374 fn. cliv; objections of
intuitionists, 383; Well-Ordering
Theorem, 128, 359-360
Zermelo-Fraenkel (ZF) axiomatic
set theory, 339, 344-348, 344
fn. cxxxii; relation to Axiom of
Choice (AC) and the Continuum
Hypothesis (CH), 389

ABOUT THE AUTHOR

Robert G. Bill was a researcher in fire and fire protection for twenty-five years at FM Global, a major industrial property insurer which operates the world's largest full-scale fire research facility. There, he was Assistant Vice President and Director of Research for Fire Hazards and Protection, overseeing research in areas of flammability, fire spread, material reactivity, and fire protection systems. Previous to joining FM Global, he was an Assistant Professor in the Department of Mechanical Engineering at Columbia University conducting research in turbulent combustion. He had received BS, MS and PhD degrees in Mechanical Engineering from Cornell University. His publications include research in the areas of fluid mechanics, micro-meteorology, combustion, and fire protection. In 1994 and 2003, he received the National Fire Protection Association's Bigglestone Award for communication of scientific concepts in fire protection. From 2002 to 2008 he served on the executive committee of the International Association for Fire Safety Science and in 2009 was elected as a lifetime honorary member equivalent to the grade of Fellow of the Society of Fire Protection Engineering. Currently retired, Dr. Bill enjoys time with family, community volunteering, playing the violin, and walking his fox terrier while continuing to be fascinated by the universe of mathematics.

CPSIA information can be obtained at www.ICGtesting.com
Printed in the USA
BVOW03s0639030415

394514BV00001B/37/P